Power BI for Finance

Design effective dashboards, models, and forecasts
for finance teams

Martin Kratky

‹packt›

Power BI for Finance

Copyright © 2025 Packt Publishing

Portfolio Director: Pavan Ramchandani
Relationship Lead: Tejashwini R
Program Manager: Divij Kotian
Content Engineer: Akanksha Gupta
Technical Editor: Vidhisha Patidar
Copy Editor: Safis Editing
Indexer: Pratik Shirodkar
Proofreader: Akanksha Gupta
Production Designer: Jyoti Kadam
Growth Lead: Priya Bhanushali

First published: November 2025

Production reference: 1141125

Published by Packt Publishing Ltd.
Grosvenor House
11 St Paul's Square
Birmingham
B3 1RB, UK.

ISBN 978-1-83763-501-6
www.packtpub.com

To my parents, who encouraged me to follow my own path, even when it led far from theirs.

- Martin Kratky

Contributors

About the author

Martin Kratky has over 20 years' experience advising clients and implementing analytics and planning systems for some of the largest organizations in the world. He has worked with Power BI from the start, developing the initial, finance-related Power BI demo models. Martin has led more than 100 Power BI implementations and has 8 entries in the Power BI Partner Showcase.

He is the co-founder of Managility, a specialized consulting company for analytics and planning implementations, as well as the developer of Acterys, an integrated suite of applications and Power BI visuals for the Power BI ecosystem. Martin lives in the Northern Rivers region in Australia and is an avid mountaineer, skier, and surfer.

I hope you found some useful tips and improvements on how to use Power BI for your ongoing work as a finance professional in this book. I would like to express my deepest gratitude to all the people that were part of putting this book together: my team at Managility, in particular, Hesam Ziaei and Thomas Tucha; the Packt team—Akanksha Gupta, Shreya Moharir, Arindam Majumder, Hemangi Lotlikar for their patience and invaluable feedback. Any errors and shortcomings are, of course, my responsibility alone. Please let me know if you find any or have feedback on how to do things in a better way.

About the reviewers

Goutama Bachtiar is an accomplished technology advisory leader with over two decades of experience in GRC, IT, cybersecurity, and AI. He is a Fellow of several global institutes, including the Royal Society of Arts, Manufactures and Commerce, FINSIA, and OneTrust, among others. Goutama serves as a Research Fellow, Global Awards Judge, and Advisory Board Member for the EC-Council, AICERTS, and Packt Publishing. Since 2013, he has been exploring the intricacies of data science, applying these skills to transform data into actionable insights—particularly in IT audit engagements.

He has co-authored three books and one Body of Knowledge and has served as a reviewer for seven others, notably for O'Reilly, Wiley, Elsevier, Packt, Manning, and IASA.

I dedicate this book review to my indispensable circle: Jewbelle, Yezki, Gosso, Belle, Jolie, and Zowie, who made this all possible and to whom I owe more than words can express. High fives and a round of applause for the Packt team for their direction and guidance throughout the review.

Ankit Kukreja brings over a decade of experience in data analytics and finance, supported by an MBA in Finance. Currently serving as a Senior Consultant at Wipro, and with prior experience at Accenture and CLIX Capital, Ankit has delivered impactful Power BI solutions that enable data-driven insights and business optimization. His early tenure at BlackRock Services provided a strong foundation in risk analysis and process efficiency.

Certified in Power BI, Power Platform, and Microsoft Azure, Ankit is also a recognized Super User in the global Power BI Community. Additionally, he has contributed as a technical reviewer for the books *The Complete Power BI Interview Guide* and *Architecting Power BI Solutions in Microsoft Fabric*.

I would like to express my heartfelt gratitude to my parents, whose values laid the foundation for who I am; to my wife, for her unwavering support and belief in me; and to my child, who inspires me every day to keep learning and growing.

Table of Contents

Preface

Since its inception in 2015, Power BI has evolved into the market-leading solution for self-service analytics. Its unparalleled analytical capabilities, breadth, and flexibility offer significant advantages for financial professionals who have traditionally relied on spreadsheet-based solutions. Most existing literature on Power BI focuses on generic technical details. With this book, my aim is to provide practical guidance for finance practitioners on how to address a wide range of financial concepts and challenges effectively. I have drawn on lessons learned from working on projects since Power BI's inception, including developing the initial demo samples as well as on more than twenty years of experience implementing management information and planning systems.

Finance is undergoing a fundamental transformation. The role of finance professionals is evolving—from number crunchers to strategic advisors, from report generators to insight providers. Power BI is a key enabler of this transformation, and by mastering it, you're positioning yourself at the forefront of this change.

The journey from traditional financial reporting to modern analytics may not always be easy, but it's immensely rewarding. The tools and concepts in this book are designed to help you build solutions that deliver real business value, empower decision-makers, and free you from repetitive tasks so you can focus on higher-value analysis.

I hope this book serves as a practical and inspiring guide as you move forward in your Power BI and finance journey. Every expert was once a beginner. Keep learning, keep building, and keep pushing forward.

Who this book is for

This book is for financial practitioners looking to improve process efficiency and address a variety of common financial reporting and planning requirements using Microsoft Power BI.

What this book covers

Chapter 1, Introducing Power BI For Finance, lays the groundwork for a robust Power BI environment tailored specifically to finance professionals. It focuses on two core pillars: building a clean, scalable data model and then applying the financial logic that turns raw numbers into actionable insights.

Chapter 2, Financial Logic with Power BI, explains how to develop Power BI DAX calculations that enable financial calculation logic.

Chapter 3, Business Information Design, introduces the principles of effective financial dashboard design and their practical implementation in Power BI

Chapter 4, Financial Reporting, explains how to build comprehensive financial statements in Power BI, focusing on the Income Statement (Profit & Loss), Balance Sheet, and advanced reporting techniques.

Chapter 5, Power BI & Excel, explains how Excel and Power BI can be used together to optimize financial *tasks*, highlighting the optimal separation of tasks in each solution.

Chapter 6, Multi Currency Handling, explains how to handle multi-currency scenarios in Excel and Power BI, focusing on integrating currency rate data and performing currency conversions using both spot and historic rates as well as implementing live exchange rates via an API.

Chapter 7, Group & Board Reporting, outlines the best practices for effective group reporting, covering progress against strategic objectives, key project and product development metrics, financial performance, and sales/customer KPIs.

Chapter 8, Rolling Reporting Forecasts, explains how to implement rolling reporting and forecasting in Power BI, focusing on dynamically updating forecasts as new data becomes available.

Chapter 9, Discounted Cash Flow Public Company Valuation, explains how to perform discounted cash flow (DCF) valuation for public companies using Power BI, including importing financial statement data, transforming and cleaning the data in Power BI, and then applying DAX calculations to project future free cash flows and discount them to present value.

Chapter 10, Price Volume Mix Analysis, shows how Price Volume Mix (PVM) analysis helps organizations understand how changes in price, sales volume, and product mix affect overall revenue, especially for businesses offering diverse products or services.

Chapter 11, Writeback & Planning in Power BI, explains how Power BI can be used for write-back and financial planning with Acterys and Microsoft Dynamics 365 Extensions.

Chapter 12, Case Study Planning Model, outlines the process of building a complete planning model using Acterys/Dynamics BPP and integrating it with Power BI.

Chapter 13, Advanced Analytics & Machine Learning, explores advanced analytics and machine learning techniques, focusing on extracting actionable insights, uncover patterns, and predict outcomes in financial contexts.

Chapter 14, Using Language Models and Copilot in Power BI to Improve Financial Analysis, explains how LLMs and Microsoft Copilot are transforming financial analysis in Power BI by automating report creation, optimizing DAX calculations, and generating business insights through natural language interaction.

To get the most out of this book

The book is organized into four parts:

1. **Power BI Stack for Finance:** The initial part introduces Power BI's benefits for finance users, covering data integration, modeling, and logic.
2. **Financial Reports and Dashboards:** Focuses on report creation, charts, and data presentation
3. **Advanced Financial Topics:** Covers handling multiple currencies, consolidating group data, building dynamic rolling forecasts and company valuation work
4. **Planning and Forecasting:** shows how to build models to plan for the future, use advanced analytics, machine learning, and LLMs for financial applications

This book assumes that the users are familiar with the main components of Power BI: Power Query, the Power BI service, DAX and how to use Power BI visuals.

For absolute beginners, there is a vast pool of knowledge available to study prior to reading this book. I recommend consulting Microsoft's learning materials, the latest, high ranked YouTube channels, as well as a myriad of Power BI related blogs out there.

Download the example code files

The code bundle for the book is hosted on GitHub at https://github.com/PacktPublishing/Power-BI-for-Finance. We also have other code bundles from our rich catalog of books and videos available at https://github.com/PacktPublishing. Check them out!

Download the color images

We also provide a PDF file that has color images of the screenshots/diagrams used in this book. You can download it here: https://packt.link/gbp/9781837635016.

> **Note:** Since this book has many full-window screenshots to show the Power BI UI, we recommend that you view the images online for the best experience: either through this PDF image file or by unlocking the free ebook.

Conventions used

There are a number of text conventions used throughout this book.

CodeInText: Indicates code words in text, database table names, folder names, filenames, file extensions, pathnames, dummy URLs, user input, and Twitter handles. For example: "The total revenue calculation is a bit more interesting as we need to change the filter context of the Accounts table (ALL(Accounts) clear any filter on that table) to always refer to the total revenue with a CALCULATE statement."

A block of code is set as follows:

```
ACT = sum(Transactions[NetAmount_GC])
BUD = sum(Budget[NetAmount_GC])
```

Bold: Indicates a new term, an important word, or words that you see on the screen. For instance, words in menus or dialog boxes appear in the text like this. For example: "To add the data bar, we click again on the **Sum of Balance** context, choose **Conditional formatting**, and then **Data bars**:"

> Warnings or important notes appear like this.

> Tips and tricks appear like this.

Get in touch

Feedback from our readers is always welcome.

General feedback: If you have questions about any aspect of this book or have any general feedback, please email us at customercare@packt.com and mention the book's title in the subject of your message.

Errata: Although we have taken every care to ensure the accuracy of our content, mistakes do happen. If you have found a mistake in this book, we would be grateful if you reported this to us. Please visit http://www.packt.com/submit-errata, click **Submit Errata**, and fill in the form.

Piracy: If you come across any illegal copies of our works in any form on the internet, we would be grateful if you would provide us with the location address or website name. Please contact us at copyright@packt.com with a link to the material.

If you are interested in becoming an author: If there is a topic that you have expertise in and you are interested in either writing or contributing to a book, please visit http://authors.packt.com/.

Share your thoughts

Once you've read *Power BI for Finance*, we'd love to hear your thoughts! Scan the QR code below to go straight to the Amazon review page for this book and share your feedback.

https://packt.link/r/1837635013

Your review is important to us and the tech community and will help us make sure we're delivering excellent quality content.

Free Benefits with Your Book

This book comes with free benefits to support your learning. Activate them now for instant access (see the "*How to Unlock*" section for instructions).

Here's a quick overview of what you can instantly unlock with your purchase:

PDF and ePub Copies	Next-Gen Web-Based Reader
Free PDF and ePub versions	**Next-Gen Reader**

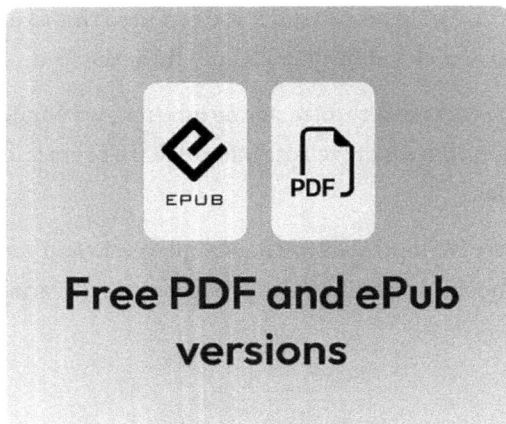

Access a DRM-free PDF copy of this book to read anywhere, on any device.

Use a DRM-free ePub version with your favorite e-reader.

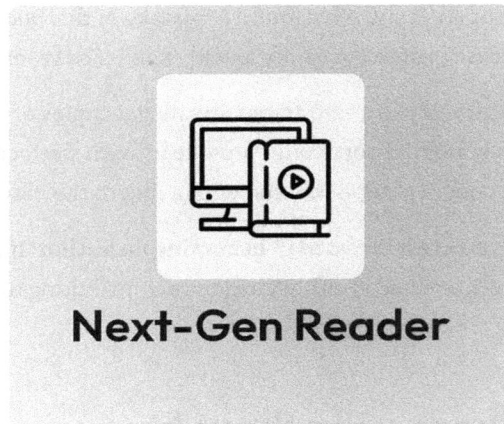

Multi-device progress sync: Pick up where you left off, on any device.

Highlighting and notetaking: Capture ideas and turn reading into lasting knowledge.

Bookmarking: Save and revisit key sections whenever you need them.

Dark mode: Reduce eye strain by switching to dark or sepia themes.

How to Unlock

Scan the QR code (or go to packtpub.com/unlock). Search for this book by name, confirm the edition, and then follow the steps on the page.

Note: Keep your invoice handy. Purchases made directly from Packt don't require one.

Part 1

Power BI Stack for Finance

The first section of the book lays the groundwork for a robust Power BI environment that is tailored specifically to finance professionals. It focuses on two core pillars: building a clean, scalable data model and then applying the financial logic that turns raw numbers into actionable insights.

This part of the book includes the following chapters:

- *Chapter 1, Introducing Power BI for Finance*
- *Chapter 2, Financial Logic with Power BI*

1

Introducing Power BI for Finance

In this opening chapter, we will cover the components of the Power BI ecosystem and how they can enable more effective processes for finance users in comparison to traditional tools and in particular, spreadsheet-based approaches.

We will also go into detail on the key pillar on which the quality of any Power BI model relies: the structure of the data model. An inadequate modeling approach leads to severe issues with report, visualization, and calculation logic designs, performance, and overall usability. We will cover the dimensions (master data tables) that form the foundation for everything else.

In this chapter, we'll cover the following main topics:

- What are the essential building blocks in Power BI?
- How does Power BI help finance users?
- Core data modeling concepts for financial purposes
- A practical walk-through, building a financial data model
- Model size considerations

Free Benefits with Your Book

Your purchase includes a free PDF copy of this book along with other exclusive benefits. Check the *Free Benefits with Your Book* section in the Preface to unlock them instantly and maximize your learning experience.

Technical requirements

Here are the things required to make the most of this chapter:

- **Chapter files**: You will find the datasets and Power BI files used in this chapter in the book's official GitHub repository here: `https://github.com/PacktPublishing/Power-BI-for-Finance`.

- **Software requirements**: Most examples covered in this book require only the free Power BI Desktop version, but I strongly recommend Pro to profit from Power BI service features like publishing reports on the web.

- **Hardware requirements**: As Power BI makes heavy use of local memory in Power BI Desktop, my recommendation is to have as much RAM as possible—at a minimum, 16 GB. My work desktop works well with 48 GB.

  With CPU, my recommendation is at least 8 core processors with 3+ GHz clock speed; 16/24 cores will give you even better results. With screen resolution, again, *the more the merrier* to consistently enable a full, detailed view of your dashboards, even when multiple side panes are displayed. I am using a resolution of 3,840 x 2,160 pixels on my work desktop, but 2,560 x 1,440 and a dedicated GPU should suffice for most requirements.

What is Power BI?

Since 2015, Microsoft's Power BI platform has grown to be the leading solution for data analytics.

I assume that you are familiar with the key concepts of the Power BI platform, so here is just a brief overview of its components. The Power BI platform comprises the following:

- **Power BI Desktop app**: This is a free development environment. It enables analysts to build data models, logic, interactive reports, and dashboards. The data in a Power BI model is either preprocessed and stored in Microsoft's proprietary **Analysis Services** format (Import mode) or queried at runtime (Direct Query mode) from supported data storage technologies such as Azure/SQL Server, SAP HANA, and others. Power BI includes its own calculation language called **Data Analysis Expressions** (**DAX**), which enables users to define calculations that are stored in the model (PBIX file or published to the Power BI service).

- **Power Query:** This is a sub-application integrated in Power BI Desktop where power users can integrate and transform data from different data sources into a composite data model optimized for analytical purposes. The definition of the transformation steps is stored in a format called **M**. The relevant M statements are either automatically generated by the Power Query UI or can be manually maintained by users using the M syntax.

- **Power BI visuals:** These are an extensible set of visualization options that are included in Power BI Desktop or can be added from a commercial marketplace. The Power BI visuals are resizable objects that can be positioned on a Power BI report or dashboard to display the required data (fields of the data model) in the desired format, such as tables, charts or diagrams, indicator cards, and so on. Beyond these core options, specialized visuals also support advanced functionality, including artificial intelligence features like key influencer detection or regression analysis.

- **The Power BI service**: A cloud-based application where a power user can publish a report from Power BI Desktop for regulated (restricted by access rights) consumption with a web browser. Alternatively, a Power BI Desktop report can also be shared in the Power BI Desktop .pbix file format. Access to the data in this file is then only restricted by access to the underlying data sources. The detailed user rights to particular granularities in the data model (for example, a specific scenario, product group, or legal entity) that can be set in the Power BI service (**row-level security**, or **RLS**) do not apply in this case on Power BI Desktop. Besides report distribution, the Power BI service also fulfills a variety of data governance tasks like user group definitions, data access and security maintenance, administration of data sources, and the like.

Next, let's see how we can expand the capabilities of Power BI even further by using **Microsoft Fabric**.

Microsoft Fabric: enhancing Power BI

In 2023, Microsoft launched Microsoft Fabric as an integrated analytics platform that builds upon the capabilities of Power BI and extends it with additional tools and functionalities designed to provide a more comprehensive solution for data management, analytics, and business intelligence. Microsoft Fabric combines the power of Power BI, Azure Synapse Analytics, and Azure Data Factory, offering a unified environment for data processing, storage, and visualization.

Here are the key benefits of Microsoft Fabric:

- **More scalable data processing**: Microsoft Fabric leverages the power of Azure Synapse Analytics, offering high-performance data processing and storage capabilities. This scalability allows organizations to handle large volumes of data and complex queries, which is particularly important for financial applications that require real-time insights and rapid decision-making.

- **Enhanced security and compliance**: Microsoft Fabric includes robust security features, such as data encryption, access controls, and compliance monitoring, ensuring that sensitive financial data is protected. This is crucial for financial applications that must adhere to strict regulatory requirements.

- **Enhanced scenario planning**: The advanced analytics tools available in Microsoft Fabric, such as predictive modeling and machine learning, enable finance teams to perform more sophisticated scenario planning and forecasting. This helps organizations to better anticipate future trends and make more strategic decisions.

- **Streamlined data governance**: Microsoft Fabric's integrated environment simplifies data governance by providing a single platform for managing data access, security, and compliance. This ensures that financial data is handled in a consistent and secure manner, reducing the risk of data breaches and regulatory violations.

Now that we are familiar with the key components and concepts of Power BI, we will review how they can add value for particular finance team tasks.

How does Power BI help finance users?

Building calculation models and presenting data are core requirements for finance users. The standard tool of choice for these purposes is typically a spreadsheet solution like MS Excel or Google Sheets, which enables users to build tabular business models and charts.

Spreadsheets are great for flexible analysis where users require completely flexible cell-based layouts with limited data (typically less than a million rows that can be handled in a spreadsheet) but have limitations when larger amounts of data or several different data sources are involved. Let's see how they compare with a solution like Power BI.

Spreadsheets versus Power BI

The following diagram outlines the differences between working with data stored in spreadsheets as opposed to separating the presentation (spreadsheet tables and charts) and data storage layer (spreadsheet that presents data stored in a separate database):

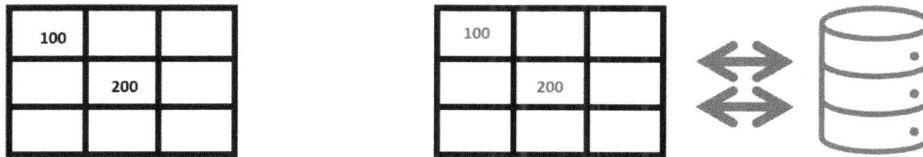

Data stored in spreadsheet in free form:
- Risks of unintended changes/overwrites/formula corruption
- Limited data volumes
- Ineffective sharing in "all-or-nothing" access to specific workbook only

Data stored in structured database:
- Governed access down to single record
- Near unlimited data volumes
- Access with different tools

Figure 1.1 – Separation of data and presentation

In a spreadsheet, there is typically no separation of data from the presentation, as opposed to an approach where the data resides separately in a database with a standardized data structure optimized for handling high volumes of transactions that are also accessible with other tools.

The spreadsheet method leads to a variety of very severe challenges for ongoing, standardized reporting and data collection requirements (such as budgeting and planning):

- **Workbook proliferation**: New or updated data typically means an additional spreadsheet, which very quickly leads to a proliferation of spreadsheet files (for example, Budget 2022 *Version 1* to *Version n*), which becomes very hard to control.

- **Access rights granularity**: No granular access rights can be assigned; a user can either see the full spreadsheet or nothing. Allowing a user access to specific parts of the data (for example, data for a particular company, product, or scenario) is impossible or very cumbersome to realize.

- **Processing performance**: Spreadsheet processes are typically slow as they run in a decentralized manner; a spreadsheet file is sent to another business unit for offline data collection. Once finished, it is sent back and then must be integrated into the overall model with data from all other business units. The user can't see how their entries will affect the total business, considering the last version of data from all other decentralized entities in real time.

- **Limited interactivity and analysis options**: Spreadsheets include great charting and dynamic matrix analysis (Pivot Tables) capabilities but lack more advanced business intelligence features available in specialized applications, such as complex data filtering, dynamic navigation within hierarchies, cross-filtering and drill-through between different tables and charts, artificial intelligence/machine learning capabilities, and so on.

In contrast, Power BI offers the following :

- **Real-time access:** Power BI offers live (i.e., automatically updating) access to a nearly unlimited number of data sources and provides a platform to transform these disparate sources into an integrated business data model.

- **Filtered views and custom aggregations**: In contrast to several spreadsheets in a single file/cloud application, where users only get access to the data details, Power BI offers the option to use filters to retrieve any combination of calculated, aggregated results from within the entire underlying data set, such as a point in time or a time span, a scenario, a legal entity, or whatever "dimension" criteria was defined in your underlying model.

- **Unparalleled interactive analytics capabilities**: This includes drill down on a table/chart (navigation into further detail), drill through (navigation to a different page or a more detailed report), and cross filtering (a selection on one chart/table is applied to others), in addition to very strong inbuilt visualization capabilities that can be enriched with a vast array of extensions and additional application options available in a commercial marketplace.

- **Two-way operations/write-back:** Power BI on its own has limited options for data collection and data write-back, but it lets us add these with extensions like Power Apps, or specialized applications from the extended Power BI ecosystem, such as Dynamics Business Performance Planning and the related Acterys offering that are also covered in this book. The best source to review and obtain these solutions is Microsoft's AppSource marketplace (`https://appsource.microsoft.com/`).

- **Dedicated application and web browser support:** Power BI reports that are published on the Power BI service only require a standard web browser for consumption. There is no need for users to install a specific spreadsheet solution that might not run on their platform, such as Microsoft Excel in Linux environments. This is admittedly less of an issue in recent years, as many spreadsheet solutions now offer browser-based access.

Conclusion

So, does Power BI replace spreadsheets completely?

Despite all the advantages we've discussed here, Power BI will not replace spreadsheet solutions completely. It is not suitable for one-off (as opposed to ongoing repeating) scenarios with limited data that require extensive flexibility regarding the tabular layout, such as layouts that can't be addressed in one or more standard tables with a symmetric row/column layout. This includes complex merger and acquisition transactions, feasibility and project investment analyses, response forms, and similar requirements that are highly varied.

Given the right approach (which you will learn from this book), Power BI offers significant efficiencies for recurring, standardized finance requirements like ongoing financial (income/balance sheet/cash flow statements) or operational reporting, budgeting and planning processes, and any scenario that requires more advanced visualizations and data analysis capabilities with, for example, machine learning features.

With that established, let's explore some of these Power BI features, starting with simple data models.

Building a data model for financial purposes

The data model is an abstraction layer that acts as an effective interface between the analyst and the raw data and is a key pillar for realizing your financial requirements in Power BI.

If your data model is not properly defined, every following step, such as defining calculation logic, report layout, and charts, will lead to unnecessarily inflated build times and limited usability for your users. In some cases, a wrong data model might even prevent you from realizing a reporting or calculation requirement at all. As seen in *Figure 1.1*, the data model integrates the data sources that you intend to use and structures how your users can access and use the data for reporting.

The optimal overall structure for a data model, unless you are working with a single, very simple file, is the **star schema**. Let's dive into that next.

Understanding the star schema approach

This approach breaks up the model into a central **fact table** with the transactions and several **dimension tables** with the master data details. This structure is typically applied in a data warehouse where data from different sources is consolidated into a database for analytical purposes. This same principle applies equally to Power BI, which incorporates a similar role as a centralized analytical model layer.

A **star schema** separates transactional data and analysis dimensions and leads to optimal performance and ease of analysis for your users. These dimension tables include all details like hierarchy relationships or attributes of a particular analysis perspective. For example, dimensions that are commonly used to analyze journal transactions of an **enterprise resource planning (ERP)**/ accounting system typically include the following:

- Accounts
- Organizational entity

- Scenario
- Time

The dimensions are connected to a fact table that contains the actual transactions, as outlined in the following figure:

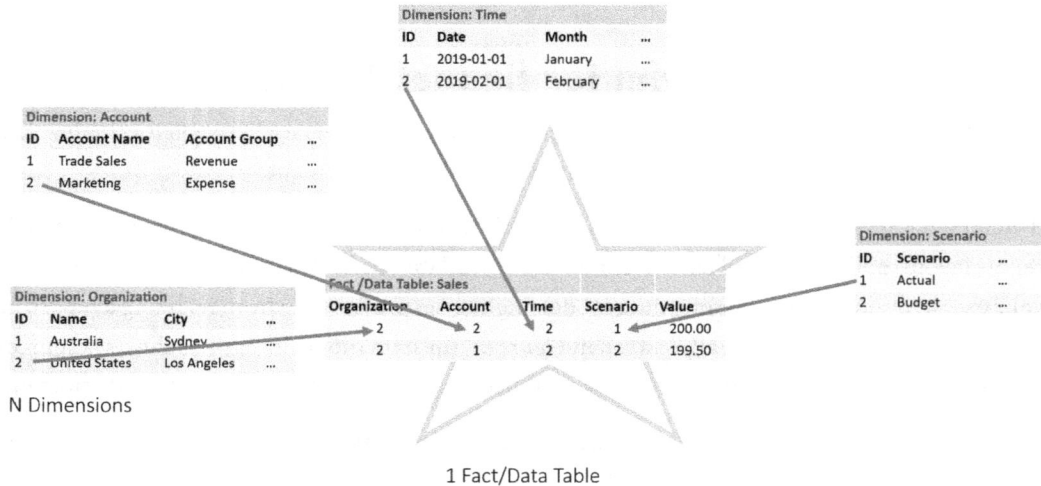

Typical Financial   "Star Schema"

Dimension: Time			
ID	Date	Month	...
1	2019-01-01	January	...
2	2019-02-01	February	...

Dimension: Account			
ID	Account Name	Account Group	...
1	Trade Sales	Revenue	...
2	Marketing	Expense	...

Dimension: Scenario		
ID	Scenario	...
1	Actual	...
2	Budget	...

Dimension: Organization			
ID	Name	City	...
1	Australia	Sydney	...
2	United States	Los Angeles	...

Fact /Data Table: Sales				
Organization	Account	Time	Scenario	Value
2	2	2	1	200.00
2	1	2	2	199.50

N Dimensions

1 Fact/Data Table

Figure 1.2 – Financial star schema

Ideally, the connection between fact and dimension tables is implemented via unique (integer) IDs. On the one hand, this provides the best performance for analysis, and on the other hand, it facilitates changes. For example, if you want to change the name of an account (and the ID stays the same), you only have to modify the account name in the dimension's Name attribute without the need to apply that change to every single journal entry that is in the fact table for that account.

This model enables users to create any possible report layout by adding row and column item hierarchies and filters, as displayed in the following diagram:

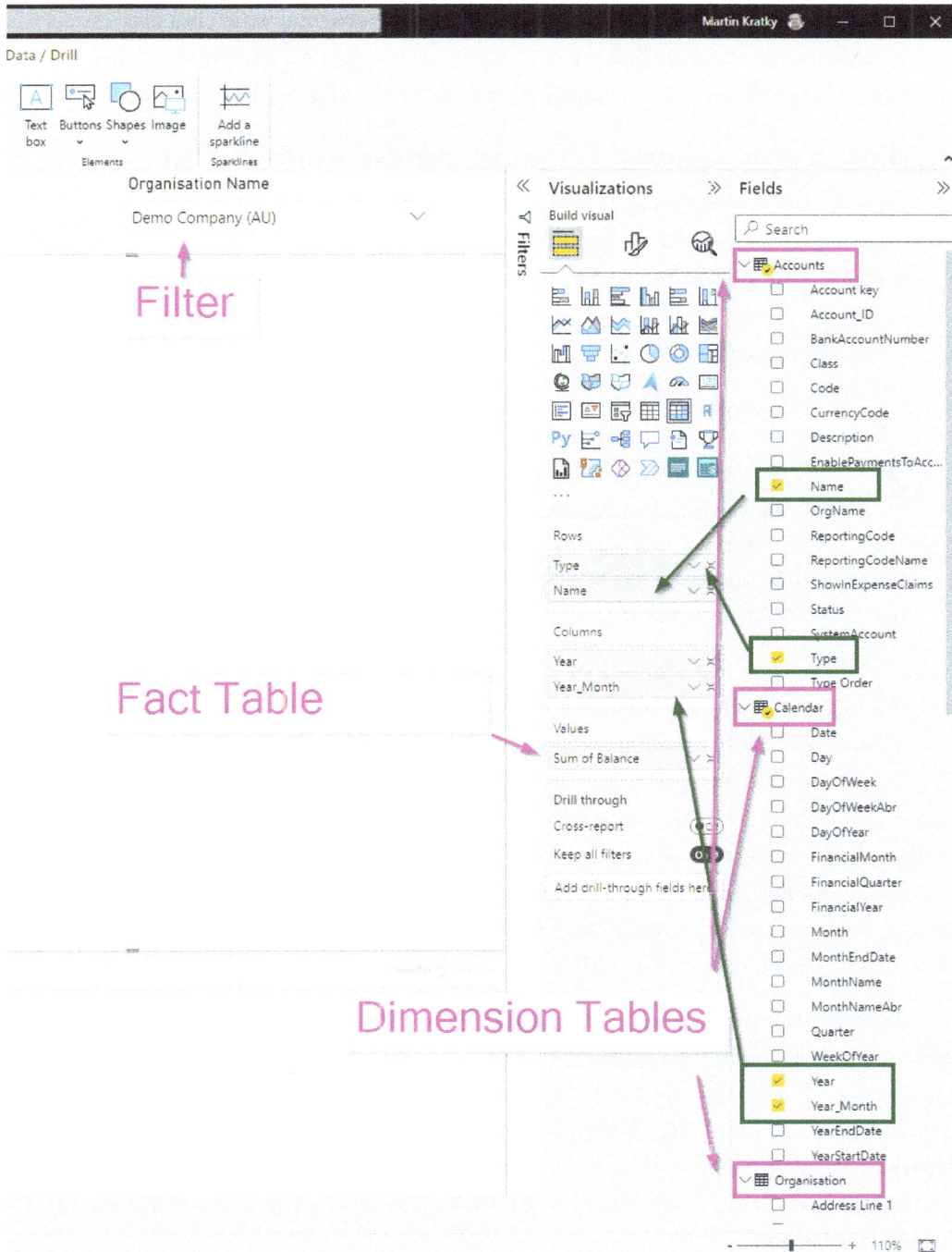

Figure 1.3 – Report based on star schema model

Several star schemata can be combined to create a **galaxy schema,** which is a data model that links multiple fact tables through shared dimension tables. But first things first. In the following section, we will cover how you can build an initial star schema for financial purposes in Power BI.

Building a star schema financial model in Power BI

In this section, you will learn how to build a financial star schema model based on sample data that is very similar in structure to a typical accounting/ERP system. The sample file is in Excel format, which is normally supported as an export option in any major accounting system.

> **A word of caution**
>
> In this book, we are using the latest Power BI Desktop/service version available in Q2 2025 and everything covered here is current as of that date. However, Power BI is a fast-developing ecosystem. Some screenshots and features might look different in your current version, and some approaches in this book might be addressed in a different way than covered here. The latest version of the sample files and notes will be updated in the README.md file on the book's GitHub site: https://github. com/PacktPublishing/Power-BI-for-Finance.

Now, you might ask, why are we not connecting to the accounting system directly? This is, in most cases, impossible or not advisable, as data structures in the source system are not set up for analysis purposes and direct access involves complex API authentications that require expert IT skills. A way around is a separate data warehouse where data is automatically loaded from the accounting system (and other sources) in a structure optimized for analysis. Some accounting system vendors offer this as a feature. In addition, there are solutions from software vendors that offer data warehouse creation in the cloud from accounting/**customer relationship management (CRM)**/billing systems that are directly accessible from Power BI as a service.

Using an Excel file is a very quick way to create a data model prototype or showcase data model building, but it involves ongoing manual efforts to create the files. For our purposes, it is the easiest way to demonstrate this. In productive systems, you wouldn't use data extracted from an ERP system but would directly connect/import data from a data warehouse or respectively prepared star/galaxy schema defined in a SQL data source. The sample `Accounting Data Set. xlsx` dataset is available for download in the book's GitHub repository. We will discuss this in the following section.

Loading Excel data through Power Query

To go through this example, you will require a current Power BI Desktop application installed on your computer. You can download the latest version of Power BI Desktop free of charge from Microsoft's current download area: `https://www.microsoft.com/en-us/power-platform/products/power-bi/desktop`. The first step is to connect the data file to your Power BI Desktop report. This is done through the Power Query data integration component that is part of the Power BI Desktop application. The easiest way to load an Excel file is from the main ribbon:

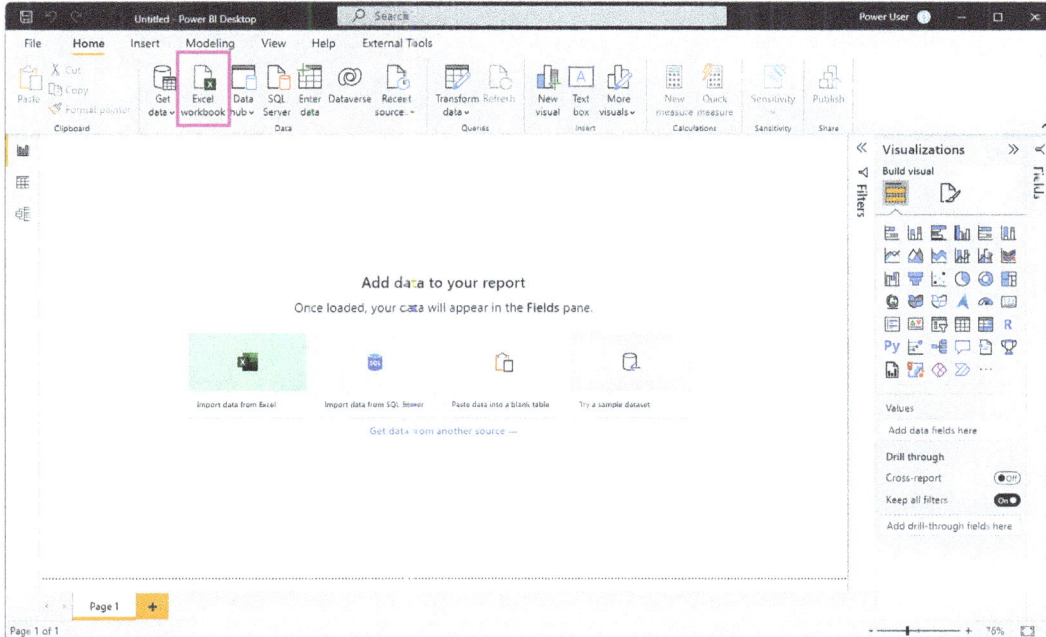

Figure 1.4 – Source selection

From here, you point to a file, and this dialog will show where you select the following four marked tables:

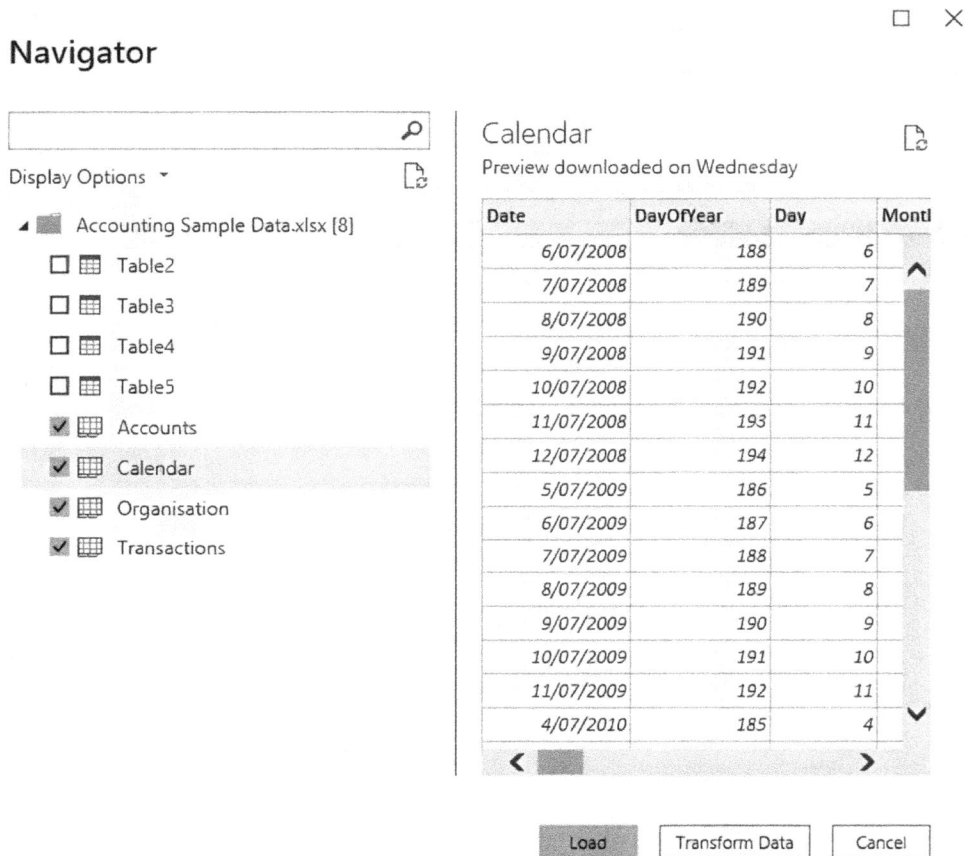

◻ ✕

Navigator

| Display Options ▾ | | | |

▲ 📰 Accounting Sample Data.xlsx [8]

◻ ▦ Table2

◻ ▦ Table3

◻ ▦ Table4

◻ ▦ Table5

✔ ▦ Accounts

✔ ▦ Calendar

✔ ▦ Organisation

✔ ▦ Transactions

Calendar
Preview downloaded on Wednesday

Date	DayOfYear	Day	Montl
6/07/2008	188	6	
7/07/2008	189	7	
8/07/2008	190	8	
9/07/2008	191	9	
10/07/2008	192	10	
11/07/2008	193	11	
12/07/2008	194	12	
5/07/2009	186	5	
6/07/2009	187	6	
7/07/2009	188	7	
8/07/2009	189	8	
9/07/2009	190	9	
10/07/2009	191	10	
11/07/2009	192	11	
4/07/2010	185	4	

| Load | Transform Data | Cancel |

Figure 1.5 – Table load

These tables are essentially components of the star schema that we have covered at the beginning of this chapter. Transactions is the *fact table* that contains sample accounting journal transactions, and Accounts, Calendar, and Organisation are related *dimension tables*. Once you have selected the tables, click on **Transform Data**. Unlike the **Load** button, this gives you an option to edit the single steps of the loading process. **Load** would immediately load the data otherwise. After you have clicked **Transform Data**, you will be in the Power Query environment and see a dialog similar to the following one:

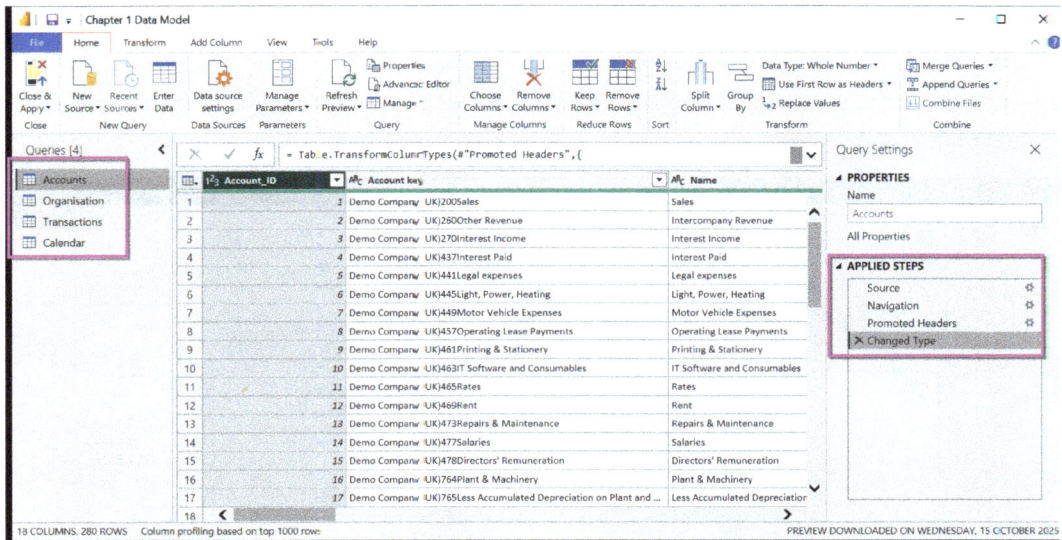

Figure 1.8 – Power Query tables and steps

What we see here now are our four tables on the left, a sample of the currently active data table in the middle, and transformation steps for that table on the right. The latter is the area where you will work to add and edit transformations of your data tables.

The `Accounts` table contains all the details of a typical accounting chart of accounts, such as account name, code, account groupings, and many more. What is important with all tables is that they have a common denominator, or in other words, a common column to connect dimension tables with the fact tables. This is normally defined on the lowest granularity of the fact table and connected to the specific ID of the respective account in the `Accounts` table, here based on an integer ID. This approach typically gives you the best performance in Power BI (likewise in a data warehouse). If your data tables don't have these IDs already in place, you can also use a common string or add an integer ID applying Power Query commands and/or scripting. As covering Power Query in detail is not the subject of this book, you can refer to the following great training materials provided by Microsoft and the Power BI community on how you can accomplish this:

- https://powerbi.microsoft.com/en-us/learning/
- https://community.powerbi.com/
- https://www.youtube.com/@yourcfoguy
- https://www.youtube.com/@PowerQuery

All tables in this sample are already structured as we need them, so the only task left is to check whether the necessary relationships between the tables are in place. For this purpose, we can switch back to the Power BI Desktop app (we can leave the **Power Query** dialog still open) and switch to the **Model** section:

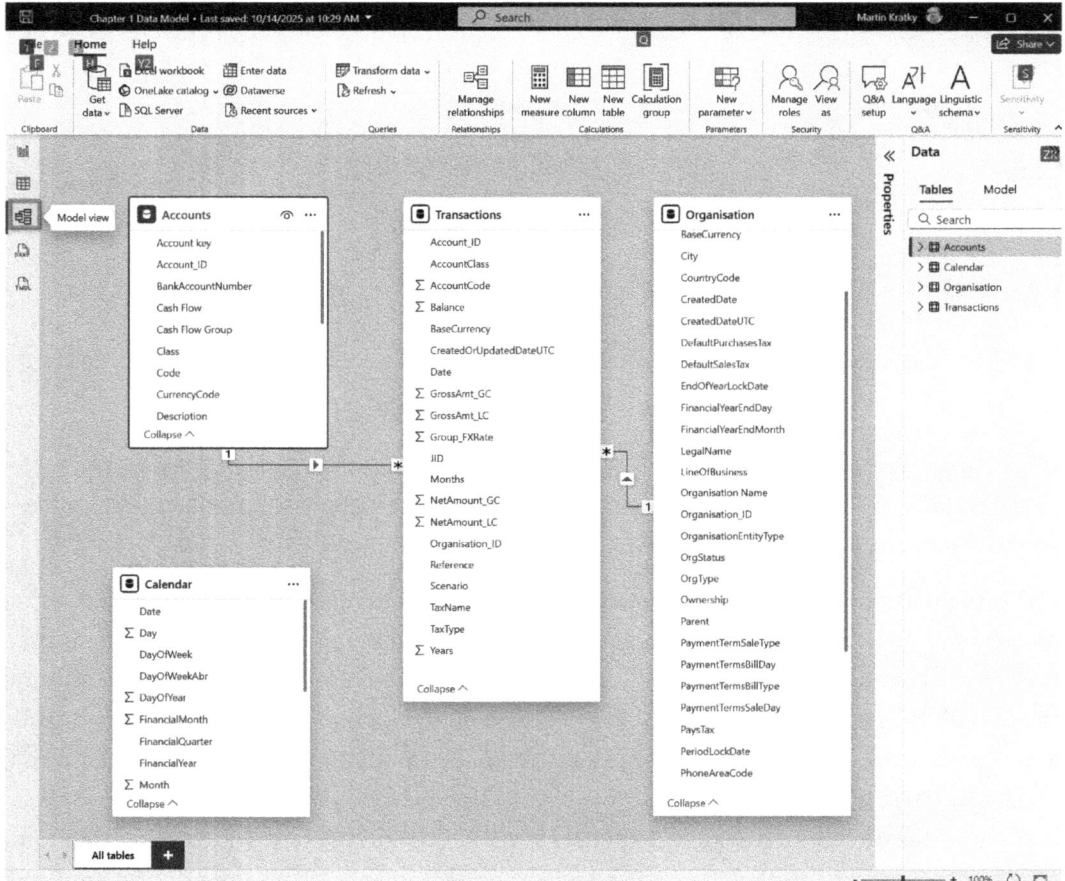

Figure 1.7 – An overview of table relationships

Here, we see our four tables, with three of them that Power BI has automatically added a relationship to. For the Calendar table, we're obliged to do this ourselves: just drag the Date field from the Calendar table to the Transactions table or use the **Manage relationships** button in the top ribbon to achieve the same in the following way. First, create a new relationship by clicking on the **New...** button:

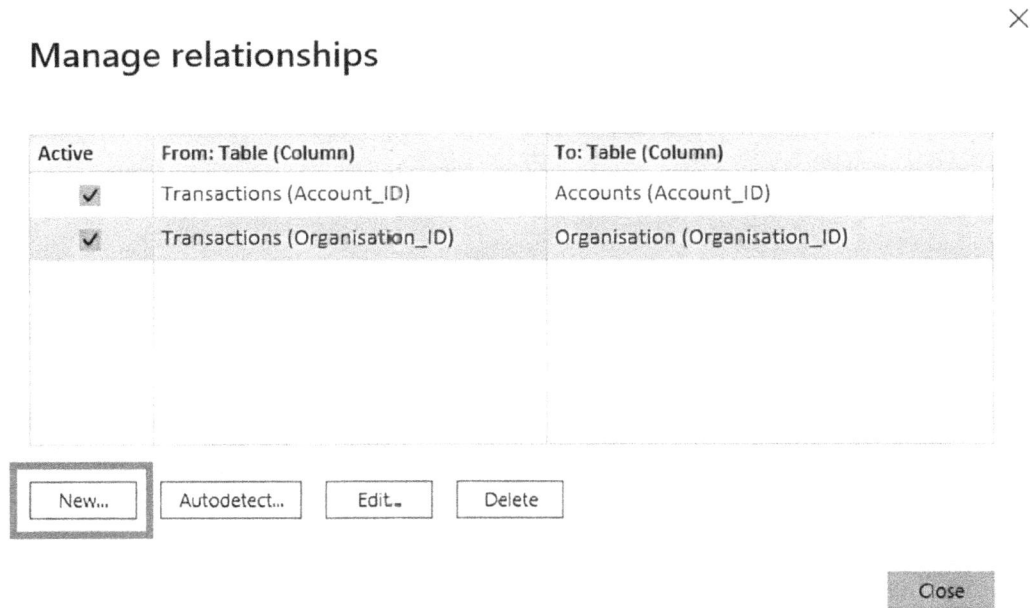

Figure 1.8 – Creating a new relationship

Then, select both the Calendar and the Transactions table and select (tick box) the Date column in each:

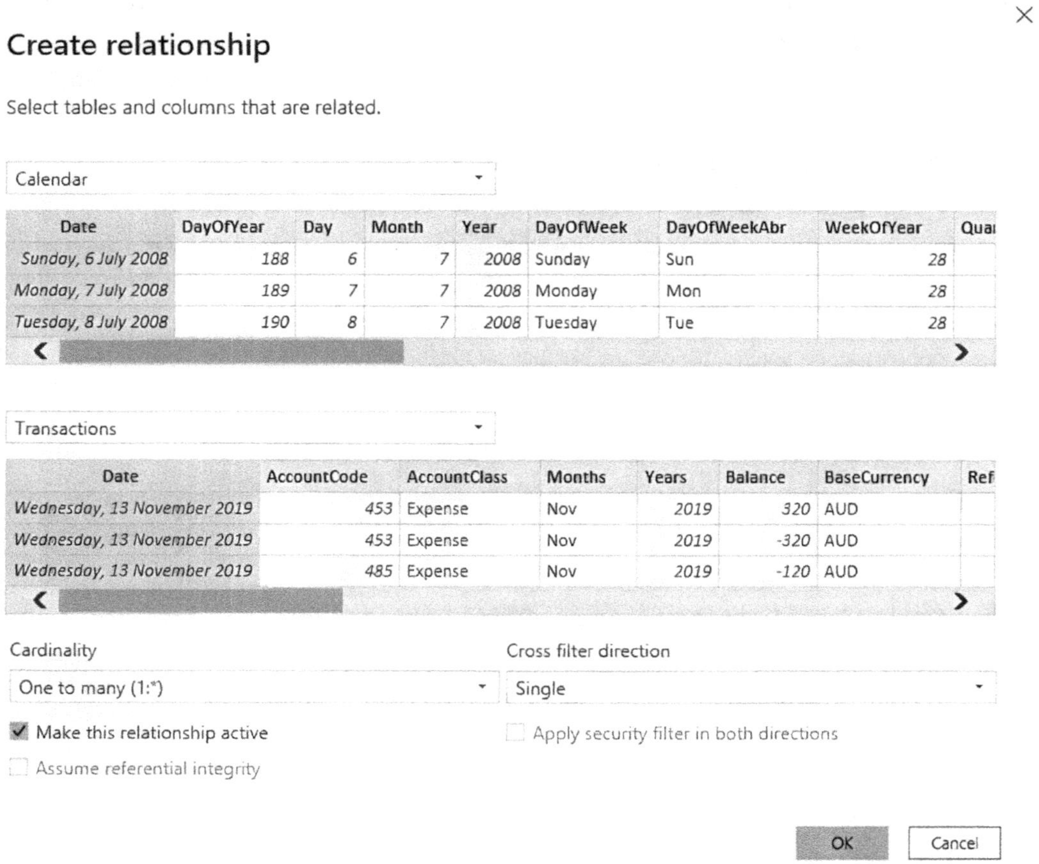

×

Create relationship

Select tables and columns that are related.

Calendar ▾

Date	DayOfYear	Day	Month	Year	DayOfWeek	DayOfWeekAbr	WeekOfYear	Qua
Sunday, 6 July 2008	188	6	7	2008	Sunday	Sun	28	
Monday, 7 July 2008	189	7	7	2008	Monday	Mon	28	
Tuesday, 8 July 2008	190	8	7	2008	Tuesday	Tue	28	

‹ ›

Transactions ▾

Date	AccountCode	AccountClass	Months	Years	Balance	BaseCurrency	Ref
Wednesday, 13 November 2019	453	Expense	Nov	2019	320	AUD	
Wednesday, 13 November 2019	453	Expense	Nov	2019	-320	AUD	
Wednesday, 13 November 2019	485	Expense	Nov	2019	-120	AUD	

‹ ›

Cardinality

One to many (1:*) ▾

Cross filter direction

Single ▾

☑ Make this relationship active

☐ Apply security filter in both directions

☐ Assume referential integrity

OK   Cancel

Figure 1.9 – Relationship definition

As a result, you will see the new relationship in place:

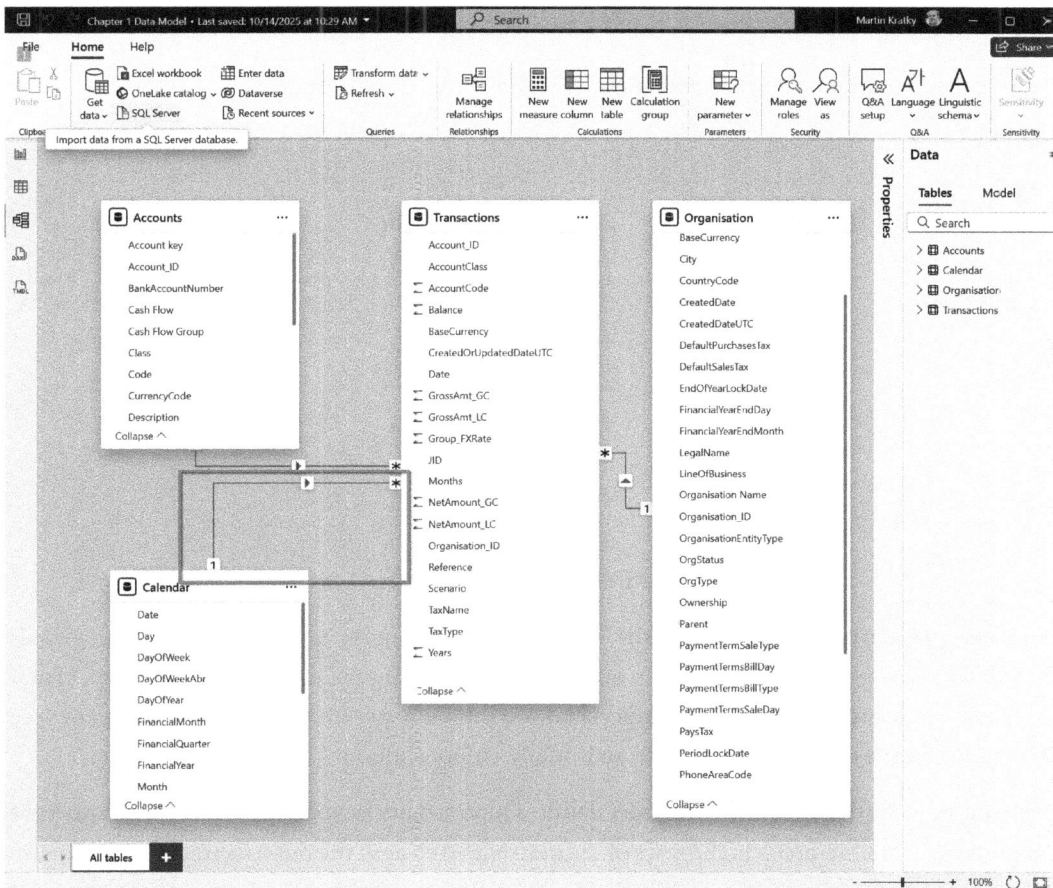

Figure 1.10 – Star schema data model

This sequence of settings was all required to establish an easy-to-use initial data model that will give us the ideal basis to build on for future calculation logic, reports, and visualization examples.

Now that we have a basic data model in place, we can build our first financial report with it.

Building a simple financial report with a star schema

Here are the steps you can follow to build a financial report with the star schema.

To get started, switch to the **Report view** section in the Power BI application.

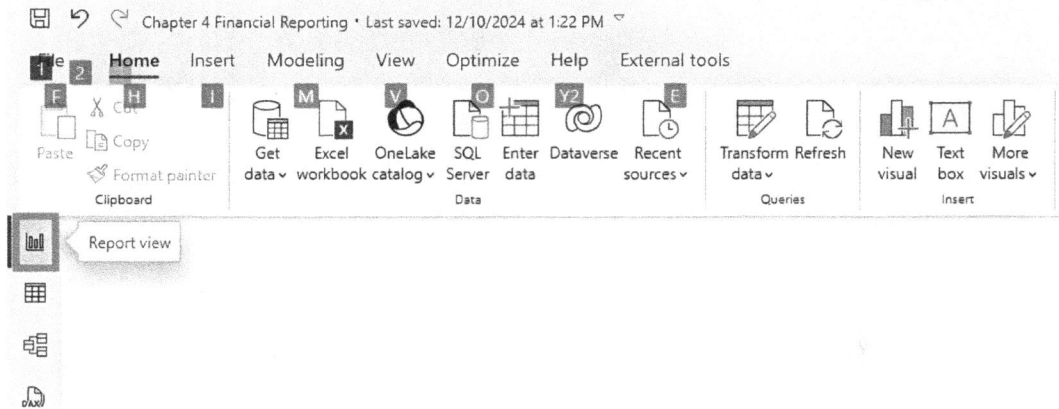

Figure 1.11 – Power BI Report View

From here, we can now add visuals as the building blocks of our report. Among the default visuals included in Power BI, a good choice as the foundation of a financial report is the **Matrix** visual. Just click on the respective symbol of the visual you intend to use in the **Visualizations** pane (see *Figure 1.12*) on the right, and it will add an initially empty container to your report canvas.

With our new Matrix visual, we can now define a report that shows a two-level (Type and Name columns) account hierarchy in the rows of the matrix as well as in the three consecutive months in the columns. In addition, we can add two **Filter** visuals at the top for which we assign Financial Year Quarter and LegalName columns from the Calendar and Organisation tables, respectively.

As a final step, we can drag a **Text Box** object from the **Insert** tab on the ribbon to the report canvas for displaying the report title. The result will look similar to this:

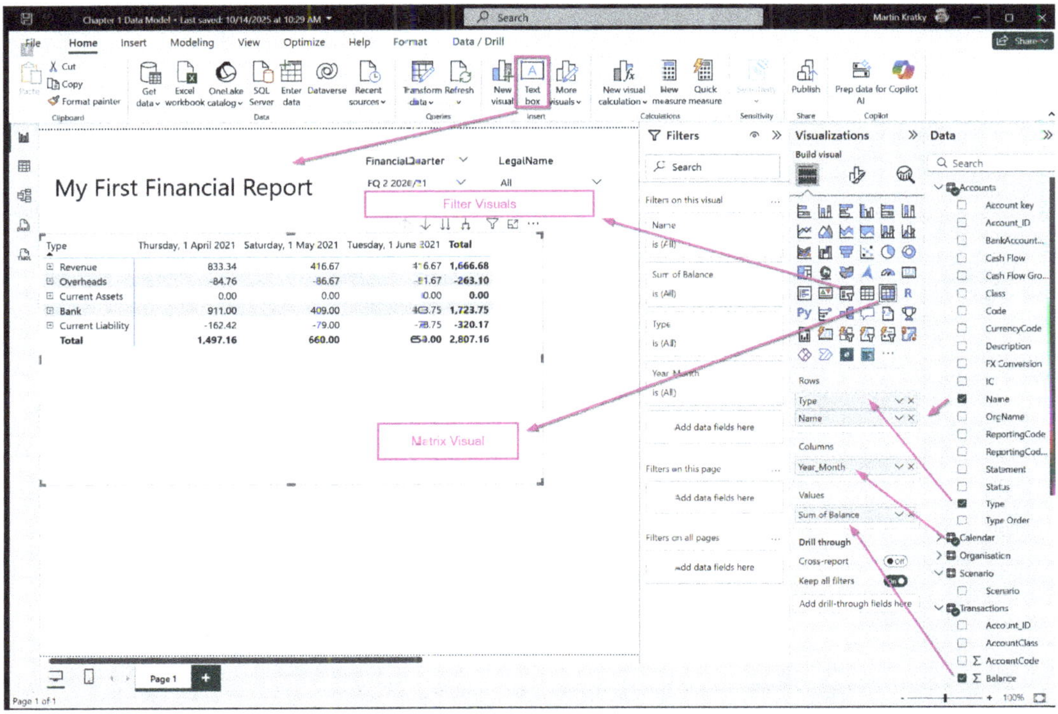

Figure 1.12 – Power BI report elements

This was a quick start, but the report obviously has a few shortcomings, and we can improve it further. Let's assume we only want to show an income statement here with the related accounts. This means we need to filter out balance sheet accounts (like the BANK entry) that are currently displayed in the report.

To accomplish this, we select the **Matrix** visual, uncheck **Select all** for the account types (the Type column) and then just select the five income statement categories (**DirectCosts, Expense, OtherIncome, Overheads** and **Revenue)** in the filter section:

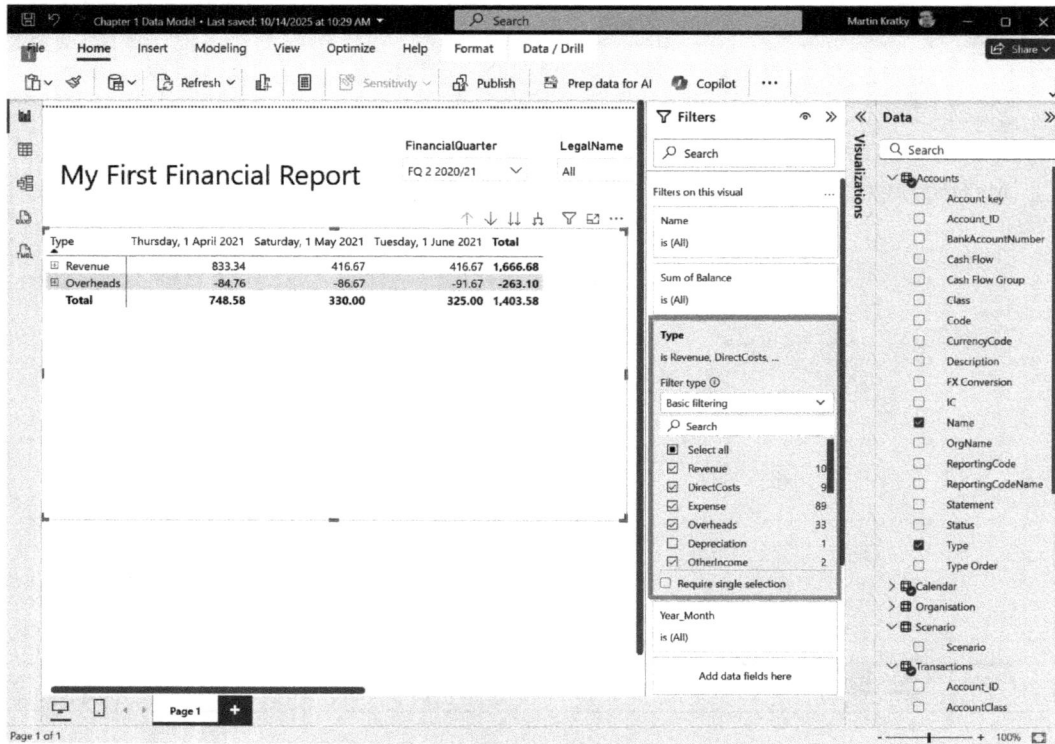

Figure 1.13 – Visual filters

A smarter option to filter only the income statement accounts would be to enhance the Accounts table by adding a new Statement column; for example, add PL for all income statement (Profit & Loss) accounts and then filter the **Matrix** visual on that column. We can either create this column directly in the underlying Excel file or create a rule based on the account type. In our case, this is straightforward: account types with an order less than 7 represent **Profit & Loss (PL)** accounts, and types with an order of 7 or higher represent **Balance Sheet (BS)** accounts. So, we simply add a custom column to assign PL to rows where the type order is less than 7, and BS to all others.

This approach has the advantage that as long as we categorize them correctly with the PL attribute, new account groups will automatically appear in the report without us having to modify filter item selection settings.

Another issue that we still have is that the order of items in the income statement is not correct. Revenue should be at the top, and all other account groups should be listed in the correct order for a financial report. This is easy to achieve in our sample as we have a column called Type Order that specifies the sequence in which we want to display the financial report items. So, we only must apply an "order by" reference to the model. We can do this by clicking on the Type column in the Accounts table and then selecting **Sort by column** from the **Column tools** tab in the ribbon, and pointing to the Type Order column:

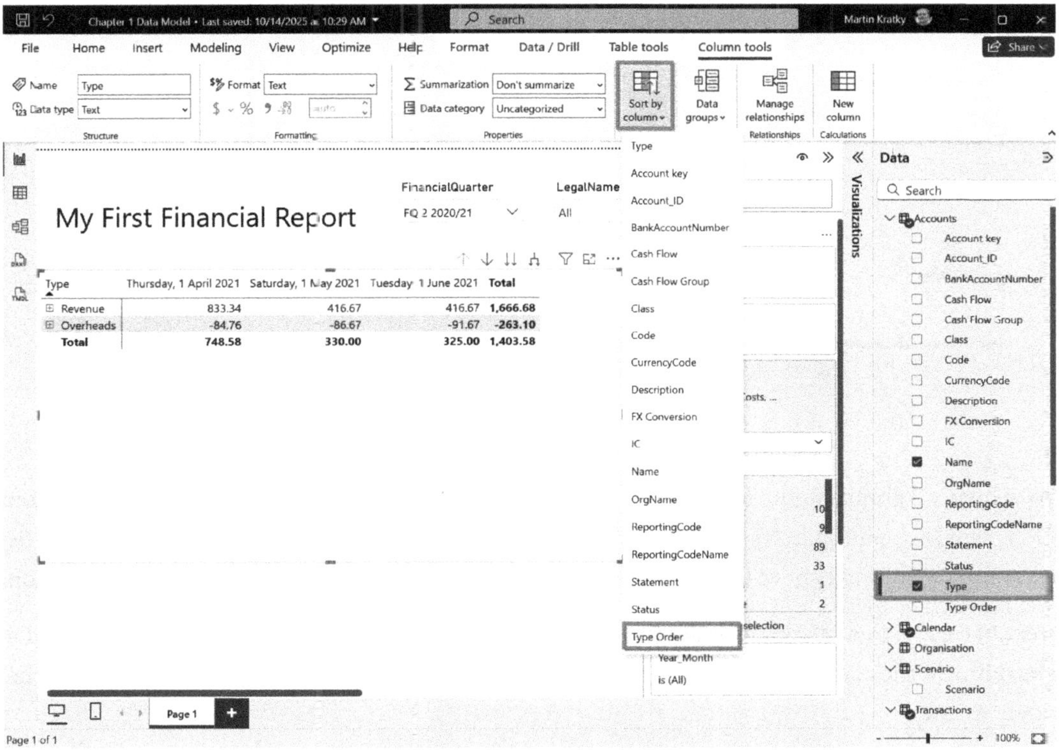

Figure 1.14 – Sort options

This now gives us a properly structured report with the account groups in the correct order:

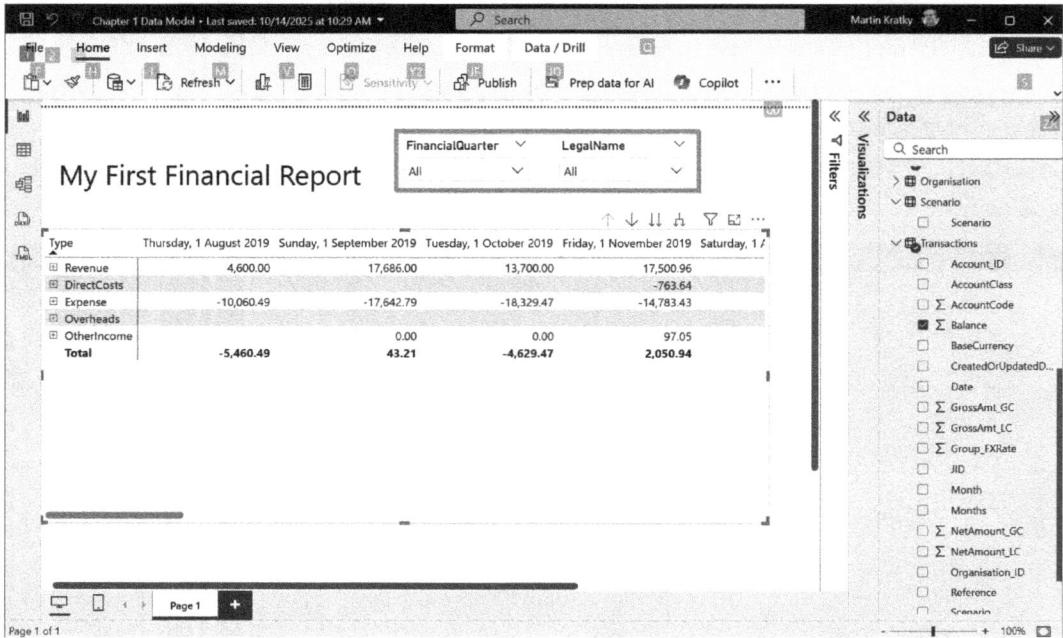

Figure 1.15 – Power BI report

To display all groups in the report, you have to switch to All Quarters in the **FinancialQuarter** filter visual as some quarters only have data for some accounts along the dimension hierarchies. Be aware, you potentially have to activate **Select all** in the filter properties before getting that option.

Next, we can add a sparkline and data bars to the report to facilitate analysis. Just select **Add a sparkline** in the context menu in the Sum of Balance column in the **Values** section (click on the down arrow):

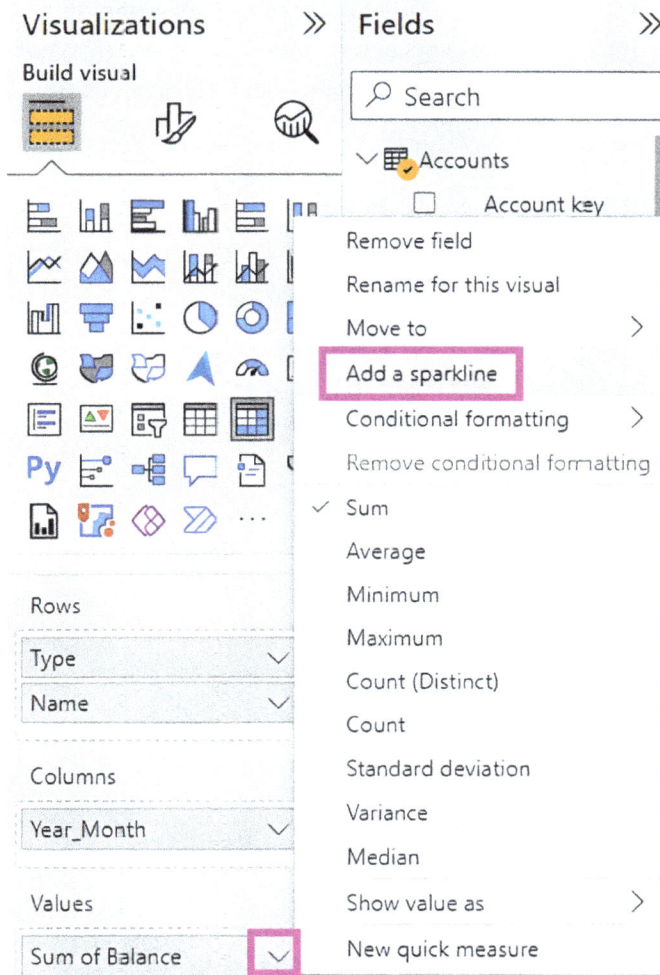

Figure 1.16 – Adding a sparkline

In the next step, we select Year_Month from the Calendar table (this would work equally with Date, but this can result in too many data points to process for Power BI). To add the data bar, we click again on the **Sum of Balance** context, choose **Conditional formatting**, and then **Data bars**:

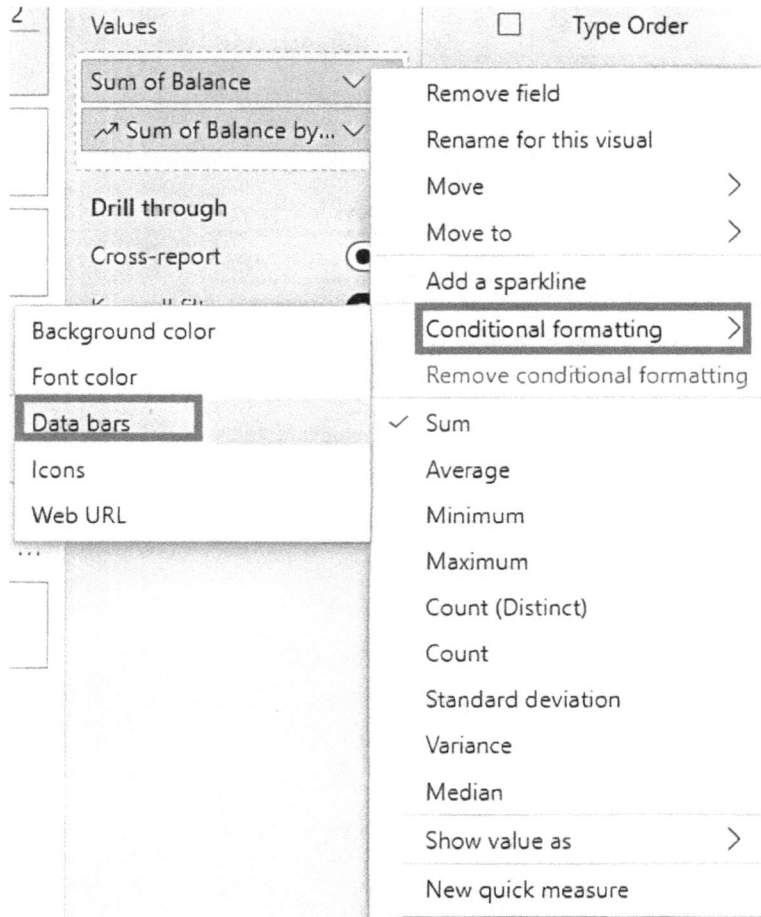

Figure 1.17 – Conditional formatting

Change the color of the negative bar to a reddish tone to clearly outline the difference to positive values:

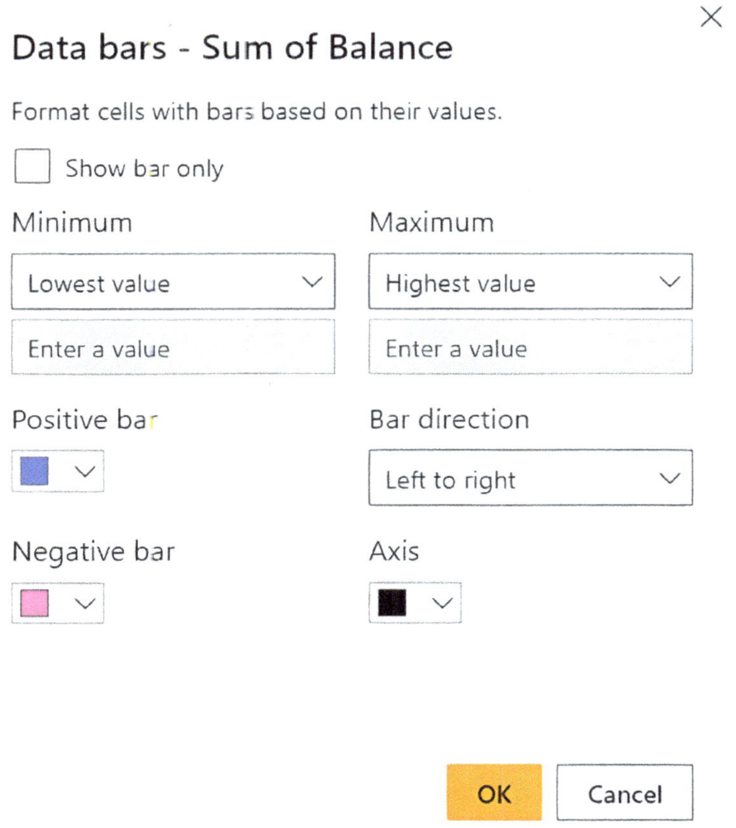

Data bars - Sum of Balance

Format cells with bars based on their values.

☐ Show bar only

Minimum	Maximum
Lowest value ⌄	Highest value ⌄
Enter a value	Enter a value

Positive bar   Bar direction

■ ⌄   Left to right ⌄

Negative bar   Axis

■ ⌄   ■ ⌄

OK   Cancel

Figure 1.18 – Positive/negative colors

As a final touch, we can change the **Subtotal label** at the bottom from **Total** to **EBIT (Earnings Before Interest and Tax)** in the **Visual** properties section:

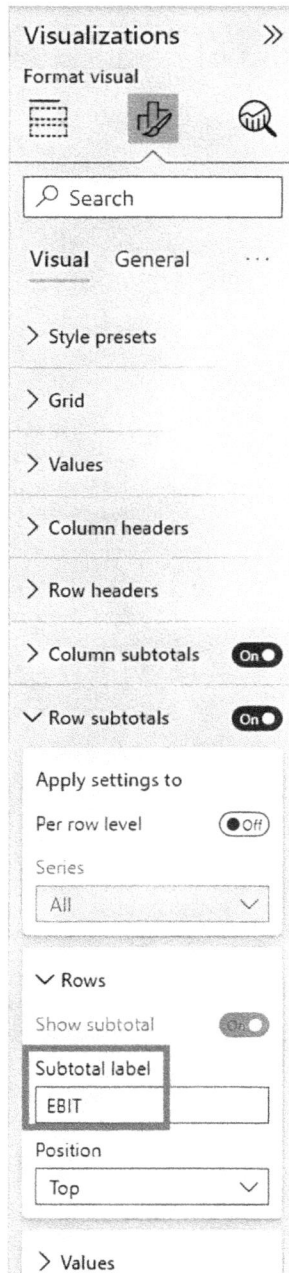

Figure 1.19 – Custom subtotal name

This change of name for the total is correct as we have revenue and cost with positive and negative signs (a contentious approach that some accountants might not like, but for simplicity in this example, hopefully is permissible):

That is it! We now have a dynamic financial report that only took us a few minutes to create:

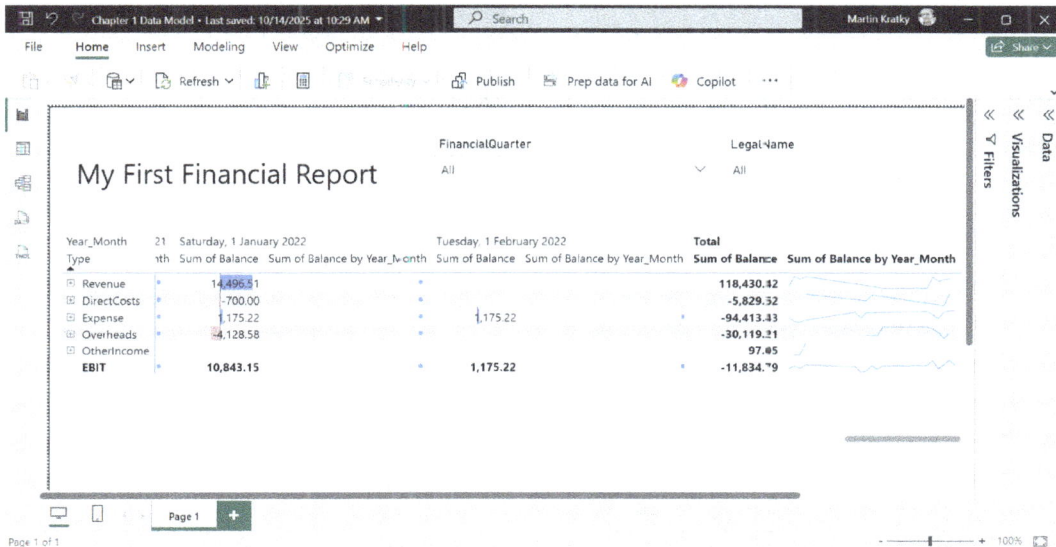

Figure 1.20 – Final report layout

This, though, is a very simplified approach that doesn't incorporate custom subtotal calculations, such as calculating a gross profit and others. Also, more advanced formatting options (for example, row-specific number formats and line handling) are not taken into account for now. We will cover all those in the dedicated *Financial Reporting* chapter (*Chapter 4*).

In the following section, we will review how we can amend the current model based on actuals with additional plan data.

Adding scenario dimensions and budget/plan data

A common requirement in finance is to compare your actuals with plan-related data, for example, an annual budget that we can add to our data model. In our current sample and in most other cases, the data for the plan will reside in a separate system, typically spreadsheets or a specialized planning software solution. In this section, I will cover the optimal modeling approach for integrating this type of data.

The typical challenge here is that the plan data is not available in the same granularity as the actuals from your accounting system. This typically involves the following:

- The time detail (e.g., budget by month versus date-specific transactions in your ERP system)
- The accounts (budgets are not done on the detailed chart of accounts)

In the following example, I will cover a typical scenario where budget data is available on a monthly basis but otherwise matches the actuals. Here, we assume that budgets were already prepared in the accounting chart of accounts structure. In a scenario where this is not the case, the options are either to manually map budget accounts in the source or introduce relationships on a different level than the lowest granularity (e.g., on account group level). This, though, can get relatively complex. Marco Russo covers this case very well in this article: https://www.sqlbi.com/articles/budget-and-other-data-at-different-granularities-in-powerpivot/.

Here, we will only cover a simpler example where only the date hierarchies don't match. For that, we have the same options as with Accounts, where we added an additional attribute for account grouping. The quickest and easiest way is to just introduce a match on the lowest granularity level, or in other words, add a Date column on the same detail as our Calendar table. We can do this either in Excel (which is very easy to accomplish for finance pros who are likely experts with that solution) or in Power Query.

The file that contains our budget numbers is called Budget Sample.xlsx. We can load that the same way as in the previous example by using the **Excel workbook** button. Once we load that in Power Query, we see that in this file, the headers were not automatically recognized. So, as a first step, we need to specify that we want to use the first row as headers:

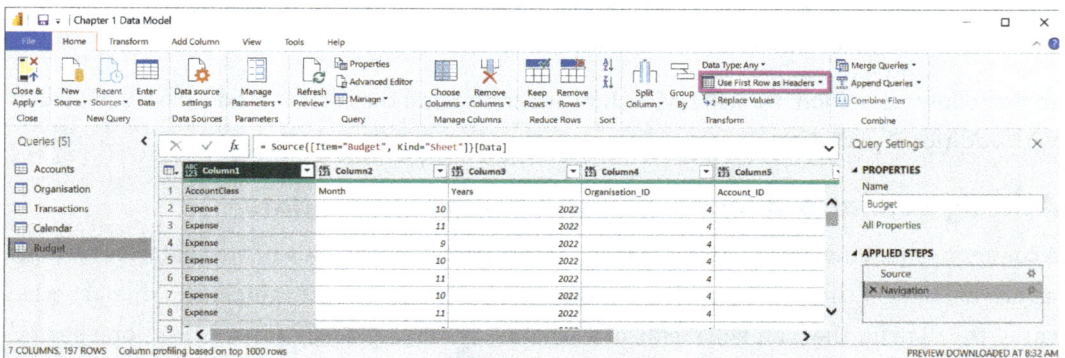

Figure 1.21 – First row as header

In the next steps, we need to make sure we can link the Budget table with the main Actuals one. The only missing key (the ID column) here is the Date key. While the other fields in the Budget table can be matched to dimensions already present in the Actuals table, the Budget table currently lacks a proper Date field—it only contains separate year and month values. An easy way to accomplish this (without complex DAX) is to just transform the existing date information into a Date field. Power Query is a good way to go: we just add a new column that concatenates the first day of the month number (1), the month, and the year. We can add a new custom column in Power Query from the **Add Column** menu:

Figure 1.22 – Adding a custom column

From here, we can now add a new column named Date and enter the definition of the column. What helps us here is the M function, Date.FromText, which converts a text string into a date value. So, we concatenate the time information in focus and add 1 for the first day of the month:

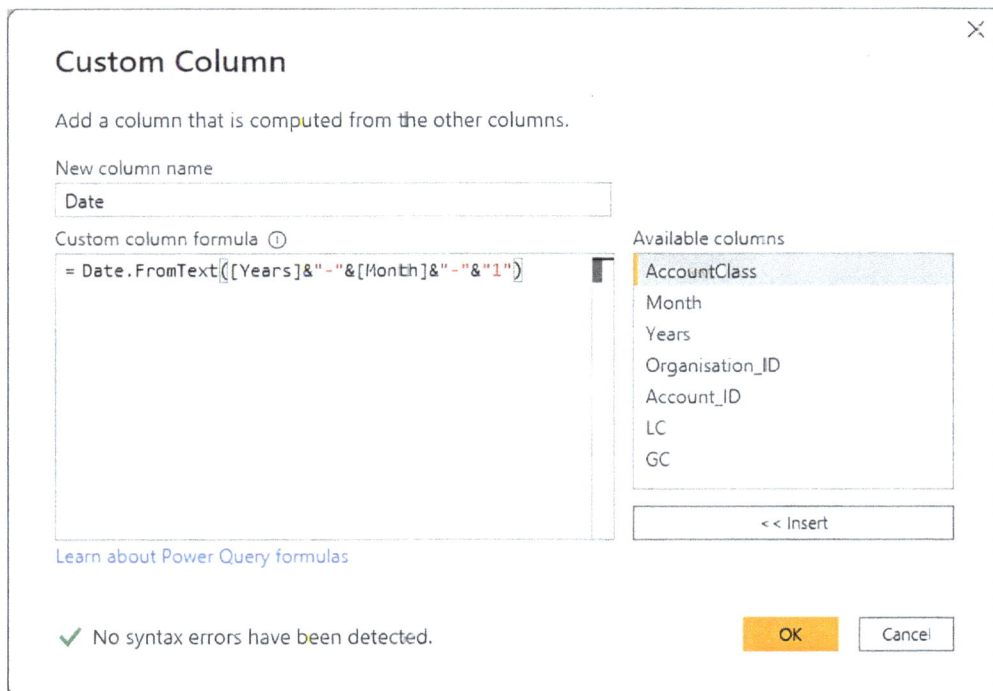

Figure 1.23 – Adding M calculation

When we press the **OK** button, we unfortunately run into an error:

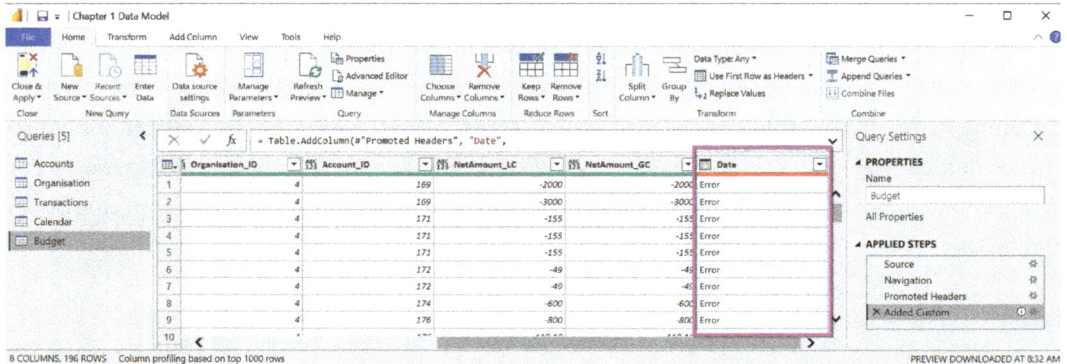

Figure 1.24 – Column errors

Clicking on the error text, we get the following explanation:

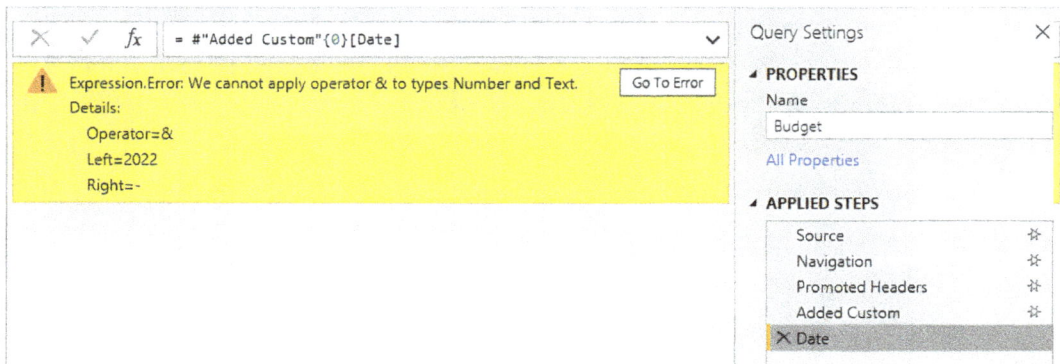

Figure 1.25 – Error details

The reason for this error is that the Year and Month columns are not specifically defined as Text types. We can easily change that by selecting the two columns (multi-column select requires holding the *Ctrl* key here) and assigning them the data type of Text:

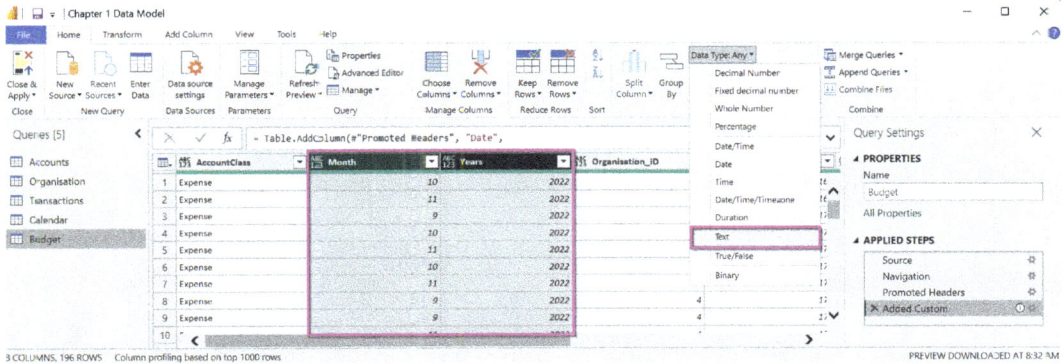

Figure 1.26 – Changing the column type

Now, we see that this operation was added to the end of the list of operations in the **APPLIED STEPS** pane, which doesn't help us, as this transformation needs to happen before the **Column Add** action. We can address this by dragging **Changed Type** before the **Added Custom** step:

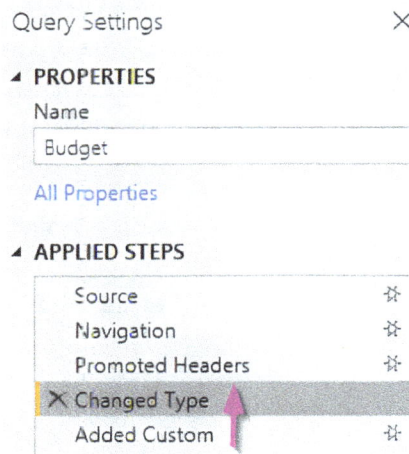

Figure 1.27 – Step sequence change

After that, we see that our added column shows the date correctly. There is just one step missing: we need to change the format to a date to correspond to our `Calendar` and fact tables. We can easily do that by selecting the column and changing that to `Date` in the **Data Type** definition in the ribbon:

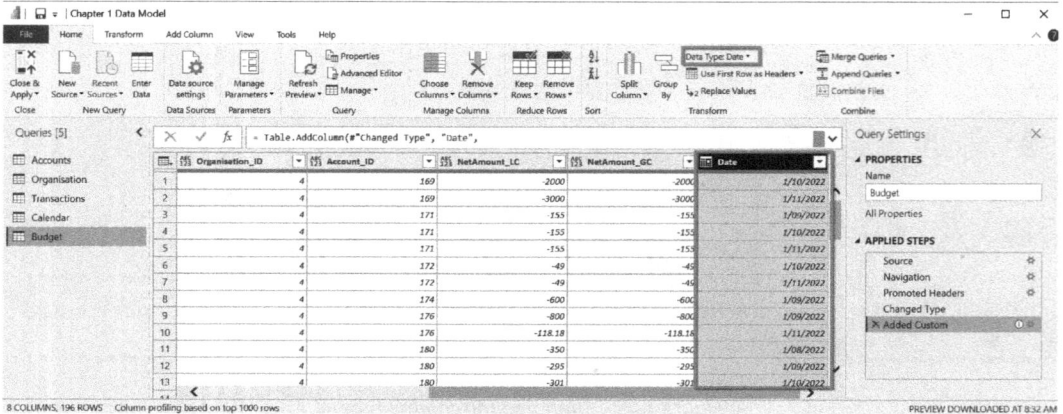

Figure 1.28 – Date type column

Now that we have the table in a format at the same granularity, the best option is to merge the Actuals table with our Budget table into a single combined (fact) table. Another option would be to use two separate fact tables. But if there is an option to bring the two tables into the same granularity for all dimensions (differences in fact table columns normally don't matter and can be handled), I would always recommend a single fact table as it makes handling both, calculation logic and reporting, much easier and less complicated to maintain.

If you really want to use multiple fact tables for scenarios, it is imperative that *all* dimensions have relationships with all these fact tables. Otherwise, any report that uses measures from multiple tables will work incorrectly. That's because a filter in a dimension that is only used in one fact table and wouldn't apply to the other ones. This makes the results incomparable. In the following section, we will look at how this can be done.

Merging Actuals and Budget tables

As explained before, we need to merge tables to facilitate calculations and keep our data model as simple as possible. Specifically, we need to merge our new Budget table into our existing Actuals table. In order to keep our existing reports working right, we need to ensure that we handle scenario filters correctly, by either filtering these to just Actuals or adding a new Scenario dimension to the report for displaying multiple scenarios. Let's get started with the following steps:

1. First, we need to modify the structures of our two fact tables and add a new Scenario column with the Power Query Editor. Let's start with the Transactions table where we add a custom column by clicking the **Custom Column** button in the **Add Column** ribbon. In that new column, we can now assign every record with the Actual scenario by typing ="Actual":

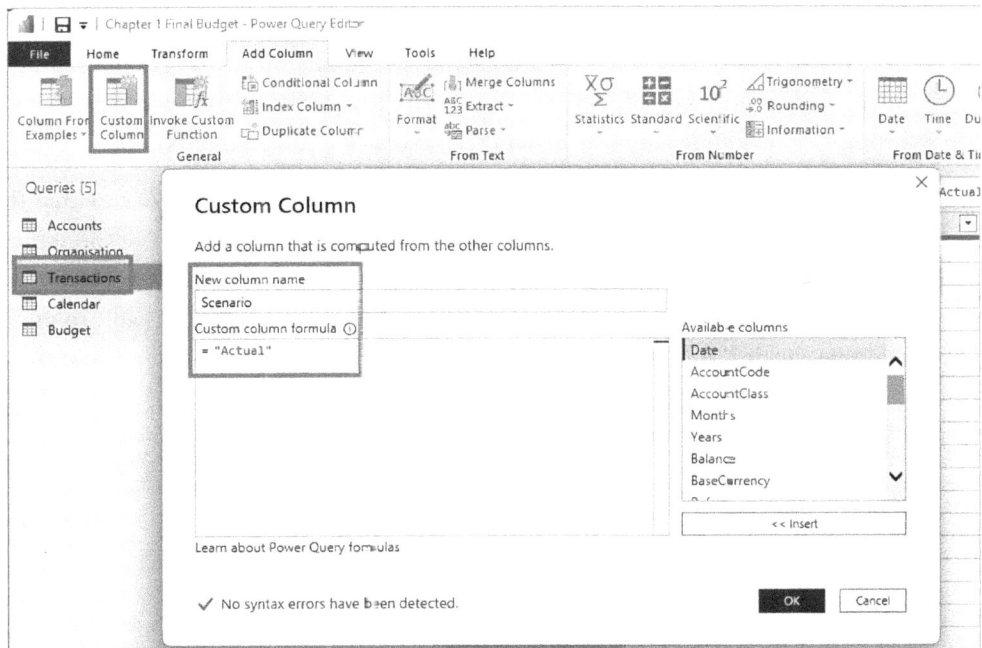

Figure 1.29 – Custom Column formula

We do the same for the Budget table but assign "Budget" in this case:

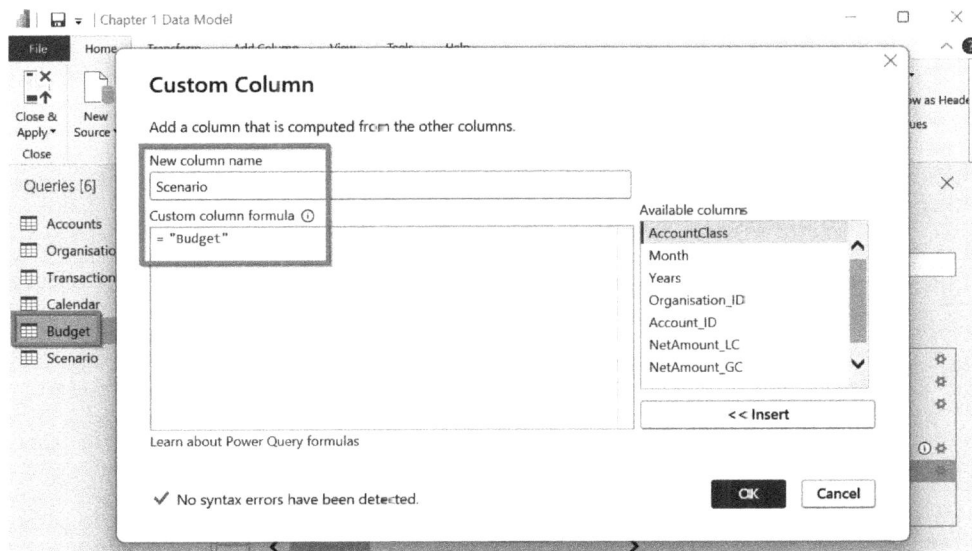

Figure 1.30 – Budget custom column

There is an argument to use IDs for the scenarios as they will be processed faster when the filters from a dimension table are applied. But this would have no measurable effect in our model and is typically not an issue in financial models, as those in most cases don't comprise very large amounts of data (i.e., exceeding 100m records).

2. To merge the two tables effectively into each other, we need to make sure that the main Value fields in the two columns match. In our example we assume that the actual values come as the net amount in **group currency (GC)** represented by the NetAmount_GC field in the Transactions table. So, we rename the GC field in the Budget table to the same by double clicking and typing NetAmount_GC:

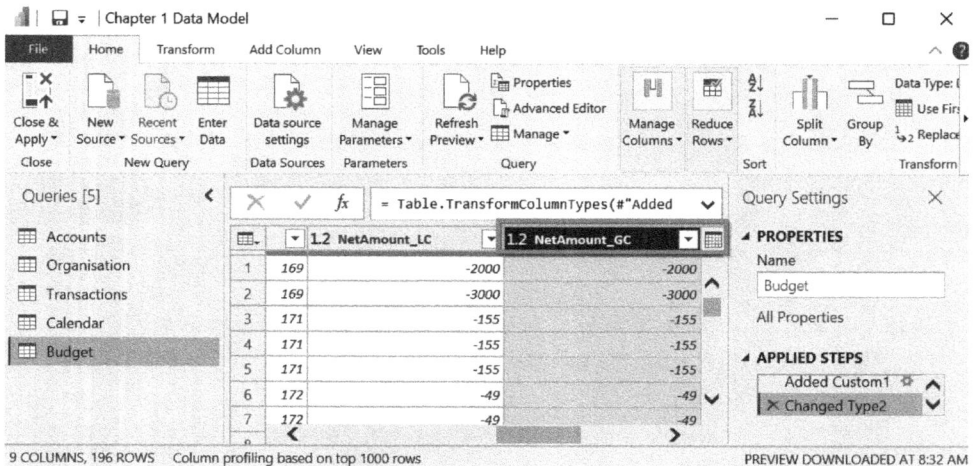

Figure 1.31 – Merging tables

These steps enable us now to merge the two tables into one by appending the records from the Budget table to the actual Transactions table:

3. To accomplish we have only to select the Transactions table and then select **Append Queries** from the ribbon.

4. In the following dialog box we select the Budget table:

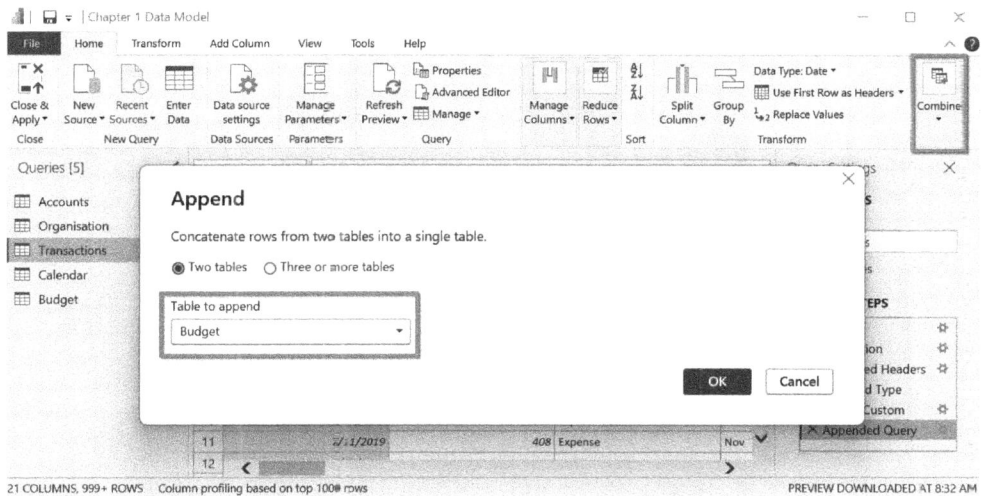

Figure 1.32 – Append table

Now, we see that our Transactions table includes the Budget records as well:

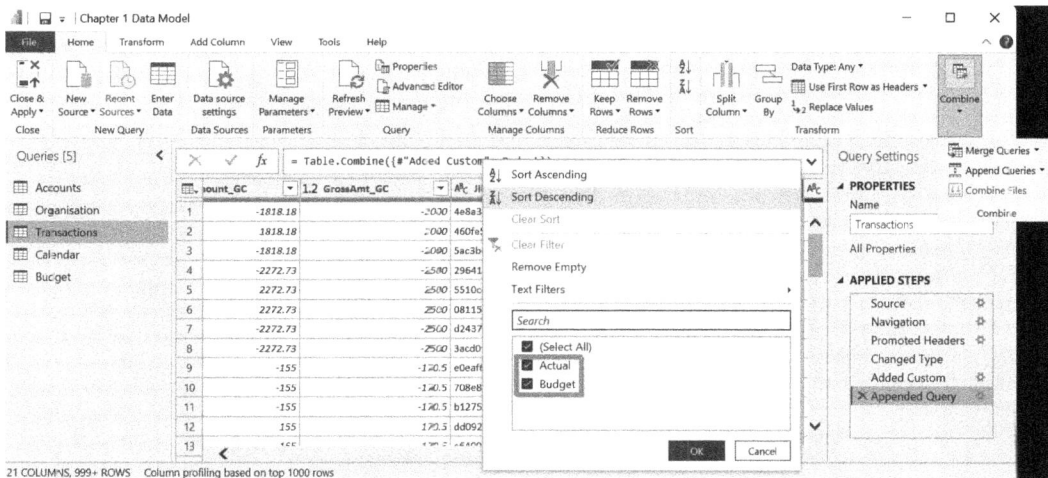

Figure 1.33 – Populated custom column

Theoretically, we could work with that table and use the new Scenario field from the Transactions table. Apart from the fact that it's not good practice from a data model perspective, this will slow filtering (slicing) performance down as applying a filter directly on the Scenario table will always process the entire Transactions table. We need to add an additional Scenario dimension that only contains the distinct scenarios in our model: Actual and Budget. There are now different ways to achieve that. The quickest is to just create a duplicate of the Transactions table, only keep the Scenario column, and run a distinct filter on that:

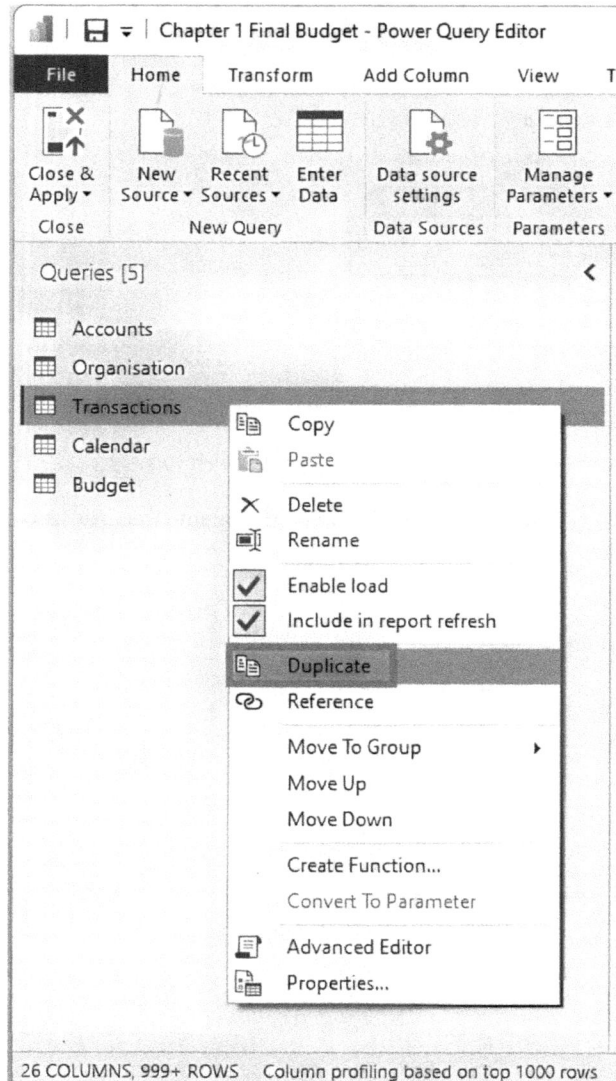

Figure 1.34 – Power Query table duplication

The other option to add a Scenario dimension table is to create it from scratch in the data model.

1. Rename that table to Scenario and just keep the Scenario column:

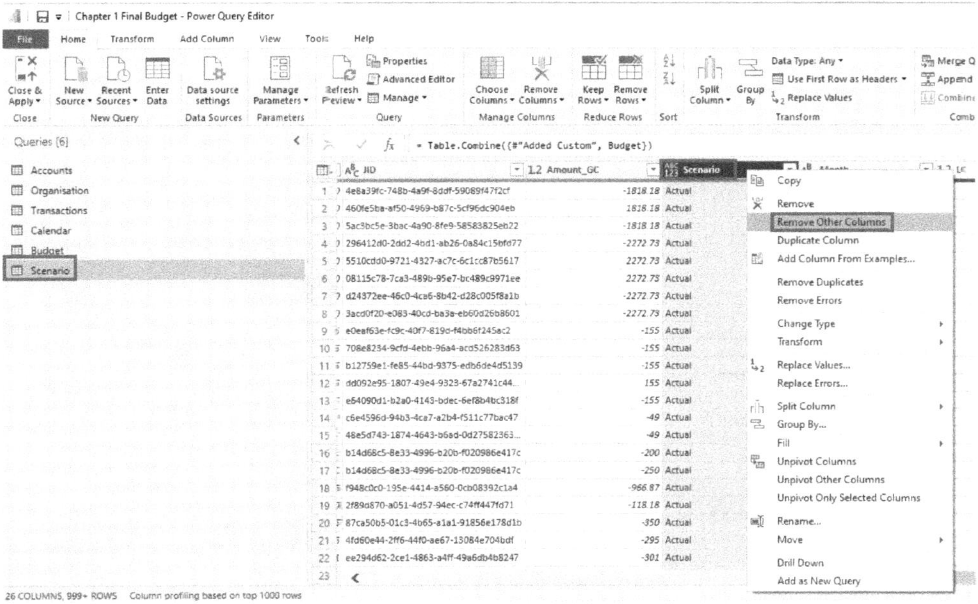

Figure 1.35 – Duplicate table

2. We only need the distinct scenarios, so we remove duplicate values:

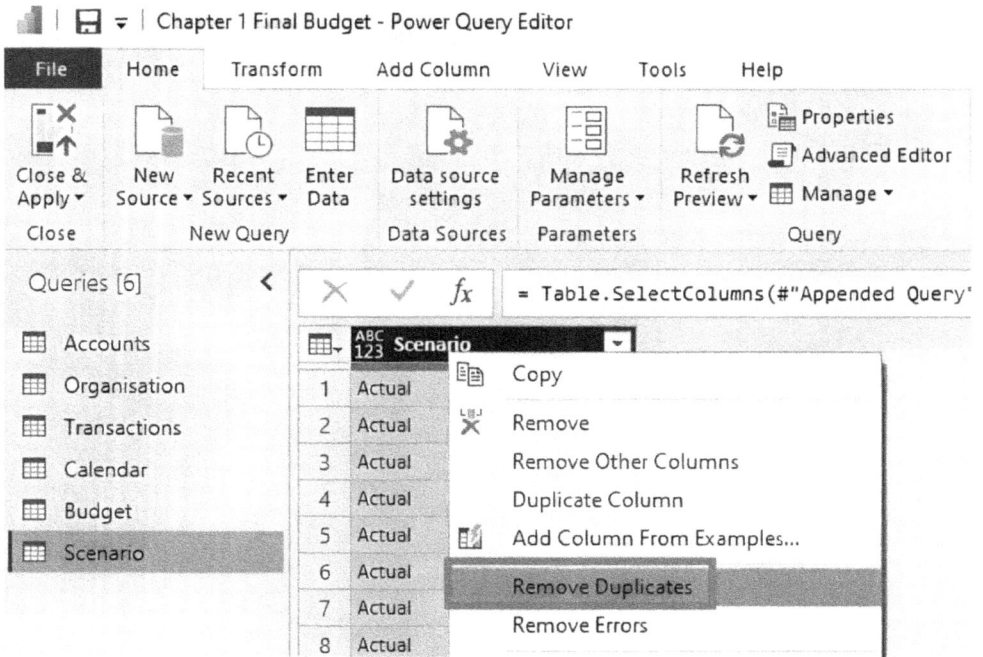

Figure 1.36 – Removing duplicates

3. The final step is to add the relationship between the new Scenario dimension and the Transactions table in the **Model** pane:

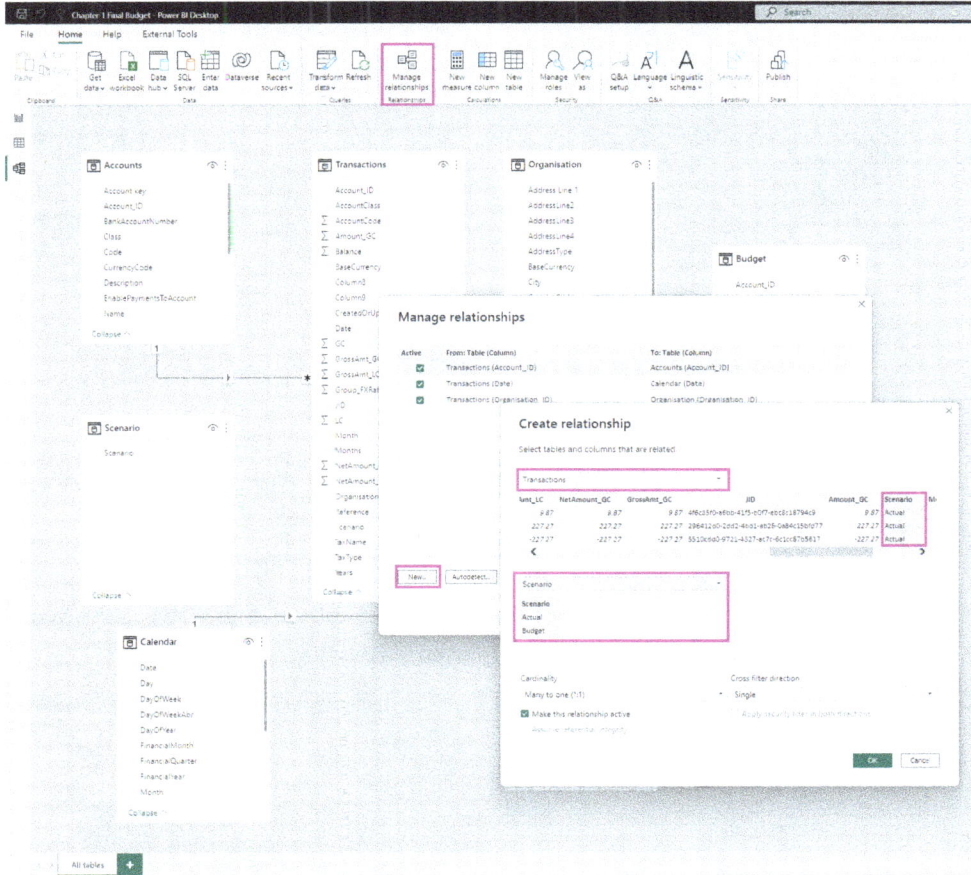

Figure 1.37 – Adding relationship for the Scenario table

4. Now, we can enhance our report layout by adding the budget scenario; we only need to add the Budget dimension as another field in the **Columns** canvas of the **Visualizations** pane:

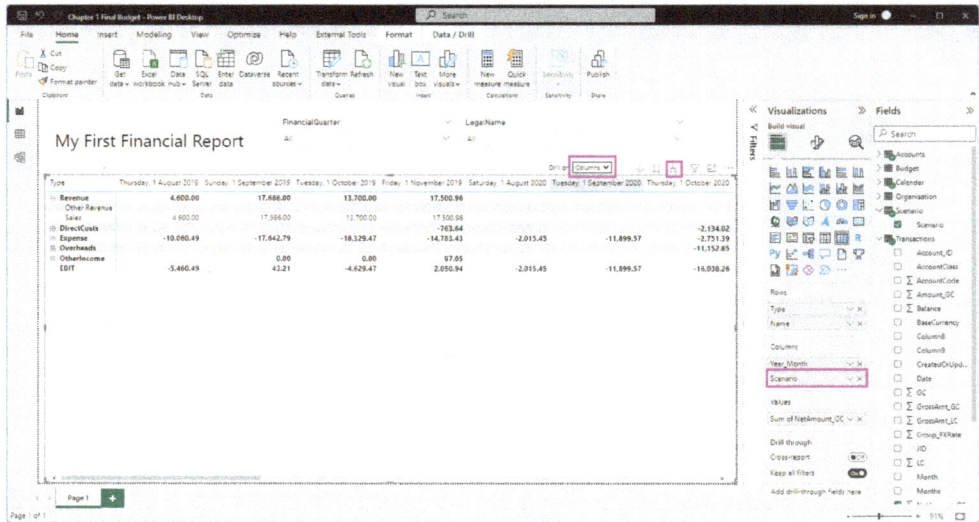

Figure 1.38 – Column drill down

This will apparently not change much, but if we perform a column drill-down in the **Matrix** visual, we will see the Actuals and Budget data displayed correctly where data exists:

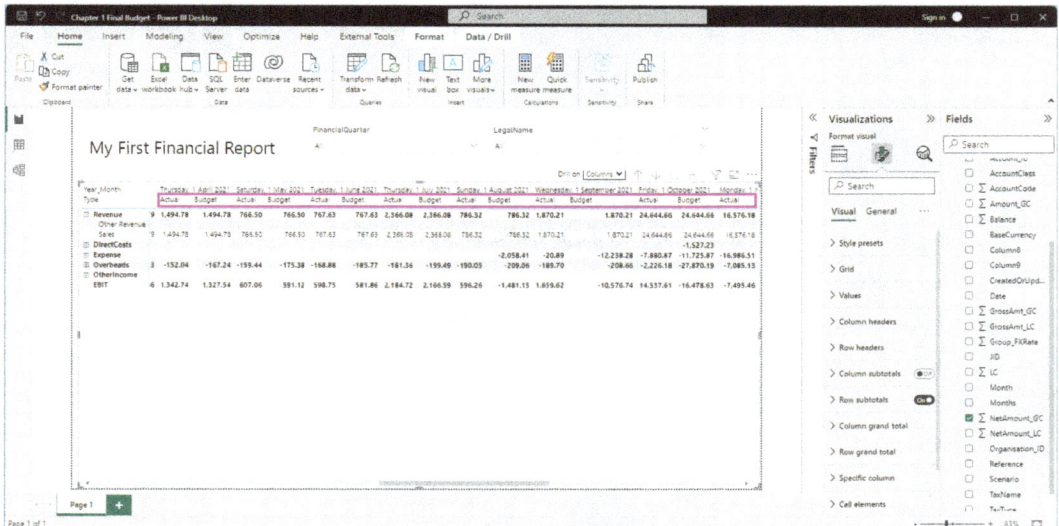

Figure 1.39 – Expanded columns

Showing column subtotals doesn't make much sense in this context, so I have hidden those in the **Matrix** visual's **Properties** pane.

These examples reflect some of the typical challenges you will face with financial data models in Power BI. Let's summarize:

- In nearly all cases, a star schema that separates dimensional and transactional data is the optimal approach. We will see in the coming chapters how much easier this makes calculations.
- You should focus on having as few as possible dimensions with only the columns you really need. If there is a one-to-one relationship between elements in one dimension and another, then these should be part of the same dimension.

Model size considerations

In preparation for the book, we have had a bit of interest in how to deal with data volumes. In my experience with Power BI from the start in hundreds of financial projects, this has never been an issue if (and that's a big IF) the data model is structured properly with clear separation of data, fact and dimension tables. Power BI can deal with data tables with billions of rows, particularly in conjunction with using new storage options in Fabric. I have rarely seen tables for common financial application scenarios that exceed the millions of rows. Power BI Desktop is only limited by the available memory in your machine. Even on 16 GB RAM machines, I have seen 100 million row tables handled reasonably well. The performance is not fantastic, but it works.

Should you really get to the limits, explore **DirectQuery** (connecting to the data store directly and not importing the data into Power BI) and Fabric options.

Summary

In this chapter, we have covered the benefits that finance users can obtain by using Power BI for financial analysis and reporting that have standardized requirements, such as recurring reporting/interactive dashboards and analytical tasks.

We then reviewed the optimal data model structure for financial requirements and covered typical modeling techniques based on a sample dataset included with the book. We then focused on the integration of budget data that resides in a different data source at a different granularity and demonstrated how to best integrate this data with our main fact table. Finally, we covered how to set up a simple financial statement with our data model.

In the next chapter, we will look at implementing typical financial calculations and logic in Power BI that will make our report more insightful using additional visualization options available in Power BI.

Get This Book's PDF Version and Exclusive Extras

Scan the QR code (or go to packtpub.com/unlock). Search for this book by name, confirm the edition, and then follow the steps on the page.

Note: Keep your invoice handy. Purchases made directly from Packt don't require one.

2

Financial Logic with Power BI

In this chapter, we will cover the different calculation options available for realizing financial logic with practical examples. After we have introduced the two main options directly available in Power BI—**calculated columns** and **Data Analysis Expressions (DAX)** (https://learn.microsoft.com/en-us/dax/) calculations—we will cover typical practical use cases and examples.

The chapter has the following main sections:

- Power BI calculations options
- Calculated columns
- Financial calculations with DAX measures
- Financial ratios
- Variance calculations

Technical requirements

To demonstrate the different calculation options in this chapter, we will build on the demo model that we developed in *Chapter 1*, where we were working with the Accounting Sample Data.xlsx Excel file with demo accounting transactions.

As with all sample content in this book, all related files from examples covered in this chapter are available in the GitHub repository: https://github.com/PacktPublishing/Power-BI-for-Finance.

You can review all calculation examples in the Chapter 2 Calculations.pbix report file.

Power BI calculations options

In Power BI, you can use three options to run calculations with your data model:

- **Calculations in your source database:**

  - **How it works:** Calculations defined in your source database—for example, views, stored procedures, and so on in a relational data warehouse.

  - **Advantage:** When using a SQL database source, users profit from a widely used calculation language (T-SQL) that provides functionalities not available in calculated columns or DAX.

  - **Disadvantage:** They can't be edited in Power BI.

- **Calculated columns:**

  - **How it works:** Column-based calculations on a row level using the M language in Power Query that apply to one table only. Processed at time of model refresh.

  - **Advantages:**

    - Can be added and edited with wizards and an editor in Power Query.

    - Can be used as filters in slicers.

  - **Disadvantages:**

    - Higher memory consumption and refresh times than DAX.

    - They work only on the row level in the specific table where they were designed.

- **Measure calculations:**

  - **How it works:** Calculations on any level across all your tables in Power BI models using the DAX language. Processed at query time.

  - **Advantages:**

    - Can be added and edited with wizards and an editor in Power BI Desktop.

    - Work on any level (e.g., single rows and aggregations).

  - **Disadvantages:**

    - More complex calculations require learning efforts.

    - Can't be used as filters (e.g., for categorization data).

Calculations in the source typically require the expertise of specialists for the respective system and are not a topic of this book, so we will look first at calculated columns with a few finance-related examples.

Calculated columns

As previously mentioned, a typical use case for calculated columns is categorizing accounts with the particular financial statement to which they belong. Examples of such assignments are *Revenue* to *Income Statement (Profit & Loss)*, *Equity* to *Balance Sheet*, and *Cash Receipts* to *Cashflow Statement*. As this involves a categorization on the row level, the only automated option is a column calculation.

In our sample file, we can open Power Query with the **Transform Data** button on the ribbon and select the **Accounts** table, which contains our account details and account hierarchy:

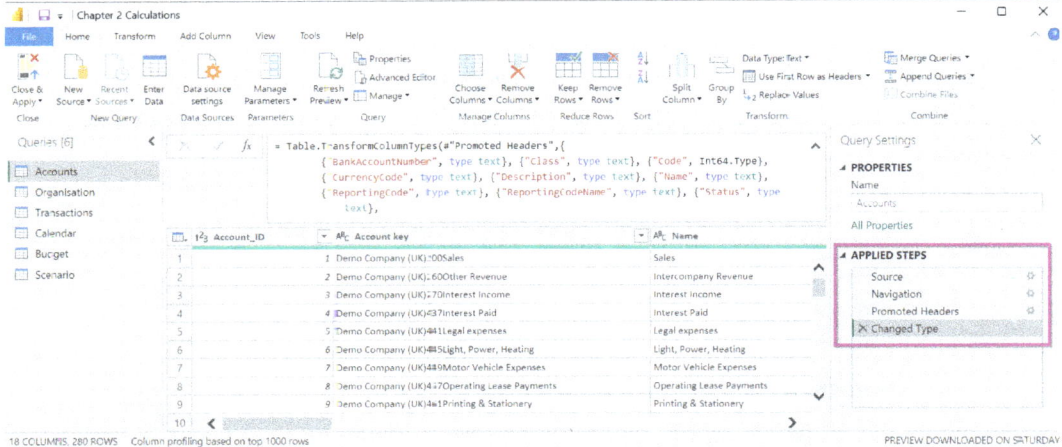

Figure 2.1 – Accounts table in Power Query

We see now the existing transformation steps in the right-hand **Query Settings** pane that Power Query has added automatically when we added the Excel file as per the *Technical requirements* section.

Our aim is now to add a new Statement category as a new column with the respective categorization to which financial statement (Income/Balance) it belongs. There are now a few options to do this: you can either add conditional columns with IF statements (e.g., IF Class = Expense then Income Statement) or use a smarter **Column From Examples** option.

This is a Power BI feature supported by machine learning methods, where you add a categorization in a row, and Power Query will learn from your entries. To get started, add a new column with the **Column From Examples** button from the Power Query ribbon:

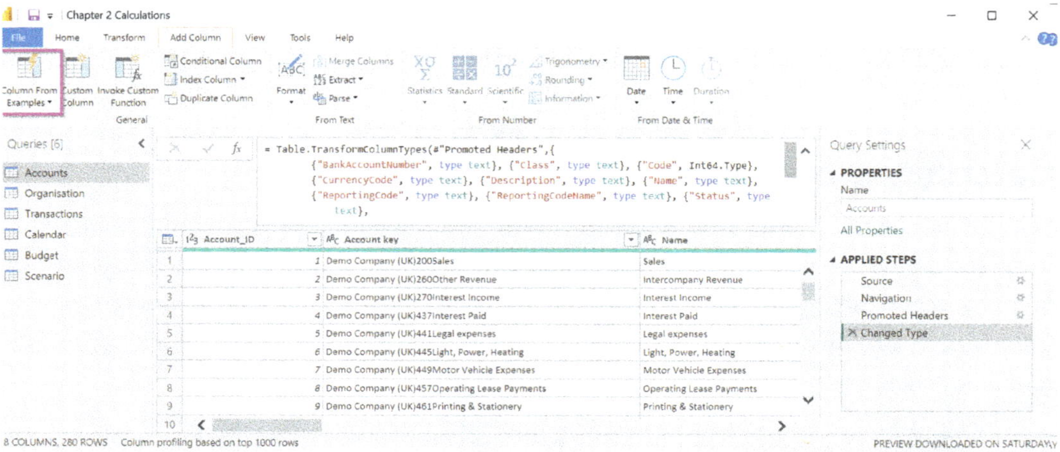

Figure 2.2 – Adding Column From Examples

This will add a new custom column on the rightmost side of the table. Double-click on the column header and change the name to Statement. Then, just enter the correct statement classification for the first account of each category. You will see Power Query automatically populate the correct classifications after a few entries.

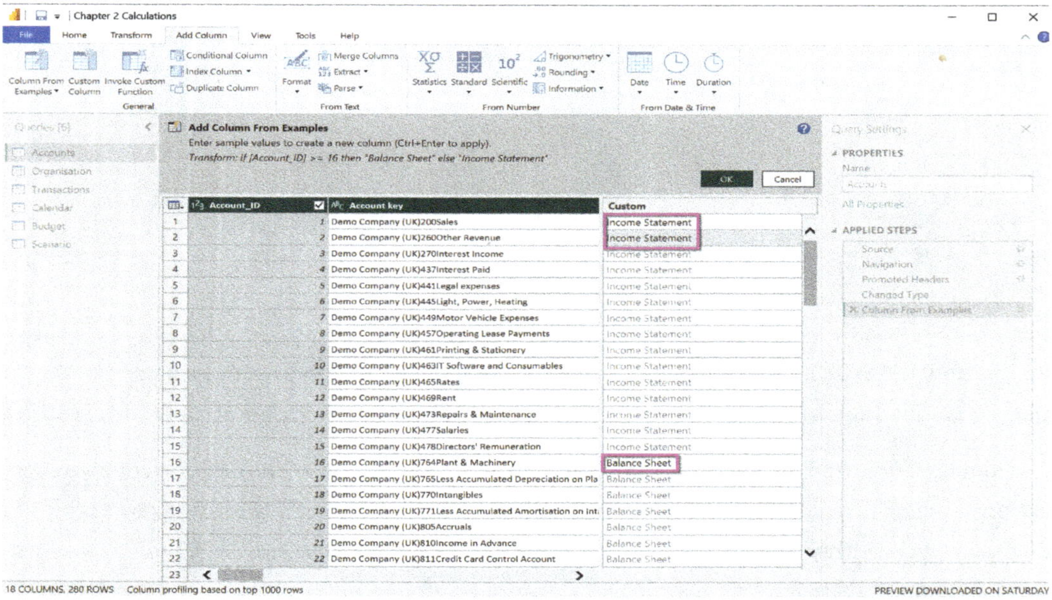

Figure 2.3 – Entering values (Balance Sheet/Income Statement) in example rows

Now, we can go back to our existing report in Power BI Desktop, add the new Statement column to the filter pane on the right, and choose, for example, just the Income Statement category. This will automatically filter either all visuals on the report or can be applied to just filter a specific visual:

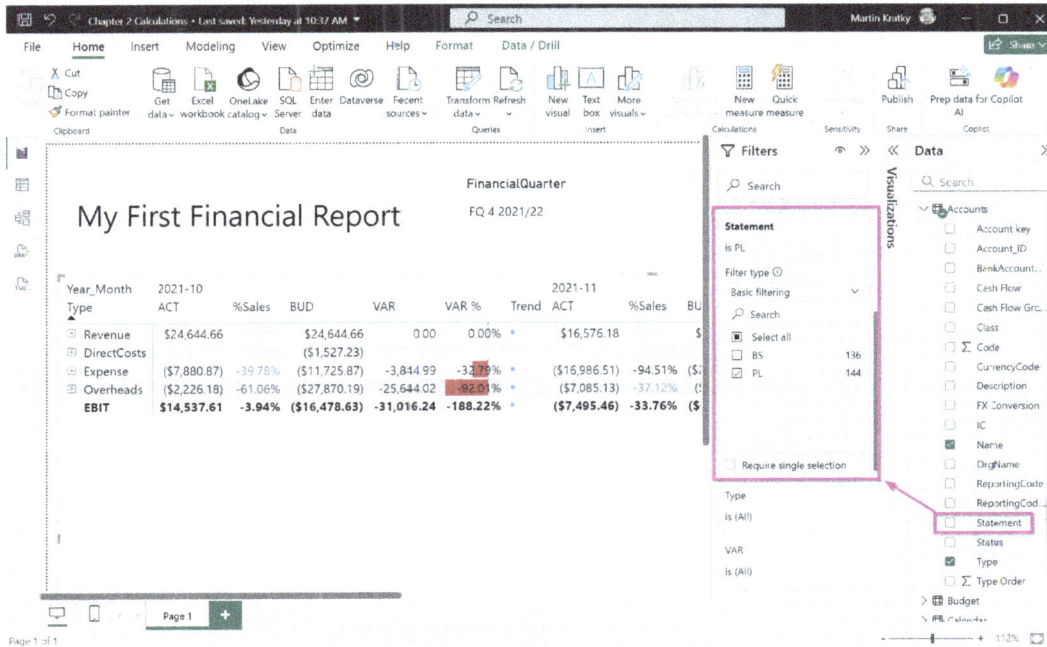

Figure 2.4 – Adding Statement filter

This was a simple example of a column calculation. There are many other use cases where you want to add financial calculations on a row level, such as currency conversions, tax calculations, price x volume, and so on. In many cases, you will be able to realize these with measures (covered in the following section) as well. Measures are typically more efficient as they consume less memory, though they are often more complex to create.

Financial calculations with DAX measures

Power BI DAX measures are calculations that use the Power BI DAX language, a library of functions and operators that can be combined to build formulas and expressions in Power BI, Analysis Services, and Power Pivot in Excel data models.

DAX measures are created in the DAX formula bar in the Power BI model designer with the following general structure:

Measure to be calculated = Calculation function with its respective arguments

Here is an example:

```
Total sales = SUM(Sales[Amount])
```

This formula will calculate the sum total of all records in the [Amount] column in the current filter context. Filter context is a very important (and unfortunately not trivial) concept in Power BI that defines what conditions apply to a result set. For example, if a filter for a particular store in the table with sales amounts is set, then our DAX calculation will only calculate the sum for the store(s) selected.

This book assumes that you are familiar with the basics of DAX. For readers who are new to DAX or want to take their knowledge to the next level, I recommend all the works (books they have authored, blogs, and training available at https://www.sqlbi.com/) by Marco Russo and Alberto Ferrari.

The section will initially cover generally useful financial ratios, and following on from that, we will look at different variance calculations that cover handling time and scenario-based cases.

Financial ratios

Initially, I would like to cover how you can realize typical financial ratios that determine profitability, liquidity, leverage, and so on in DAX. Let's start with the *percentage of revenue*, which is a great measure to compare to industry benchmarks or tracking of outliers. This calculation needs to work on the single row level, but is also not additive (i.e., we can't add up percentages), so we need to use a DAX measure-based calculation. This measure needs to return the ratio of the current context's (which is defined by filters chosen by the report user or designer) revenue to the total revenue, expressed as a percentage.

To correctly calculate the total revenue percentage, we need to adjust the *filter context* (in other words, the filters that apply to the current cell, i.e., what account, at what date, etc.), as we always want to use the total revenue, regardless of the current filters, we must override this context. The quintessential DAX formula to do that is CALCULATE(). It allows you to run a calculation in a specific filter context. So, our calculation needs to aggregate to the current sum of balances in the current context and divide this by the total revenue in an unfiltered context:

The current value is NetAmount in local or group currency. As we likely want to use a group-wide view, it makes more sense to use the group currency, as only that will show us the correct value across different companies that use different currencies. So, it is best to use the NetAmount_GC column itself or create an explicit measure:

```
GC = SUM(Transactions[NetAmount_GC])
```

In Power BI, it is not necessary to explicitly define this measure, as we can use just the column reference. It will also make other DAX calculations that utilize the same measure a little easier to read, as we can just use the reference to GC. In addition, as of the time of writing, this is required when you want to use the group currency value calculation in Excel, as here, using an implicit measure (just the [NetAmount_GC] column itself) is not supported.

The total revenue calculation is a bit more interesting as we need to change the filter context of the Accounts table (ALL(Accounts) clears any filter on that table) to always refer to the total revenue with a CALCULATE statement:

```
Total Revenue = CALCULATE (
  SUM([GC]),
    ALL (Accounts),
    Accounts[Class] = "Revenue")
```

We can now add the two measures together with DIVIDE():

```
% Revenue = DIVIDE([GC],[Total Revenue])
```

We could also have written the function in one calculation, but it's good practice in DAX to build on other DAX calculations to improve readability (by reducing complexity) and reusability. Another option would have been to use variables introducing the VAR syntax statement of the DAX language, like this:

```
%Sales =
VAR TotalRevenues =
CALCULATE (sum(Transactions[NetAmount_GC]),
    ALL (Accounts),
    Accounts[Class] = "Revenue")
RETURN
DIVIDE([GC],TotalRevenues)
```

The final step is to format this measure as a percentage and add it to our report. We can also apply a font color conditional format to help the user see the most relevant cost components. As our costs come with a negative sign, we need to have a dark color as the lowest and a light color for the highest value. For more relevance, it's also a good idea to set the maximum at 0; otherwise, there won't be much differentiation, as the light color will only apply to the positive 100% of the revenue:

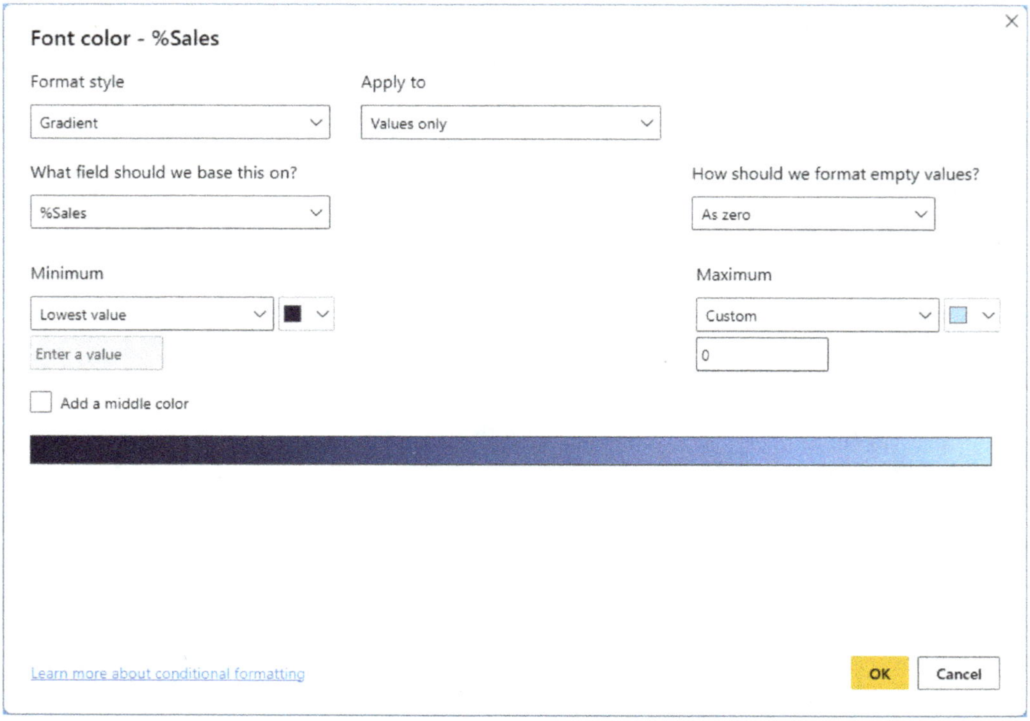

Font color - %Sales   ✕

Format style   Apply to

[Gradient   ∨]   [Values only   ∨]

What field should we base this on?   How should we format empty values?

[%Sales   ∨]   [As zero   ∨]

Minimum   Maximum

[Lowest value   ∨] [■ ∨]   [Custom   ∨] [▫ ∨]

[Enter a value   ]   [0   ]

[ ] Add a middle color

Learn more about conditional formatting   [OK] [Cancel]

Figure 2.5 – Applying conditional format to % Sales

Our report now makes it much easier for the audience to see outliers at a glance and relevant trends in the data:

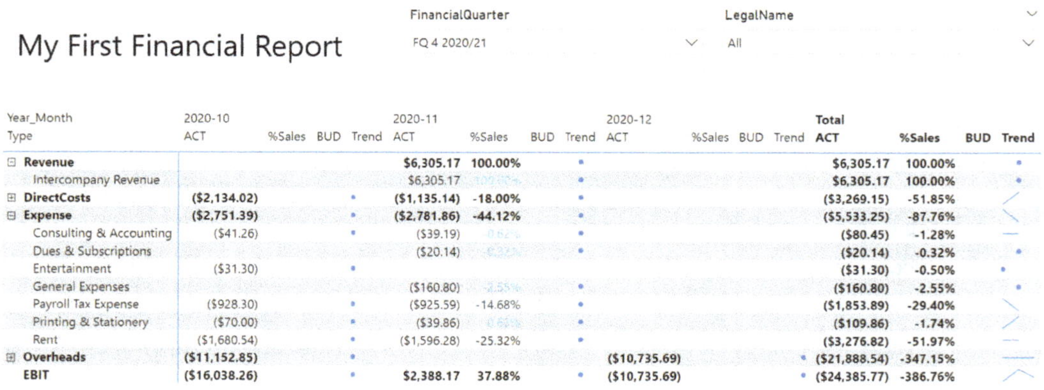

My First Financial Report

	FinancialQuarter							LegalName								
	FQ 4 2020/21							All								

Year_Month	2020-10				2020-11				2020-12				Total			
Type	ACT	%Sales	BUD	Trend	ACT	%Sales	BUD	Trend	ACT	%Sales	BUD	Trend	ACT	%Sales	BUD	Trend
⊟ **Revenue**					**$6,305.17**	**100.00%**		•					**$6,305.17**	**100.00%**		•
Intercompany Revenue					$6,305.17			•					$6,305.17	100.00%		
⊞ **DirectCosts**	**($2,134.02)**			•	**($1,135.14)**	**-18.00%**		•					**($3,269.15)**	**-51.85%**		⟋
⊟ **Expense**	**($2,751.39)**			•	**($2,781.86)**	**-44.12%**		•					**($5,533.25)**	**-87.76%**		⟍
Consulting & Accounting	($41.26)			•	($39.19)			•					($80.45)	-1.28%		—
Dues & Subscriptions					($20.14)			•					($20.14)	-0.32%		•
Entertainment	($31.30)			•									($31.30)	-0.50%		•
General Expenses					($160.80)	-2.55%		•					($160.80)	-2.55%		•
Payroll Tax Expense	($928.30)			•	($925.59)	-14.68%		•					($1,853.89)	-29.40%		⟍
Printing & Stationery	($70.00)			•	($39.86)			•					($109.86)	-1.74%		⟋
Rent	($1,680.54)			•	($1,596.28)	-25.32%		•					($3,276.82)	-51.97%		—
⊞ **Overheads**	**($11,152.85)**			•					**($10,735.69)**			•	**($21,888.54)**	**-347.15%**		—
EBIT	**($16,038.26)**			•	**$2,388.17**	**37.88%**		•	**($10,735.69)**			•	**($24,385.77)**	**-386.76%**		⌃

Figure 2.6 – Financial report with conditional format and sparklines

With a few simple steps, we have now transformed our raw data into a clear report that shows our organization's performance over time (EBIT), where expenses and revenues are trending with sparklines and the relevance as a portion of sales of revenue and expense accounts.

In the following section, we will look at another very relevant topic for financial applications: how to handle scenario and time-based variances.

Variance calculations

Typical calculations in financial reports include variances, which calculate the difference between two scenarios, time periods, and so on.

Let's initially look at an actual budget variance.

Comparing scenario-based variances

As Power BI doesn't support dimension calculations like adding a new row to a table that calculates based on other elements in that table, we need to define generic measures for all scenarios that we want to compare and finally, the calculations for their variance—in our case, we can use the separate fact tables (which would require relationships with all dimensions to both fact tables!):

```
ACT = sum(Transactions[NetAmount_GC])
BUD = sum(Budget[NetAmount_GC])
```

The better option is to use our combined fact table with Actual and Budget details. This is a little bit more complicated as we need to use two CALCULATE() DAX measures that filter on the respective scenario; otherwise, the filters for one scenario would suppress the other:

```
ACT = CALCULATE([GC],ALL(Scenario),Scenario[Scenario]="Actual")
BUD = CALCULATE([GC],ALL(Scenario),Scenario[Scenario]="Budget")
```

As you can see, we are also using an ALL() function here that removes any filter from the scenario table. This avoids the BUD measure showing as empty when an active filter from the Scenario table, different from the BUD scenario, is applied.

Now, we can just define the calculation as follows:

```
VAR = IF(Transactions[ACT]<>BLANK(),[BUD]-[ACT])
```

This calculation will work in our context, where costs were multiplied by a negative sign. In a situation where you only get the balances, this needs to be adapted so that it treats expenses and revenues correctly. One option here is a DAX calculation with an IF statement that applies a sign depending on the account type. We are also using an IF() statement to check and to only calculate if there are actuals to avoid the report getting too cluttered.

To calculate the relative variance, we can use the following:

```
VAR % = DIVIDE([VAR],abs([BUD]))
```

By using the abs() function that returns the absolute value, we make sure that the calculations return a positive value for positive effects (higher revenue) and a negative one for deviations.

We apply a percentage format, and again, we can enhance understanding by adding a bar chart. The visualization will be improved by setting fixed values for the upper and lower thresholds:

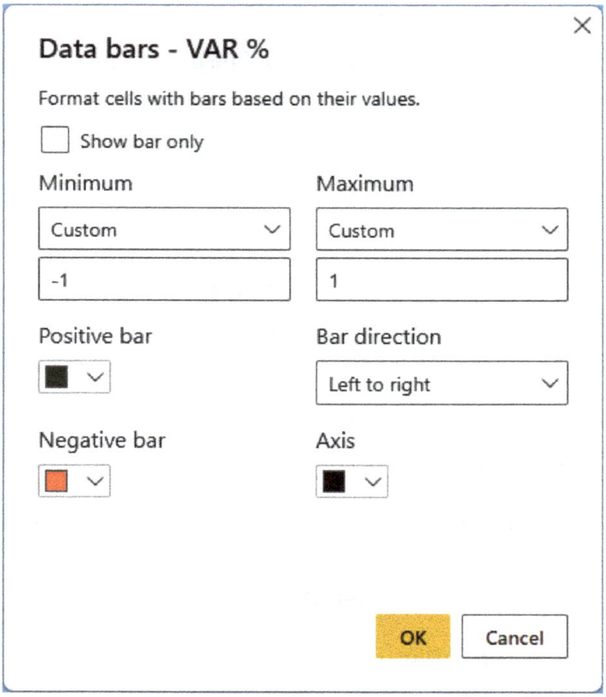

Figure 2.7 – Conditional format for variance calculation

We get the following result:

Year_Month	2021-10				2021-11							2021-12				
Type	BUD	VAR	VAR %	Trend	ACT	%Sales	BUD	VAR	VAR %	Trend	ACT	%Sales	BUD	VAR	VAR %
⊟ Revenue	$24,644.66	0.00	0.00%	■	$16,576.18	100.00%	$23,511.87	6,935.69	29.50%	■	$24,069.57	100.00%	$26,476.52	2,406.95	9.09%
Intercompany Revenue							$6,935.69								
Sales	$24,644.66	0.00	0.00%	■	$16,576.18		$16,576.18	0.00	-0.00%	■	$24,069.57		$26,476.52	2,406.96	9.09%
⊟ DirectCosts	($1,527.23)					-2.13%	($855.25)				($3,394.68)	-14.10%	($3,734.14)	-339.47	-9.09%
Cost of Goods Sold	($1,527.23)						($855.25)								
Purchases											($3,394.68)	-14.10%	($3,734.14)	-339.47	-9.09%
⊞ Expense	($11,725.87)	-3,844.99	-32.79%	■	($16,986.51)	-94.51%	($20,901.02)	-3,914.51	-18.73%	■	($1,466.51)	-6.09%	($1,613.16)	-146.65	-9.09%
⊞ Overheads	($27,870.19)	-25,644.02	-92.01%	■	($7,085.13)	-37.12%	($7,793.64)	-708.51	-9.09%	■	($14,949.13)	-92.34%	($31,725.90)	-16,776.78	-52.88%
EBIT	($16,478.63)	-31,016.24	-188.22%	■	($7,495.46)	-33.76%	($6,038.04)	1,457.41	24.14%	■	$4,259.25	-12.54%	($10,596.69)	-14,855.94	-140.19%

Figure 2.8 – Report with additional calculations and visualizations

Here, the users now get a clear picture of the absolute and relative variances at a glance, supported by visualization techniques such as data bars.

Comparing time-based variances

Next, I would like to cover a typically used time-based variance: the difference from the prior year. This is again a standard DAX calculation where we compare two time periods—in this case, the previous year (-1 on the YEAR level) with the DATEADD( ) DAX function:

```
PY ACT = CALCULATE (
        [ACT],
        DATEADD ( 'Calendar'[Date], -1, YEAR ),
        ALL ( 'Calendar'[Date] )
    )
```

As a final step, we can add a year-to-date (YTD) calculation where we calculate the total from the start of the financial year to the latest date (MAX ('Calendar'[Date])) in the active Calendar date selection:

```
YTD ACT =
VAR StartOfFYYear =
    SELECTEDVALUE ( 'Calendar'[YearStartDate] )
RETURN
    CALCULATE (
        Transactions[ACT],
        FILTER (
            ALL ( 'Calendar' ),
```

```
        'Calendar'[Date] >= StartOfFYYear
            && [Date] <= MAX ( 'Calendar'[Date] )
    )
)
```

This calculation will accommodate financial years that have a start date different from the standard calendar year start on the first of January. Our Calendar dimension already contains financial year start and end dates as columns in the table.

Summary

In this chapter, you have learned about the different options to realize basic financial logic calculations for profitability, actual/plan, and time-based variances in Power BI.

This was, of course, only an initial basic introduction to the special financial application chapters; starting from *Chapter 6*, we will look at more advanced options in detail.

Having looked at data integration and model structure in the previous chapter and financial logic in this one, we now have all the necessary building blocks in place for the next chapter. In the upcoming chapter, we will cover general principles and specific examples on how to best present the data in the data model.

Part 2

Financial Reports and Dashboards

Having established a solid data foundation in *Part 1*, *Part 2* focuses on turning that data into meaningful visual stories. It covers how to design business-information dashboards, build standard financial reports, and leverage Excel for ad-hoc analysis or further distribution.

This part of the book includes the following chapters:

- *Chapter 3, Business Information Design*
- *Chapter 4, How to Realize Financial Reporting in Power BI*
- *Chapter 5, How to Best Integrate Excel and Power BI for Financial Requirements*

3

Business Information Design

Before we move on to a more detailed treatment of financial statements, I will cover general information design principles that apply to any report/dashboard design in Power BI. The fundamental goal of business information design is effective communication, which typically entails two key objectives:

- The recipient understands the key messages as quickly as possible
- The information is relevant and actionable

The chapter is broken down into two sections – general principles and the implementation in Power BI. Specifically, we will cover the following:

- General design recommendations
- Table recommendations
- Chart recommendations
- Power BI design case study
- Power BI specific settings

A big inspiration for the design-related recommendations was the works of Edward Tufte, Steven Few, and Rolf Hichert, and the **International Business Communication Standards (IBCS)** framework that was developed under his guidance. The IBCS are a comprehensive set of guidelines designed to standardize and improve the clarity, consistency, and effectiveness of business communication, particularly in charts, tables, reports, and presentations. A key objective is to address the widespread problem of unclear and inconsistent data visualization in corporate environments.

IBCS provides specific rules for chart design, color usage, notation, and structure that make business information easier to understand and compare across different documents and organizations. The standards emphasize principles such as semantic notation (using consistent symbols and colors to convey meaning), proper scaling, clear labeling, and logical arrangement of data elements. By following IBCS guidelines, users can create more professional, readable, and actionable visual communications that reduce misinterpretation, speed up decision-making processes, and ensure that stakeholders can quickly grasp key insights from complex data presentations. If you are interested in further details on the topic, I highly recommend checking out their works and the IBCS website: `https://www.ibcs.com/`.

Technical requirements

As with all sample content in this book, all related files from examples covered in this chapter are available in the GitHub repository: `https://github.com/PacktPublishing/Power-BI-for-Finance`.

General design recommendations

The objective of effective business information design is that our audiences understand the key messages and implications in the quickest possible way. In the next subsections, we will look at the principles that help us achieve effective business information design.

1. Minimize ink-to-data ratio

A general principle that is stressed by all information design experts is to minimize noise when communicating business information. In other words, any embellishments that are not relevant to the message of your data are to be avoided. This includes, among others, graphical elements, shapes, and effects with no meaning, using background pictures, and so on.

In some cases, there are arguments to add design elements such as varying light/dark background shades to facilitate reading between different rows in tables. In charts, usage of 3D effects, frames around chart elements (e.g., outlines for bar charts), and excessive use of different font formatting (without consistent reasons) never assist clarity.

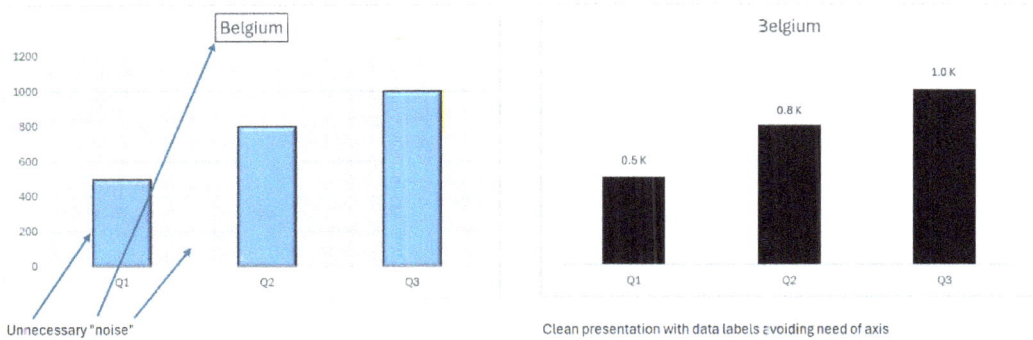

Figure 3.1 – "Noisy" and clean presentation

2. Consistent chart use

Another key principle for effective business information is consistency with all report elements. This starts with a consistent approach to chart and table designs. For example, IBCS recommends using vertical bars for any data with time periods on the *x* axis and horizontal ones for other types of data (e.g., an overview of a product). This helps users to differentiate at a glance whether the data covers time periods or performance at a particular point in time.

In summary: whatever conventions you use from a chart type perspective, make sure they're used in the same way organization-wide on any platform, no matter whether it's Power BI, PowerPoint, printed annual reports, and so on. The following report layout (*Figure 3.2*) is a good example of a clear report with conventions to help users understand the scenario at a glance: whether this is a plan or actual data (white bar versus black bar under the column title), as well as "micro charts" that display the relevance of variances without having to read a number.

Income Statement Q2 2024	ACT	BUD	Variance (Δ)	Variance (%)
– Revenue	$156,879.71	$184,446.99 -27.57K		-14.9%
Sales	$156,879.71	$184,446.99 -27.57K		-14.9%
– DirectCosts	($8,769.75)	($8,258.90)	-510.84	-6.2%
Cost of Goods Sold	($3,269.15)	($2,382.48)	-886.67	-37.2%
Purchases	($5,500.60)	($5,876.42)	+375.83	+6.4%
=Gross Profit	$148,109.96	$176,188.08 -28.08K		-15.9%
+ Expense	($103,311.54)	($96,513.91)	-6.80K	-7.0%
+ Overheads	($55,595.55)	($77,043.10)	+21.45K	+27.8%
=EBIT	($10,797.12)	$2,631.08	-13.43K	510.4%
=EBIT %	(6.88 %)	1.43 %	-0.08	-582....

Consistent scenario visualization

Consistent variance display (ABS/%)

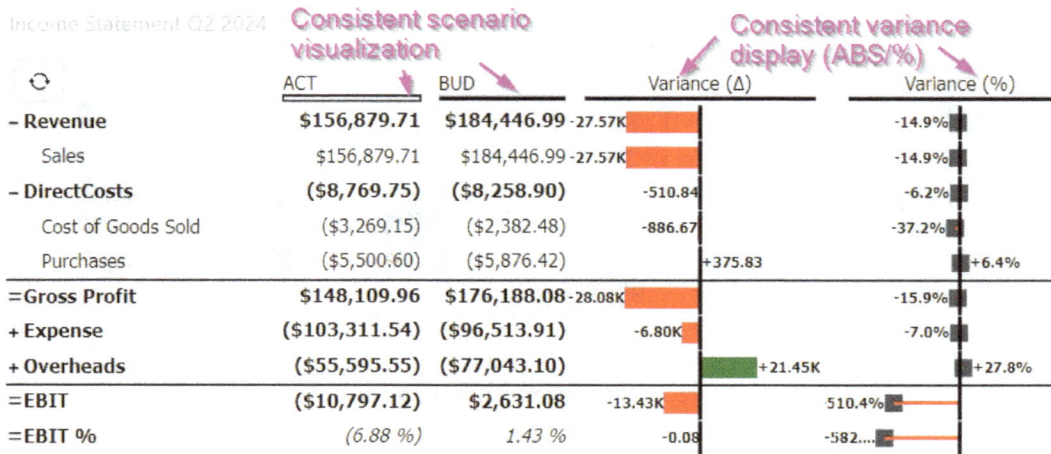

Figure 3.2 – IBCS-inspired sample report

3. Consistent color use

Like the chart type principle, colors should be used consistently across all your business communication and definitely within the pages of a Power BI report file. IBCS (https://www.ibcs.com/ibcs-standards-1-2/) postulates using color only to express variances – for example, green for positive and red for negative. Otherwise, data in charts should only be displayed in variations of black – for example: solid black for actuals, white for budget, gray for prior years, and hatched for forecast, and so on. This view is contentious and is not generally followed, which I think is acceptable if a consistent approach is used. What is not acceptable, though, is to be inconsistent – for example, using a color for a particular product group and then the same color for something completely different. It is also not advisable to use what could be confused with the signal colors red and green.

4. Comparability

A widely accepted design principle postulated by most business information design experts is to be mindful that the information that you are conveying is correctly scaled, or, in other words, the results are really comparable. This is particularly relevant in dashboards that typically contain multiple chart visualizations. All of these should use the same scale, for the same measures (e.g., monetary amount), or, in other words, have the same maximum value on the x or y axis, as only under these conditions is the information presented correctly.

For example, when you use charts to compare results, it's typically a good idea to use the same maximum scale on the *y* axis to correctly show the relevance of results. In *Figure 3.2*, each chart has a different scale, which, at a glance, looks like Belgium has a similar importance as the US and France, when, in reality (as shown in *Figure 3.3*), that is not the case:

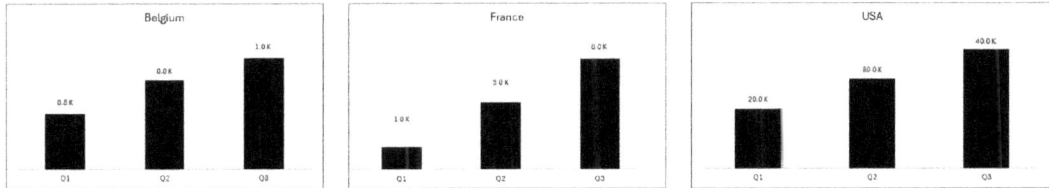

Figure 3.3 – Charts using different y scaling

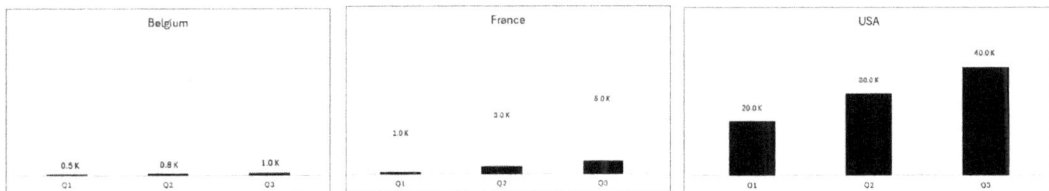

Figure 3.4 – The same y axis scaling showing relevance correctly

Both of the preceding charts could still be done better, as we will demonstrate in the coming sections.

In the next section, we will review important principles for table designs, where the right approach can also lead to much improved clarity and a reduction in the processing time to obtain insights for recipients.

Table recommendations

Out of the box, Power BI includes two visuals for tables: table and matrix. These typically format tables reasonably well. What the table visuals can't control is your number formatting. Here, the designer needs to make sure that the values/measures are formatted in a way that enables users to understand the information in the quickest way.

My recommendations are as follows:

- Use fonts with equal width to display financial numbers where decimals are aligned. These include Calibri, Segoe UI, Open Sans, and Consolas

- Utilize scaling with **Display these** visual properties when it is not necessary to display full numbers. Or define your own custom formats – for example, here are some custom format strings for values and measures:

  - Numbers in millions with brackets for negative numbers #,##0,.0;(#,##0,.0).

  - Scaling abbreviations at the end such as "M" or "K", but I would only do that if you have different scaling factors in the table; otherwise, it's better to use the scaling in the title, for example, "Sales in Millions."

Typically helpful for financial reports is enabling drilldown in the **Rows** and **Headers** +/- icons properties. Another option that is relevant for financial reports is the option to rename the subtotal label for row subtotals. For example, when you are adding up revenues and expenses and you want to use **EBIT** as the description, as opposed to the default, **Total**, as shown in the following screenshot:

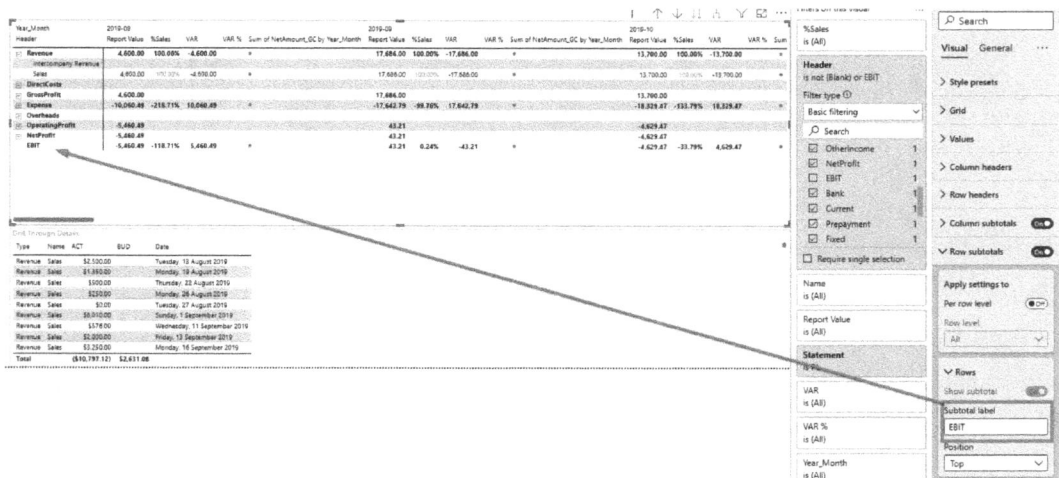

Figure 3.5 – Overriding standard Power BI labels

Chart recommendations

In this section, I will be covering more detailed recommendations on how to improve the clarity of your chart designs.

Cutting off axes

Chart axes need to start at zero. An unfortunately still common practice, even in reputable business publications, is to start the axis of a chart with multiple bars arbitrarily near one of the bars "To show the difference better." This, of course, is simply wrong, as it conveys an incorrect picture of reality. A small change in a chart with a cut-off axis can show as a significant one despite being irrelevant when you see the total value from zero. This is particularly wrong (in my opinion, an outright lie about the facts) when multiple charts with cut-off axes are used in comparison.

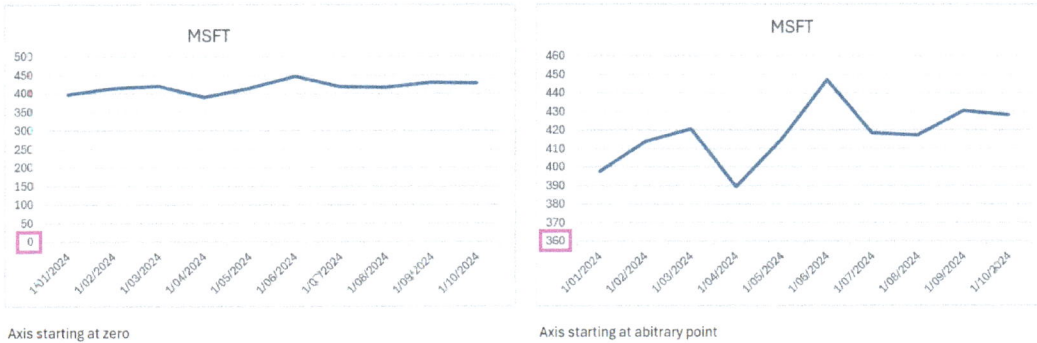

Figure 3.6 – Cut off y axis compared to starting at zero

Use labels as opposed to axis markers

Default Power BI bar and line charts use a y axis with markers and labels. This is acceptable when a large number of x elements are involved. When the number of x elements allows you to display labels, then this is a better way, as it gives the user the exact value, and they don't have to scan between the axis marker and the chart element.

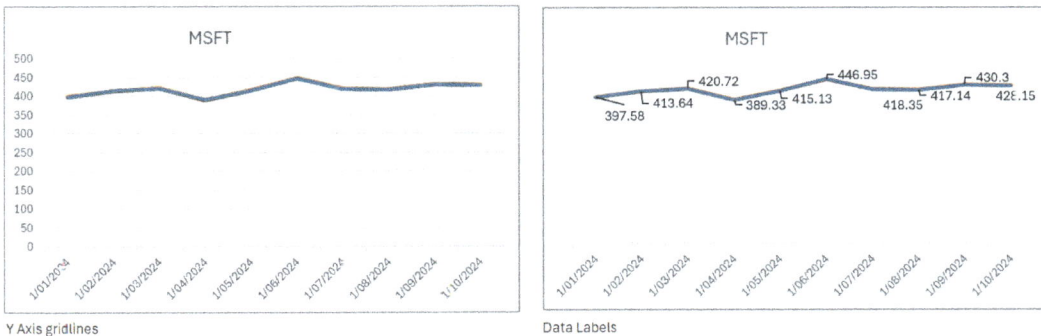

Figure 3.7 – Chart with data labels

Power BI design case study

In the following Power BI report (also available in the sample report for Chapter 3 in the book's GitHub repo), I have compiled a horror show of what not to do (unfortunately, not too far away from what I have seen organizations use in reality):

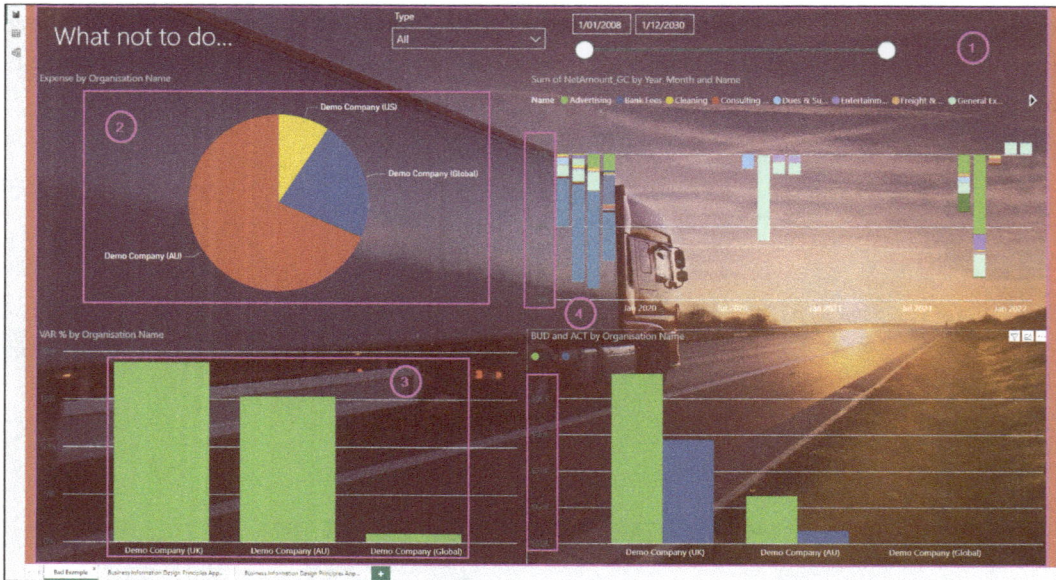

Figure 3.8 – What your report should NOT look like

Let's have a look at how we can address the different issues with *Figure 3.8* in detail:

1. The background picture adds zero information value and just makes it harder to understand the data. It contradicts recommendation *#1*: minimize data/ink ratio.

2. The pie chart is a chart type that, in general, should be avoided as it is not conducive to quickly understanding data. Human brains have a much harder time sorting areas than a simple length comparison. A sorted bar chart will always make it clearer and facilitate comparison between different visuals.

3. The first problem here is the use of the signal color green. This should only be done in conjunction with events with a positive variance/status. The second one is the chart type: what's displayed here is a percentage that's different from the amounts in the other visuals on the right. So, it would be better to clearly differentiate by, for example, using a very thin bar that is clearly different from an amount bar, as IBCS postulates. Another area for improvement here is to remove the display of the y axis and add data labels to the data points. As we are only displaying a small number of elements on the x axis, it is no problem to show the label with the exact amount on the chart. This avoids forcing the user to scan back and forth between the chart point and axis.

4. The final area to improve is the use of a vertical bar. IBCS suggests using vertical bars for time-related displays and horizontal bars for everything else.

There are three problems in the charts:

- First, the scale is not consistent; 40K dollars in the bottom chart has the same length as 20K in the top one.

- Second: the bottom chart cuts off the *y* axis at 50K. This should always be avoided.

- Finally, the top chart is nearly impossible to understand for a user without a lot of reviewing and interaction on the chart. Here, it would be much better to use a small-multiples display to avoid users having to go back and forth between the legend and bars and enable instant understanding of the situation.

The following Power BI report page from the book sample shows how the same dashboard can be expressed much more cleanly and clearly:

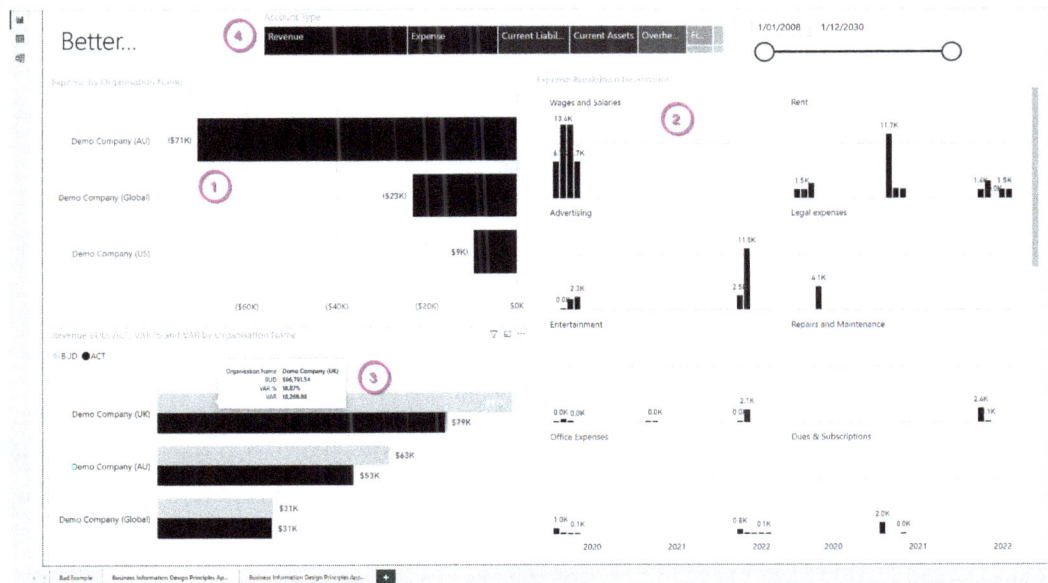

Figure 3.9 – Report with effective business design guidelines applied

Let's see what went right in the report:

1. Usage of a horizontal bar chart that's sorted by the amount immediately tells the user the ranked results without having to potentially compare different pies that are potentially not even legible as they are too small in comparison to other pies. No axis labels and gridlines are necessary as the users can clearly see the amounts as data labels.

2. As opposed to the close-to-useless stacked bar in the previous example, here the user can immediately compare the different accounts and identify trends over time.

3. In this chart, I am combining the two charts at the bottom in the previous example. This is something that you should always ask yourself as a designer: Do I really need to use multiple visuals, or can this be combined into one? In this case, by using tool tips, the user has a very simple way to see the exact relative variance amount that was previously on a second chart.

Admittedly, if your objective is to display trends over time, there could be an argument for a separate display. Using the bars is as good as it gets when requiring variance analysis with the visuals that come with Power BI by default. There are better options with custom visuals developed by third parties. For example, my company has developed the Acterys Variance Chart (free for personal use), which displays variance in the following way, applying the principles for variance display by IBCS:

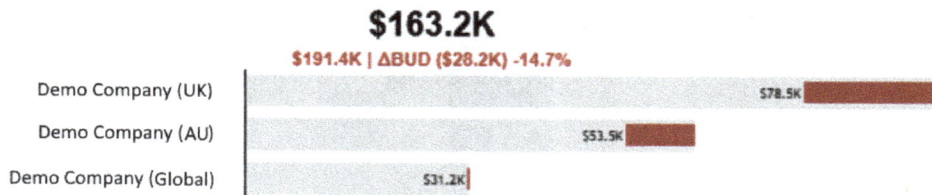

Figure 3.10 – Variance display with Acterys Variance

4. For the Account Type filter, I have switched the previous Type filter into a tree map visualization with the Absolute Balance measure. This adds value in that users can not only select, but also see the relevance of a filter. I will explain this concept further in detail in a following section.

Recommendation for default

In this section, I will cover a few general recommendations to improve your Power BI report designs.

Power BI settings

Use a canvas resolution of 1920x1080 px. Currently, the default resolution for Power BI is 1280x720 px. This is unnecessarily low, and I recommend setting this to the most common screen resolution of 1920x1080 px as follows:

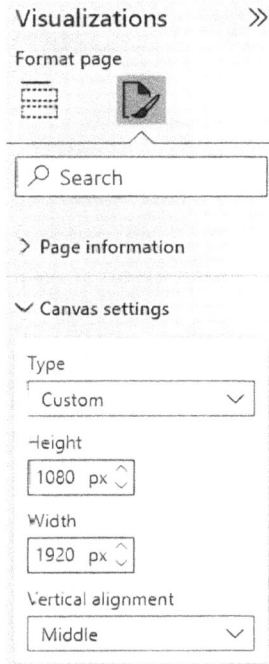

Figure 3.11 – Power BI canvas settings

Power BI layouts

You have the option in Power BI to use a canvas background picture. I recommend using this as it facilitates the positioning of visuals on the canvas and makes your reports look more professional. The exact layout will depend on your requirements. As a general guideline, we use templates with two areas – a title and a report area – or three areas, with an additional navigation bar:

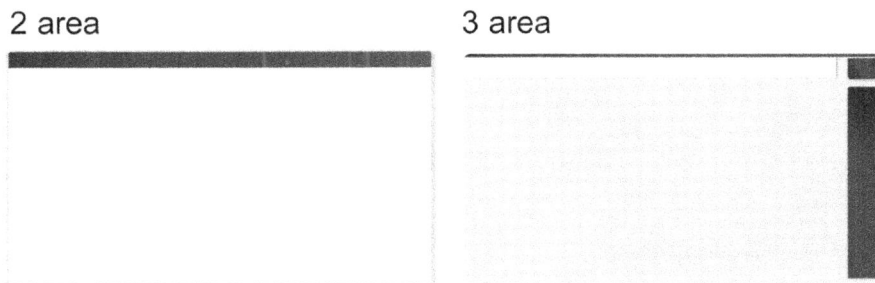

Figure 3.12 – Power BI layout designs

Both samples are available for download from the book's GitHub repository: `https://github.com/PacktPublishing/Power-BI-for-Finance`

Themes

Themes in Power BI are a collection of design and formatting standards that apply to your report as the default settings. You can either use templates built into Power BI or develop your own theme. This is done through a JSON file that you can upload to Power BI. This contains general settings such as color palettes and ones that are specific to the visual. In this file, you can apply all the principles (ink/data ratio, consistency, axis formatting, data label usage, etc.) discussed previously in this chapter. I won't go into details on usage as the JSON file structure changes frequently, which is well explained here: https://learn.microsoft.com/en-us/power-bi/create-reports/desktop-report-themes.

As a good starting point, I recommend the Microsoft Power BI Community Themes Gallery (https://community.fabric.microsoft.com/t5/Themes-Gallery), which contains very good examples that you can adapt to your own requirements. You can also find one of my dark-themed designs there, which is a bit easier on the eyes, by searching for "Acterys."

Filter

A contentious topic in the community is whether to use filters/slicers on the report or use the **Filters** panel. In my view, there is no definitive answer to this. If you have enough space on the report to use slicers, there is nothing wrong with using them – they are very intuitive for users. The Power BI **Filters** panel provides more filtering options, but not all users might be familiar with it. You will need slicers on the report, though, if you want to share the report in a static format such as PDF, as the filter details are not visible then.

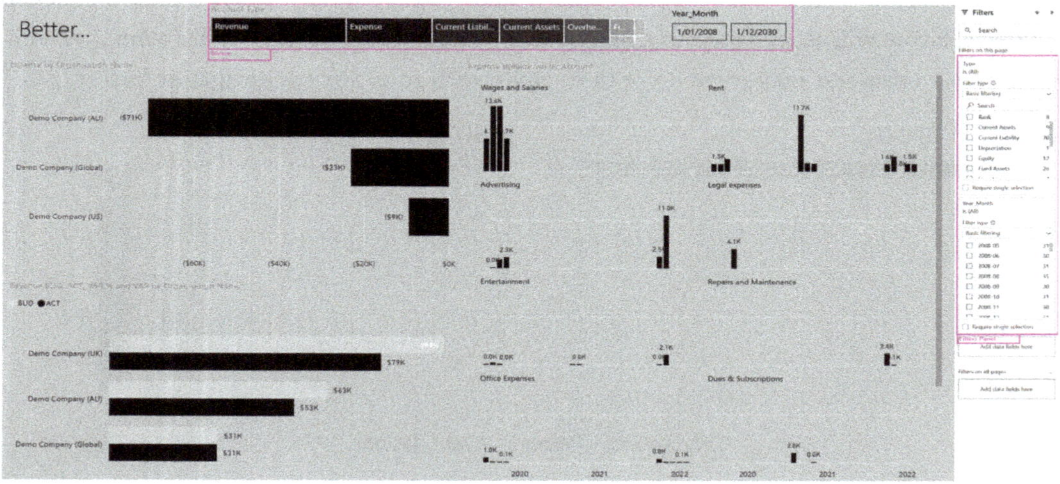

Figure 3.13 – Slicers versus Filters panel

Another thought to keep in mind is using a Power BI visual as a filter element. This works with a limited number of filter elements (<10). For example, as opposed to using a standard drop-down box, you can use a tree map visual where users can see the relevance of two filter options (**Annual** and **Monthly** payments) using a revenue measure that was added to the visual, for two product segments:

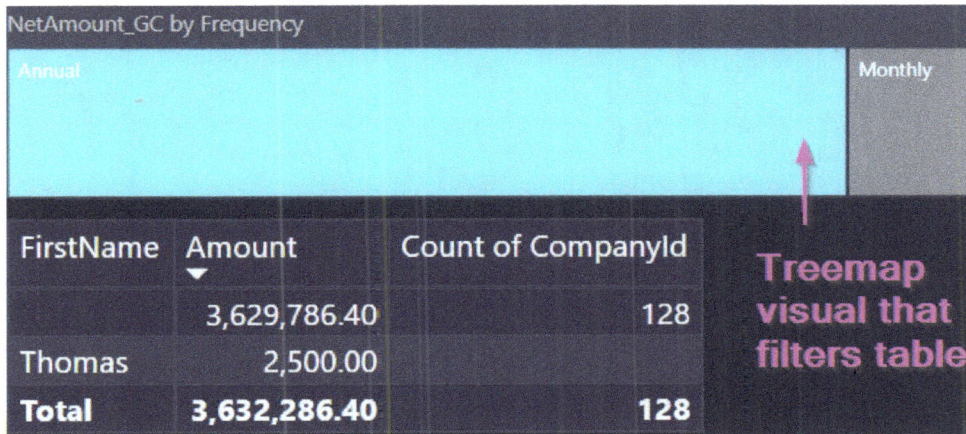

Figure 3.14 – Using a treemap as a filter

Summary

In this chapter, we covered general business information design recommendations to improve clarity and minimize the time it takes for the audience to process key insights. In particular, we reviewed table and chart designs that avoid noise, ensure comparability, and use design elements consistently. In the next chapter, we will look at more specific options for interactive financial report designs and the related calculation logic.

4

How to Realize Financial Reporting in Power BI

In the previous chapters, we were working on the foundations for well-designed financial models in Power BI. In this chapter, we will cover options for how to best realize interactive financial reports that cover typical accounting requirements. Initially, we will review options for realizing profit and loss and balance sheet statements using core Power BI calculation (DAX) options alongside Power BI standard visuals. Following that, we will showcase how specialized visuals, such as Reporting (part of Dynamics 365 Finance business performance planning and Acterys), can facilitate simpler design and improved layout options.

In this chapter, we're going to cover the following main topics:

- Creating an interactive income statement/profit and loss report
- Developing a balance sheet
- Implementing asymmetric reports

Technical requirements

You will find the datasets and Power BI files used in this chapter in the book's official GitHub repository here: https://github.com/PacktPublishing/Power-BI-for-Finance.

The Power BI visuals covered in this chapter can be added directly from Power BI or through Microsoft AppSource. We'll cover both methods in the chapter.

Creating an interactive income statement/profit and loss report

So far, our financial reports in the previous chapters were missing some key elements of a financial statement, in particular, subtotal calculations.

In most cases, the basis for creating a financial statement report is a table that contains all transactions from the relevant accounting system(s). We have already used a table with account balances in *Chapter 1* and can continue to build on that.

The required subtotal aggregations (like total revenues, expenses, etc.) are available through the Type field/column in the Accounts dimension table. If we require a different aggregation of the accounts, it will need to be added to that table as another mapping.

Adding subtotals, such as Gross Margin calculated by subtracting **Cost of Goods Sold** (**COGS**) from Total Revenues, can't currently be implemented by just using dimension tables.

Unlike the **Multi-Dimensional Expressions** (**MDX**) calculation language in the previous version of the Tabular analytics engine (OLAP MD (Multi-Dimensional)), the DAX language doesn't support manual row calculations in a dimension.

When using Power BI, which only supports DAX and the included standard visuals, we have to use a more complex approach, which I will cover in the following section.

As always, there are different options to implement logic in DAX. The approach that I cover here only requires two DAX statements and is much simpler than other solutions that I have seen proposed in the community (for example, calculating each subtotal with a separate DAX statement).

Report structure table

The approach is based on a separate report structure table with fields for aggregations (Header), subtotals, order, calculation type, and statement, and is linked to the Accounts dimension by the Header column.

The table should have the following structure:

Order	Header	Calculation Type	Report
0	Revenue	1	PL
1	Sales	1	PL
2	DirectCosts	1	PL
3	GrossProfit	2	PL
4	Expense	1	PL
5	Overheads	1	PL
6	Depreciation	1	PL
7	OperatingProfit	2	PL
8	OtherIncome	1	PL
9	NetProfit	2	PL
10	EBIT	2	PL
11	Bank	1	BS
12	Current	1	BS
13	Prepayment	1	BS
14	Fixed	1	BS
15	Inventory	1	BS

Order	Header	Calculation Type	Report
16	CurrentLiability	1	BS
17	NonCurrent	1	BS
18	TermLiability	1	BS
19	Liability	1	BS
20	Equity	1	BS

Table 4.1 – Financial statement structure sub-table

To add this, you can use the **Enter Data** option in the Power BI Desktop ribbon and copy and paste the report structure rows from the Report Structure.xlsx spreadsheet in the GitHub repository.

This can either be a data entry table in Power BI or a table in your data source. (Third-party solutions like **Acterys** enable you to edit and create this table directly from a web browser or reports published on the Power BI service.)

The columns are important here. The records will vary depending on your report's definition. The records define your report headers, Header, which will need to match the account grouping, AccountGroup, in your chart of accounts table. In the columns, we also define how to treat them. Calculation Type specifies whether the subtotal is a standard aggregation (1) or a calculated running total (2), such as Gross Profit. The Report field contains the detailed information of the respective statement (for example, PL for profit and loss and BS for balance sheet).

Once you have the Report_Structure table, you need to create a relationship between its Header field and the Type field in the Accounts table by either dragging these fields on top of each other or connecting the two in the **Manage Relationships** dialog in the **Model View** ribbon. The end result in Power BI **Model View** should look like this:

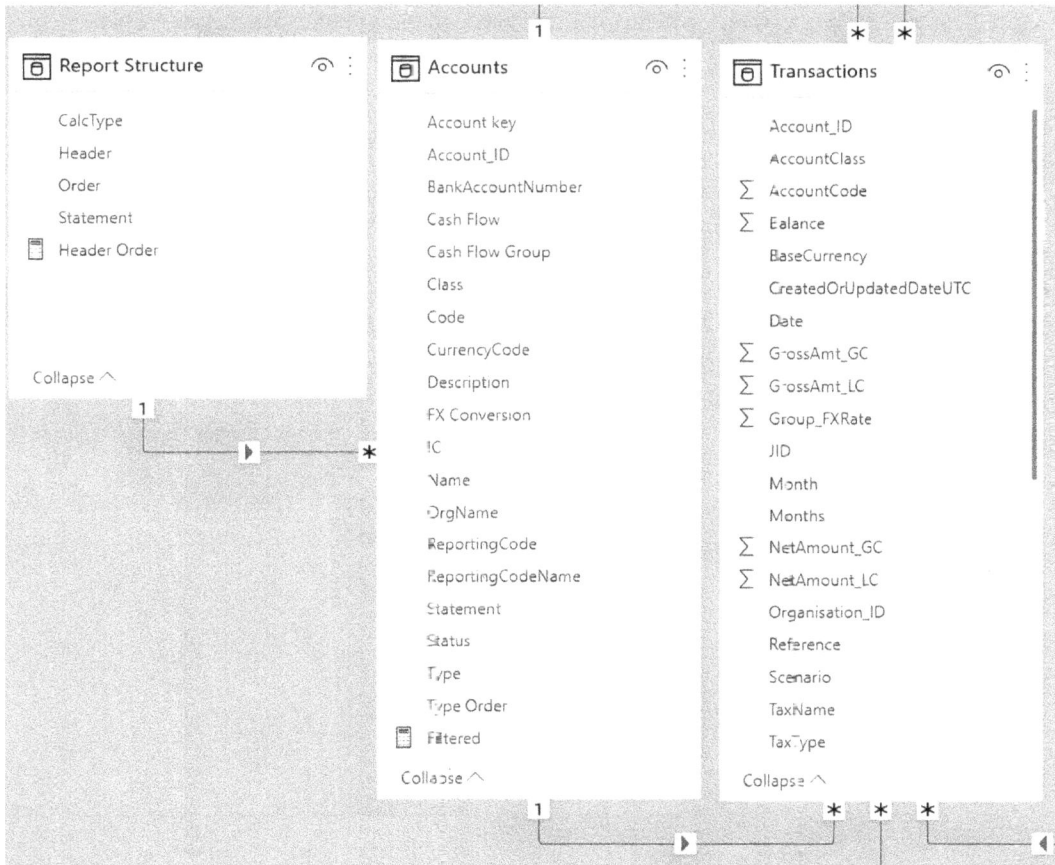

Figure 4.1 – Relating the Report Structure sub-table with the Accounts dimension table

Now that we have the required model structure in place, we can look at the required DAX calculations for our financial statements.

DAX measures

Initially, we have to create logic to handle the sequence of the report items correctly. Following that, we will look at the calculation for the subtotals (e.g., Gross Margin, EBIT, etc.):

1. As a basis for our other calculations, we first need to add a calculated column, Header Order, to our Report_Structure table:

    ```
    Header Order =
    MAX ( Report_Structure[Order] )
    ```

    This is necessary to know the current order position of the header.

2. The next step is to add a measure called `Filtered` to our chart of accounts table:

    ```
    Filtered = ISFILTERED(Accounts[Name])
    ```

    This is useful for hiding accounts that we don't want to display in the report.

3. Next, we add a DAX measure for `Running Total` and `Report Value`. `Report Value` is the main measure that will act as your value/amount field in the report.

In a nutshell, the DAX measure will check whether the `Calculation Type` value is 1 to create an aggregation of the accounts, or 2 to calculate a running total up until that header order position point. As we are applying the sign (positive or negative) to be used in the calculation for each account value type in the right way, all subtotals of the PL are just a running total of the previous groups.

The running total measure will add up all header elements up until that respective header's order point (i.e., smaller than `Report_Structure[Order]`):

```
Running Total =
IF (
    HASONEFILTER ( Report_Structure[Header] ),
    CALCULATE (
        SUM ( 'GL_Table'[Amount] ),
        FILTER (
            ALL ( Statement_Structure ),
Report_Structure[Header Order] < VALUES ( Report_Structure[Order] )
        )
    ),
    BLANK ()
)
```

In the final step, we need to bring all aspects of the calculation together in the `Report Value` DAX measure:

```
Report Value =
IF (
    AND ( MAX ( Statement_Structure[Calculation Type] ) = 1, [Filtered] ),
    BLANK (),
    SWITCH (
        MIN ( Statement_Structure[Calculation Type] ),
        BLANK (), BLANK (),
```

```
        1, CALCULATE ( SUM ( 'GL_Table'[All Scenarios] ) ),
        2, [Running Total]
    )
)
```

Once we have this logic defined, we can replace the static reference to group currency value in the Actuals (ACT) calculation with the Report Value DAX measure and just rename that to ACT. As a second step, we replace the Type field from the Accounts table with the Header field from our new Report_Structure table to show the subtotals calculations correctly.

We can now add a few improvements, such as your existing variance calculations, and have a versatile, interactive income statement layout with all subtotals showing correctly as a final product:

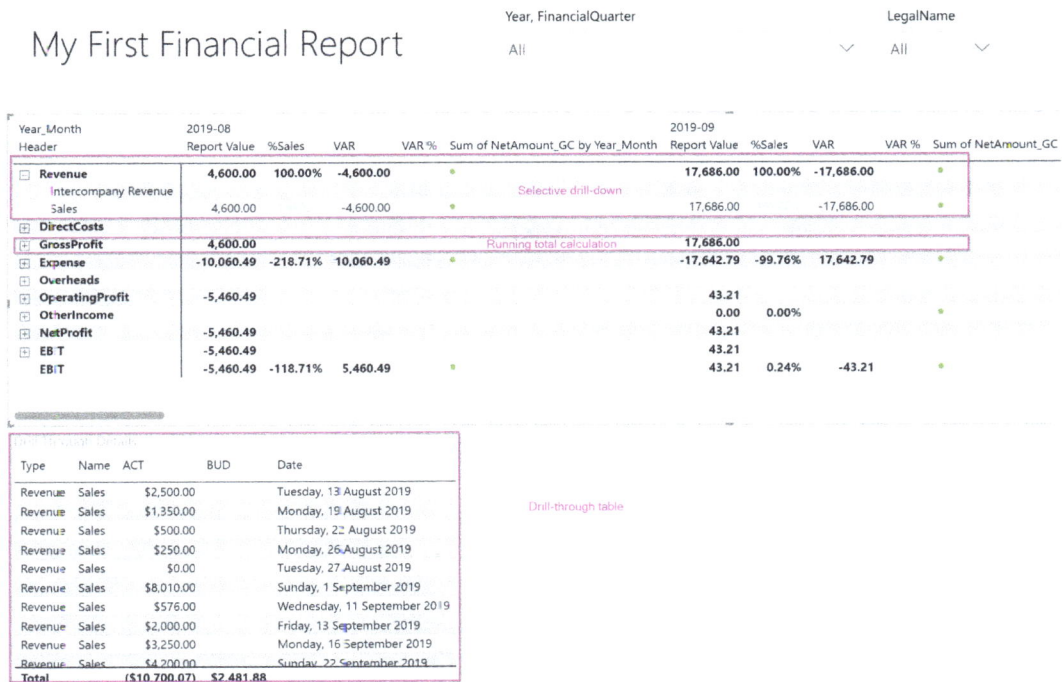

My First Financial Report

| Year, FinancialQuarter | LegalName |
| All | All |

| Year_Month | 2019-08 | | | | | 2019-09 | | | | |
Header	Report Value	%Sales	VAR	VAR %	Sum of NetAmount_GC by Year_Month	Report Value	%Sales	VAR	VAR %	Sum of NetAmount_GC
⊟ **Revenue**	**4,600.00**	**100.00%**	**-4,600.00**	•		**17,686.00**	**100.00%**	**-17,686.00**	•	
Intercompany Revenue					*Selective drill-down*					
Sales	4,600.00		-4,600.00	•		17,686.00		-17,686.00	•	
⊞ **DirectCosts**										
⊞ **GrossProfit**	**4,600.00**				*Running total calculation*	**17,686.00**				
⊞ **Expense**	**-10,060.49**	**-218.71%**	**10,060.49**	•		**-17,642.79**	**-99.76%**	**17,642.79**	•	
⊞ **Overheads**										
⊞ **OperatingProfit**	**-5,460.49**					**43.21**				
⊞ **OtherIncome**						**0.00**	**0.00%**			•
⊞ **NetProfit**	**-5,460.49**					**43.21**				
⊞ **EBIT**	**-5,460.49**					**43.21**				
EBIT	**-5,460.49**	**-118.71%**	**5,460.49**	•		**43.21**	**0.24%**	**-43.21**	•	

Type	Name	ACT	BUD	Date
Revenue	Sales	$2,500.00		Tuesday, 13 August 2019
Revenue	Sales	$1,350.00		Monday, 19 August 2019
Revenue	Sales	$500.00		Thursday, 22 August 2019
Revenue	Sales	$250.00		Monday, 26 August 2019
Revenue	Sales	$0.00		Tuesday, 27 August 2019
Revenue	Sales	$8,010.00		Sunday, 1 September 2019
Revenue	Sales	$576.00		Wednesday, 11 September 2019
Revenue	Sales	$2,000.00		Friday, 13 September 2019
Revenue	Sales	$3,250.00		Monday, 16 September 2019
Revenue	Sales	$4,200.00		Sunday, 22 September 2019
Total		**($10,700.07)**	**$2,481.88**	

Drill-through table

Figure 4.2 – Financial report and drill-down table

The sample file with the result (called Chapter 4 Financial Reporting.pbix) can be found in the book's GitHub repository.

Drill-through tables

A useful item to add here is a **drill-through table**, as shown in *Figure 4.2* on the right side. This is a separate table visual on the same Power BI report page that contains the detailed transactions. When a user clicks on a cell in the financial report, the filters will apply to the detail table and display the transactions behind the value in the report.

Custom tooltips

Another option to set up a detailed report that can provide even further analytical insights is setting up a custom tooltip for the financial report. Before we set up the tooltip, we have to create the new report page by clicking on the + symbol at the bottom, on the right of the report tabs. Once we have added the new report page in the same report, we need to qualify that as a tooltip page by enabling it as a tooltip in the report page properties:

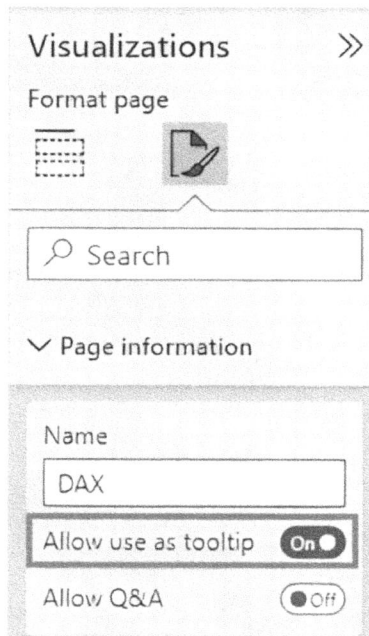

Figure 4.3 – Activating the tooltip property

Once this is set, we see that the report page size was reduced to 320 px x 240 px. The reason is that the tooltip is typically a much smaller dialog that shows when the user hovers over a specific visual detail. For our purposes, this size should be increased. My recommendation is to change it to 400 px x 400 px:

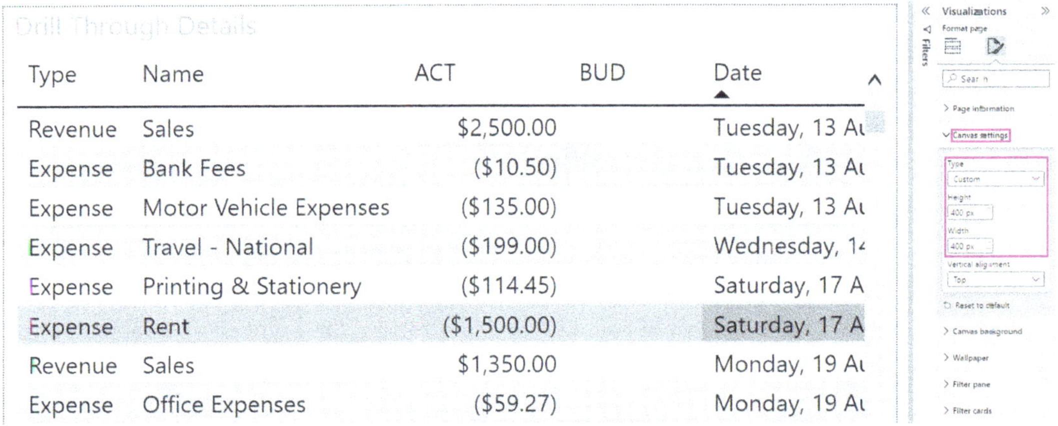

Figure 4.4 – Tooltip page settings

On this new page, we can now add a Power BI table visual that will be shown when the user points the mouse on a cell on the main report. We just need to define what detail columns we want to show by dragging them from the available dataset tables. For our financial report purposes, we add the Account Type, Account Name, two scenarios (ACT and budget (BUD)) and Date fields.

After that, we can go back to the main **Income Statement** report and set up the custom tooltip by specifying the drill-through page in the properties of the report visual:

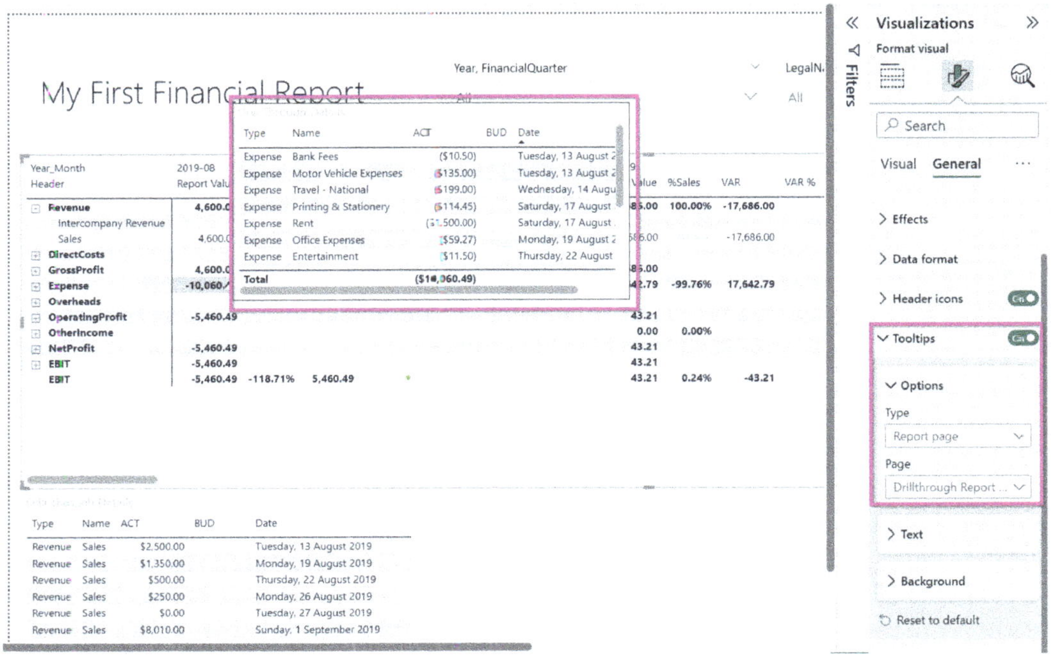

Figure 4.5 – Financial report with custom tooltip drill through

When the user now navigates to a cell on the report, the drill-through tooltip will show with the respective records, enabling the user to see exactly what the source transactions are behind the value.

Adding a trendline to the tooltip

In addition to showing the detail records, it can be very insightful for the user to add a trend indicator to the tooltip that displays how the specific row item is evolving over time. For this, we can add a chart to the tooltip report that displays the trend. This, though, is not as simple as it looks, as our report cells are filtered by a time detail. This time-related filter will also be applied to the chart, so using that would just show data for one date. As a workaround, we can use another time dimension that is related to the main time dimension on the level of detail for which we want to display the trend (e.g., the year). The additional time dimension can be created with a DAX calendar function (CALENDAR( )), or we can use a date table that is already in our model, Closing Date. As the new timetable has no Year column, we can add that with a column function, Year = YEAR('Closing Date'[Date]), which refers to the Date field in that table.

We also need to create a new measure that removes the filter that is automatically applied when a detail is selected from the main date table. We can do that by using the following:

```
DAX ACT ex Calendar = IF(
        HASONEVALUE('Calendar'[Year]),
CALCULATE(
  [Report Value],
    ALL('Calendar'),
        'Calendar'[Year] = SELECTEDVALUE('Calendar'[Year])
    ),CALCULATE([Report Value], ALL('Calendar'))
)
```

The 'Calendar'[Year] filter enables us to only show the current year in the tooltip as opposed to the entire time range. The IF( ) function at the start ensures that the DAX is working when no year is selected. Now, when a user moves the mouse cursor to a cell in the report, they get the transaction details and a trend chart:

My First Financial Report

Year, FinancialQuarter

All

Year_Month Header	2019-08 Report Value	%Sales	VAR	VAR %	Sum of NetAmount_GC by Year_Month	2019-09 Report Value	%Sales	VAR	VAR %
⊞ Revenue	4,600.0					17,686.00	100.00%	-17,686.00	
⊞ DirectCosts									
⊞ GrossProfit	4,600.0					17,686.00			
⊞ Expense	-10,060.4					-17,642.79	-99.76%	17,642.79	
⊞ Overheads									
⊞ OperatingProfit	-5,460.4					43.21			
⊞ NetProfit	-5,460.4					43.21			
⊞ EBIT	-5,460.4					43.21			
EBIT	-5,460.4					43.21	0.24%	-43.21	

Tooltip drill-in data:

Type	Name	ACT	BUD	Date
Revenue	Sales	$2,500.00		Tuesday, 13 August 2019
Revenue	Sales	$1,350.00		Monday, 19 August 2019
Revenue	Sales	$500.00		Thursday, 22 August 2019
Revenue	Sales	$250.00		Monday, 26 August 2019
Revenue	Sales	$0.00		Tuesday, 27 August 2019
Total		$4,600.00		

Name ● Sales

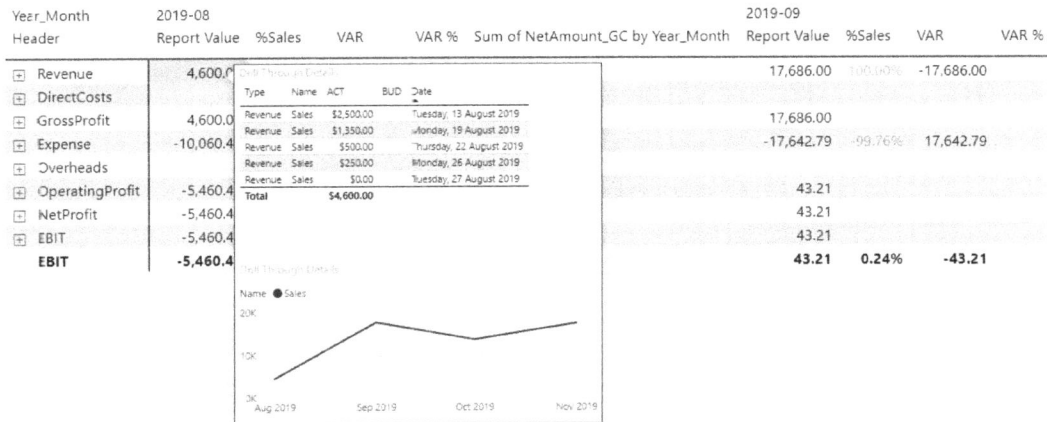

Figure 4.6 – Combined table chart custom tooltip

Using custom visuals for reporting

A much simpler approach to using DAX, as described before, is using custom visuals that were developed specifically for financial reporting purposes. These do not use any DAX but offer ways to calculate subtotals in the visual, which is also much faster in calculation performance. Currently, there are a few visuals that enable that. As I have been involved in the development of the Acterys **Reporting** visual that was also selected by Microsoft as part of Dynamics 365, I will use this as an example here. Every reader of this book is also entitled to a single, free license of the visual for personal use. Please send proof of purchase of this book to sales@acterys.com.

Initially, we can add the **Reporting** visual from the AppSource marketplace or directly in Power BI. To add it from Power BI, click on the ellipsis at the bottom of the **Visualizations** section and click on **Get more visuals**:

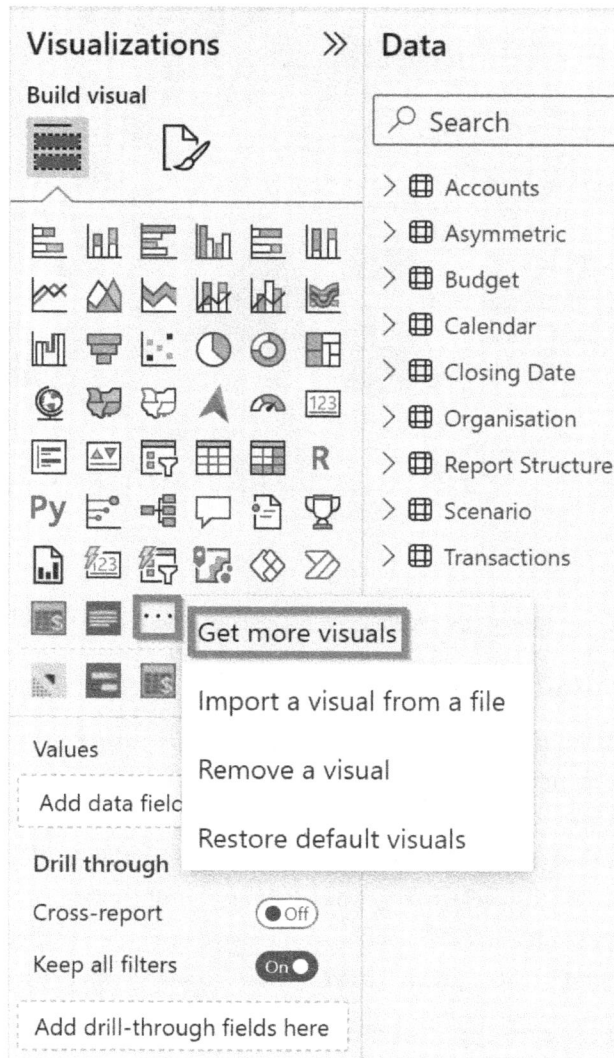

Figure 4.7 – Adding a custom visual from Power BI

Then, search for Dynamics 365 Finance business performance planning reporting or Acterys Reporting:

Power BI visuals   ×

ⓘ By clicking 'Add' and/or 'Download Sample' and downloading a visual, you agree to the provider's Terms and Conditions and Privacy Policy on the visual's page and agree Microsoft can share your account details to provider for their transactional purposes. Use of Microsoft's AppSource is subject to the Microsoft Commercial Marketplace Terms and Privacy Statement.

All visuals   Organizational visuals   AppSource visuals

Explore all available visuals to magnify your business insights Learn more

Filter by   All   Sort by: Popularity ∨

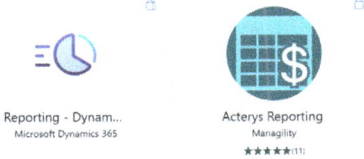

Reporting - Dynam...   Acterys Reporting
Microsoft Dynamics 365   Managility
                                       ★★★★★(11)

Figure 4.8 – Adding Dynamics 365 Finance business performance planning or Acterys Reporting

Alternatively, you can go to the **AppSource** marketplace and search for Acterys Reporting:

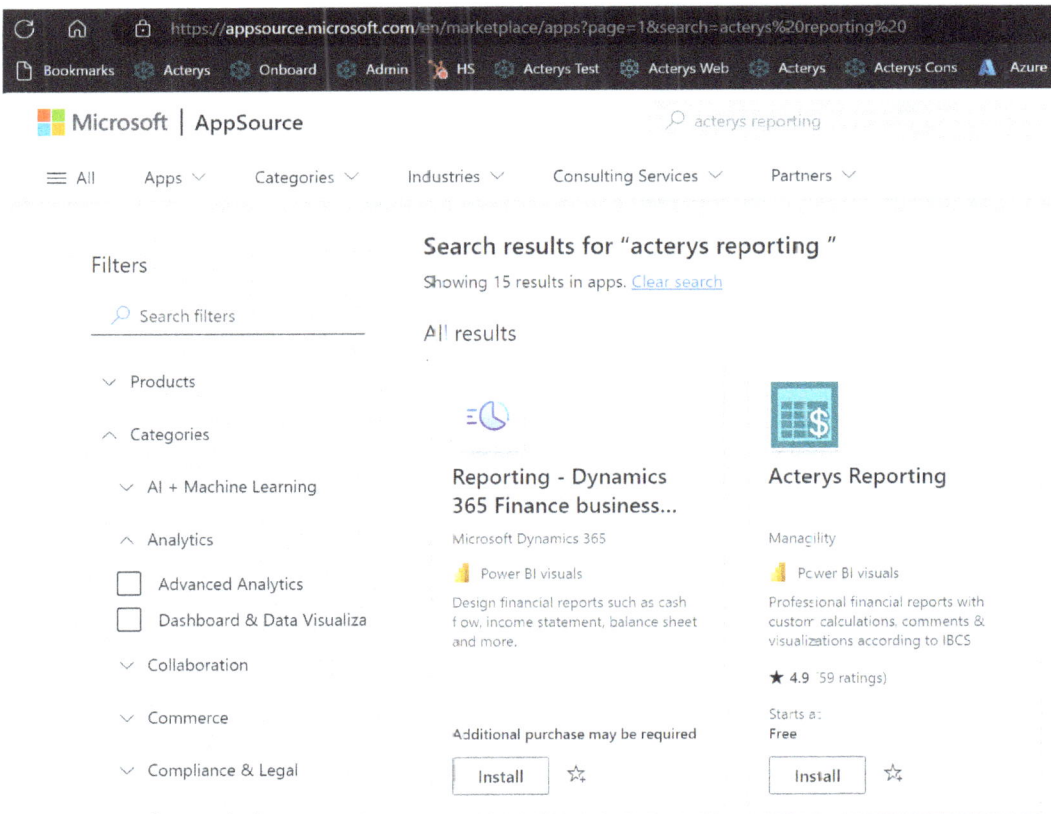

https://appsource.microsoft.com/en/marketplace/apps?page=1&search=acterys%20reporting%20

Bookmarks   Acterys   Onboard   Admin   HS   Acterys Test   Acterys Web   Acterys   Acterys Cons   Azure

Microsoft | AppSource   acterys reporting

☰ All   Apps ∨   Categories ∨   Industries ∨   Consulting Services ∨   Partners ∨

Filters

🔍 Search filters

∨ Products

∧ Categories

  ∨ AI + Machine Learning

  ∧ Analytics

    ☐ Advanced Analytics

    ☐ Dashboard & Data Visualiza

  ∨ Collaboration

  ∨ Commerce

  ∨ Compliance & Legal

  ∨ Customer Service

Search results for "acterys reporting "

Showing 15 results in apps. Clear search

All results

Reporting - Dynamics 365 Finance business...

Microsoft Dynamics 365

📊 Power BI visuals

Design financial reports such as cash flow, income statement, balance sheet and more.

Additional purchase may be required

[Install] ☆

Acterys Reporting

Managility

📊 Power BI visuals

Professional financial reports with custom calculations, comments & visualizations according to IBCS

★ 4.9 (59 ratings)

Starts at:
Free

[Install] ☆

Figure 4.9 – Adding the Reporting visual from AppSource

Once the visual is added, the only settings to configure are the row hierarchies (Type and Name) for the actual (ACT) and budget (BUD) measures, as well as selecting PL in the **Statement** filter on our report:

Figure 4.10 – Configuring the row hierarchies for actual and budget measures

This gives us an initial simple layout where we can drill down with the standard Power BI functionality:

ACT and BUD by Type and Name

	ACT	BUD
– Revenue	**$163,184.88**	**$191,382.68**
Other Revenue	$6,305.17	$6,935.69
Sales	$156,879.71	$184,446.99
– DirectCosts	**($8,769.75)**	**($8,258.90)**
Cost of Goods Sold	($3,269.15)	($2,382.48)
Purchases	($5,500.60)	($5,876.42)
+ Expense	**($103,311.54)**	**($96,513.91)**
+ Overheads	**($55,595.55)**	**($77,043.10)**
+ OtherIncome	**$97.05**	**$106.76**

Figure 4.11 – Interactive income statement

Adding our subtotal calculations is now easy to accomplish with the edit functionality that the context menu at the top right-hand side provides us. Here, we can now just right-click at the position where we want to add the calculation and select **Add Row Before** or **Add Row After**:

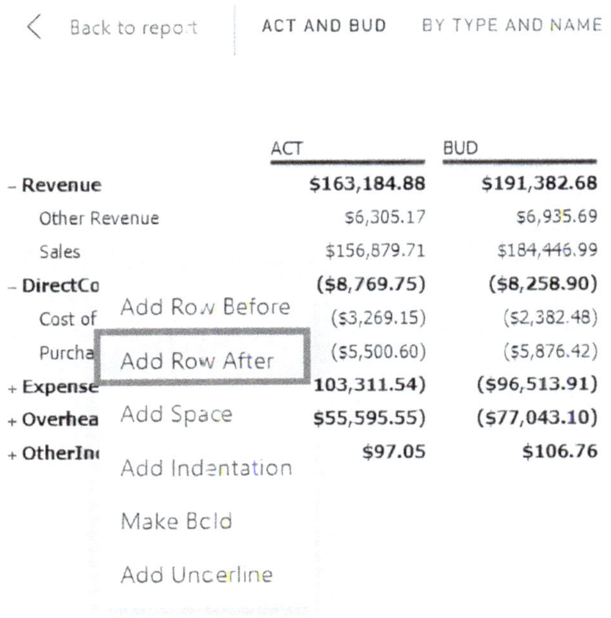
Back to report
ACT AND BUD
BY TYPE AND NAME
ACT
BUD
- Revenue $163,184.88 $191,382.68
Other Revenue $6,305.17 $6,935.69
Sales $156,879.71 $184,446.99
- DirectCo ($8,769.75) ($8,258.90)
Cost of ($3,269.15) ($2,382.48)
Purcha ($5,500.60) ($5,876.42)
+ Expense 103,311.54) ($96,513.91)
+ Overhea $55,595.55) ($77,043.10)
+ OtherIn $97.05 $106.76
Add Row Before
Add Row After
Add Space
Add Indentation
Make Bold
Add Underline

Figure 4.12 – Adding a custom calculation/subtotal

From here, we can just define the calculation by clicking on the header row that we want to use in the calculation, using the mathematical operator (if necessary, there is also a wide array of functions available), and applying a format. For example, in order to calculate the gross profit, we add the following:

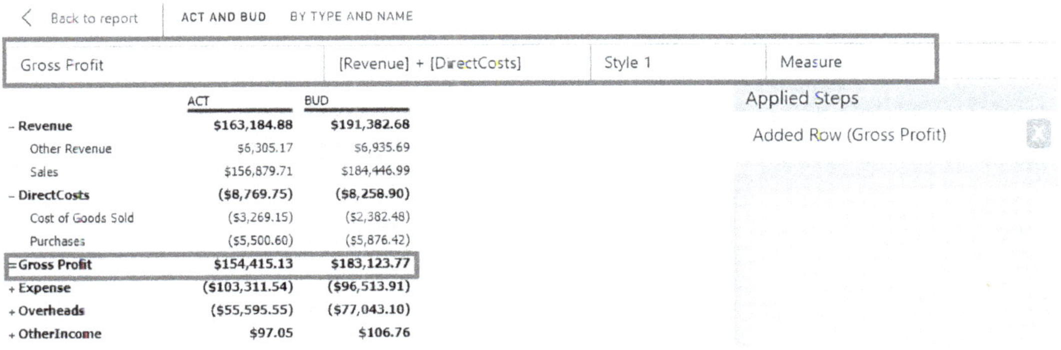
Back to report
ACT AND BUD
BY TYPE AND NAME
Gross Profit
[Revenue] + [DirectCosts]
Style 1
Measure
Applied Steps
Added Row (Gross Profit)
ACT
BUD
- Revenue $163,184.88 $191,382.68
Other Revenue $6,305.17 $6,935.69
Sales $156,879.71 $184,446.99
- DirectCosts ($8,769.75) ($8,258.90)
Cost of Goods Sold ($3,269.15) ($2,382.48)
Purchases ($5,500.60) ($5,876.42)
= Gross Profit $154,415.13 $183,123.77
+ Expense ($103,311.54) ($96,513.91)
+ Overheads ($55,595.55) ($77,043.10)
+ OtherIncome $97.05 $106.76

Figure 4.13 – Calculation of the Gross Profit subtotal

A proper financial report should also contain underlines to support structuring and reading it well. The Acterys Reporting visual enables you to edit/add that at any position in the report (right-click on position and click on **Add underline**) or add them via styles (i.e., a predefined format that you can easily apply from the calculation):

	ACT	BUD
Revenue	**$163,184.88**	**$191,382.68**
Other Revenue	$6,305.17	$6,935.69
Sales	$156,879.71	$184,446.99
DirectCosts	**($8,769.75)**	**($8,258.90)**
Cost of Goods Sold	($3,269.15)	($2,382.48)
Purc	($5,500.60)	($5,876.42)
Gross Add Row Before	**$154,415.13**	**$183,123.77**
Expen Add Row After	103,311.54)	($96,513.91)
Overh	$55,595.55)	($77,043.10)
Other Add Space	**$97.05**	**$106.76**
Add Indentation		
Make Bold		
Edit Underline		
Remove Underline		

Figure 4.14 – Adding underlines

To finish our report, we can add EBIT (**Earnings Before Interest and Tax**) and EBIT % calculations, and voila, we have a perfectly formatted report (with the **Format** option in the calculation bar, we can also apply a percentage format for the EBIT ratio):

EBIT %		[EBIT]/[Revenue]	Style 1	0.00 %

	ACT	BUD		Applied Steps
– **Revenue**	**$163,184.88**	**$191,382.68**		Added Row (Gross Profit)
Other Revenue	$6,305.17	$6,935.69		
Sales	$156,879.71	$184,446.99		
– **DirectCosts**	**($8,769.75)**	**($8,258.90)**		Added Row (EBIT)
Cost of Goods Sold	($3,269.15)	($2,382.48)		
Purchases	($5,500.60)	($5,876.42)		
= **Gross Profit**	**$154,415.13**	**$183,123.77**		Added Row (EBIT %)
+ **Expense**	**($103,311.54)**	**($96,513.91)**		
+ **Overheads**	**($55,595.55)**	**($77,043.10)**		
+ **OtherIncome**	**$97.05**	**$106.76**		
= **EBIT**	**($4,394.90)**	**$9,673.52**		
= **EBIT %**	**(2.69 %)**	**5.05 %**		

Figure 4.15 – Report with calculated rows

The Acterys Reporting visual also offers very useful optional micro chart variance visualizations, which follow the rules of the **International Business Communication Standards (IBCS)** principles. You can switch between these by clicking on the `Variance` header:

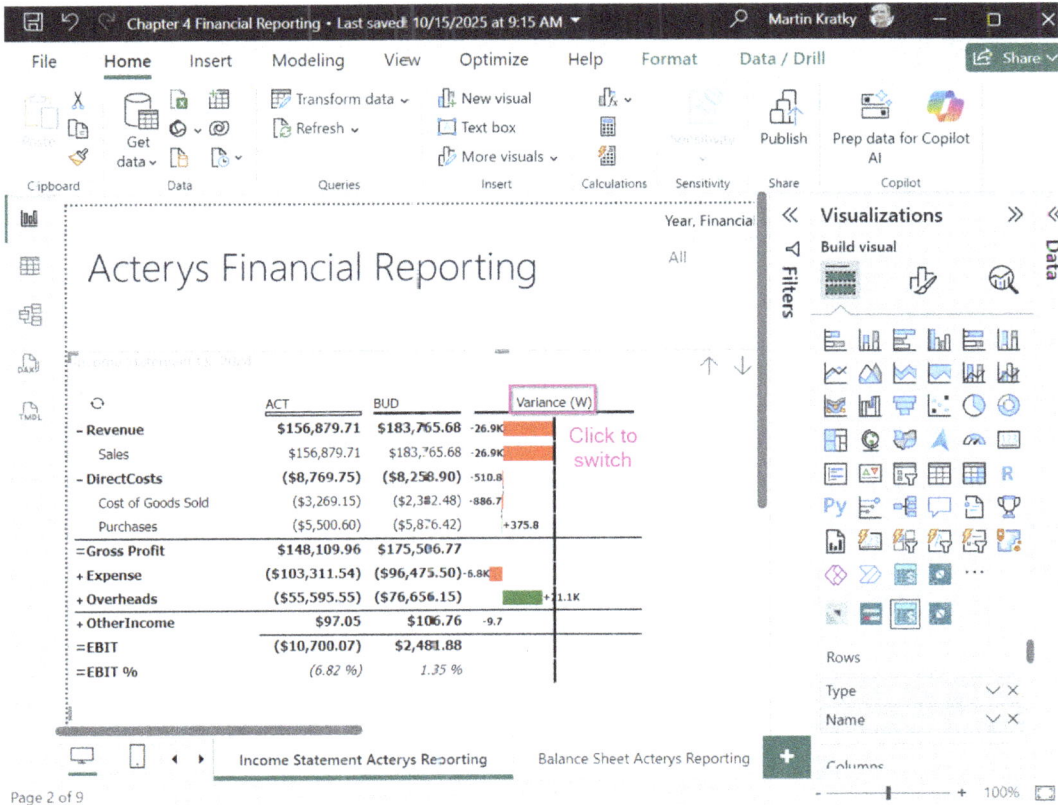

Figure 4.16 – Adding a micro chart visualization

Next, we will focus on how we can realize a balance sheet in Power BI.

Developing a balance sheet

This report is a little bit more complicated as it displays stock/point in time data (value of assets at a specific date, such as 31st of December XXXX) as opposed to an aggregable movement measure (revenue over a period, such as revenue in December, i.e., between 1/12/XX and 31/12/XX). The data in the Profit & Loss/Income Statement reports covered in the previous section can be summarized across all hierarchies of our financial calendar. The balance sheet looks at the value of assets/liabilities and equity at a specific cut-off date and covers data since the inception of the organization. This means that the balance sheet data (different from the income statement) is not additive over time periods, and you need to ensure that your time/calendar hierarchies are calculated correctly.

This can be addressed by how you handle the granularity of data. My recommendation is to use as much as possible balance sheet movement data (i.e., not the balance but the changes in the time period), as this makes time handling easier. On the other hand, this also means you need to either have all movements since inception or you have to work with opening balances. For example, you can load the balance sheet opening balances into the first period (or a specific opening balance period) of your calendar and then use movements in subsequent periods. When applying movement granularity, the only calculation that you need to add is a DAX measure that sums up all movements up to the cut-off point. This point is typically the latest date in the current time context. The DAX code to calculate this is as follows:

```
Balance sheet = CALCULATE(sum(Transactions[Amount_
GC]),FILTER(all('Calendar'[Date]),'Calendar'[Date]<=max('Calendar'[Date])))
```

If you only get balance data (e.g., quarterly balance sheets from a web source), you can either transform data at load time, which is not trivial in **Power Query**, or you can achieve this with lag/lead functions in a **SQL** data warehouse. Another option is to use DAX functions to calculate movements from balance data, in principle; aggregate the values since the last empty value in the current period with a DAX syntax similar to the following:

```
Balance = CALCULATE(SUM('Balance Sheet'[Value]),
LASTNONBLANK('Date'[Date],SUM('Balance Sheet'[Value])))
```

With that calculation, it will work correctly over all time hierarchies. You obviously have to use the right measure only in the relevant report type (e.g., the calculated DAX movement measure in Power BI visuals that contain the income statement and cashflow statement, and the balance calculation in the balance sheet).

Once you have the right calculations in place, the final task is adapting the layout. In a balance sheet, you typically have **Assets** and **Liabilities**. My recommendation here is to use two table visuals (just copy and paste the existing) and filter one on your assets grouping(s) in your Account dimension, and the other on the rest, as shown here:

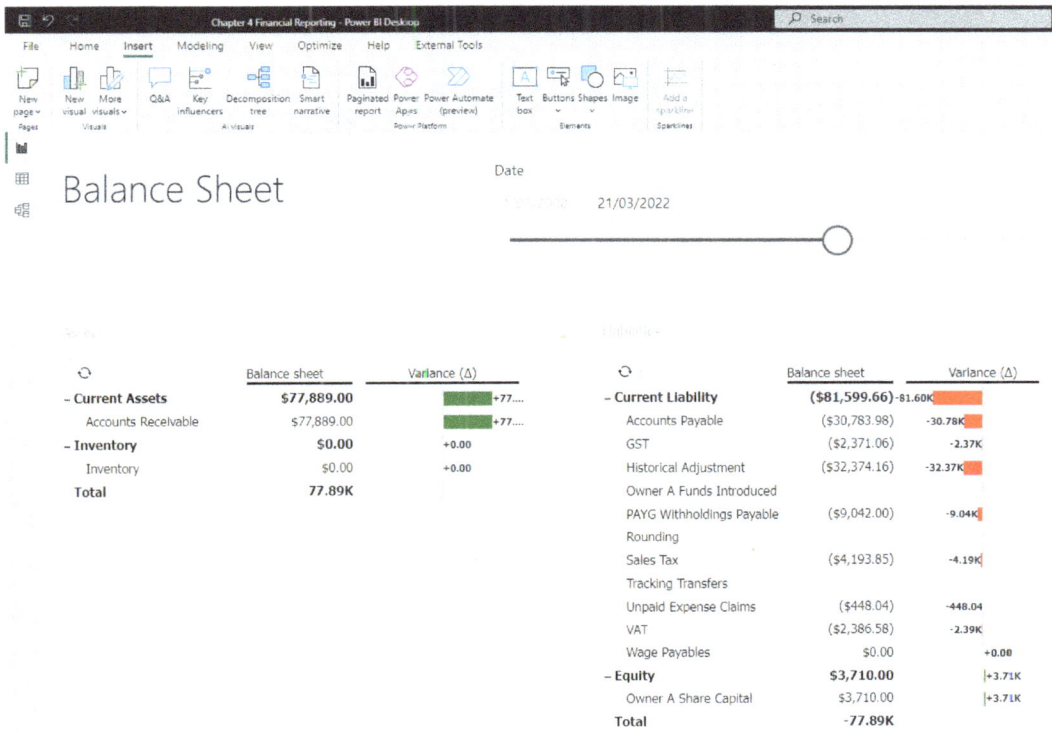

Figure 4.17 – Balance Sheet report

In the previous sections, we reviewed how to design standard financial statements in Power BI. In the next section, we will review how to approach asymmetric reporting requirements.

Implementing asymmetric reports

A special reporting requirement is the implementation of asymmetric reports in Power BI.

An **asymmetric report** uses a combination of either rows or columns where the child node content differs between the parent nodes. For example, for a nested two-dimensional display of Year with 2020 and 2021 members, and Scenario type Actual and Budget members, we only want to display some of the scenarios for each year as opposed to both for each year:

Year	2020	2021
Type	Actual	Budget
⊞ Revenue	6,305.17	86,066.67
⊞ DirectCosts	-3,269.15	-6,116.62
⊞ Expense	-19,448.27	-48,536.74
⊞ Overheads	-21,888.54	-69,072.56
EBIT	**-38,300.79**	**-37,659.25**

Figure 4.18 – Asymmetric report

Normally, the Power BI matrix, similar to most visuals in Power BI and the Pivot Table in Excel, will display the nodes symmetrically: a nested row or column element can only show the same elements for all parents. For example, if you have selected Actual and Budget, they will be displayed for all elements (years in this case). In the Excel Pivot Table, there is a way out with using **MDX sets** for the sources that support it (e.g., PowerPivot and SSAS MD). We will cover this in the next chapter.

In Power BI, one option is to define a static DAX measure that filters the required combination (for example, Year and Scenario). This has a variety of limitations (e.g., drill down won't be available anymore), and it's not easy to make it dynamically react to filter changes.

A better option is to use a separate report definition table and a DAX measure. To do that, the first step is to add the two-dimension table columns/fields from our dataset used in the asymmetric combination in the matrix or Pivot Table:

Asymmetric Report

FinancialQuarter

All

Year	2019	2020	2021		2022	
Type	Actual	Actual	Actual	Budget	Actual	Budget
⊞ Revenue	53,486.96	6,305.17	75,595.03	86,066.67	27,797.72	105,316.00
⊞ DirectCosts	-763.64	-3,269.15	-3,394.68	-6,116.62	-1,342.28	-2,142.28
⊞ Expense	-60,816.18	-19,448.27	-26,354.78	-48,536.74	3,307.70	-47,977.17
⊞ Overheads		-21,888.54	-25,790.27	-69,072.56	-7,916.74	-7,970.54
⊞ OtherIncome	97.05					106.76
EBIT	**-7,995.81**	**-38,300.79**	**20,055.30**	**-37,659.25**	**21,846.39**	**47,332.77**

Figure 4.19 – Standard matrix display

Now we can see that the Scenario and Year fields are added to the columns of the matrix, and the visual shows all the available combinations of scenarios/years. As zero suppression (i.e., hiding rows/columns with no data) is turned on, not all the available combinations will show. This, however, is not what we want. We only want to show the budget for 2021.

To achieve the desired report layout, we need a DAX measure with a separate report definition table. The report definition will contain the combinations we want to show.

The DAX measure will then, based on our report definition table, only return data for the desired Time/Scenario combinations and will produce blanks for the combinations that we don't need.

Configuring the report definition table

To enable the asymmetric table, we need to create a new definition table that contains the details of what we want to display in our report with the following steps.

Step 1: Specifying the desired combinations

In our case, we need to create a definition table that contains the required Scenario and Time (Year) combinations. The table can be created using a data entry table in Power BI, a linked table in Excel, or with a third-party solution such as Acterys that enables you to edit dimensions and add dimension table columns directly in the model.

To add the table in Power BI, just click on **Enter data** in the ribbon:

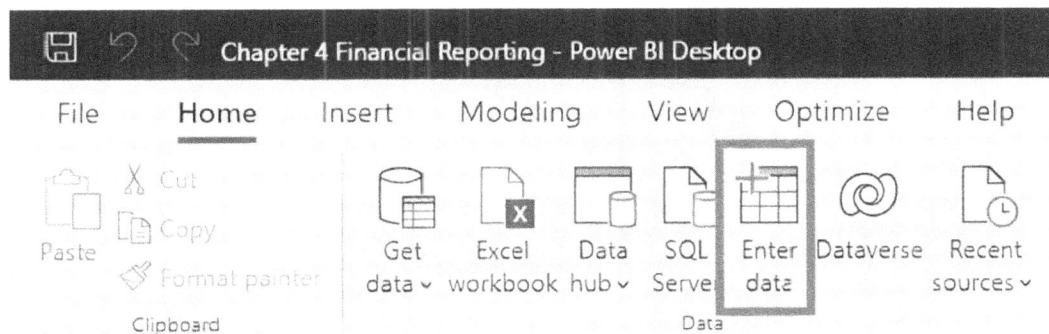

Figure 4.20 – Creating the definition table

We will create a new table with three columns (Scenario, Report Year, and Order) as well as populate these with two rows that contain the definition of what we want to display (Actual for 2020 as the first item, and Budget for 2021 as the second):

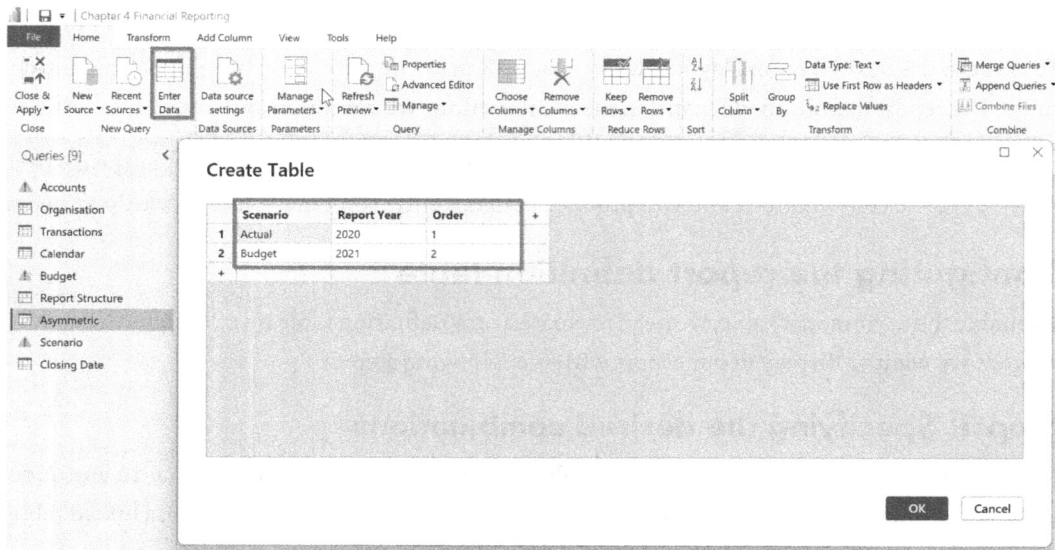

Figure 4.21 – Entering report definition

We can then link this new table to the main Transactions table in the Power BI **Model View** section by either dragging the two Scenario fields onto each other or creating a relationship between them in the **Manage relationships** section in the Power BI ribbon:

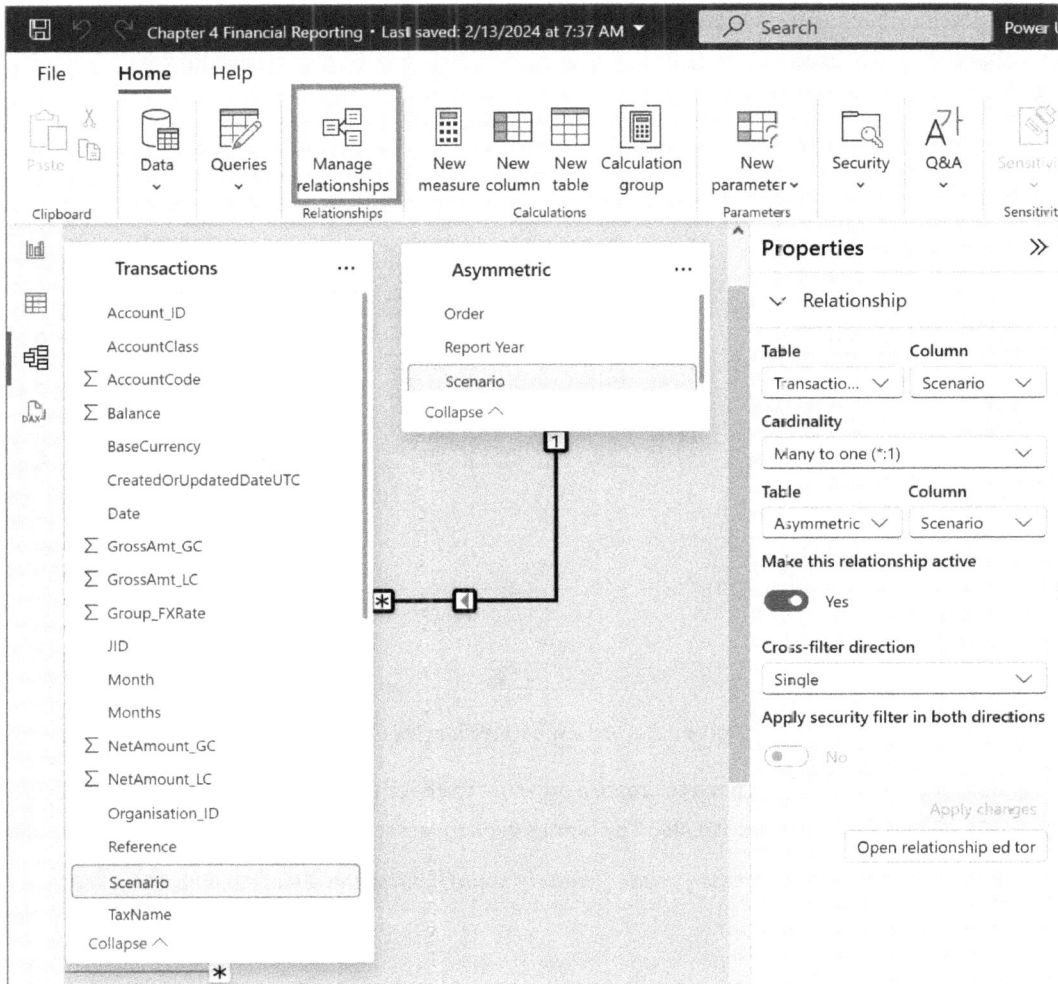

Figure 4.22 – Creating a relationship between the definition and the Transactions table

Step 2: The DAX measure to show or hide a combination

Now that we have our definition, we just need a DAX measure with an `IF` function that produces blanks if encountering an undesired combination and a normal aggregation otherwise. First, we need a measure to check whether the desired combination is being encountered:

```
showYear = IF(max('Calendar'[Year]) in VALUES(Asymmetric[Report
Year]),TRUE(),FALSE())
```

In the preceding measure, we check whether the Year/Scenario combination is valid. To show the effect of this measure, let's display this measure in the matrix. Only the valid Year/Scenario combinations produce a True value:

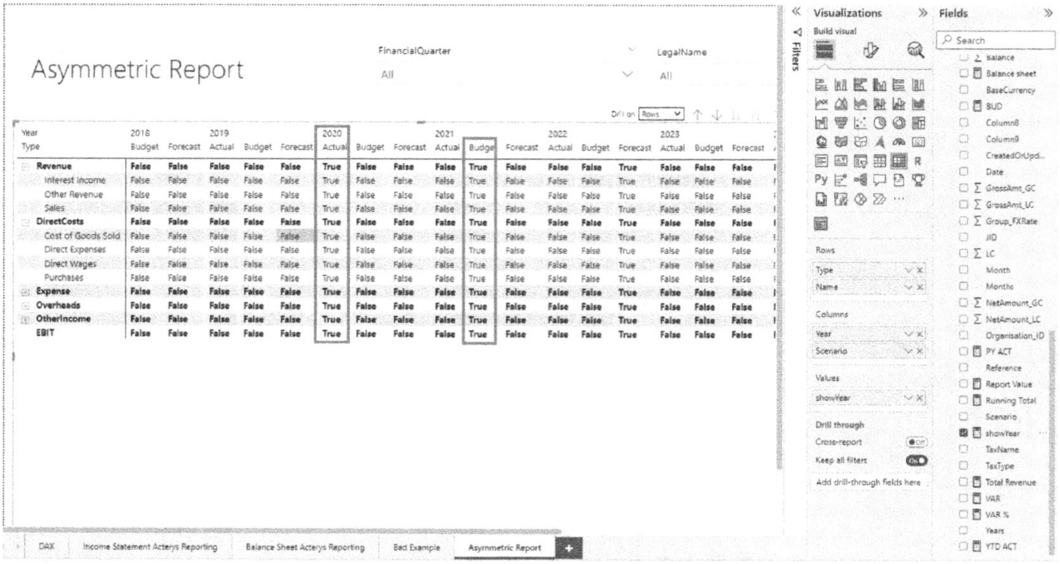

Figure 4.23 – Review of DAX measure output

The next step is easy. We just need to create a measure to check the showYear flag, and if True, do a normal sum, and if False, pass a BLANK. The blanks get suppressed by the matrix visual/Pivot Table:

```
Asymmetric = if([showYear],sum(Transactions[NetAmount_GC]),BLANK())
```

The resulting report now displays the desired asymmetric report with a drill-down option in the rows:

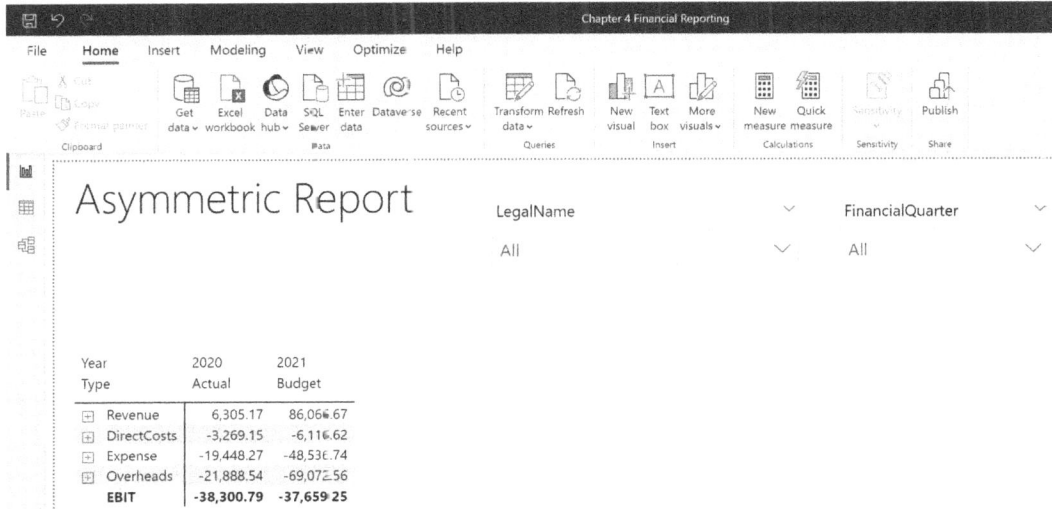

Figure 4.24 – Asymmetric report as per definition

In this section, we have reviewed options to create asymmetric reports in Power BI using a definition table and DAX logic that displays the desired combinations.

Summary

In this chapter, we covered different options to realize comprehensive financial statements in a typically required presentation style with either DAX calculations or special Power BI visuals. It might take a bit more initial effort, but in contrast to static spreadsheets, it will enable automatically updating reports that require no maintenance efforts in conjunction with all the analytics and visualization features that Power BI offers, such as using smart tooltips (as covered in this chapter) that provide unparalleled insights for the report user.

In the following chapter, we will look at how Power BI and Excel interact. Excel also offers a flexible alternative for realizing financial statements.

Get This Book's PDF Version and Exclusive Extras

UNLOCK NOW

Scan the QR code (or go to packtpub.com/unlock).
Search for this book by name, confirm the edition, and
then follow the steps on the page.

*Note: Keep your invoice handy. Purchases made directly
from Packt don't require one.*

5

Integrating Excel and Power BI for Financial Requirements

Excel is arguably the most widely used business application and a key tool for any finance professional. There are extensive arguments on social media and other channels about how Power BI can address financial requirements better than a spreadsheet. Many of them focus on why one is "better than the other." From my experiences over the last nearly 10 years, the optimal approach is to use both effectively together.

As discussed in *Chapter 1*, recurring and standardized Excel tasks that benefit from more advanced, interactive visualization/analytics capabilities are better handled in Power BI. Financial professionals, though, often have one-off requirements that require quick, flexible solutions, such as the following examples:

- Formula calculations that would take way more time to realize in Power BI
- Flexible, non-symmetric layouts that can't be addressed in a matrix
- Handling and adding unstructured content
- Charting requirements that require more flexibility than available in Power BI visuals (e.g., adding other elements and shapes to a chart)

For these requirements, Excel is still the better option. In this chapter, I will cover scenarios in which Excel and Power BI can work effectively together to facilitate typical financial tasks.

We will cover the following topics:

- Working with your Power BI data in Excel
- Creating a live link in Excel
- Working with dynamic columns

Technical requirements

For the examples in this chapter, we will use `Chapter 5 Power BI Excel.xlsx` from the book's official GitHub repository here: `https://github.com/PacktPublishing/Power-BI-for-Finance`. As the Power BI-Excel integration requires access through the Power BI service, at least a Pro license is required.

Working with your Power BI data in Excel

You have two options to work with your Power BI data in Excel: a static file export from any visual in Power BI or a live link to the Power BI data. For a one-off requirement in which you want to do an analysis in Excel with your data only at that particular point in time, a static export is sufficient. For any case where you might need updated data or want to do this analysis again, a live link to the data in Power BI is a much better option. Every finance professional will be familiar with how to work with static data in Excel, so we will only cover the live link option in this book.

Creating a live link in Excel

Using Power BI data in Excel requires publishing the Power BI Desktop `.pbix` file to the Power BI service. From there, you can create a live connection to Excel by either going to the dataset or, from any point, choosing **Analyze in Excel** in the **Export** options:

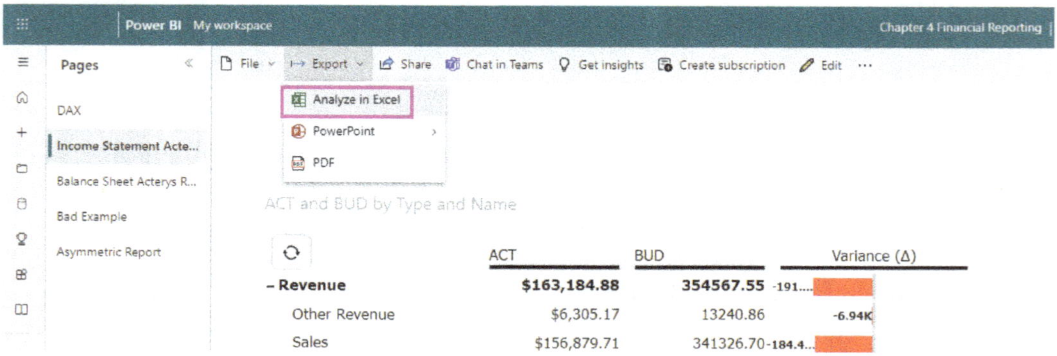

Figure 5.1 – Connecting your Power BI dataset with Excel

Either option creates an Excel file that you can open with Excel Desktop or Excel Online. It contains a connection to your Power BI dataset with all tables and measures in the model:

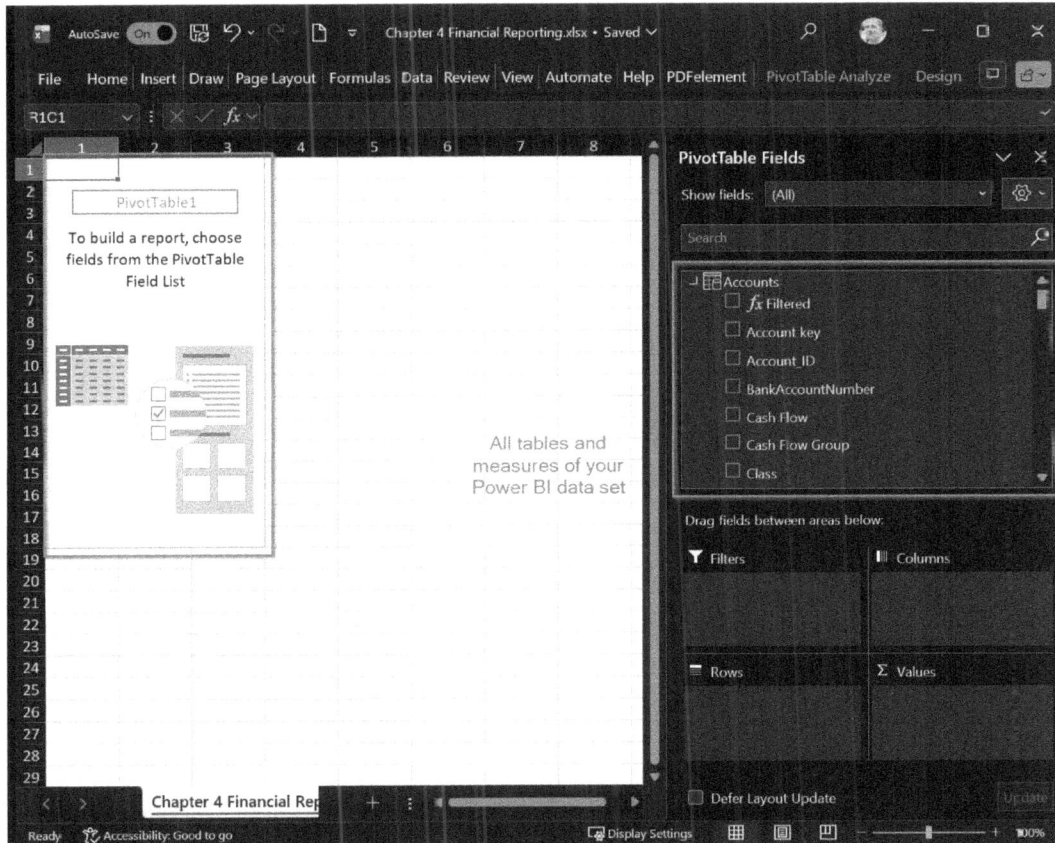

Figure 5.2 – PivotTable field configuration

From here, you can now create a report as an Excel Pivot Table in the same way as in the Power BI matrix by just dragging the measures in the Values field and columns from your tables into Filters, Columns, and Rows. This PivotTable is now connected to your data model. Click **Refresh** in Excel to automatically update the table with the latest data in the Power BI dataset.

For example, to replicate our simple income statement (without the subtotal calculations) in Power BI, covered in *Chapter 1* of the book, we just add the respective dimension in the rows, fields, and columns and assign our two measures for actuals (ACT) and budget (BUD). As a result, we will get the following:

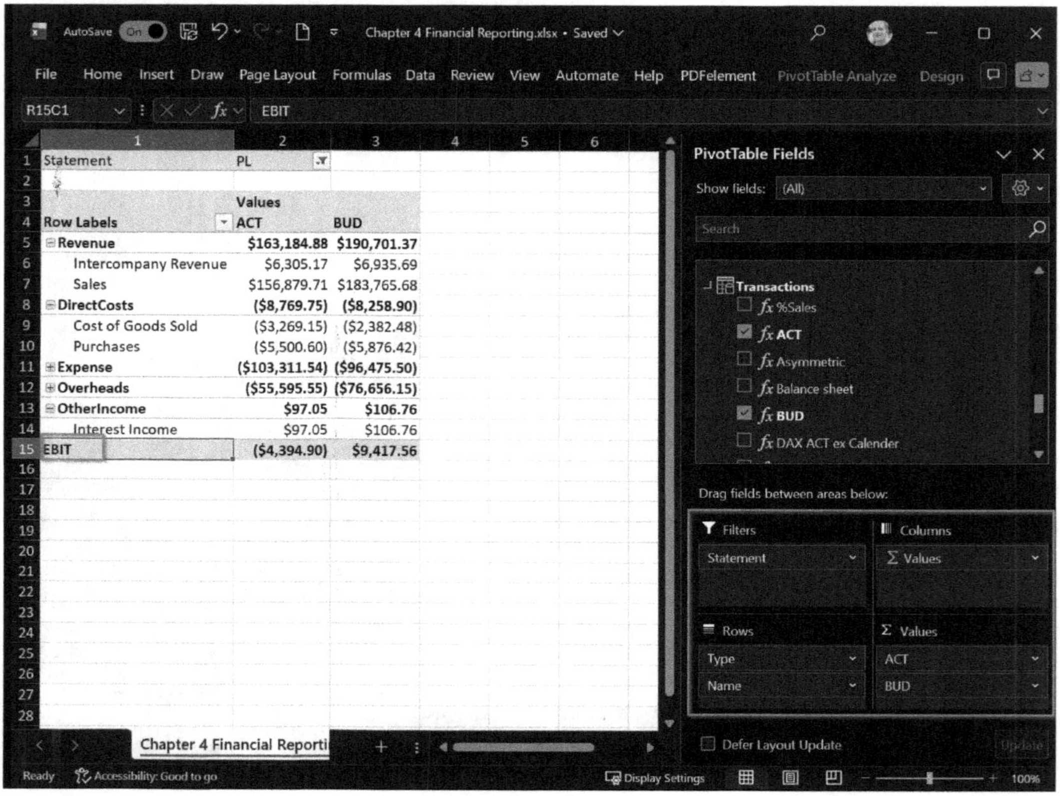

Figure 5.3 – Sample Pivot Table report with Power BI data

To make it a bit clearer, I have added empty rows at the right and top and renamed what the Pivot Table calls Grand Total as EBIT at the bottom left. This is not bad, but it doesn't give us much benefit over the Power BI solution. We can add value, though, by using a special functionality that is only available in Excel: we can convert this Pivot Table report into a formula report where, in contrast to the relatively rigid structure of a Pivot Table, we retrieve all the parts of the report as formulas, which gives us much more flexibility. To convert the report to formulas, first, duplicate the current Excel worksheet page (so that we still have the Pivot Table). Then, select any cell of the Pivot Table; this should make the **PivotTable Analyze** tab active. Under this tab, click on the arrow next to **OLAP Tools** to open the submenu and click on **Convert to Formulas**:

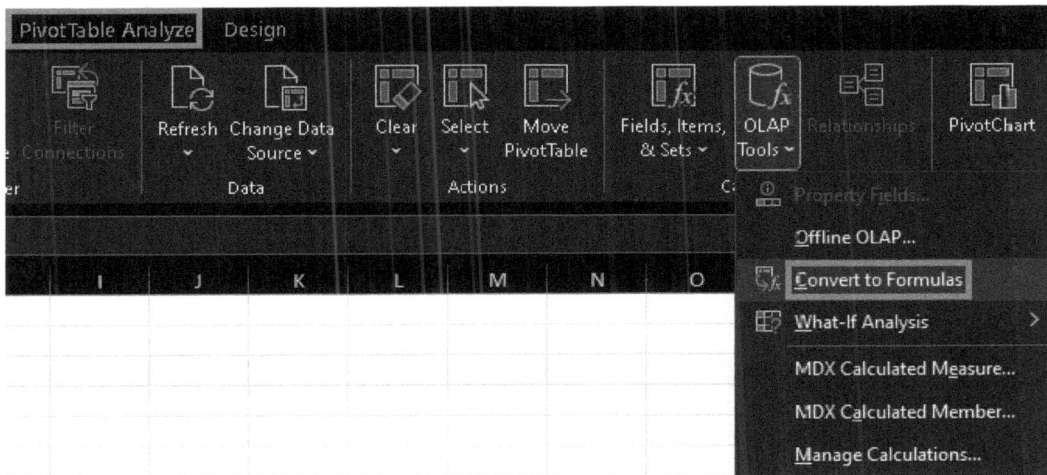

Figure 5.4 – Conversion to formulas

In the next dialog box, press **OK**. We will leave the filters as a Pivot Table, as that allows us to dynamically change them. Otherwise, they would be converted to formulas as well.

Now we see the same report, but it is represented by formulas for every part of the report apart from the filters:

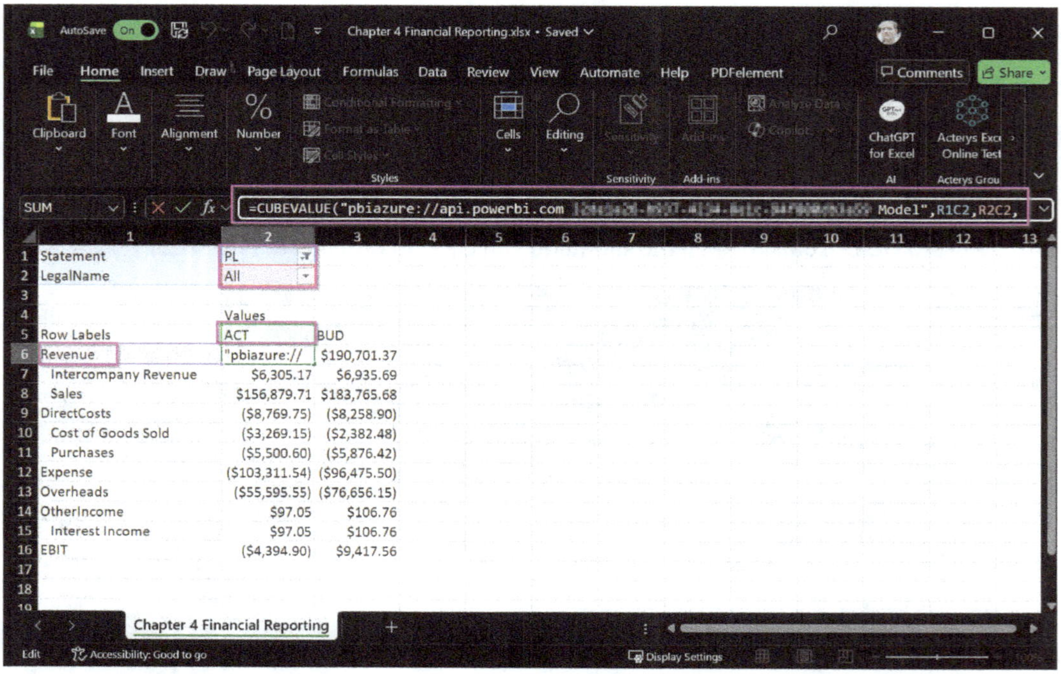

Figure 5.5 – Formula report

Every cell with values in the report (fields that were put in the Values area in the Pivot Table) is now a CUBEVALUE() formula that uses, as arguments, connection (which is our Power BI dataset) and *1* to *n* dimensions member fields. In the formula in cell C7 in *Figure 5.5,* Revenue from the Type field in Accounts (cell B7), PL from Statement (cell C2), and All in LegalName (cell C3), as well as the ACT measure, are referenced, and the value of these coordinates is displayed in the report in that cell.

When we look at cell B7, we see that a formula is also used here, in this case, CUBEMEMBER(), which uses two arguments: the connection and a reference to the dimension element consisting of table, column, and field name:

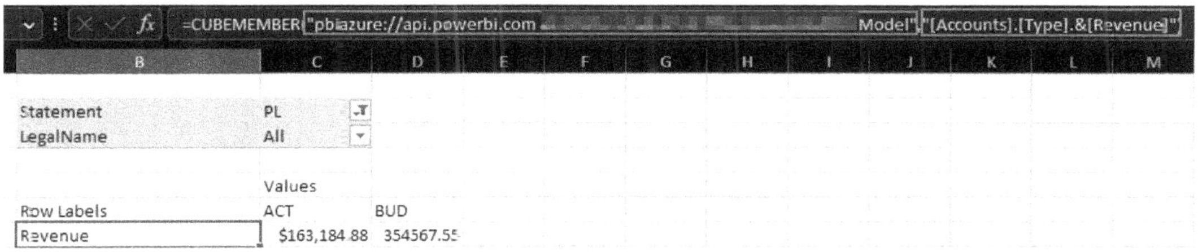

Figure 5.6 – The CUBEMEMBER() formula

The top section with the filters is actually a very limited Pivot Table where you can still change filters, for example, to a different organization by clicking on the arrow at the top right of the LegalName filter field and then selecting the element(s) that you want to use:

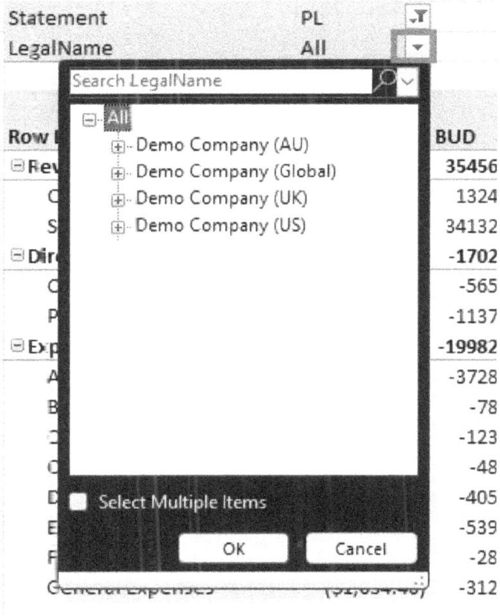

Figure 5.7 – Filter selection

This alone is not much improvement to the Power BI matrix or the Pivot Table. However, we now have all the flexibility of Excel to edit this report. The rigid structure of a matrix no longer limits us. We can add any formatting exactly as we want it, add new or edit formulas, and add any other Excel feature to this table, which makes it even more helpful from a financial perspective, as we can see in the following screenshot and the sample file:

E7		✓ : ✕ ✓ *fx*	=C7-D7								
	A	B	C	D	E	F	G	H	I	J	K	L
1												
2		Statement	PL									
3		LegalName	All									
4												
5												
6			ACT	BUD	VAR	VAR %						
7		Revenue	$163,184.88	354567.55	-191383	-54%						
8		Other Revenue	$6,305.17	13240.86	-6935.69	-52%						
9		Sales	$156,879.71	341326.70	-184447	-54%						
10		DirectCosts	($8,769.75)	-17028.65	8258.905	-49%						
11		Cost of Goods Sold	($3,269.15)	-5651.63	2382.48	-42%						
12		Purchases	($5,500.60)	-11377.02	5876.424	-52%						
13		Gross Margin	168685.4757	365944.58	-197259	-54%						
14		Expense	($103,311.54)	-199825.45	96513.91	-48%						
15		Advertising	($17,518.97)	-37288.64	19769.67	-53%						
16		Bank Fees	($387.30)	-780.78	393.4812	-50%						
17		Cleaning	($611.00)	-1236.61	625.6053	-51%						
18		Consulting & Accounting	($256.72)	-488.90	232.1812	-47%						
19		Dues & Subscriptions	($2,006.13)	-4057.61	2051.479	-51%						
20		Entertainment	($2,531.42)	-5396.28	2864.865	-53%						
21		Freight & Courier	($136.79)	-287.26	150.4684	-52%						
22		General Expenses	($1,634.46)	-3123.66	1489.201	-48%						
23		Income Tax Expense	$0.00	0.00	0	#DIV/0!						
24		Legal expenses	($4,090.91)	-9090.91	5000	-55%						
25		Light, Power, Heating	($1,505.64)	-3057.37	1551.733	-51%						
26		Motor Vehicle Expenses	($1,779.06)	-3648.13	1869.072	-51%						
27		Office Expenses	($2,302.37)	-4583.44	2281.068	-50%						
28		Payroll Tax Expense	($1,853.89)	-3788.38	1934.493	-51%						
29		Printing & Stationery	($450.64)	-883.89	433.2451	-49%						
30		Rent	($21,945.22)	-44669.33	22724.11	-51%						
31		Repairs and Maintenance	($2,522.44)	-5297.12	2774.681	-52%						
32		Subscriptions	($120.00)	-240.00	120	-50%						
33		Telephone & Internet	($424.50)	-867.49	442.9935	-51%						
34		Travel - National	($1,034.06)	-2129.62	1095.565	-51%						
35		Wages and Salaries	($40,200.00)	-68910.00	28710	-42%						
36		Overheads	($55,595.55)	-132638.64	77043.1	-58%						
37		OtherIncome	$97.05	203.81	-106.755	-52%						
38		Interest Income	$97.05	203.81	-106.755	-52%						
39		EBIT	($4,394.90)	5278.61	-9673.52	-183%						
40												

Figure 5.8 – Additional formatting options in the formula report

This is great as it overcomes the limitations that we had in Power BI, and we now have total flexibility with formatting on a cell level with all the features of Excel. All this is done with a live connection to the database, so one workbook can replace hundreds of others, and you can query any report combinations from the central Power BI dataset in one Excel file.

This looks like a godsend for financial pros but has limitations, as the elements in rows and columns are static. As these are now formulas referring, for example, to a specific account or period, any changes to these dimensions, such as a new account, will not be added to the report automatically. Instead, the report admin has to do this manually.

Equally, rows and columns don't automatically update to filters as in the Pivot Table. For example, if you switch to an organization that doesn't have values for particular account rows, you can't easily implement zero suppression.

There are a few options to make your formula reports dynamic by making the references used in the formula dynamic. I will cover that in the following section.

Working with dynamic columns

Let's create a copy of our Pivot Table and modify the layout to include a filter for Year and show months in Columns:

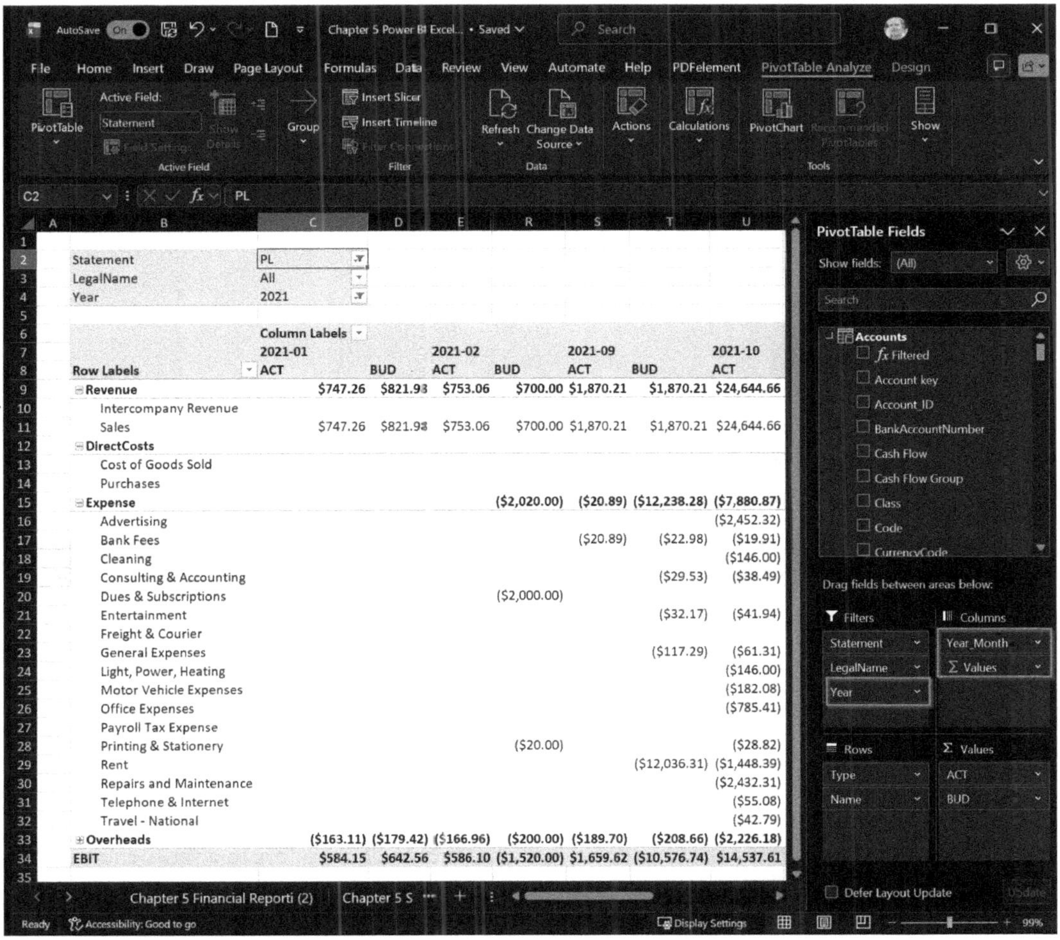

Figure 5.9 – Pivot Table with Month and Scenario in rows

Make sure that the order of the Values field is below the Year_Month field; otherwise, the report will show the months grouped by scenario as opposed to both scenarios per month.

Once we have the report correctly in place, we can convert it to formulas again, as described in the previous section.

When we change the Year filter now to 2021, we see that columns won't update and still show the months for the year with which we created the report. Also, we don't get any data. Let's have a look at the formula and see why:

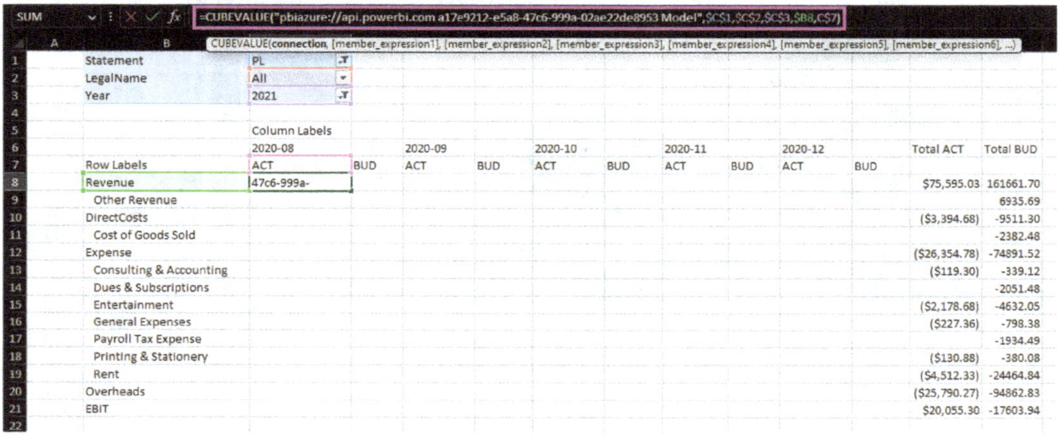

Figure 5.10 – The CUBEVALUE() formula

We see that the formula is referring to all filters, the row (B8), but only one column cell, C7; there is no reference to the Year_Month field in C6. Let's look at C7:

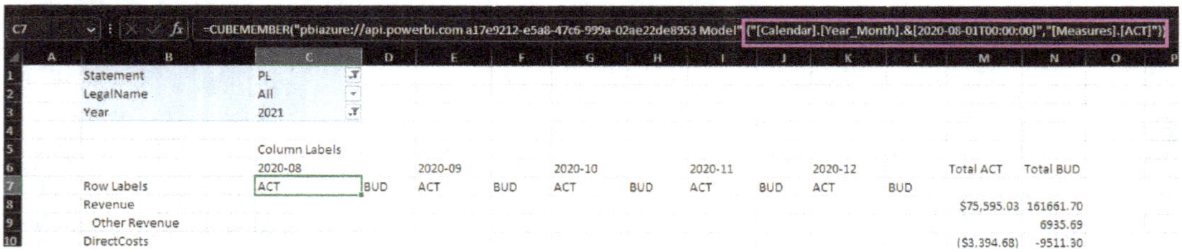

Figure 5.11 – The CUBEMEMBER() formula

Here, we see that the formula that the Pivot Table has created now refers to a set (denominated by curly brackets { }) referring to a static Year_Month reference, 2020-08-01, and the ACT measure.

Up to this day, I haven't found anyone who can give me a good explanation of what the point of a combined reference is. A reference to both cells would be much more logical to handle, and we see we can do that by replacing this reference with two arguments and changing cell C7 to only refer to the ACT measure:

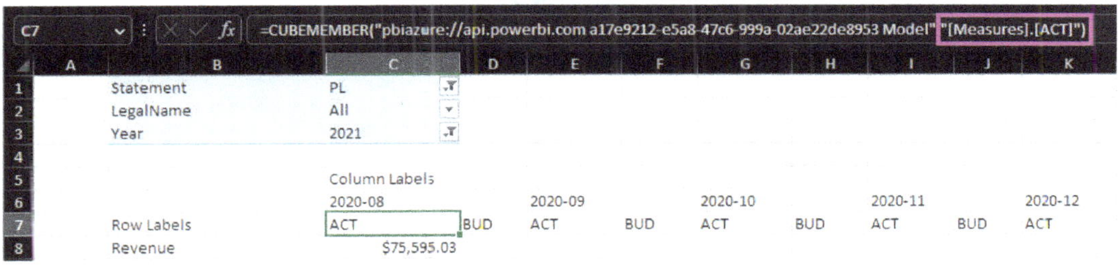

Figure 5.12 – Changes to CUBEMEMBER()

To have the reference to the month, we just add another argument to the formula referring to cell C6:

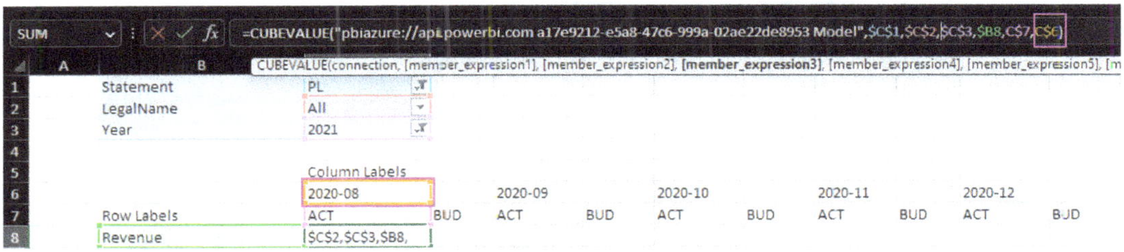

Figure 5.13 – Reference to new cell C6

You see that I am using a partly absolute reference with an absolute ($6) one for the row, but a relative one (C) for the column. The reason for that is that this allows me to easily copy this formula to any other cell on the report with correct referencing.

Interestingly, we see now that the value in the Revenue cell (C8) is empty:

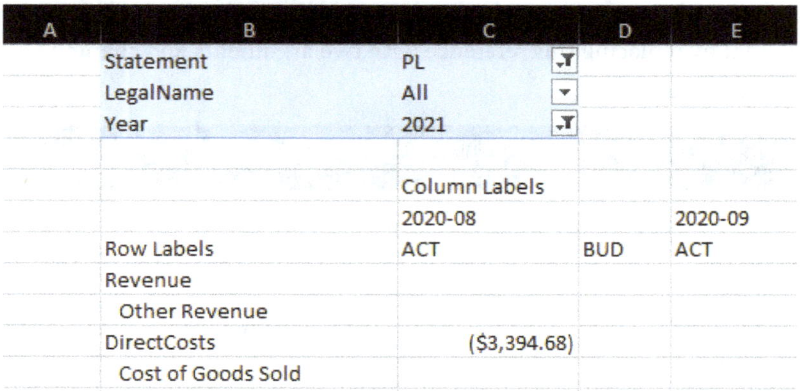
A
B
C
D
E
Statement
PL
LegalName
All
Year
2021
Column Labels
2020-08
2020-09
Row Labels
ACT
BUD
ACT
Revenue
Other Revenue
DirectCosts
($3,394.68)
Cost of Goods Sold

Figure 5.14 – Empty CUBEVALUE() cell

The reason is that we have conflicting references (`Year` `2021` and `Year_month` `2020-08`). There is no value in that combination as it doesn't exist.

Let's change the `Year` back to `2020` and copy our formula down (a double-click on the bottom corner of `C8` does that automatically for you) to see whether our formula works. Now, we see that it does:

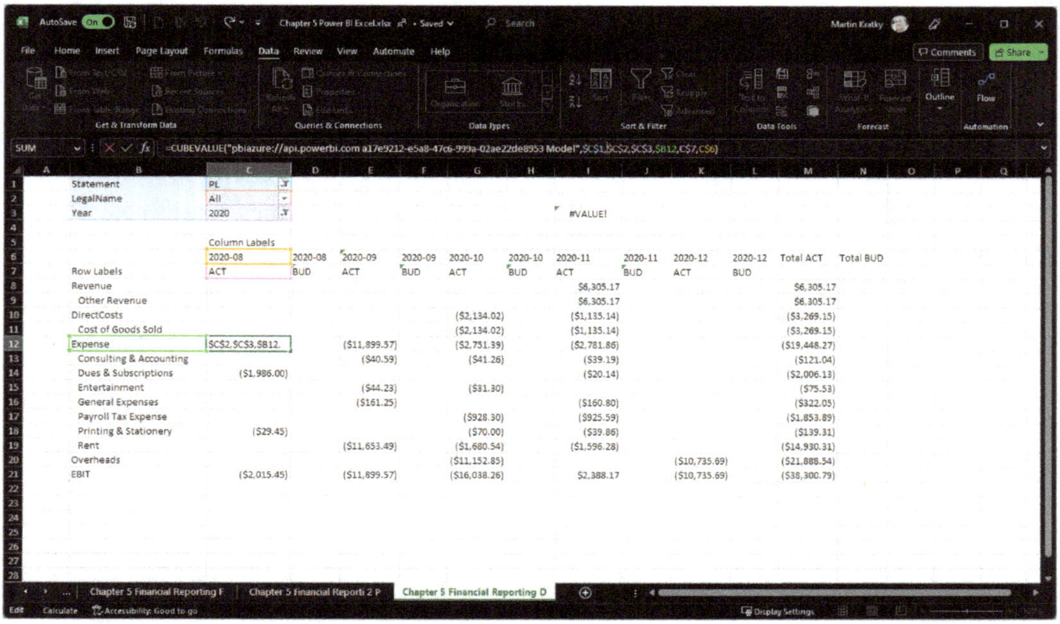
Statement
PL
LegalName
All
Year
2020
Column Labels
Row Labels
Revenue
Other Revenue
DirectCosts
Cost of Goods Sold
Expense
Consulting & Accounting
Dues & Subscriptions
Entertainment
General Expenses
Payroll Tax Expense
Printing & Stationery
Rent
Overheads
EBIT
Total ACT
Total BUD

Figure 5.15 – CUBEVALUE() updated

There was really no data in cell C8. Now, we need to find a way to avoid getting into a "conflict" between the selected year in the filter and the months in rows. As we have formulas, we can just use our Excel know-how: we just need to update the formula in the Month row header to refer to the year selected. We can do this by just concatenating the argument in the formula:

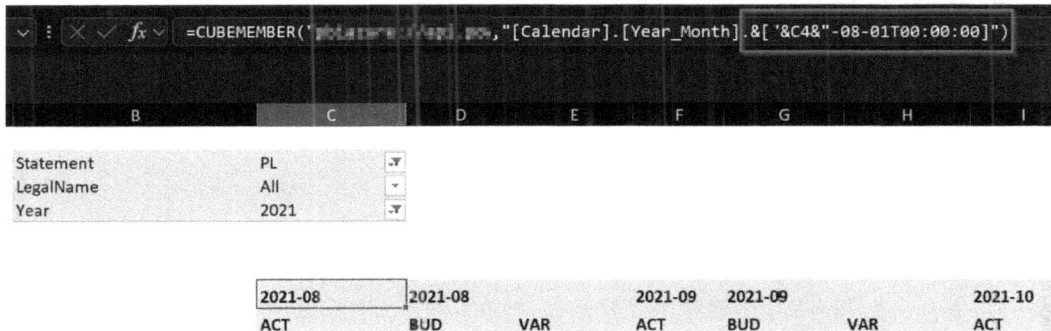

Figure 5.16 – Concatenated formula

The approach just adds the reference to cell C3, which contains the selected year. We just need to enclose the text before and after in quotation marks (") and concatenate them with an ampersand (&). The principle is always the same. If we had used a calendar reference with a simple month number, this would have been easier, but this is a good exercise, as there is no other way around than this in other cases with non-numeric date references.

We can now replicate this for all other row headers and remove the reference to the year in the filter in CUBEVALUE formulas. It doesn't hurt, but it is redundant, and it's a good idea to have your formulas structured in the simplest form possible. Equally, we can replace the ACT and BUD measure headers with our updated formula. Now, the results should match what we have (*had* if we didn't copy it) in the Pivot Table in *Figure 5.9*.

When we switch now to the year 2021 in the filter, we see our report works correctly with dynamic headers, but there is one catch:

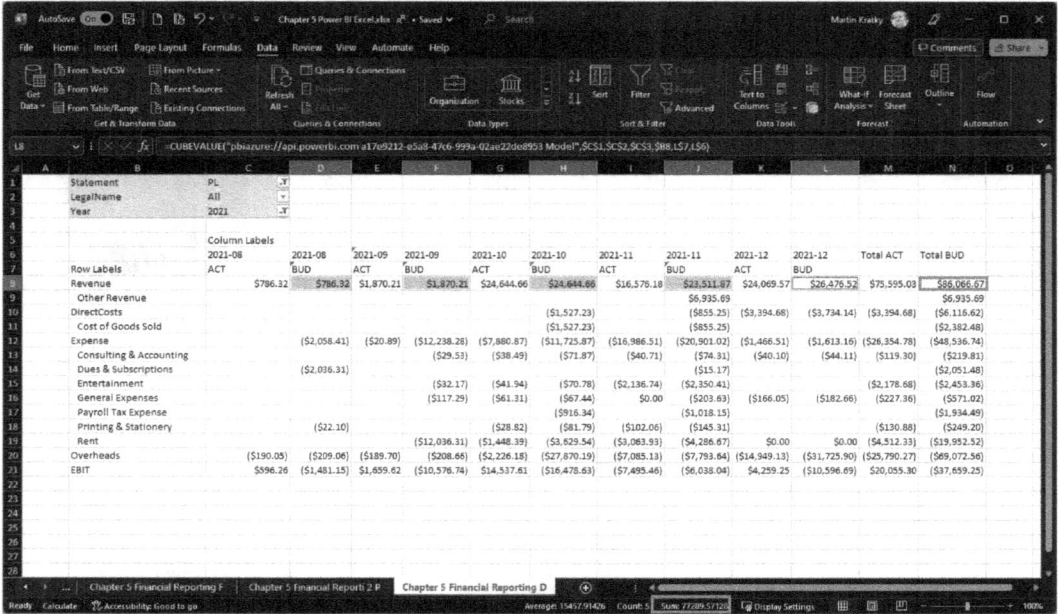

Figure 5.17 – Formula report with dynamic headers

The formulas, for example, the totals in columns M and N, return what the references in the formula are, not the "visible totals" of months 8 to 12 as used in our case. If you want to show the correct total of the visible fields, you have to modify the respective cells to Excel formulas that, in this case, would just sum up the cells with the budget or actuals.

Let's try that:

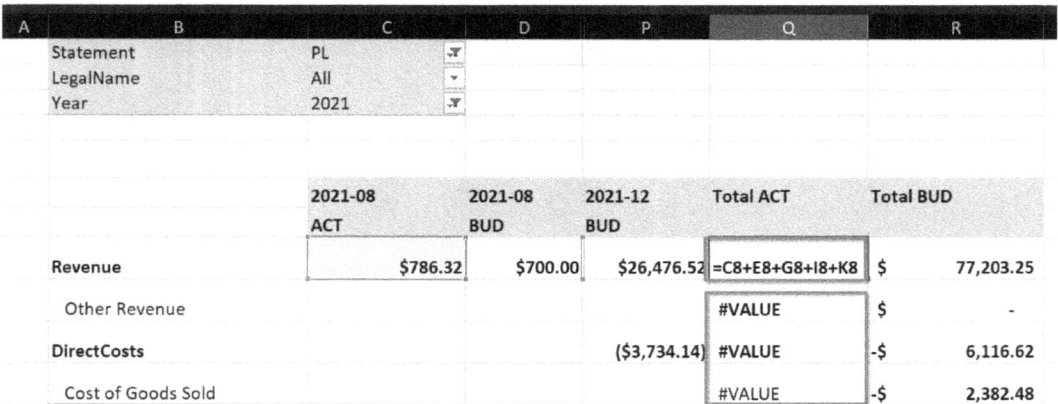

Figure 5.18 – Errors in totals columns

Strangely enough, we are now getting #VALUE! errors from cell Q9. The reason for that is an unexpected (but correct) behavior with CUBEVALUE functions, which return empty cells as opposed to a number when there is no value in the database. Blank is correct, as showing a zero would imply that a zero is in the database, which is not the case. So, we must deal with that. We can avoid this error message by enclosing our cell references to CUBEVALUE() formulas with N(), which prevents the #VALUE! error from getting shown:

A	B	C	D	P	Q	R
	Statement	PL				
	LegalName	All				
	Year	2021				
		2021-08 ACT	2021-08 BUD	2021-12 BUD	Total ACT	Total BUD
	Revenue	$786.32	$700.00	$26,476.52	=N(C8)+N(E8)+N(G8)+N(I8)+N(K8)	$ 77,203.25
	Other Revenue				#VALUE	$ -
	DirectCosts			($3,734.14)	#VALUE	-$ 6,116.62
	Cost of Goods Sold				#VALUE	-$ 2,382.48
	Expense		($2,020.00)	($1,613.16)	#VALUE	-$ 48,498.33

Figure 5.19 – Updating references with N()

Understanding #VALUE! and #N/A errors in Excel

When you are working with connected data sources in Excel, you often encounter specific error messages. In this section, we'll explore the reason and how to address the two most often occurring issues.

#VALUE! error

The #VALUE! error occurs when Excel cannot perform calculations with the given input. Common causes include the following:

- Using text in mathematical formulas (as in the preceding example, where the returned result is a text in a mathematical formula)
- Referencing cells with formatting issues
- Using functions with incorrect argument types; for example, =SUM("Revenue",5) will return #VALUE! because "Revenue" isn't a number

#N/A error

The #N/A error appears when Excel can't find a referenced value or when a function can't produce a valid result. Common causes include the following:

- VLOOKUP or HLOOKUP not finding a match
- The MATCH function failing to find a value
- Missing data in lookup tables
- The INDEX function with out-of-range arguments; for example, =VLOOKUP("Test", A1:B10, 2, FALSE) will return #N/A if "Test" isn't in column A

Here's how to avoid these errors:

- Use data validation to restrict input types
- Check data types before calculations
- Wrap functions with IFERROR() to handle exceptions
- For lookups, use IFNA() to provide fallback values
- Clean data before analysis (remove spaces and fix formatting)
- Use the ISTEXT() and ISNUMBER() functions to verify data before calculations
- For VLOOKUP, consider using TRUE for approximate matches when appropriate

Implementing these practices will significantly reduce errors and make your spreadsheets more robust.

After having this applied to both the ACT and BUD visual totals, we can now make this report more useful with a few modifications as before and add a sparkline so that users can immediately see the trend. This is a bit tricky as our range includes non-adjacent cells. When we try to set that in the sparkline, we get an error:

		2021-08 ACT	2021-08 BUD	2021-12 BUD	Total ACT		Total BUD	ACT Trend
Revenue		$786.32	$700.00	$26,476.52		27387.50214 $	77,203.25	
Other Revenue						0 $	-	
DirectCosts						1527.231075 -$	6,116.62	
Cost of Goods Sold							2,382.48	
Expense							48,498.33	
Consulting & Accounting							219.81	
Dues & Subscriptions						2000 -$	2,015.17	
Entertainment						-45.28321097 -$	2,453.36	
General Expenses				($182.66)		-172.4692063 -$	571.02	

Create Sparklines
Choose the data that you want
Data Range: C8,F8,I8,L8,O8
Choose where you want the sparklines to be placed
Location Range: S9
OK   Cancel

Microsoft Excel
⚠ Data source reference is not valid.
OK

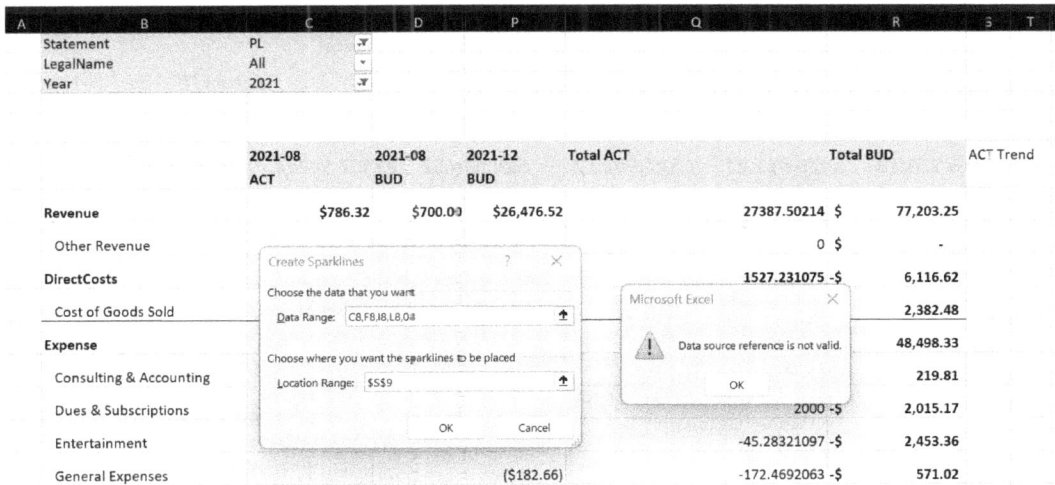

Figure 5.20 – Sparklines don't work in non-contiguous cells

One way out here is to define a named range in Excel that includes our Actuals cells. The easiest way is to type the new range in the name box at the top left:

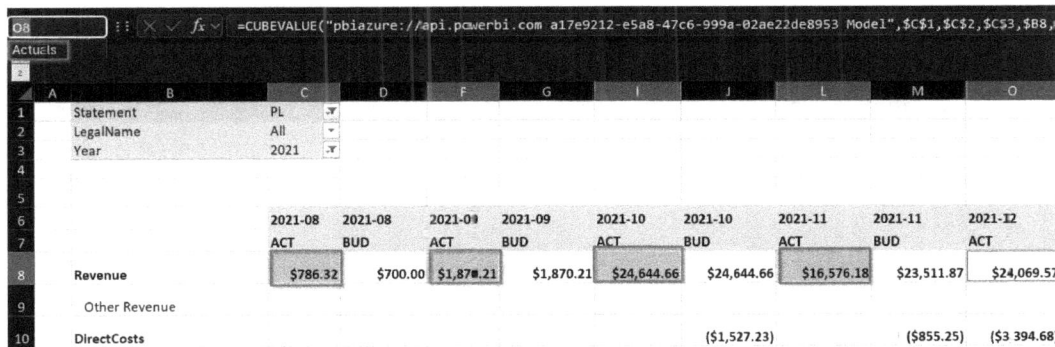

O8
Actuals
=CUBEVALUE("pbiazure://api.powerbi.com a17e9212-e5a8-47c6-999a-02ae22de8953 Model",C1,C2,C3,$B8,C

		2021-08 ACT	2021-08 BUD	2021-09 ACT	2021-09 BUD	2021-10 ACT	2021-10 BUD	2021-11 ACT	2021-11 BUD	2021-12 ACT
1	Statement PL									
2	LegalName All									
3	Year 2021									
8	Revenue	$786.32	$700.00	$1,87■.21	$1,870.21	$24,644.66	$24,644.66	$16,576.18	$23,511.87	$24,069.57
9	Other Revenue									
10	DirectCosts					($1,527.23)		($855.25)		($3 394.68)

Figure 5.21 – Defining a range

Once we have that, we just need to refer to the named range when we add the sparkline:

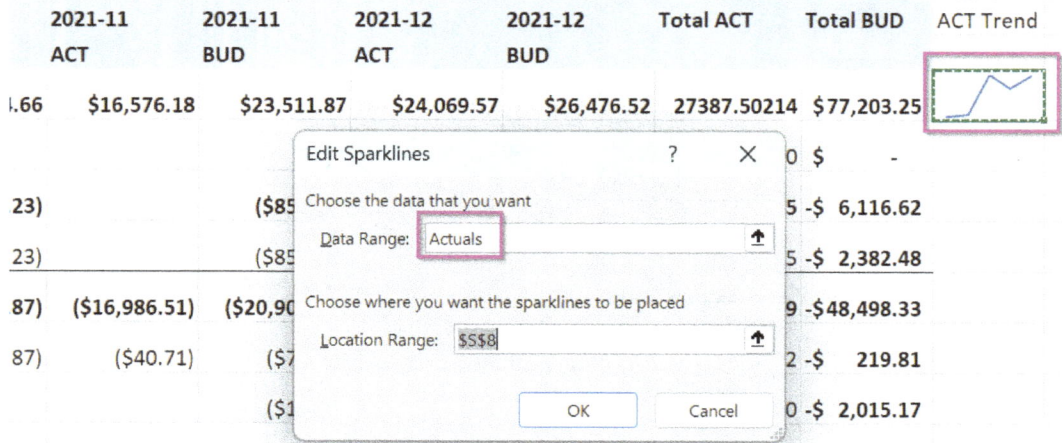

2021-11 ACT	2021-11 BUD	2021-12 ACT	2021-12 BUD	Total ACT	Total BUD	ACT Trend
.66 $16,576.18	$23,511.87	$24,069.57	$26,476.52	27387.50214	$77,203.25	

Edit Sparklines   ?   X

Choose the data that you want

Data Range: | Actuals |

Choose where you want the sparklines to be placed

Location Range: | S8 |

OK   Cancel

0 $	-	
5 -$	6,116.62	
5 -$	2,382.48	
9 -$	48,498.33	
2 -$	219.81	
0 -$	2,015.17	

Figure 5.22 – Reference to the Actuals cell range

This works, but the problem is that if we want to have this sparkline for all rows in our report, we need to set the name range for all these rows. Not exactly practical. So, the more effective way out is to create a new table with adjacent values:

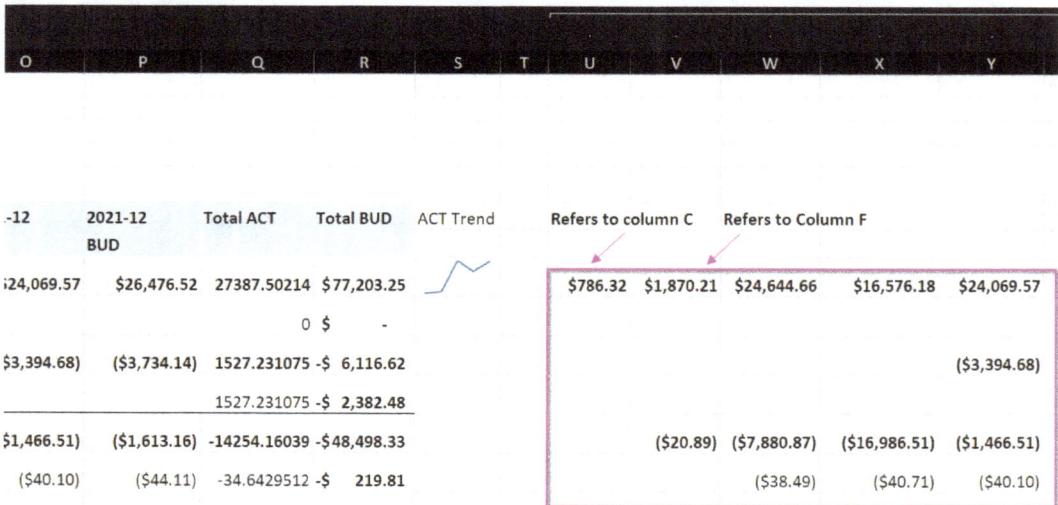

O	P	Q	R	S	T	U	V	W	X	Y

-12	2021-12 BUD	Total ACT	Total BUD	ACT Trend		Refers to column C		Refers to Column F		
;24,069.57	$26,476.52	27387.50214	$77,203.25			$786.32	$1,870.21	$24,644.66	$16,576.18	$24,069.57
		0	$ -							
$3,394.68)	($3,734.14)	1527.231075	-$ 6,116.62							($3,394.68)
		1527.231075	-$ 2,382.48							
$1,466.51)	($1,613.16)	-14254.16039	-$48,498.33				($20.89)	($7,880.87)	($16,986.51)	($1,466.51)
($40.10)	($44.11)	-34.6429512	-$ 219.81					($38.49)	($40.71)	($40.10)

Figure 5.23 – Avoiding setting multiple ranges

Now, we can refer the adjacent cells in that table to the sparkline:

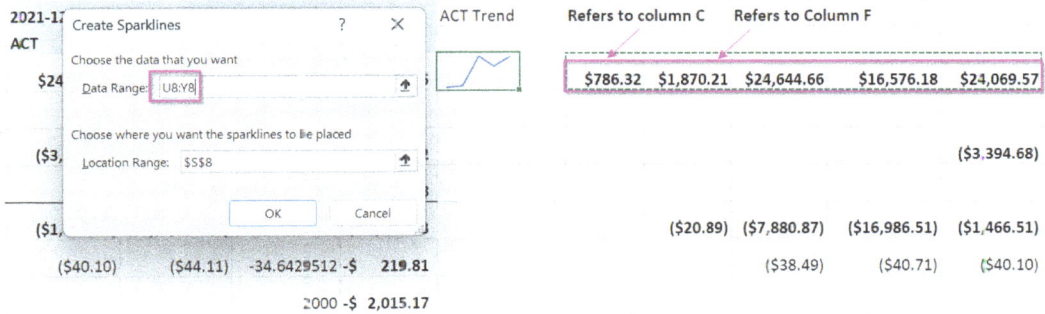

Figure 5.24 – Adding a sparkline

Just copy the sparkline down, and then you can add a grouping to hide the sparkline table that's cluttering our worksheet by selecting its columns and using **Group** in the **Data** ribbon:

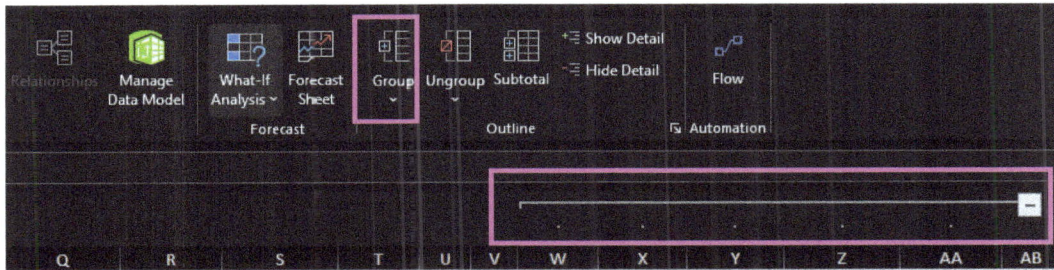

Figure 5.25 – Sparkline report

When we try to hide the table, we will see that the sparklines disappear. This is the default behavior. We can change this by clicking on a sparkline cell and selecting **Edit Data** in the **Sparkline** ribbon, and then **Hidden & Empty Cells...**:

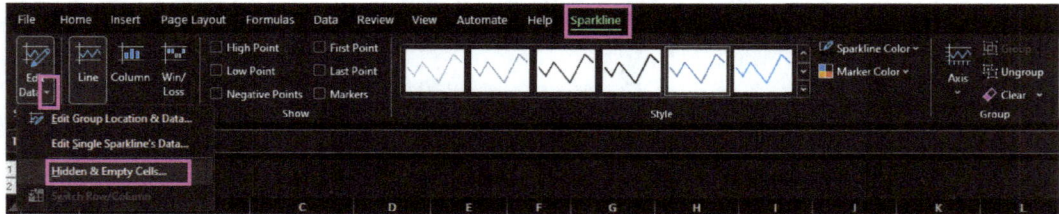

Figure 5.26 – Handling empty cells

After we have added a few other useful improvements, such as table formatting, hiding grid lines, and adding a conditional format to the variance, we get a professional-looking dynamic report on your Power BI data:

Statement	PL																
LegalName	All																
Year	2021																

	2021-08 ACT	2021-08 BUD	2021-08 VAR	2021-09 ACT	2021-09 BUD	2021-09 VAR	2021-10 ACT	2021-10 BUD	2021-10 VAR	2021-11 ACT	2021-11 BUD	2021-11 VAR	2021-12 ACT	2021-12 BUD	2021-12 VAR	Total ACT	Total BUD	ACT Trend
Revenue	786	700	86	1870	1870	0	24645	24645	0	16576	23512	-6936	24070	26477	-2407	67947	77203	
Other Revenue			0			0			0			0			0	0	0	
DirectCosts			0			0	-1527		1527	-855		855	-3395	-3734	339	-3395	-6117	
Cost of Goods Sold			0			0	-1527		1527	-855		855			0	0	-2382	
Expense	-2020		2020	-21	-12238	12217	-7881	-11726	3845	-16987	-20901	3915	-1467	-1613	147	-26355	-48498	
Consulting & Accounting			0	-30		30	-38	-72	33	-41	-74	34	-40	-44	4	-119	-220	
Dues & Subscriptions	2000		2000			0			0	-15		15			0	0	-2015	
Entertainment			0	-32		32	-42	-71	29	-2137	-2350	214			0	-2179	-2453	
General Expenses			0	-117		117	-61	-67	6	0	-204	204	-166	-183	17	-227	-571	
Payroll Tax Expense			0			0		-916	916	-1018		1018			0	0	-1934	
Printing & Stationery	-20		20			0	-29	-82	53	-102	-145	43			0	-131	-247	
Rent			0	-12036		12036	-1448	-3630	2181	-3064	-4287	1223	0	0	0	-4512	-19953	
Overheads	-190	-200	10	-190	-209	19	-2226	-27870	25644	-7085	-7794	709	-14949	-31726	16777	-24640	-67798	
EBIT	596	-1520	2116	1660	-10577	12236	14538	-16479	31016	-7495	-6038	-1457	4259	-10597	14856	13557	-45210	

Figure 5.27 – Final report

As we saw in this example with dynamic columns, an extension is possible with CUBE formulas, but it has its limits. Useful dynamic row handling in Excel is nearly impossible with standard features. For that reason, my company, Acterys, has developed an Excel add-in (that is now also part of Microsoft Dynamics business performance planning) that includes a smart pivot grid supporting dynamic drill down in rows, zero suppression, and most importantly, write back and planning to a central database. We will cover Acterys and Dynamics' business performance planning in a later chapter. For details, please check out `https://acterys.com` and `https://learn.microsoft.com/en-us/shows/dynamics-365-fasttrack-architecture-insights/business-performance-planning`.

Summary

In this chapter, we have covered an option for how to access your Power BI data in Excel, either in Pivot Tables or as Excel formula reports. Excel formula reports give the users near limitless flexibility to format reports but have limitations when it comes to structure updates. Starting in the next chapter, we will cover how to realize special financial requirements in Power BI, starting with multi-currency handling.

Part 3

Advanced Financial Topics

In this section, we move beyond the core data model and basic reports into more sophisticated financial analyses that many organizations rely on for strategic decision-making, risk management, and investor communication. This part covers handling multiple currencies and consolidating group data, as well as building dynamic rolling forecasts and performing valuation work such as discounted cash flow (DCF) analysis. Finally, we explore how to implement price–volume–mix variance analysis to better surface market-driven insights.

This part of the book includes the following chapters:

- *Chapter 6, Handling Multi-Currency Requirements in Power BI*
- *Chapter 7, Management, Group, and Board Reporting*
- *Chapter 8, Rolling Reporting Forecasts*
- *Chapter 9, Discounted Cash Flow Public Company Valuation*
- *Chapter 10, Price Volume Mix Analysis*

6

Handling Multi-Currency Requirements in Power BI

In this chapter, we will cover how to realize multi-currency handling scenarios – a very typical requirement for finance professionals, not just in multi-national companies. We will start by looking at how to integrate currency rates from a data provider. After that, we will carry out different currency logic calculations using Power BI DAX. Particularly, we will be looking at how to best address spot and historic currency treatment requirements.

In this chapter, we will cover the following main topics:

- Sourcing rate data
- Loading currency rates
- Addressing API challenges

Technical requirements

As with all of the sample content in this book, all related files are available in the GitHub repository: https://github.com/PacktPublishing/Power-BI-for-Finance.

Sourcing rate data

In some cases, like in the sample data in the initial chapters, you might be lucky to have rate information included in your source data records. This is not always the case, and in some cases, the rate that you get is not the rate that you need, such as when you need to apply calculations at the current spot rate and not the historic rate included in the transaction. In these instances, you need to source rates from a provider. Power BI has a number of options to source data with connectors (integrations to a variety of data sources that you see when you use the **Get data** option on the **Home** ribbon in Power BI Desktop) from online providers. Unfortunately, currently, there is no standard solution for currency data. The other options are the offerings from generic data service providers through an **Application Programming Interface** (**API**). This is a volatile area as the services and their policies change constantly. I will cover here a free option that uses the `https://app.freecurrencyapi.com/` service (with whom I have no affiliation), which, at the time of writing, works fine, but I can't guarantee that this will always be the case.

Loading currency rates

The **FreecurrencyAPI** service provides currency rates via an API. For limited amounts of data, there are no charges. For our use case, we only need the current rate that is provided in the free plan, as we have the historic rate in our data source. Should you require historic rates, you can use sources like this historical currency converter: `https://www.oanda.com/fx-for-business/historical-rates`, download the data in CSV format, and easily add it to Power BI.

To establish a live connection, we need the API service URL and an API key. You get the key from `https://freecurrencyapi.com/` after you have created a free account. The key is available on your dashboard on the service when you have logged in:

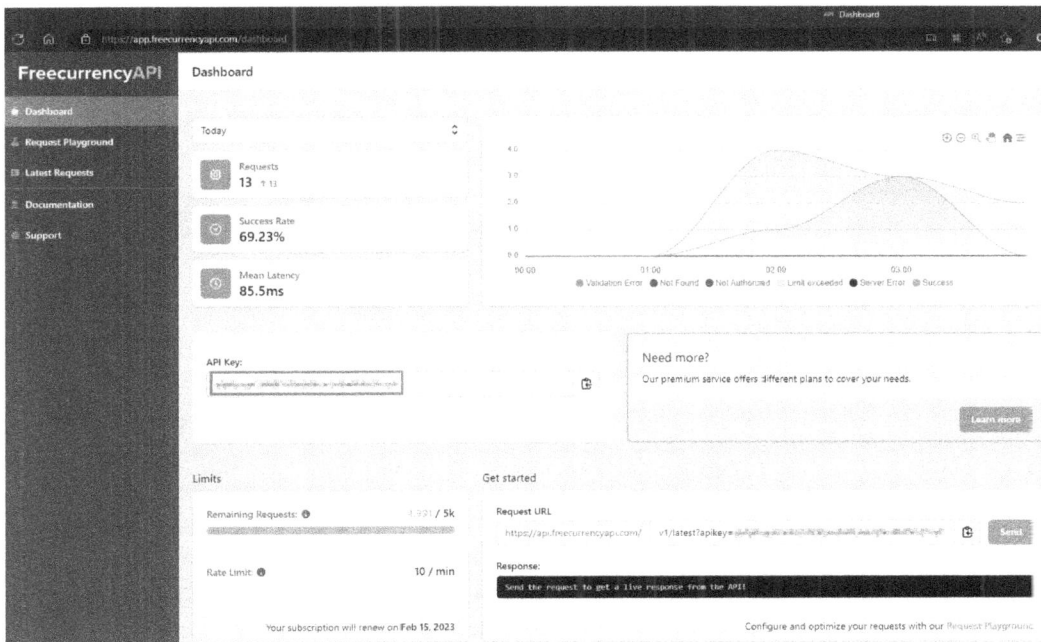

Figure 6.1 – Getting FreecurrencyAPI key

With APIs, there are typically different *endpoints* (a link to the provider) that will provide you with specific services. In the case of FreecurrencyAPI, you can find details here: `https://freecurrencyapi.com/docs`. The one that is relevant in our case to retrieve the latest rates is a `GET` method (i.e., will return data) that is aptly named **latest**; the full URL to call it is `https://api.freecurrencyapi.com/v1/latest`.

Now, you may think you could just use this link and Power Query will return the data. Unfortunately, it is a bit more complicated than that.

Addressing API challenges

I will guide you through some pitfalls of using APIs that will hopefully prevent you from spending the same hours that I have spent figuring things out initially.

If no authentication or parameters are involved, connecting to a web source is fairly easy in Power BI by working with the URL to the source and selecting the table. With APIs that require authentication either to avoid misuse (mostly overuse) or simply because they are commercial, with a subscription password, the process is more complex.

You would normally expect Power BI to provide an option to handle authentication keys, and it does, but unfortunately, the expected approach doesn't work.

As we have already done, data sources can be connected in the **Get data** menu on the **Home** ribbon.

Here, we now select the **Web** option:

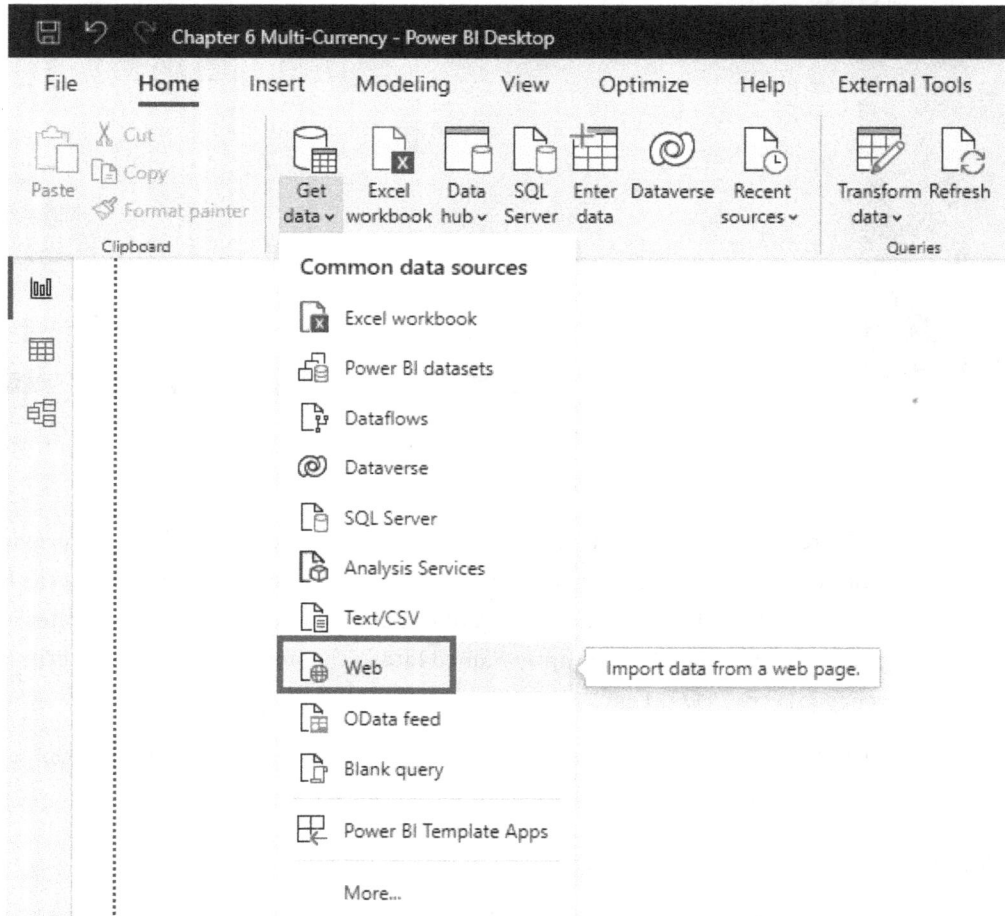

Figure 6.2 – Choosing a web source

Following that, we see a dialog box with **Basic** and **Advanced** options:

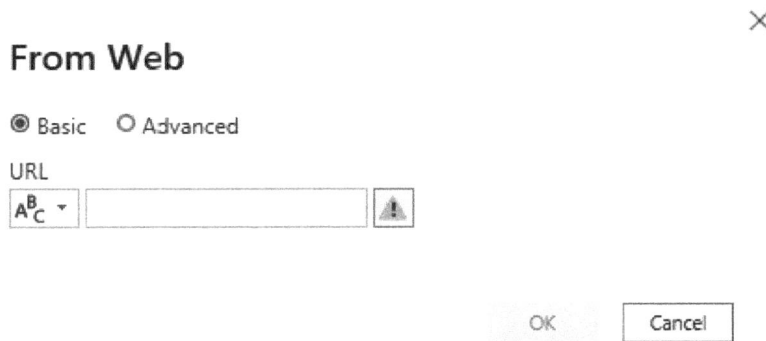

Figure 6.3 – Choosing the access type

Basic will work for us, as long as we construct the URL string correctly. The first part of the entry in the **URL** field is the URL of the service and our required endpoint, https://api.freecurrencyapi. com/v1/latest. But that alone won't get us far, as once we press **OK**, we get this:

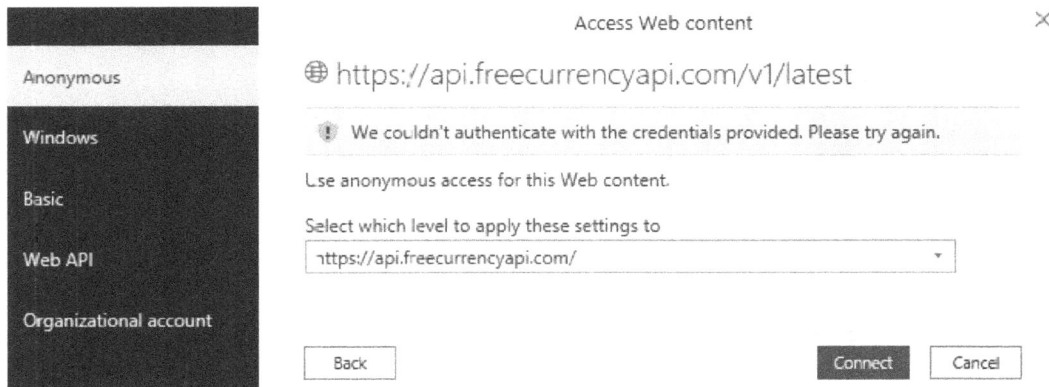

Figure 6.4 – Entering the API link

Now, you might think, "OK, let's go to the **Web API** tab and put in our key":

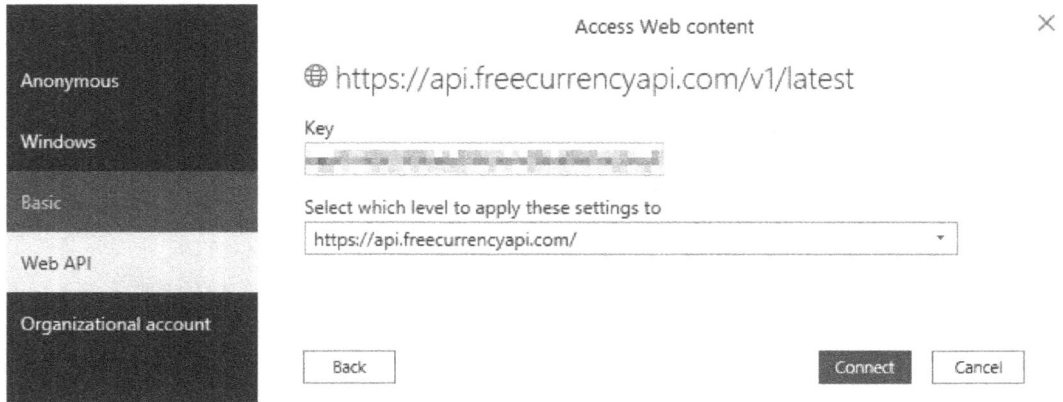

Figure 6.5 – Web API mode

Yes, that sounds right. But unfortunately, again, it isn't. At the time of writing this book, you get this error:

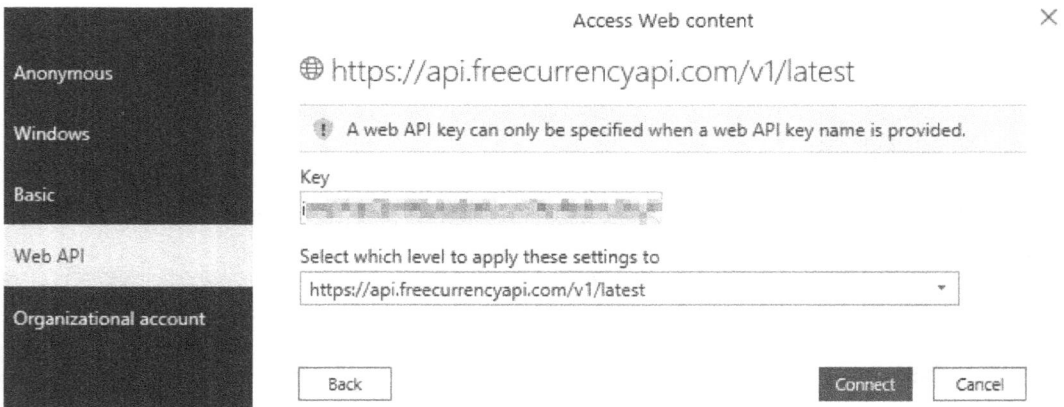

Figure 6.6 – Error with Web API

This, admittedly, is hard to understand, but there is an explanation. The parameter for the API key varies with each web service, and Power BI doesn't know which one to use. The strange thing, though, is that this could be easily resolved with another parameter box.

So, we have to go down a different route. The easiest one that I found (after too many frustrating hours…) is to construct the link with the relevant parameters on our own. This might be straightforward for IT experts, but for the average finance person, it likely isn't. I will spare you the frustration; here is the correct link: `https://api.freecurrencyapi.com/v1/latest?apikey=YourAPIKey&base_currency=AUD`.

The last parameter defines the base currency and is optional. If you don't specify it, the data will be provided in USD. As our group currency is AUD, we have to specify it.

Now, the best option is to just start by adding the web source again and use the correct link:

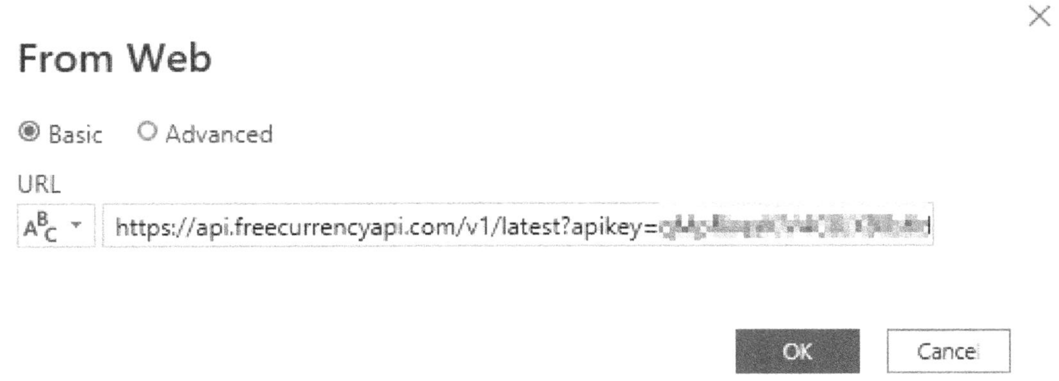

Figure 6.7 – Adding the API key parameter

The key comes straight after the = sign. What is important to know here is that parameters in a REST API are added using a ? (denotes a parameter) and & (to add another parameter). This is a typical challenge for new users.

So, if all was entered correctly, you will see the following:

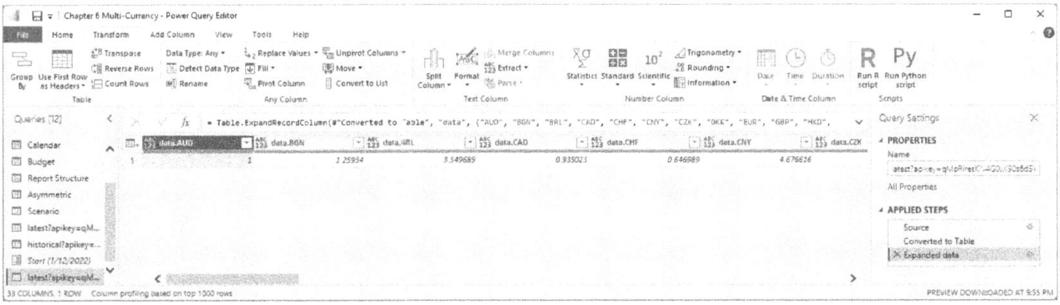

Figure 6.8 – Power Query connection established

This needs a bit more work. What we need are just the currency symbols, so the first step to fix this is to go to the expanded data step properties and remove the prefix by deleting the word *data* here:

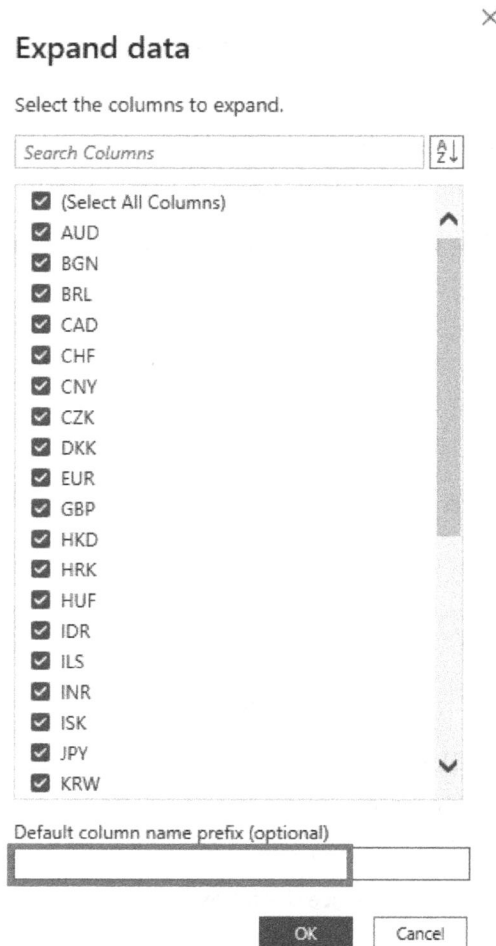

Figure 6.9 – Remove column prefix

Now we see that the headers only contain the currency rate codes:

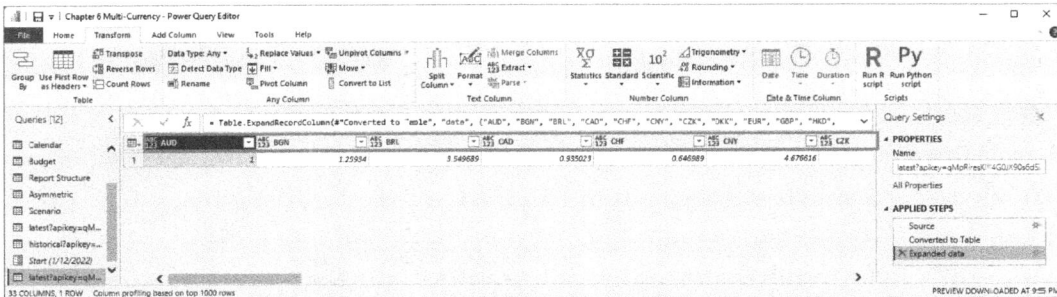

Figure 6.10 – Correct column names

To meet our calculation requirements, we need to convert this table into a two-column layout with the code and the rate. We can do this by selecting all the columns and clicking on **Unpivot Columns** in the **Transform** ribbon. The final step is to give this query a better name by double-clicking on the table name and entering Latest Rates. Now, we see that we get the data as needed:

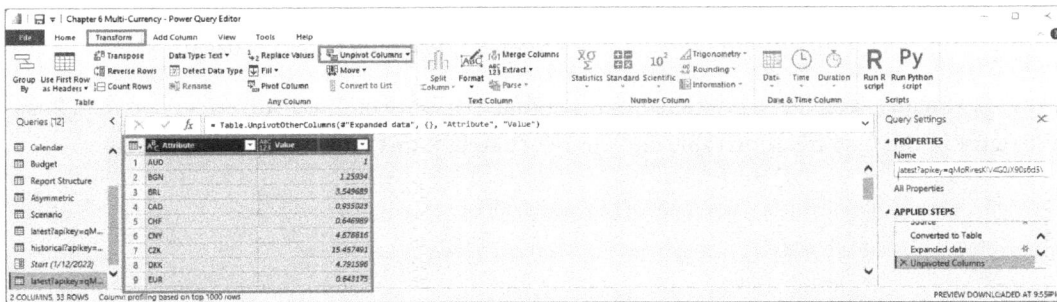

Figure 6.11 – Unpivoted list

From here, it's now relatively straightforward; we just need to construct a calculation that multiplies the local currency by the rate.

We already have the base currency for each organization in the Organisation table, which is, in general, the best approach for managing this:

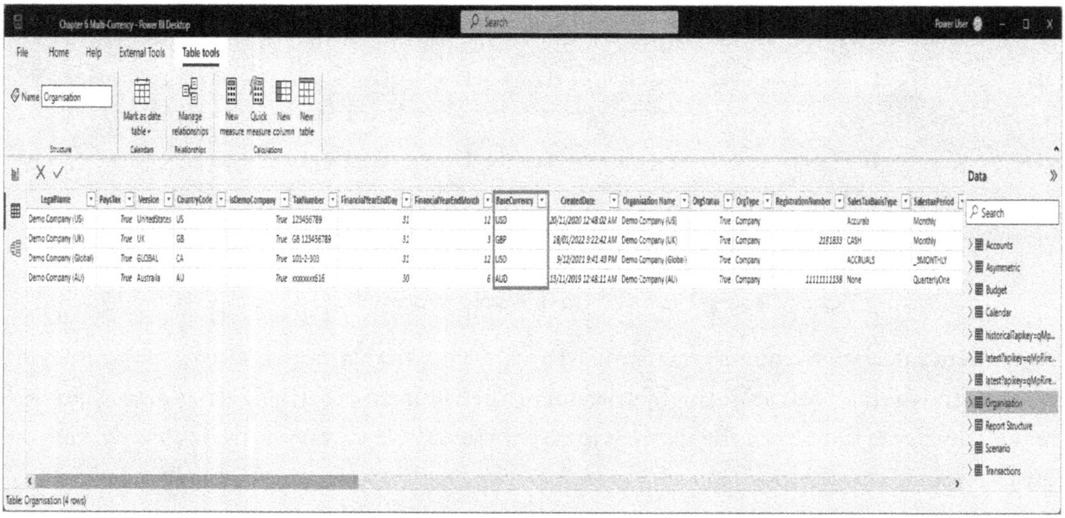

Figure 6.12 – Ensure the currency code in the Organisation table matches

Now we can just establish a relationship (dragging **Attribute** on **BaseCurrency**) between **Base-Currency** in the **Organisation** table and our new **Latest Rates** table:

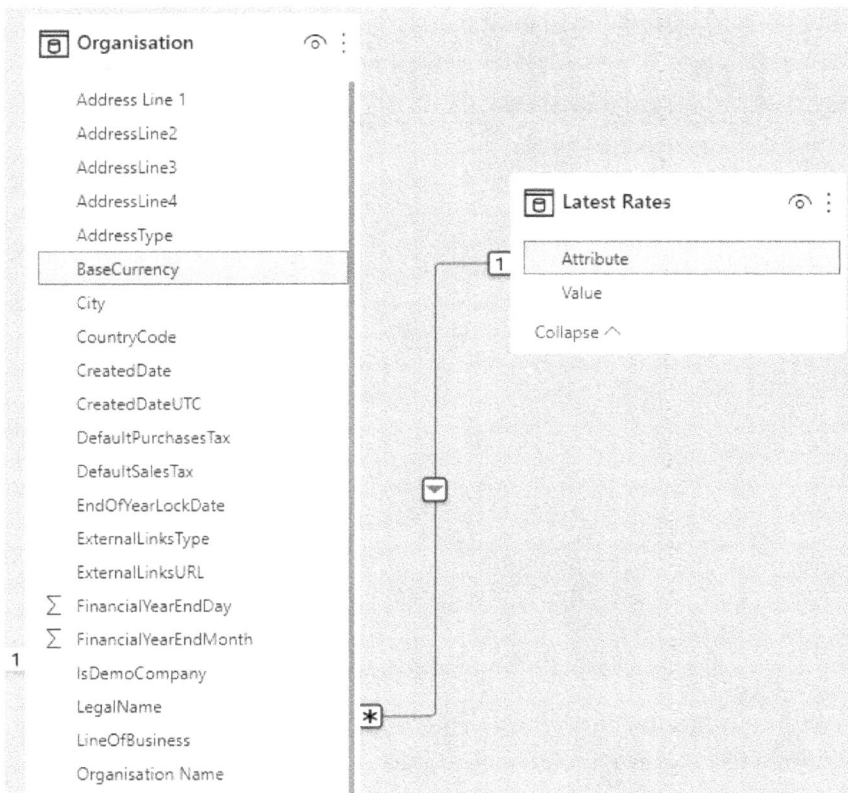

Figure 6.13 – Relationship between Organisation and Latest Rates tables

Finally, we create a new DAX measure in the Current Rate Amount transactions table:

```
Current Rate Amount = sumx(Transactions,Transactions[NetAmount_LC]/
RELATED('Latest Rates'[Value]))
```

This calculation divides the local currency amount by the respective rate. It is important to understand that it can only be applied to base-level records. On aggregated levels (e.g., all companies,
date aggregations such as quarter, etc.), the records need to be added up as per the respective
hierarchy, for example, month to quarter. This can be achieved with SUMX(), which applies calculations only on the rows in the current context.

When we add the new calculation to our report, we see that it works (despite quite a change between the currency rate in the sample data and the current one):

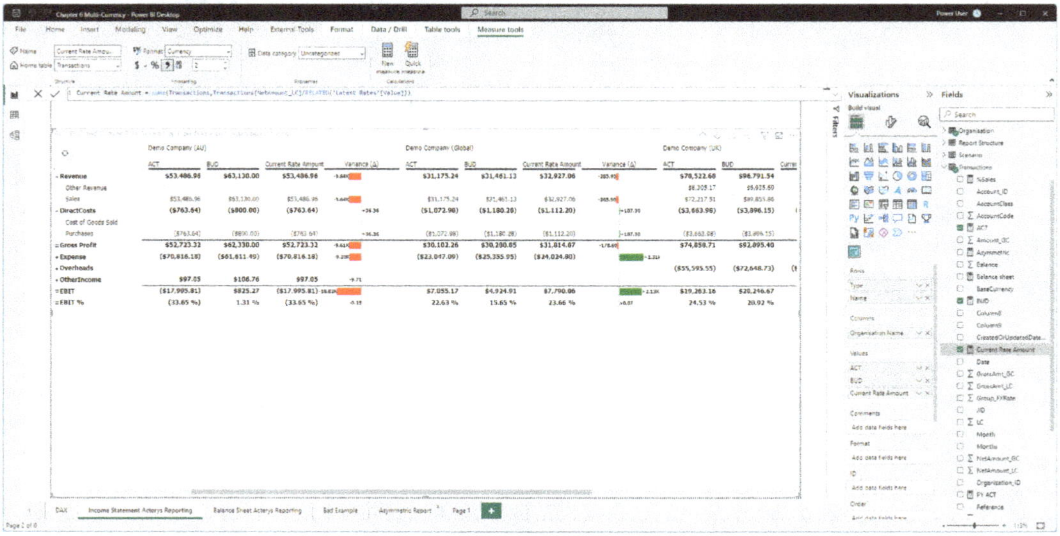

Figure 6.14 – Local and group currency report

In a real requirement, this calculation will likely only be used for some accounts, for example, balance sheet accounts that require spot rates. In that case, you must add a flag to your accounts table that specifies whether the account should use the spot rate or not and adjust your DAX to only apply to accounts with this flag. This is typically just an additional *if* check. In this section, we have covered how to apply the logic for current foreign exchange rates. In some cases, we have to use historic rates or averages. This will be discussed in the final section.

Handling historic and average rates

For currency calculations that require historic rates, the best option is to get them from the source. For example, most ERP systems will provide this with a rate column in the accounting transaction. In that case, you can then just add a column that multiplies the rate and local amount. If that is not available, you need to maintain your own rates table that contains the rates for the entire history of your transactions and apply the historic rate on the date of the transaction. Transactions that require average rates (e.g., interest expense payable on foreign currency debt) need a Currency Rates table with the following fields:

- Conversion Date
- Currency From

- Currency To
- Conversion Rate

With that, you can then use a DAX calculation such as the following:

```
[Monthly Average Conversion Rate] =
var CurrentDate = 'Exchange Rates'[Conversion Date]
var CurrencyFrom = 'Exchange Rates'[Currency From]
var CurrencyTo = 'Exchange Rates'[Currency To]
Var MinDate = EOMONTH( CurrentDate, -1) + 1
Var MaxDate = EOMONTH( CurrentDate )
var Result =
    AVERAGEX(
        FILTER(
            'Exchange Rates', true
            && 'Exchange Rates'[Currency From] = CurrencyFrom
            && 'Exchange Rate Master'[Currency To] = CurrencyTo
            &&  MinDate <= 'Exchange Rates'[Conversion Date]
            &&  'Exchange Rate Master'[Conversion Date] <= MaxDate
        ),
        'Exchange Rates'[Conversion Rate]
    )
return
    Result
```

This calculation yields the monthly average conversion rate.

For each row in the Exchange Rates table, it calculates the average conversion rate for the month that the current conversion date falls in, but only for the same currency pair (CurrencyFrom → CurrencyTo).

Summary

In this chapter, we covered typical currency conversion requirements with the integration of a live currency rates API. We learned the following main points:

- Having a well-defined data model in place with either the applicable conversion stored in the transaction table or a separate FX rate table

- An understanding of how you construct calls to data service APIs, particularly how to use parameters

- An understanding of how to implement the optimal DAX for the conversion logic

In the next chapter, we will look at another very common financial requirement: how to implement budgeting and planning.

Get This Book's PDF Version and Exclusive Extras

UNLOCK NOW

Scan the QR code (or go to packtpub.com/unlock). Search for this book by name, confirm the edition, and then follow the steps on the page.

Note: Keep your invoice handy. Purchases made directly from Packt don't require one.

7

Management, Group, and Board Reporting

In previous chapters, we discussed some of the essential building blocks of group reporting, including an effective data model and business logic. This includes merging data from different organizational entities and converting local currencies to a group standard.

In this chapter, we will cover additional specific management, group, and board reporting requirements, such as reporting structure, ratios, and reporting layouts (scorecards), as well as addressing business logic aspects such as intercompany elimination and some generally useful tips and tricks.

Specifically, we will cover the following topics:

- Designing the group reporting structure
- Handling accounts receivable/payable
- Presenting information in a scorecard
- Implementing management consolidation/group reporting
- Integration with Word for board reporting

The covered examples and tips will assist you with presenting management reports more effectively and making your processes that integrate data from multiple companies more efficient, with fewer maintenance efforts required.

Technical requirements

For the examples in this chapter, we will use `Chapter 7 Board Report Sample.docx` from the book's official GitHub repository here: `https://github.com/PacktPublishing/Power-BI-for-Finance`.

Designing the group reporting structure

The required content for group and board reports varies greatly depending on company size and legal standards. A concept that is often used is the **balanced scorecard**, which tracks performance across all key aspects of the organization, including the following:

- Progress against strategic objectives
- Operational business, project, and product metrics
- Financial performance against targets and forecasts for the remaining fiscal periods
- Sales/customer success KPIs

Next, let's dive into each of these and see what they entail.

Measuring strategic objectives

Strategic goals in general entail the key elements of the organization's purpose. They are high-level objectives that define what the organization aims to achieve over the medium to long term. These goals translate the organization's mission and vision into specific, measurable targets that guide decision-making.

Documentation of strategic plans

Strategic plans are typically documented through several documents that outline the organization's chosen direction and priorities. These documents include the mission, vision, values, strategic goals, strategies for achieving them, and resource allocation plans. The content here is mostly unstructured and typically not managed in Power BI.

Measurement of strategic goals

Strategic goals are measurable goals derived from the aforementioned unstructured documents. They are typically measured through **key performance indicators (KPIs)** that provide quantifiable metrics linked to strategic objectives. From a presentation point of view, they typically include the goal need, additional explanations and comments, the current actual, and a target. Often, for quick understanding, status indicators are included as per the following example:

1 Key Strategic Goals					
Item #	Goal	Comment	Actual	Target	Status
1.1	Customer satisfaction improvements	The launch of our new customer support system has tested very positive in initial surveys and has led to an increase in Net Promoter Score (NPS), a customer loyalty metric that measures the likelihood of a customer recommending a given business.	NPS: x	y	✓
1.2	Employee retention		Actual churn rate (what % of employees were lost)	x	

Table 7.1 – Example of strategic KPIs

Operational performance metrics (e.g., process, sales, marketing, and customer metrics) are typically a combination of structured content (i.e., numeric actual/target values) and unstructured data, such as comments that provide further explanations, and ideally, recommendations:

2 Key Operational Goals					
Item #	Goal	Comment	Actual	Target	Status
2.1	Manufacturing ready for the launch of product X	Main manufacturing line components are ready. Slight delays with the loading dock due to regulatory requirements. We are confident that the go-live date on XX/XX will be delayed by 2 weeks.	Go live: Q2/23	Q3/23	

Table 7.2 – Example of operational KPI

For more generic content such as financials, I have listed some of the commonly used metrics in the following table, broken down by statement type (income/balance sheet/cash flow) and using actual result, target, comment, and a status indicator as details:

Financial Performance					
Statement	Metric	Actual	Target	Comment	Status
Income	EBIT				
	EBIT margin				
	Gross margin				
Cash Flow	Operating cash flow				
	Cash flow from investing/financing				
Balance Sheet	Working capital				
	Accounts receivable/ payable aging schedules				

Table 7.3 – Financial KPIs

The calculations for the financial statement metrics are straightforward, as already covered in *Chapters 1, 3,* and *4.* In the following section, we will look at more specific examples.

Handling accounts receivable/payable

Accounts receivable/payable details are generally required in management and board reports. The related data is typically available in the invoice summary and bills/payable invoice summary tables. For realizing interactive **aging tables** (a breakdown of the age of debts and receivables) in Power BI, I recommend the following approach with sample data available in the Chapter 7 PBIX file. Here, you will find an **Invoice Summary** table that is based on a real ERP and likely not too dissimilar to your own requirements. This table contains the fields that we typically need for our aging tables:

Status	A flag that specifies the status of the invoice (paid, authorized, voided, etc.)
Due Date	Date when the invoice is supposed to be paid
Amount Due	What amount of the invoice is due (if that is not available, then this needs to be calculated)

Table 7.4 – Receivables/debtor aging table structure

As nearly always in Power BI, there are different options to implement the relevant calculations. My approach is to use Power BI **calculated columns** as they are very easy to implement (even easier than Power Query, which is one of the other options). I am just adding two calculated columns here:

```
Days Outstanding = DATEDIFF('Invoice Summary'[DueDate],Now(),DAY)
```

This calculates the days from the due date of the relevant invoice to today, and an aging group that categorizes the outstanding invoices based on four buckets (<30 days, <60 days, <90 days, and finally, <120 days):

```
Aging Group =
            IF(
                'Invoice Summary'[Days Outstanding] <=0,"0",
                    IF('Invoice Summary'[Days Outstanding]<30,"<30 DAYS",
                        IF('Invoice Summary'[Days Outstanding]<60,"< 60
DAYS",
                            IF('Invoice Summary'[Days Outstanding]<90,"<
90 DAYS",
                                IF('Invoice Summary'[Days
Outstanding]<120," < 120 DAYS"," > 120 DAYS")
                                    )
                                )
                            )
                        )
```

The Days Outstanding bucket categories can, of course, be customized to your specific requirements. In our demo case, we have receivable and payable invoices in the same table. In other cases, this could be split up into multiple tables, but the approach for implementing the logic is generally the same.

From a layout perspective, we can then add our calculations and invoice table fields to the report, splitting into payable/receivable, a breakdown by aging buckets, as well as a transaction table below the two charts to see the details when a user clicks on an object in the chart visuals:

Debtor/Creditor
Details

| Organisation Name | ∨ | FinancialYear, Year Month | ∨ |
| All | | All | |

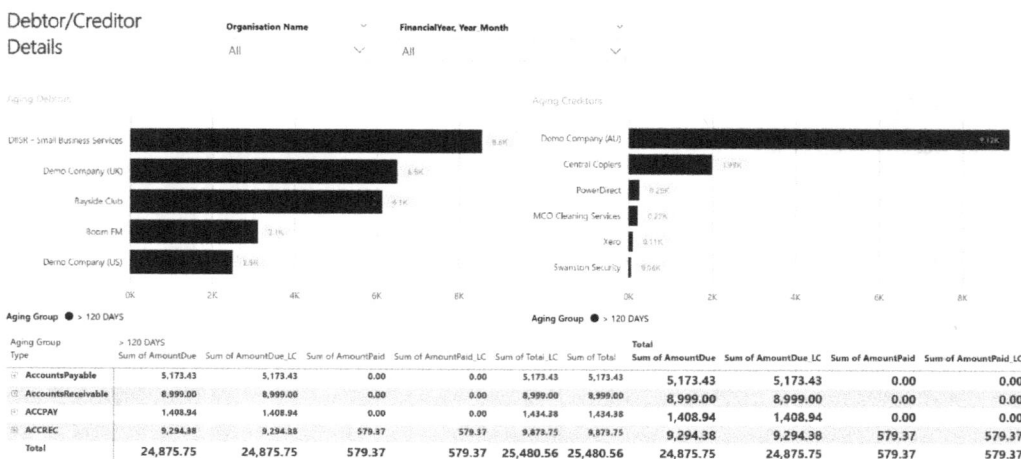

Figure 7.1 – Aging table design

In this section, we have looked at some of the building blocks for management reports. In the next section, we will cover options on how to present and visualize comprehensive scorecards that provide an encompassing picture across all organizational performance aspects.

Presenting KPIs in a scorecard

Again, there are various options to present comprehensive scorecards in Power BI: this can range from utilizing a simple matrix visual and dedicated built-in KPI visuals to commercial third-party offerings.

Before we go into details, we need to have the data structures in place. For this example, we assume we have a single table with measures and groupings similar to the content covered in the previous section in place:

Aspect	Metric	Actual	Target	Status	Comment	Period
Strategic	Net promoter score	90	92	2		1/01/2025
Strategic	Employee retention	91	90	1		1/01/2025
Finance	EBIT	10,100,000	9,000,000	1		1/01/2025

Aspect	Metric	Actual	Target	Status	Comment	Period
Finance	Days sales outstanding	35	20	3	Problems with payment delays for two key customers	1/01/2025
Marketing	Organic search hits per period	10,000	8,000	1	Over target because of the very positive reception of our blog posts	1/01/2025
Marketing	Blog posts written	10	8	1		1/01/2025
Strategic	Net promoter score	94	92	2		1/02/2025
Strategic	Employee retention	88	90	2		1/02/2025
Finance	EBIT	9,200,000	9,000,000	1		1/02/2025
Finance	Days sales outstanding	22	20	2		1/02/2025
Marketing	Organic search hits per period	7,000	8,000	1	Public holiday period	1/02/2025
Marketing	Blog posts written	6	8	2		1/02/2025

Table 7.5 – Sample scorecard metrics table for Power BI

This table is available as an *Enter Data* table in the Chapter 7 sample file created from the **Home** tab and is editable in Power Query.

We can use it now with a lesser-known Power BI visual developed by Microsoft that is freely available in the App Store: Power KPI Matrix.

To add this to our report, we can just go to **Get more visuals** in the **Visualizations** section.

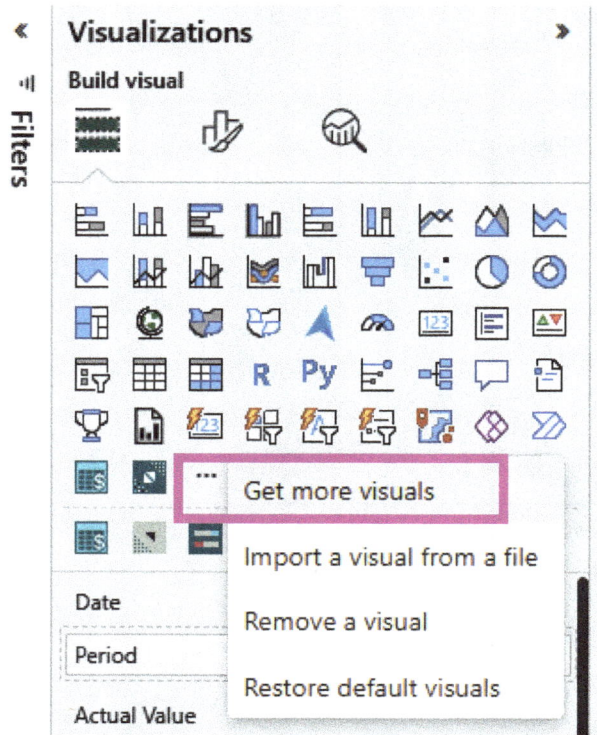

Figure 7.2 – Adding a new visual

Then, search for Power KPI and add that visual to our report:

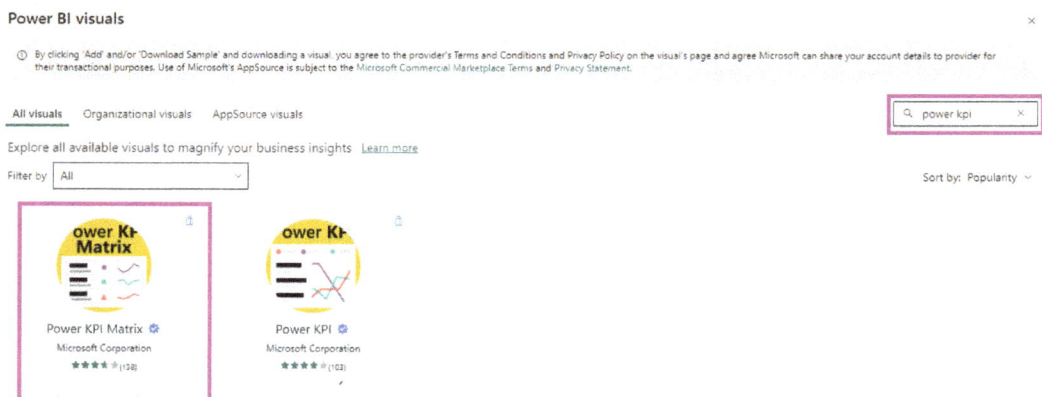

Figure 7.3 – Selecting the Power KPI Matrix

We can now add this visual to a Power BI report and configure it as per the following screenshot:

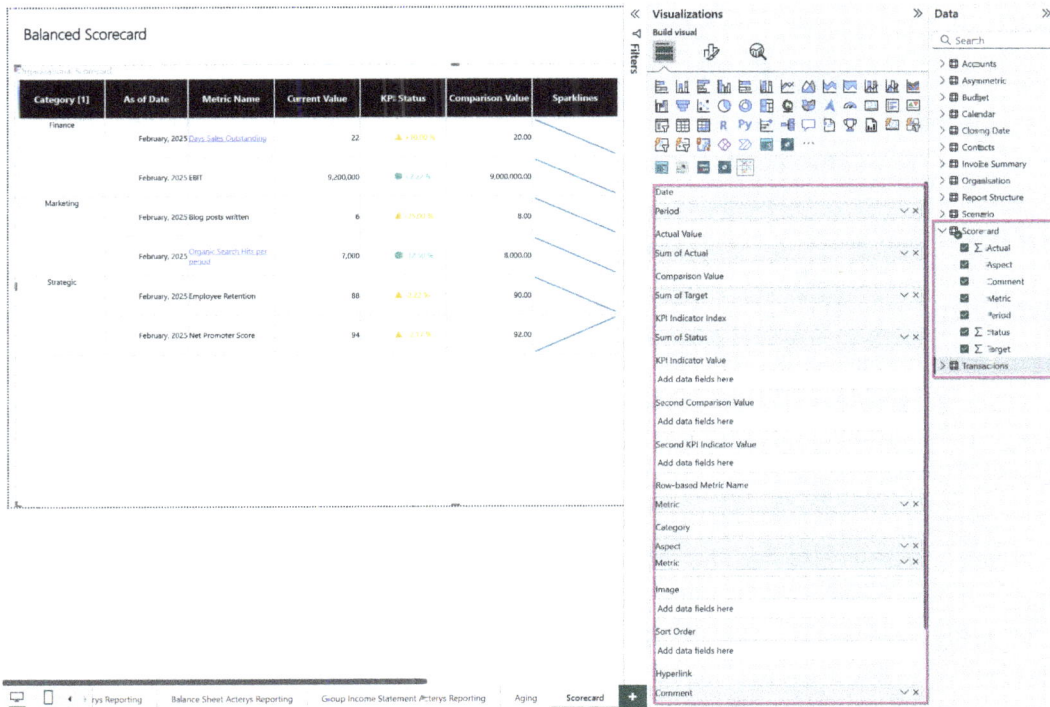

Figure 7.4 – Management scorecard

We have now created an initial scorecard with aspect/category groupings, KPI status, and sparklines. When hovering over the blue-marked KPI names, which signify that there is a comment, the related comment will show.

The data table structure in this case was already ideally formatted. Unfortunately, that is often not the case, and you will need to use the approaches covered in *Chapter 4* to combine members in existing data tables with calculated members (DAX) and add useful KPI index logic. With the latter, you will also typically have to consider how to handle the *direction of a measure* (e.g., whether higher or lower is better). A visual that I recommend considering is Acterys Smart XL, which gives you the flexibility of easily combining dynamic table content with simple Excel-based calculations.

In the following section, we will cover the challenges and options for handling the merging of data in multiple entities of an organization.

Implementing management and statutory consolidation

The key focus of both management and statutory consolidation is to enable a holistic picture across multiple entities. Our focus here will be on management reporting, which covers the relatively flexible, ongoing (typically monthly) business requirements as opposed to the more complex statutory consolidation focused on shareholders and financial authorities that is mandated by legal rules.

Account mapping in the accounts dimension table

The first step for effective group reporting is a standardized chart of accounts that maps all accounts of all entities to the group standard. With a properly defined star schema model and a single accounts dimension, this is reasonably simple: you maintain the table with a unique ID for every account in the organization. This is typically not the single account number, which is rarely unique, as *Company A* might use the same account number as *Company B*. A possible unique option is a concatenated key that contains unique company IDs and the respective account IDs. For example, *Company A* is ID *1* and account *100*, so its key would be 1100, but there are likely a lot of other conventions that really depend on your setup. A typical account dimension will look like the one we are using (which is actually based on a real ERP system):

Account key	Name	Code	Class	BankAc	Curre	Description	Reporti	ReportingCodeName	FX Conversion
1 Demo Company (UK)200Sales	Sales	200	REVENUE		GBP	Income from any no	REV.TUR.S/	Sales revenue	Historic
2 Demo Company (UK)260Other Revenue	Intercompany Revenue	260	REVENUE		GBP	Any other income t	REV.OTH	Other operating income	Historic
3 Demo Company (UK)270Interest Income	Interest Income	270	Revenue		GBP	Gross interest incor	REV	Revenue	Historic
4 Demo Company (UK)437Interest Paid	Interest Paid	437	Expense		GBP	Interest paid on a b	EXP.INT	Interest payable and similar charges	Historic
5 Demo Company (UK)441Legal expenses	Legal expenses	441	Expense		GBP	Expenses incurred c	EXP.ADM.F	Legal and professional fees	Historic
6 Demo Company (UK)445Light, Power, Heating	Light, Power, Heating	445	Expense		GBP	Expenses incurred f	EXP.EST.UT	Utility charges	Historic
7 Demo Company (UK)449Motor Vehicle Expenses	Motor Vehicle Expenses	449	Expense		GBP	Expenses incurred c	EXP.ADM.V	Vehicle running costs	Historic
8 Demo Company (UK)457Operating Lease Payments	Operating Lease Payments	457	Expense		GBP	Expenses incurred c	EXP.ADM.I	Hire & leasing of plant, equipment and v	Historic
9 Demo Company (UK)461Printing & Stationery	Printing & Stationery	461	Expense		GBP	Expenses incurred c	EXP.ADM.P	Printing, postage and stationery	Historic
10 Demo Company (UK)463IT Software and Consumables	IT Software and Consumables	463	Expense		GBP	Expenses incurred ·	EXP.ADM.S	Computer software, IT consumables and	Historic
11 Demo Company (UK)465Rates	Rates	465	Expense		GBP	Payments made to	EXP.EST.RA	Rates	Historic
12 Demo Company (UK)469Rent	Rent	469	Expense		GBP	Payments made to	EXP.EST.RE	Rent	Historic
13 Demo Company (UK)473Repairs & Maintenance	Repairs & Maintenance	473	Expense		GBP	Expenses incurred c	EXP.ADM.R	Repairs, renewal and maintenance	Historic
14 Demo Company (UK)477Salaries	Salaries	477	Expense		GBP	Payment to employ	EXP.STF.W	Wages and salaries	Historic
15 Demo Company (UK)478Directors' Remuneration	Directors' Remuneration	478	Expense		GBP	Payments to comps	EXP.STF.DIF	Directors/Partners fees and salaries	Historic
16 Demo Company (UK)764Plant & Machinery	Plant & Machinery	764	Asset		GBP	Plant and machiner	ASS.NCA.FI	Plant and machinery cost	Spot
17 Demo Company (UK)765Less Accumulated Depreciation on Plan	Less Accumulated Depreciation on	765	Asset		GBP	The total amount o	ASS.NCA.FI	Plant and machinery accumulated depre	Spot
18 Demo Company (UK)770Intangibles	Intangibles	770	Asset		GBP	Assets with no phys	ASS.NCA.IN	Intangible assets	Spot
19 Demo Company (UK)771Less Accumulated Amortisation on Inta	Less Accumulated Amortisation on	771	Asset		GBP	The total amount o	ASS.NCA.IN	Intangible assets - amortisation	Spot
20 Demo Company (UK)805Accruals	Accruals	805	Liability		GBP	Any services the bu	LIA.CUR.AC	Accruals and deferred income	Spot

Status	Type	Type Order	OrgName	Cash Flow	Cash Flow Group	IC
Active	Revenue	1	Demo Company (UK)	Operating Income	Operating Cashflow	
Active	Revenue	1	Demo Company (UK)	Operating Income	Operating Cashflow	1
Active	Revenue	1	Demo Company (UK)	Operating Income	Operating Cashflow	
Active	Overheads	4	Demo Company (UK)	Operating Income	Operating Cashflow	
Active	Overheads	4	Demo Company (UK)	Operating Income	Operating Cashflow	
Active	Overheads	4	Demo Company (UK)	Operating Income	Operating Cashflow	
Active	Overheads	4	Demo Company (UK)	Operating Income	Operating Cashflow	
Active	Overheads	4	Demo Company (UK)	Operating Income	Operating Cashflow	
Active	Overheads	4	Demo Company (UK)	Operating Income	Operating Cashflow	
Active	Overheads	4	Demo Company (UK)	Operating Income	Operating Cashflow	
Active	Overheads	4	Demo Company (UK)	Operating Income	Operating Cashflow	
Active	Overheads	4	Demo Company (UK)	Operating Income	Operating Cashflow	
Active	Overheads	4	Demo Company (UK)	Operating Income	Operating Cashflow	
Active	Overheads	4	Demo Company (UK)	Operating Income	Operating Cashflow	
Active	Overheads	4	Demo Company (UK)	Operating Income	Operating Cashflow	

Figure 7.5 – Group reporting transaction table

The details here will always vary, but I would recommend having these details when you are dealing with a group that includes organizational entities that are based in different countries:

- An account key that uniquely identifies the account in the organization (column **B** in *Figure 7.5*).

- Group standard mapping (column **C**).

- FX Logic to be applied to the specific account (column **K**).

- An order column to show accounts/groupings in the correct order, which can then be used in Power BI in the Group By column for the respective level. (column **N**).

- Cash flow groupings for the indirect cash flow method (column **Q**).

- The IC (intercompany account) column (column **R**) specifies whether this account is relevant for the purpose of eliminating intercompany transactions for consolidation purposes. This is done by using the status value of 1 for the account rows where applicable.

Organization dimension

The next crucial dimension for group reporting contains the organizational details. We already have that table in our Power BI sample model called Organisation:

Organisation ID	LegalName	PaysTax	Version	CountryCode	Ownership	Parent	OrgStatus	TaxNumber	Financial YearEnd Day	FinancialYear EndMonth	BaseCurrency	CreatedDate
1	Demo Company (US)	True	UnitedStates	US	100.00%	3	True	123456789	31	12	USD	20/11/2020 0:4
2	Demo Company (UK)	True	UK	GB	50.00%	3	True	GB 123456789	31	3	GBP	18/01/2022 3:2
3	Demo Company (Global)	True	GLOBAL	CA	100.00%	3	True	101-2-303	31	12	USD	9/12/2021 21:4
4	Demo Company (AU)	True	Australia	AU	100.00%	3	True	xxxxxxxx616	30	6	AUD	13/11/2019 0:4

Figure 7.6 – Organizational details dimension

Again, there is no "hard and fast" standard here, but you will typically require the following details as columns in the dimension table:

- Organization name
- Ownership %
- Parent-child column (specifies ownership/relationship by containing the ID of the parent of the organization)
- Financial year end

The additional fields in our sample are useful but not generally relevant.

The other dimensions for group reporting are generic and typically include scenario and time, depending on your organizational requirements. This could also include cost centers or similar classifications.

With Power BI time intelligence, variance-type logic and other time-related calculations are better realized in measures. As stated before, always aim to keep the number of dimensions to a minimum and check whether this is really a dimension (i.e., no 1:1 relationship with another existing dimension).

Intercompany elimination

In consolidated results across multiple entities, transactions between group companies need to be eliminated to get the correct aggregated results for the group. This can be a relatively complex topic as it often involves taking into account multiple journals for a single event (e.g., repayment of an intercompany loan), currency conversions, and other challenges such as revaluation requirements.

For a management consolidation, it's typically enough to just eliminate the intercompany transactions. However, in a setup where all intercompany transactions are coded to specific intercompany accounts, as we saw in *Figure 7.5*, we simply need to filter out these accounts on a group reporting page in Power BI or set up a measure that does that:

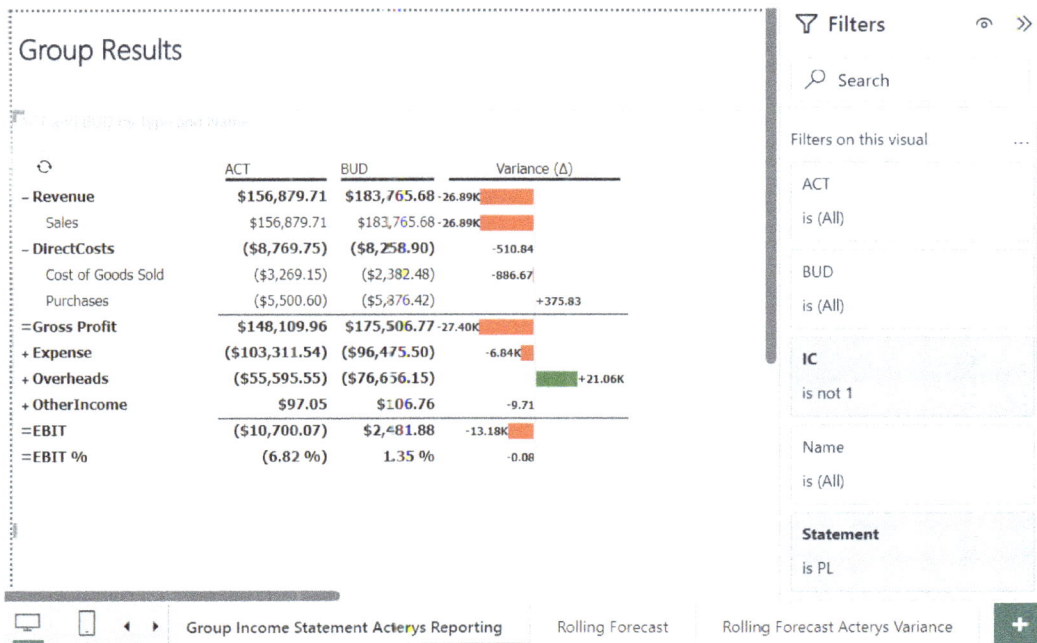

Figure 7.7 – Consolidated management report

In this section, we have covered the typical data model requirements and a simple approach for consolidated management reporting. In the final part of this chapter, we will look at the automation of the different components for a comprehensive management report that includes structured (financial) and unstructured (written commentary) parts.

Integration with Word for board reporting

Board reports typically require text commentary that can be quite lengthy. This can be either added with text boxes in Power BI and a separate PBIX file for every period or with a database-driven approach with options such as MS Power Apps or Acterys Comments/Table Edit. Both require commercial licenses, so I will not go into detail about the implementation. Another option to integrate structured and unstructured data is to use MS Word (this is technically also a separate payable license to Power BI, but one that is typically already in use).

The approach is based on **Object Linking and Embedding (OLE)**, a Microsoft standard for sharing information between different MS Office apps. There is no direct OLE option between Power BI and Word, but we can use an indirect one via Excel. As we have covered in *Chapter 5*, we can link a Power BI data set to Excel. This dataset in Excel can then be used quite easily in Word to create board reports that dynamically update when the Power BI data updates.

For example, in our Excel sample file called `Chapter 5 Power BI Excel` on the **Chapter 5 Time P** tab, we can use the *Ctrl + C* shortcut (or right-click and select **Copy** from the context menu) to copy the content in cell AA9 that contains the total revenue amount to the clipboard:

	A	B	W	X	Y	Z	AA
1							
2		Statement					
3		LegalName					
4		Year					
5							
6							
7			2021-11		2021-12		Total ACT
8		Row Labels ▾	ACT	BUD	ACT	BUD	
9		⊟**Revenue**	**$16,576**	**$23,512**	**$24,070**	**$26,477**	**$75,595**
10		Other Revenue		$6,936			
11		Sales	$16,576	$16,576	$24,070	$26,477	$75,595
12		⊟**DirectCosts**		**($855)**	**($3,395)**	**($3,734)**	**($3,395)**
13		Cost of Goods Sold		($855)			
14		Purchases			($3,395)	($3,734)	($3,395)
15		⊟**Expense**	**($16,987)**	**($20,901)**	**($1,467)**	**($1,613)**	**($26,355)**

Figure 7.8 – Copying a cell to be included in the board report

This cell reference that we have copied is absolute (i.e., always cell AA9), so it's typically advisable to turn off the zero suppression (hiding rows/columns that don't contain any data) in our pivot table. This is an option that can be set for the pivot table in the **PivotTable Analyze** menu, as shown in *Figure 7.9*. In our case, it's useful to only do this for columns, as with the rows, the zero suppression helps us avoid showing a lot of empty ones.

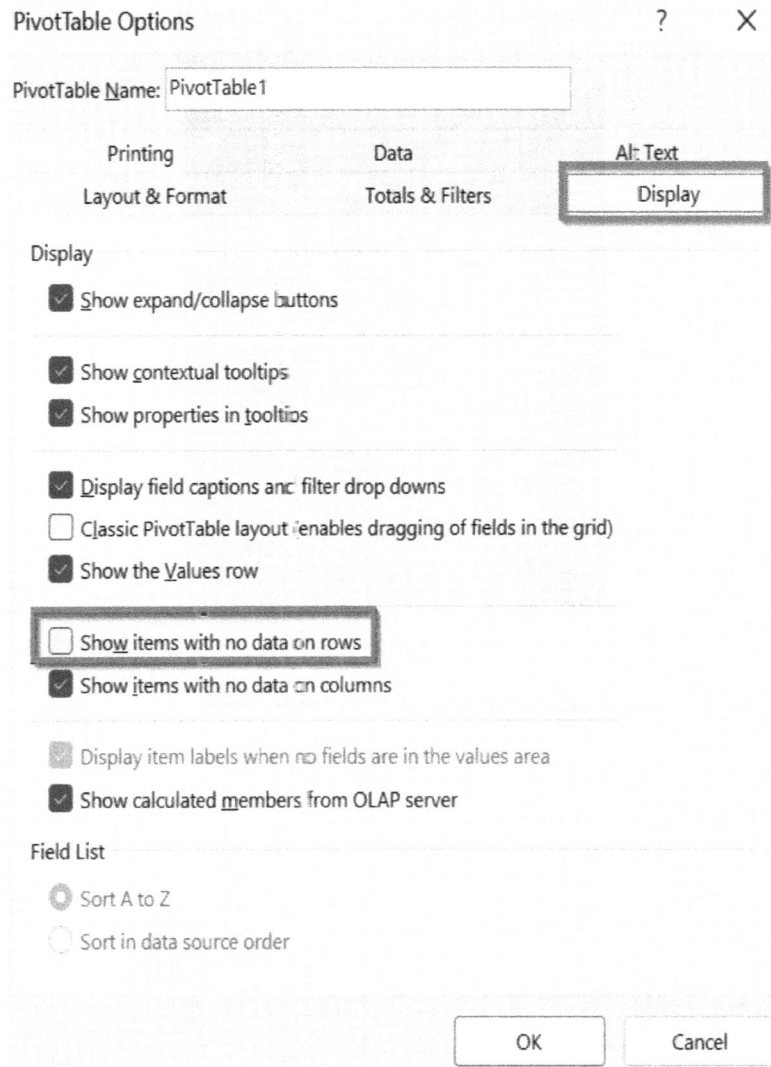

Figure 7.9 – Turning off zero suppression

This prevents you from using the wrong reference when you, for example, switch to a different year that doesn't have data for all periods.

Then, we can open a Word document, for example, the Board Report Sample.docx file, go where we want to use the dynamic link in the document, and use **Paste Special…**:

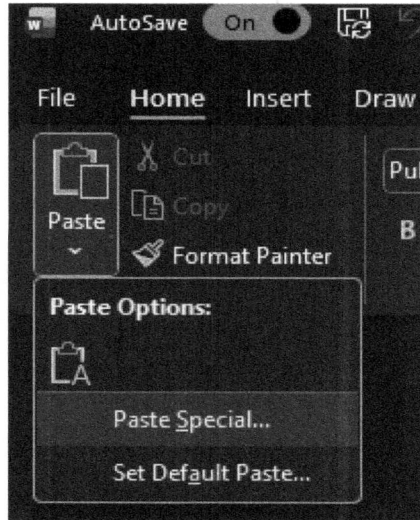

Figure 7.10 – Adding a cell to a Word board report

Then, in the following dialog, select **Unformatted Unicode Text**:

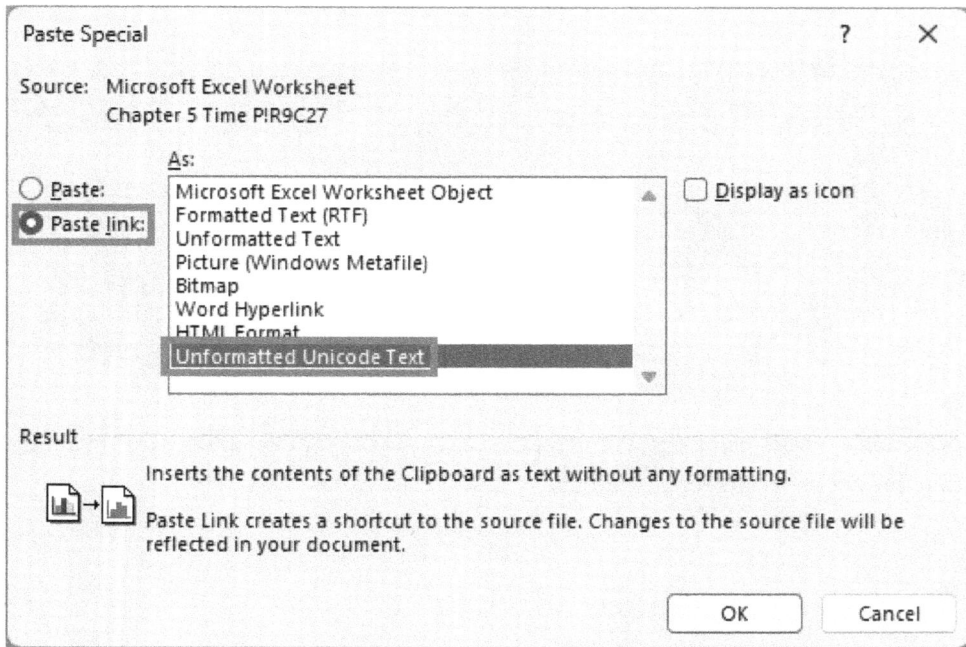

Figure 7.11 – Setting the paste type option

This will copy the reference now as a dynamic link into the document:

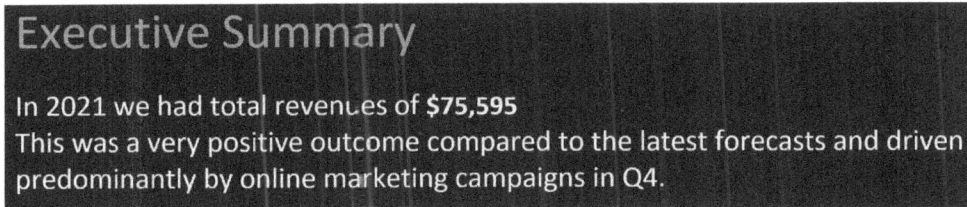

Executive Summary

In 2021 we had total revenues of **$75,595**
This was a very positive outcome compared to the latest forecasts and driven predominantly by online marketing campaigns in Q4.

Figure 7.12 – Inserted cell in Word

I have also added a reference to the year from the **Year** filter in the Excel pivot table at the beginning of the sentence, as you can see in *Figure 7.12*.

In the Chapter 5 Excel file, we can now switch the year to 2020 in the pivot table filter at the top. Once we have done that, we can go back to the board reporting Word file and update the document by choosing all content using *Ctrl + A* and then the *F9* key. After that, we see that our dynamic field references are updated:

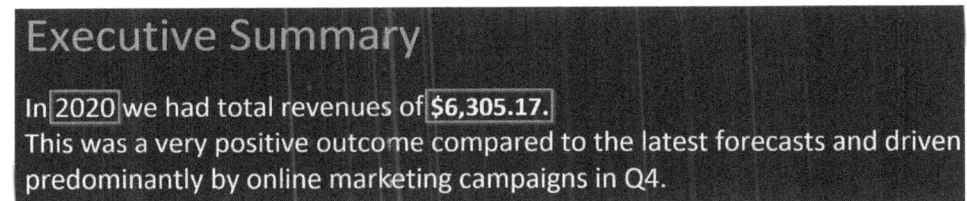

Executive Summary

In 2020 we had total revenues of $6,305.17.
This was a very positive outcome compared to the latest forecasts and driven predominantly by online marketing campaigns in Q4.

Figure 7.13 – Dynamics variables used in Word content

The text will, of course, have to be updated manually. For the ongoing process, I recommend creating a static copy of the document once the numbers are locked. This can be done by selecting the entire content of the document with *Ctrl + A* and then **Linked Object** from the right-click context, followed by **Links…**:

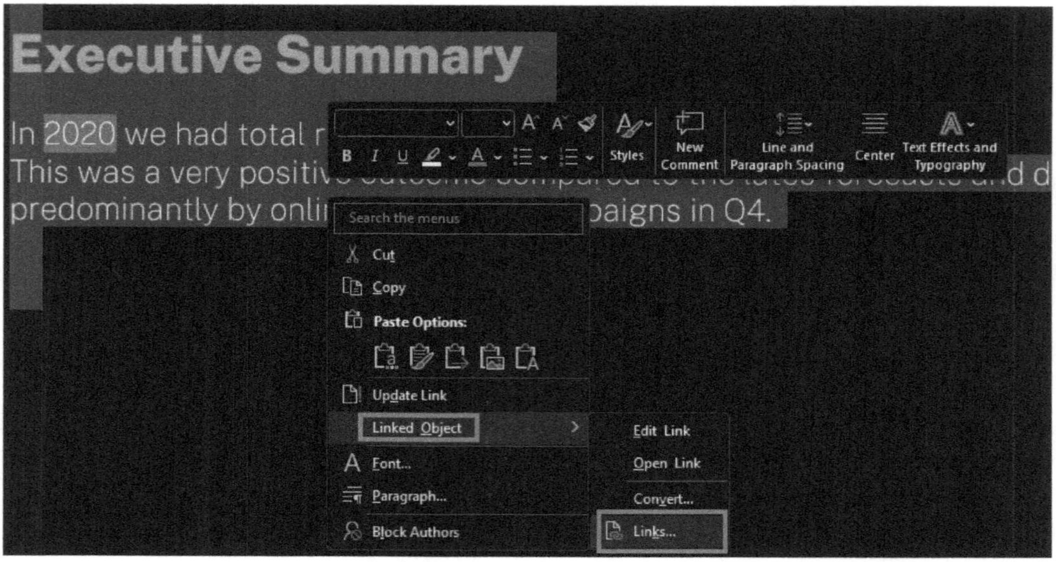

Figure 7.14 – Editing dynamic links

In the following dialog, you can convert the dynamic references to static content.

For new periods, just create a copy of the master document with the links, switch to the required period in the Excel pivot table (an Excel formula view will work in the same way), and refresh the document.

This process can likely save you time and ensure that numbers are correctly up to date. From practical experience, I must give you a little word of caution that OLE can be a bit unstable in more complex scenarios that involve larger data volumes and files.

Summary

In this chapter, we looked at options to realize comprehensive management reports/scorecards that combine strategic and financial details, including unstructured content such as comments. In the second part, we looked at the typical challenges of multi-company reporting and approaches to realizing consolidated accounts. In the final section, we looked at options to dynamically integrate content in Power BI in unstructured content such as Word documents.

In the following chapter, we will cover rolling forecasting scenarios for changing time details.

Get This Book's PDF Version and Exclusive Extras

UNLOCK NOW

Scan the QR code (or go to packtpub.com/unlock). Search for this book by name, confirm the edition, and then follow the steps on the page.

Note: Keep your invoice handy. Purchases made directly from Packt don't require one.

8

Rolling Reporting Forecasts

In dynamic business environments, traditional, fixed-period annual budget vs actual reporting often falls short in adapting to real-time changes. **Rolling forecasts** offer a solution by providing continuous updates to financial and operational plans. Rolling here refers to ongoing updates for a future time horizon, e.g., monthly, quarterly, or another defined frequency to either a specific point in time or constant period forecasts (e.g., predictions for 12 months into the future). So, reports and forecasts are updated as new data becomes available, such as monthly or quarterly. This approach allows for more accurate forecasting and a better understanding of potential risks and opportunities.

A rolling forecast often includes and calculates the numbers from different scenarios – for example, the total of actuals to a particular point (cut-off point) plus the forecasted amounts for the rest of the rolling period. Power BI is perfectly suited for implementing rolling forecasts with its powerful data visualization, modeling, and data integration capabilities.

This chapter will guide you through using Power BI to set up and manage rolling forecasts, from data preparation, report design, and using optional add-ins that add the option to edit and enter forecast values.

In this chapter, we will cover the following main topics:

- Implementing rolling forecasts with a cut-off date
- Rolling forecasts with an editing option

Technical requirements

The concepts covered in this chapter are available in the Chapter 8 Rolling Forecast.pbix sample file in the book's GitHub repository: https://github.com/PacktPublishing/Power-BI-for-Finance. This file builds on the financial reporting examples from *Chapter 4*. In this chapter, we will be using custom visuals that are part of Dynamics BPP and Acterys. These visuals can be downloaded free of charge for testing purposes directly from Power BI or from Microsoft AppSource: https://appsource.microsoft.com/.

Implementing rolling forecasts with a cut-off date

In this example, which you can also review in the chapter's sample file – we want to implement a very common requirement where a user can select a cut-off date so that the related report will display actuals until the cut-off date and then, for the rest of the months of a calendar/fiscal year, forecast or (budget) numbers. This approach enables us to get a dynamically updating full-year forecast.

To implement this logic, we first need to add an option where users can select a cut-off date. We can't use our existing date table, as that would filter the entire data set to show data for only the date that we have selected. So, as an easy option, we can duplicate our existing date table using a right-click and selecting **Duplicate** from the context menu in Power Query. In this duplicated calendar table, we only need the month's start date. This can easily be done in Power Query by adding a new custom column and using the Date.StartOfMonth() function as shown in the following screenshot:

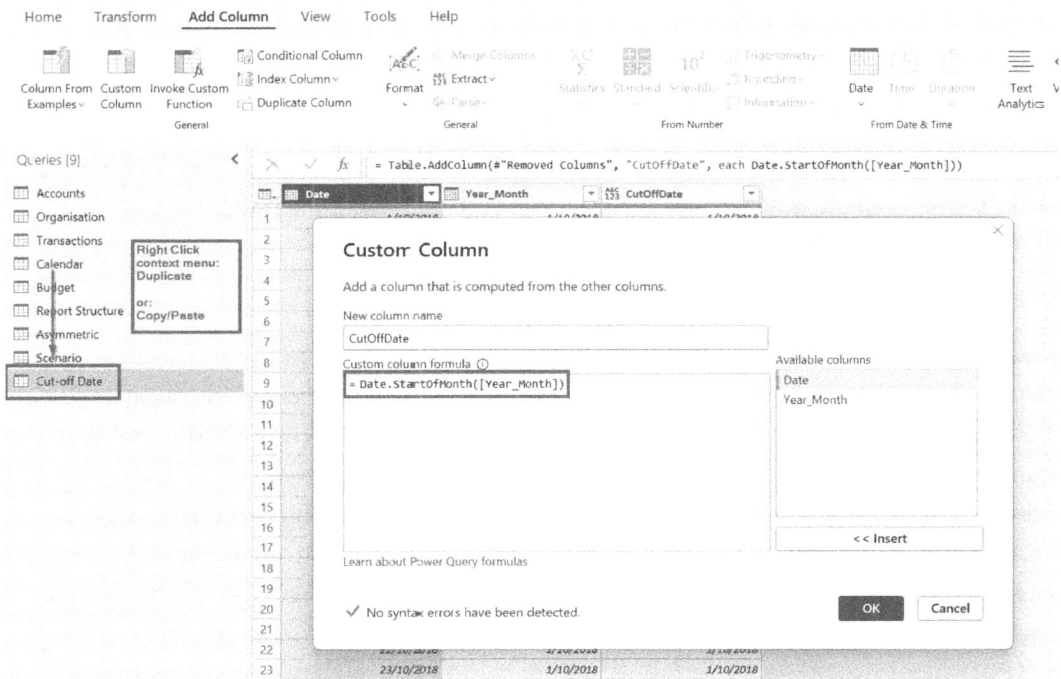

Figure 8.1 – Adding a custom column for cut-off date

Theoretically, we could use the `Date.EndOfMonth()` function as well, but that would make subsequent steps way more complicated. That is because differing end dates (between 28-31) are way more complex to handle in Power BI with DAX functions, as we are not dealing with a continuous date table. Simply having the first of every month makes it very straightforward. With this step, we now have a table from which our users can select the cut-off date they want to use for the rolling forecast.

> **Important:** The new cut-off date table can't have a relationship with the main `Transactions` data table, as that would filter only records for the closing date. For the purposes of our rolling forecast, we need to filter the table logically with a DAX statement, which we will look at in the following section.

With all the necessary data model structure in place, we can now look at the report design and logic. To achieve the dynamic display of different scenarios, we need a measure that returns the actuals until the cut-off date, followed by forecast or budget amounts for future dates.

The initial filter on actuals and forecasts is straightforward. I can filter the actuals using:

```
ACT = CALCULATE(SUM(Transactions[NetAmount_
GC]),ALL(Scenario),Scenario[Scenario]="Actual")
```

Normally, we should work with adjusted forecast values in our rolling forecast, but for our purposes, we will work with the budget scenario that I reference with the DAX:

```
FC = CALCULATE(sum(Transactions[NetAmount_
GC]),ALL(Scenario),Scenario[Scenario]="Budget")
```

Now we have the basis, but the combined requirement to show one of the two scenarios depending on the cut-off date is not trivial; it took my team and me a while to come up with a good solution. The challenge here is that we need the correct results on date hierarchies like the total year. We want to see what our new total revenue is not just the single-month results. This means we can't use CALCULATE() as that formula applies to whatever the current filter context is. In our case, we need an option that returns the actuals if the date is less than the cut-off date and the forecast/budget otherwise, but only on the row level! We can't perform the actual/forecast check on an aggregation like the entire year. This means we need to utilize a row-level context formula with SUMX(), where calculations are performed only on the row level of the used table, and the normal dimension hierarchy aggregations (e.g., total year) are applied in other cases.

The following DAX will return actuals until the active cut-off date and forecast for any period after:

```
Rolling Forecast =
VAR MAXDate = MAX('Cut-off Date'[Date])
RETURN
SUMX(
    'Calendar',
    IF( 'Calendar'[Date] >= MAXDate,
        [FC],
        [ACT]
    )
)
```

Now that we have the logic in place, we can use the standard Power BI Matrix visual and add the row metrics (in our case, the account hierarchy) as well as the column items: scenario and period (month). In the **Values** intersection, we can use the newly created **Rolling Forecast** DAX that we have just created.

Finally, we can add our new **Cut-off Date** column as a slicer to the new rolling forecast report page. Here, we see that the single months AND the totals are shown correctly:

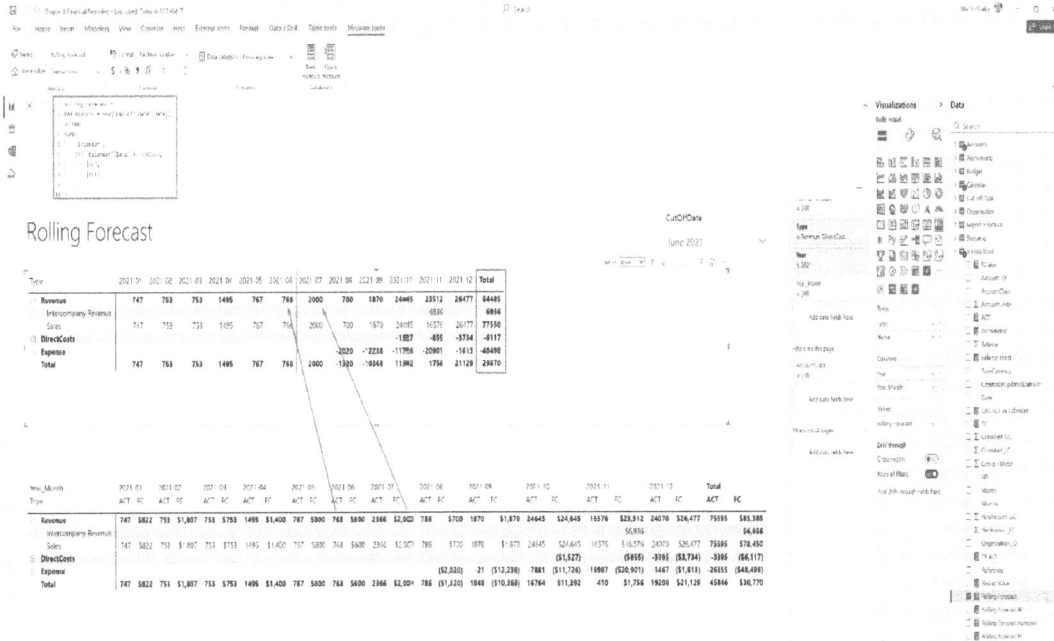

Figure 8.2 – Rolling Forecast report

Our current forecasting logic will calculate for all periods before and after the cut-off date. In some cases, you may want to only calculate the forecast for a particular date range. For that purpose, we can introduce start and end periods of the rolling forecast. In our case, we can just derive that from the cut-off date as:

```
StartofYear = DATE(YEAR(min('Cut-off Date'[CutOffDate])),1,1)
EndofYear = DATE(YEAR(min('Cut-off Date'[CutOffDate])),12,31)
```

To apply these dates, we need to add them to our forecast calculation and the variables as additional (using &&) clauses to the IF() statements:

```
Rolling Forecast Calendar Year Only =
VAR MAXDate = MAX('Cut-off Date'[Date])
RETURN
SUMX(
    'Calendar',
    IF( 'Calendar'[Date] >= MAXDate&&'Calendar'[Date] <
```

```
'Calendar'[EndofYear],
      [FC],
      IF('Calendar'[Date] <= MAXDate&&'Calendar'[Date] >=
DATE(YEAR(MAXdate),1,1),
      [ACT], BLANK()
   )))
```

In this section, we have covered an approach to achieving dynamic cut-off dates, an important element of rolling forecast reports using a closing date table and rolling forecast DAX logic. In the case covered, we assumed a fixed end date (end of the year). In the next section, we will cover an option with a constant number of future periods.

Rolling forecast with dynamic future period range

In this section, we will learn how to adapt our rolling forecast report to dynamically change (varying start and end dates) with the cut-off period. We will again need our closing date variable, which will determine the cut-off for six dynamically changing future and back periods. Initially, we will need to define the start and end variables:

```
RollingFC_PeriodStart = DATEADD('Cut-off Date'[CutOffDate],-6,Month)
RollingFC_PeriodSEnd = DATEADD('Cut-off Date'[CutOffDate],6,Month)
```

After that, we just need to modify our DAX to utilize these dates by adding the references to the start and end dates:

```
Rolling Forecast Calendar 2Q+- =
VAR MAXDate = MAX('Cut-off Date'[Date])
RETURN
SUMX(
    'Calendar',
    IF( 'Calendar'[Date] < [RollingFC_PeriodEnd],
        [FC],
        IF('Calendar'[Date] >= [RollingFC_PeriodStart],
        [ACT], BLANK()
    )))
```

Rolling forecasts with an editing option

Often, an important function of rolling forecasts is the ability to modify the forecasts for future periods. This can be achieved with the write-back features that are available in the custom visuals in Acterys and Microsoft Dynamics Business Performance Planning visuals from AppSource (all of them will require a license). We will cover these in detail in *Chapter 11*.

Here I just want to give a quick example of rolling forecasts with the Acterys/BPP visual. This visual will allow you to directly edit the values (with a variety of planning options like manual entry, relative changes, using existing allocations, etc.) in the periods after the cut-off date, either for a specific period or for the entire forecast period—a so-called *splash* across all the periods in the forecasting period. The relevant report then could look like this:

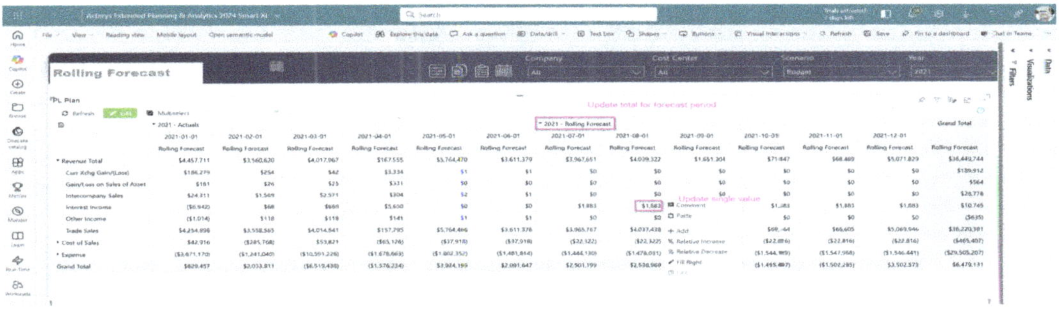

Figure 8.3 – Overview of Rolling Forecast with Acterys/BPP matrix

In this section, we've delved into the essential requirements for implementing a rolling forecast display and editing options using Acterys or Microsoft Dynamics Business Performance Planning.

Moving forward, in the final section, we'll explore how we can elevate the visualization with another custom visual.

Rolling forecasts with Acterys Variance

Acterys Variance is a free-for-personal-use Power BI visual for small multiples KPI card and variance display. It also includes an automated rolling forecast feature. To use this, just add Acterys Variance to your Power BI report from AppSource and configure the **Category** field with a time attribute (e.g., months) and add measures for your target (**Value** field) and actuals (**Comparison** field). We already have those from the samples covered in the data modelling section in *Chapter 1*. Finally, we need to enable the **Cut Off Period** option in the visual in Power BI Desktop or in the **Edit** mode in the Power BI service by applying the following settings in the visual properties. In the **Cut Off Index** drop-down dialog, the user can define at what point the cut-off line should be displayed, e.g., one position before the cut-off date would be -1:

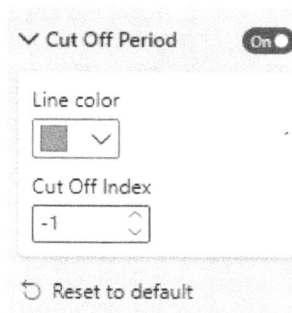

Figure 8.4 – Setting Cut Off Period

As a final option, in the next section, we will cover how you can make the forecast editable in the rolling forecast report.

Data edit option

With an Acterys or Microsoft Dynamics Business Planning license, you can activate **Edit** mode using the icon at the top of the visual, as shown in *Figure 8.5*. This allows you to edit data –including top-down changes – by dragging on the bars. The visual automatically calculates the total year forecast and provides extensive analysis options like absolute/relative variance and waterfall visualization.

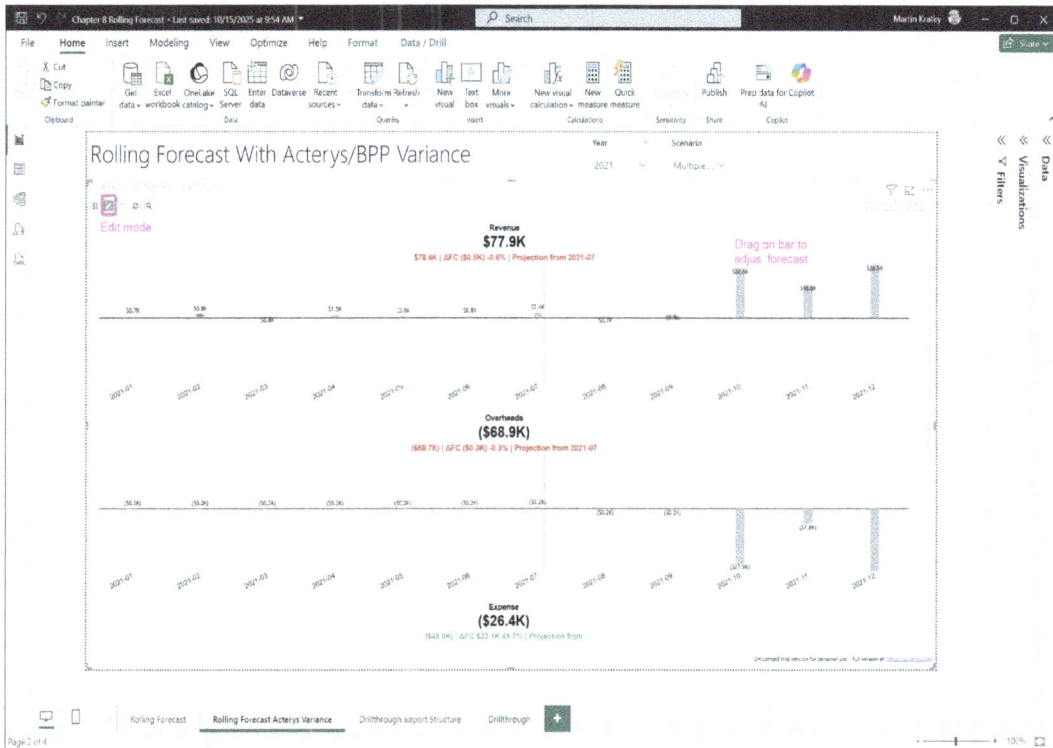

Figure 8.5 – Cut-Off visualization and edit options

Summary

In this chapter, we covered options on how to realize different rolling forecasting logic options with DAX and visualization options with different Power BI visuals. For requirements where you want to edit the rolling forecast assumptions, we have introduced how to realize this with the Acterys/ BPP matrix and variance visuals.

In the next chapter, we will explore options to realize valuations for publicly traded companies and the associated integration of financial services data.

Get This Book's PDF Version and Exclusive Extras

UNLOCK NOW

Scan the QR code (or go to packtpub.com/unlock). Search for this book by name, confirm the edition, and then follow the steps on the page.

Note: Keep your invoice handy. Purchases made directly from Packt don't require one.

9

Discounted Cash Flow Public Company Valuation

Company valuations provide a comprehensive assessment of an organization's worth, which is essential for making informed investment decisions. Investors rely on valuations to determine whether a company is undervalued or overvalued, affecting their choices on buying, holding, or selling stocks.

Company valuations also play an essential role in mergers and acquisitions. When companies seek to merge or acquire other businesses, accurate valuations ensure that the transaction is fair and beneficial for all parties involved. They help negotiate the right price and structuring deals that align with strategic goals.

In this chapter, we will look at how you can import the relevant financial details from provider sources and then implement the calculation logic for a discounted cash flow valuation.

The chapter will cover the following topics:

- Accessing data via a **REpresentational State Transfer (REST) Application Programming Interface (API)** provider
- Relevant data transformation steps
- Company value DAX calculations

Technical requirements

The concepts covered in this chapter are available in the `Chapter 9 Public Company Financials.pbix` sample file in the book's official GitHub repository here: `https://github.com/PacktPublishing/Power-BI-for-Finance`.

Sourcing financial details

Financial statement details are an essential requirement for public company valuation. Typically, at a minimum, a table contains the financial statement line (e.g., revenues), the period/interval (e.g., the total for the year 2024), and the respective value (e.g., $10 million).

Financial statement data (also called **fundamentals**) is available from a variety of sources but, unfortunately, is not easily accessible with Power BI (for example, Power BI doesn't support **eXtensible Business Reporting Language (XBRL)** data provided by the SEC), and in many cases, it is not free. For this book, the aim was to find a free option that works in a relatively simple way with Power BI and doesn't require a purchase. Unfortunately, free often means that there is no guarantee that it will stay that way, which I realized the hard way as the approach that I initially planned to cover wasn't accessible anymore during the final phase of the book.

The data service provider that I am covering (`massive.com`) is, at the time of the publishing of this book, still available free of charge but, unfortunately, the publisher of that solution (and anyone else that I am aware of) can't provide any guarantees that this will always be the case.

So, the principles that I am introducing will still be applicable in general, but it could be the case that you will need to adjust them to the particular details of the data source that you are choosing.

Loading financial data

`Massive.com` (with whom I have no affiliation) is a specialist provider of financial markets data. Customers can access the data via an API web service. To access the data in Power BI, you first have to create a free trial account via the `massive.com` website. In the process, you will be provided with a personal API key (a combination of letters and numbers) that is necessary for access. This is then used when you create a new web source in Power BI, as described next.

Constructing a web link

From the **Home** menu in **Get data**, select the **Web** source type:

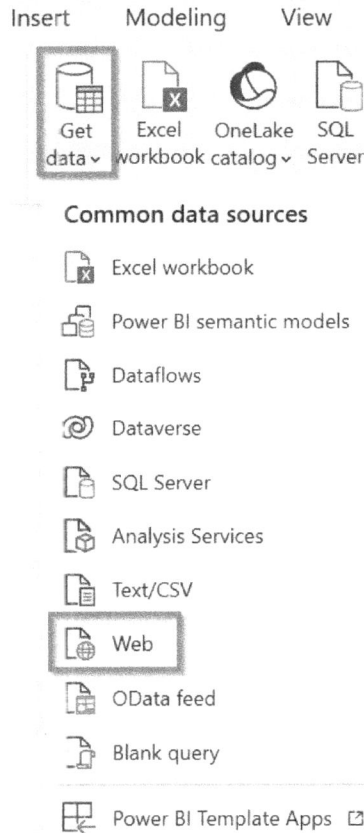

Figure 9.1 – Selecting the data source type

In the following step, we can paste an initial general query for a specific company (in this case, Microsoft with their ticker symbol, MSFT) into the URL field. You can copy the URL with the format `https://api.massive.com/stocks/financials/v1/cash-flow-statements?limit=100&sort=period_end.asc&apiKey=YOUR_API_KEY`

with your key from the Polygon documentation (`https://massive.com/docs/rest/stocks/fundamentals/cash-flow-statements`) or add your key manually into the string at the end (`apiKey=` parameter):

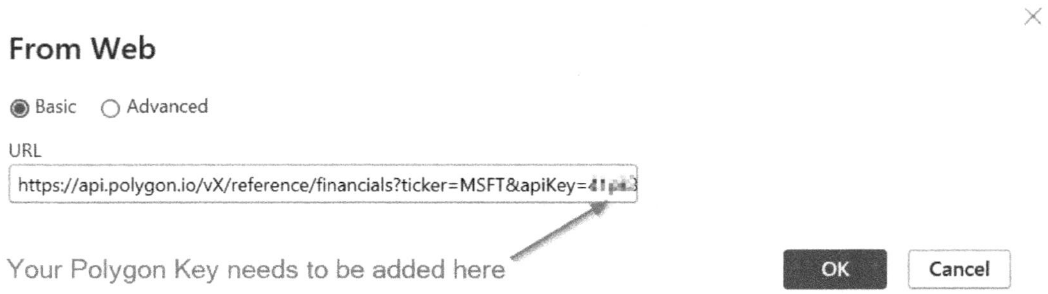

From Web

⊙ Basic   ○ Advanced

URL

https://api.polygon.io/vX/reference/financials?ticker=MSFT&apiKey=41▯▯3

Your Polygon Key needs to be added here

OK   Cancel

Figure 9.2 – Retrieval link

On the next screen, we can see the result table on which Power Query has already applied a variety of transformation steps automatically:

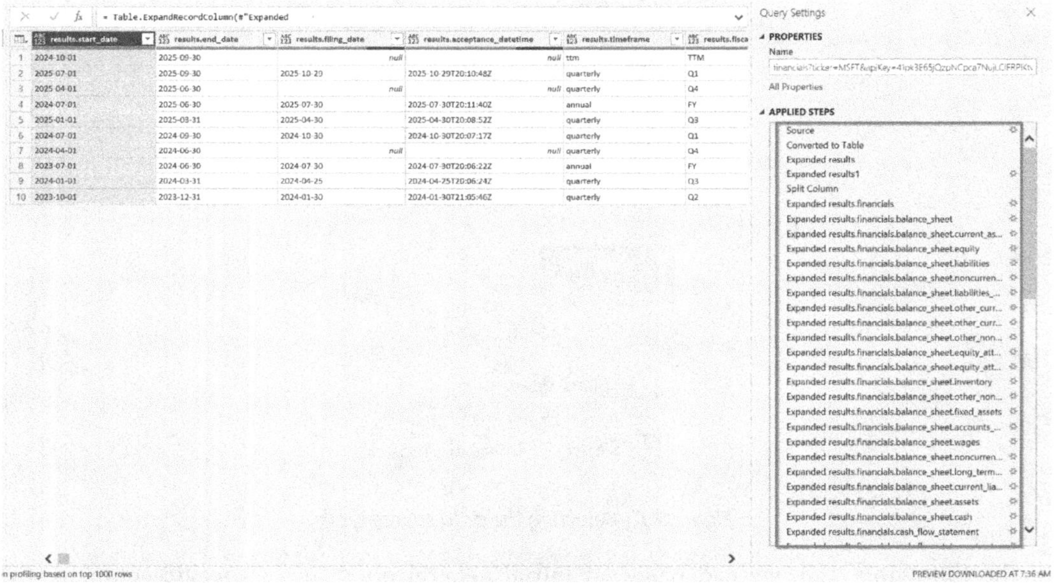

Figure 9.3 – Automatically generated Power Query steps

Many of them are not useful for our purposes. In addition, new users of API services will benefit from an explanation of some of the steps to assist general understanding. So, for that purpose, we can delete all steps from the Expanded results.financials step:

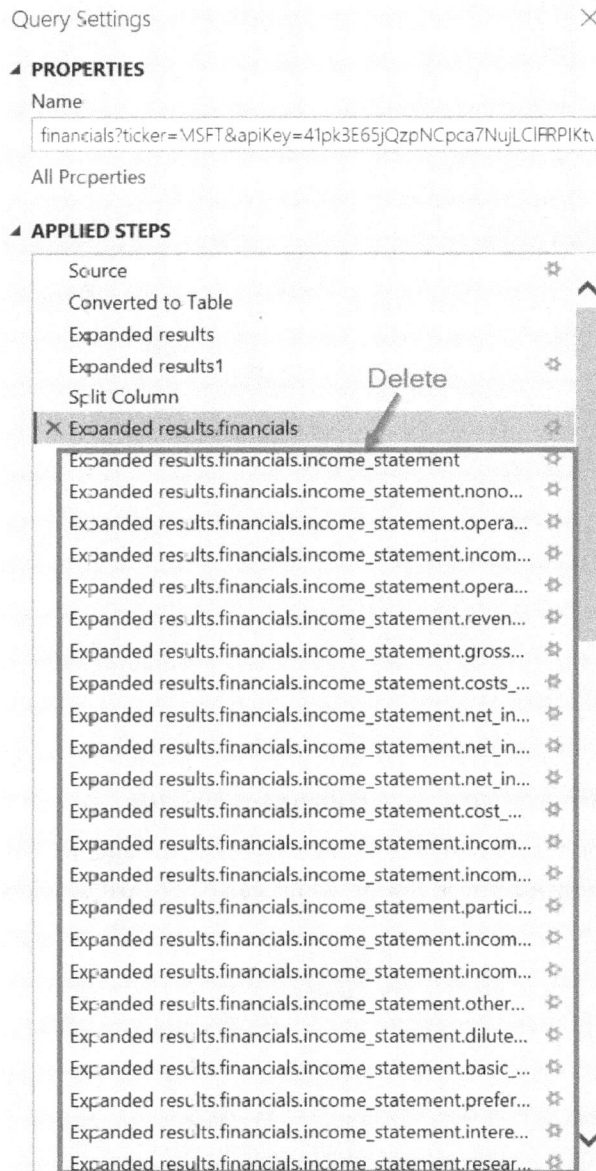

Figure 9.4 – Unnecessary steps

It is not possible to select multiple transformation steps and then press **Delete**. However, we have a helpful option of selecting the last step that we want to keep and then using the right-click option, **Delete Until End**:

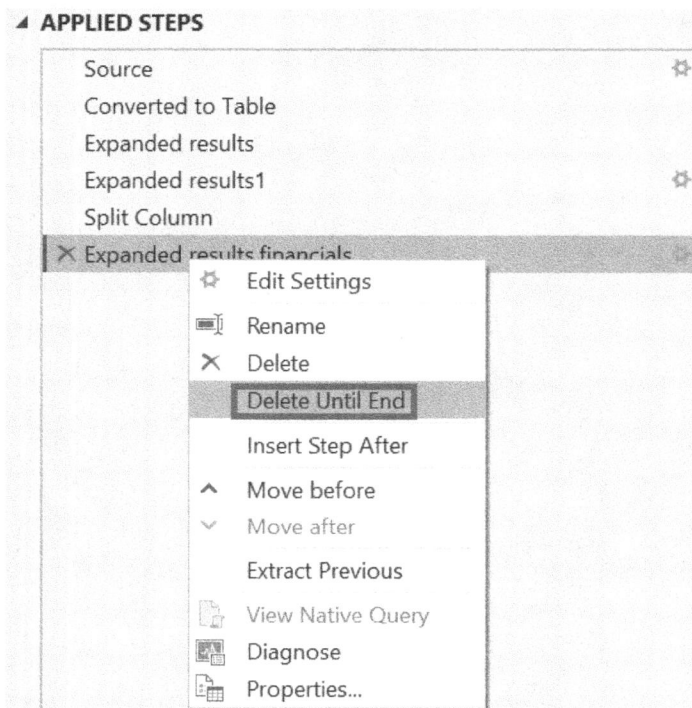

Figure 9.5 – Deleting steps until the end

Side topic: editing steps in Advanced Editor

Alternatively, if we don't want to delete all the steps until the end, we have more selective options in the Power Query **Advanced Editor**, which can be opened by clicking on the button in the **Home** ribbon:

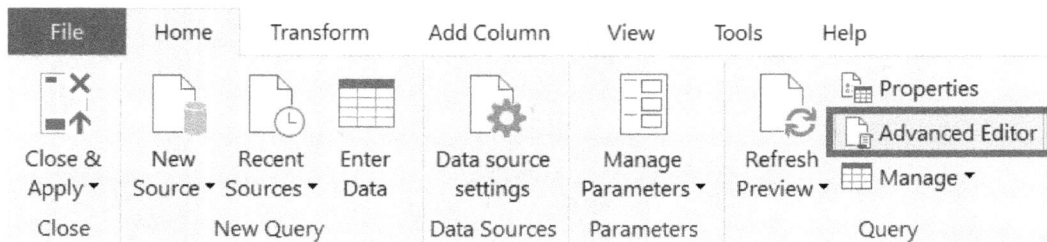

Figure 9.6 – Opening Advanced Editor

Here, we can see all the Power Query steps and edit them selectively – for instance, selectively removing some steps. As the steps cross-reference each other, you have to ensure that the integrity of the references stays in place – for example, avoiding references to the deleted steps in subsequent steps:

Figure 9.7 – Selective deletion of steps

If we assume we are deleting the four steps from #"Expanded results.financials.income_statement" to #"Expanded results.financials.income_statement.operating_income_loss", we have to replace references to those with a step that is still available (e.g., #"Expanded results.financials"); otherwise, the code steps can't be executed because of a reference that doesn't exist.

After we have deleted the steps, we can review the current table. In the first few columns, we see the **date** details:

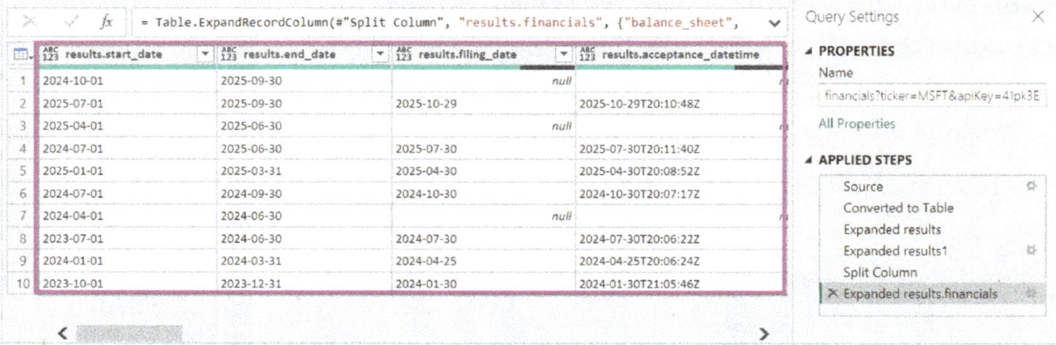

Figure 9.8 – Date details

On the right side, this is followed by the company name (e.g., Microsoft), `filing` (the report source filed with the SEC from which the data was taken), and the actual `statement` line, for example, the income (also called profit and loss) statement data in the `results.financials.income_statement` column. As we can see, these columns are stored in a cascading format (that is, as links to additional detail tables), represented as `Record` links in the JSON file structure used by the API:

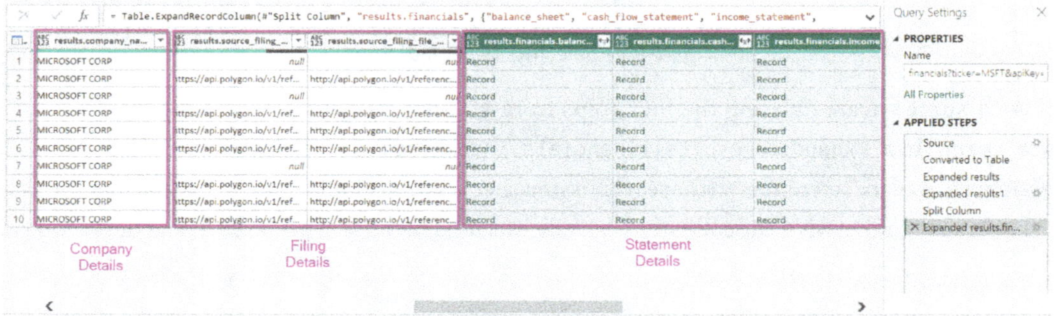

Figure 9.9 – Company details

For our purposes, and to make the structure of the table clearer (i.e., fewer columns to review), we only require the cash flow statement details. So, we can delete the other statement columns (`results.financials.income_statement`, `results.financials.balance_sheet`, and `results.financials.comprehensive_income`) by selecting them and using the *Delete* key or the right-click **Delete** menu option. The same can be done for the rest of the columns on the right, so our table will now look like this:

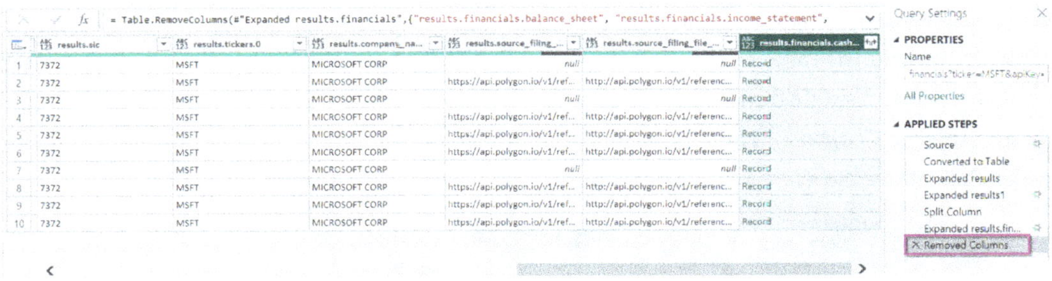

Figure 9.10 – Table after the deletion of unnecessary columns

To get to the detailed item lines, we have to expand the subsection to show the cash flow sub-table details. The best option to get to the currently hidden details is to unpivot the `results.financials.cash_flow_statement` column. We can do this by selecting the column and clicking **Unpivot Columns** in the **Transform** ribbon or using the same option in the right-click menu option on the header of this column. After this, you will see that the column has been split up into two columns (`Attribute` and `Value`):

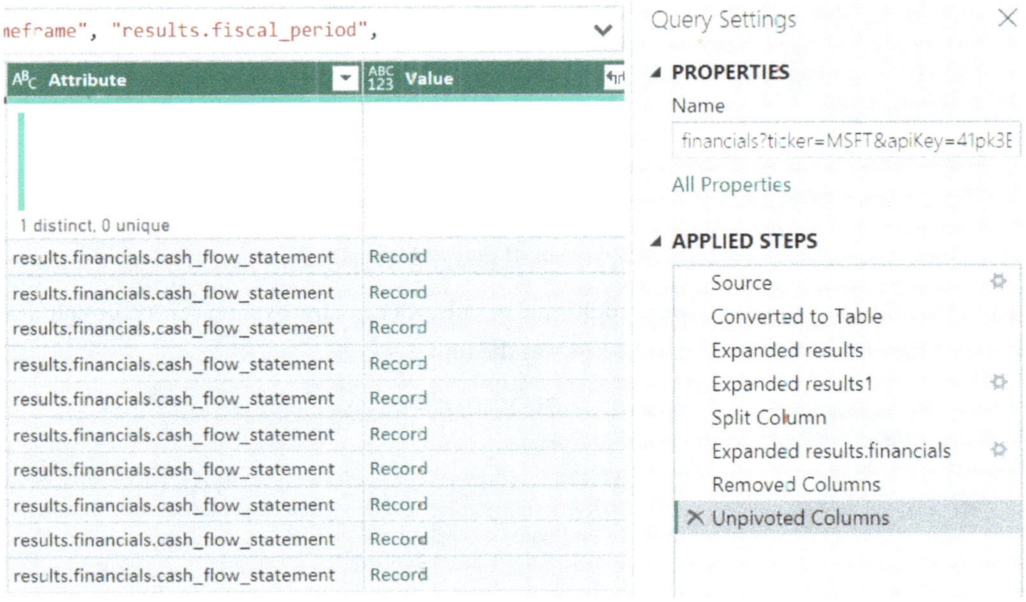

Figure 9.11 – Unpivoted Columns

We can click on the expand icon to get the statement detail value (e.g., the net cash flow amount). This will expand the table to show all the detail lines in columns. For our purposes, it is better to have them as a single dimension column, as we then have a separate measure dimension (for details, refer to *Chapter 1*). For that, we can unpivot again from the **Transform** ribbon or via the right-click menu. Now, we see all the statement line details in the Attribute.1 column:

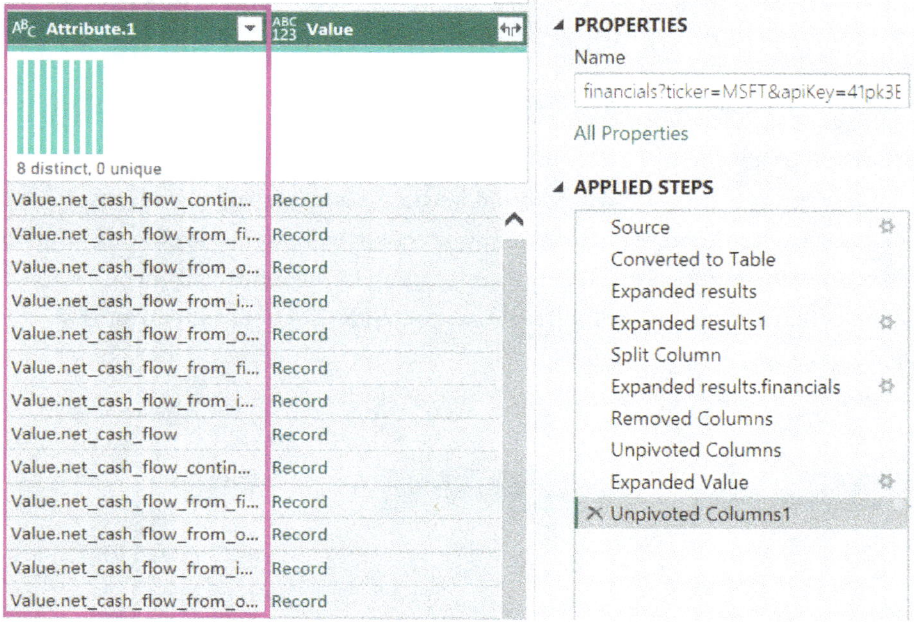

Figure 9.12 – Display of statement details

To get to the amount values and some additional details, we can now expand the Value column by clicking on the button with the two arrows at the top:

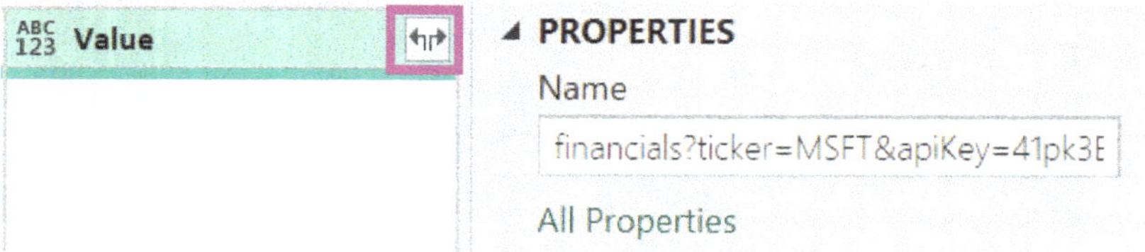

Figure 9.13 – Expanding the Value column

This will now expand the table to show the value, the unit (e.g., USD currency), a readable label of the item line, as well as the order where the line is placed in the statement:

ABC 123 Value.value	ABC 123 Value.unit	ABC 123 Value.label	ABC 123 Value.order
1738000000	USD	Net Cash Flow, Continuing	1200
-17089000000	USD	Net Cash Flow From Financing Activities, Continuing	800
1.02647E+11	USD	Net Cash Flow From Operating Activities, Continuing	200
-83820000000	USD	Net Cash Flow From Investing Activities, Continuing	500
1.02647E+11	USD	Net Cash Flow From Operating Activities	100

Figure 9.14 – Statement detail columns

There are a few further modifications to enable our calculations. Let's look at those next.

Additional format changes

Now, we have to change the date-related columns to a date format by changing the type of these four date columns to **Date** in the **Data Type** option in the **Transform** ribbon:

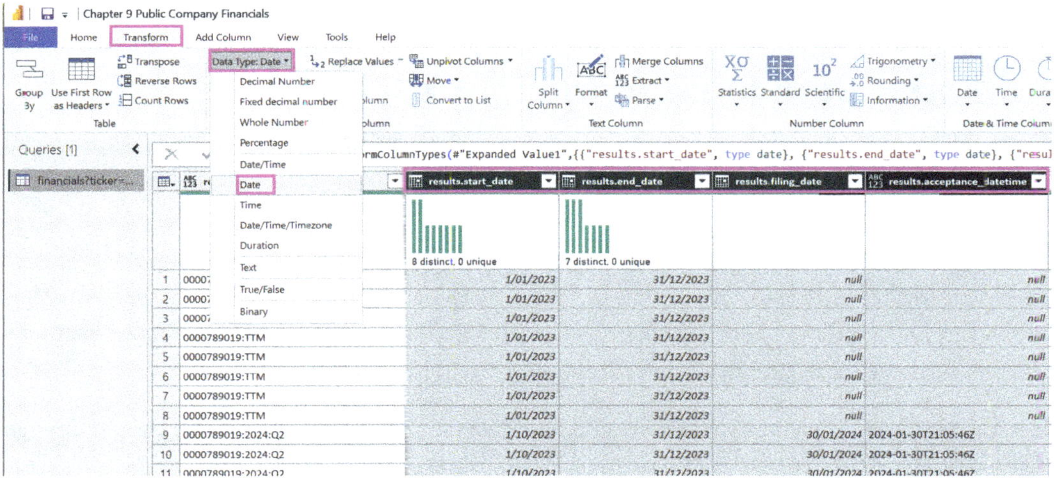

Figure 9.15 – Converting to date format

Next, we can rename our query by a double click or using **Rename** in the right-click menu and entering the desired name, CashFlow:

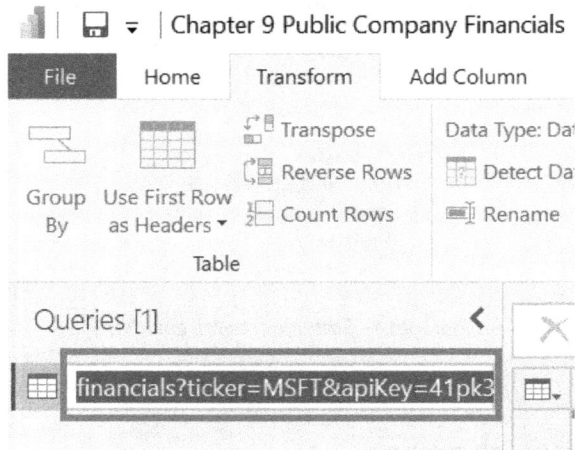

Figure 9.16 – Renaming the Power Query table

Now that we have the basis, we can look at the necessary steps to calculate the discounted cash flows required for the company value.

Adding a date table to the model

As we will require calculations with time intelligence, we require a date table. The easiest way to do this in our context is to create a new calculated table:

```
Date = Calendar(FIRSTDATE(CashFlow[results.start_
date]),LASTDATE(CashFlow[results.end_date]))
```

As you can see here, I am using an elegant way with FIRSTDATE() and LASTDATE() DAX formulas to always get the correct first and last dates in our CashFlow table.

The CashFlow table currently has start and end dates for string data types. We should change these to a date type. We can easily do this by selecting the date columns (it's helpful to do this for the filing date as well, in case we want to include that in queries) and then selecting the **Date** data type in the Power Query ribbon **Date Type** option. We can then connect our date table to the main CashFlow table.

This is best done on the **Date** field in the **Date** table and results.end_cate in the **CashFlow** table:

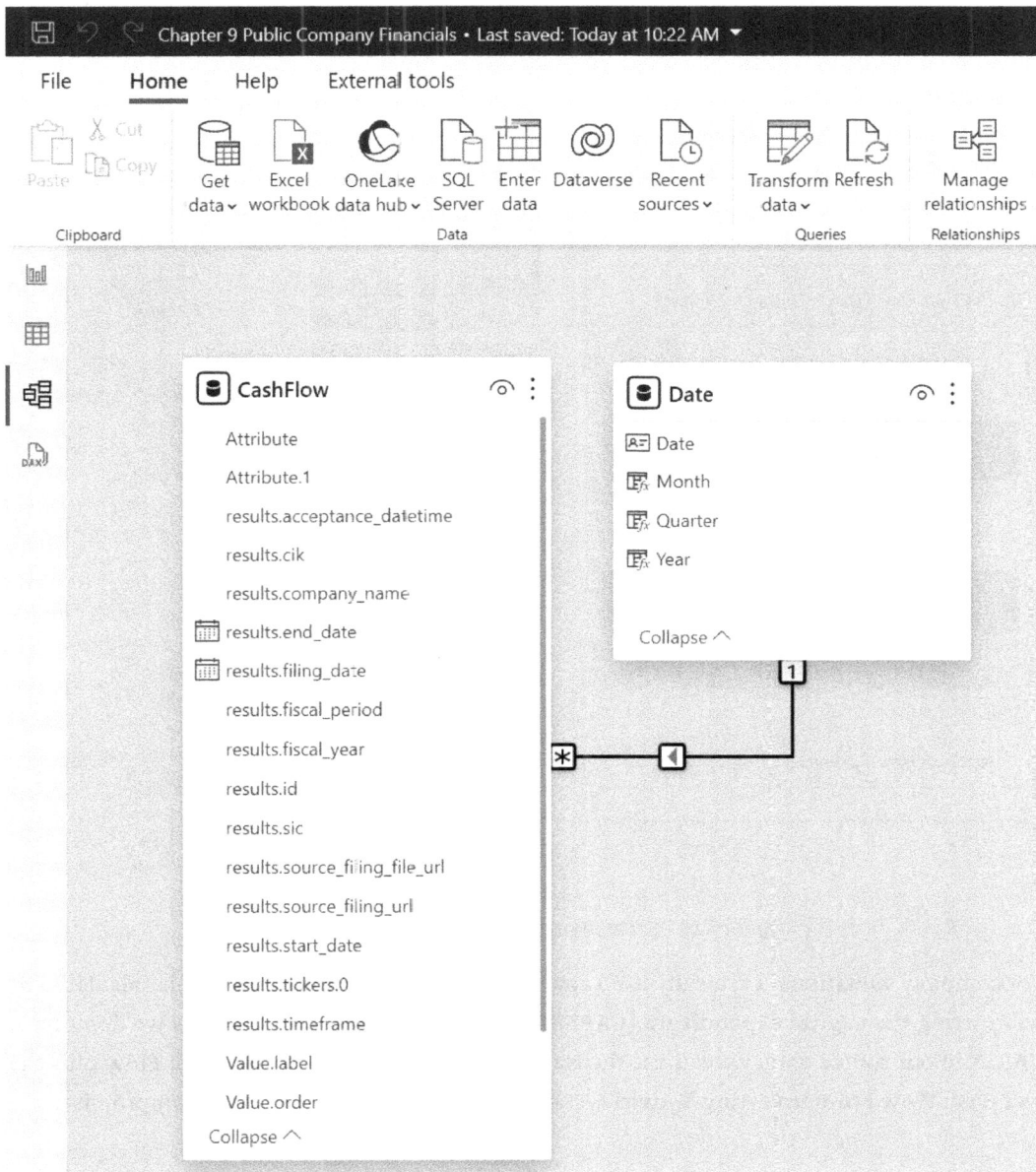

Figure 9.17 – Creating a relationship between Date fields

Now that our model is complete, we can look at the report that will contain the details that we need to calculate the company value. To keep it flexible, I will enable users to choose the cash flow statement item line(s) that they want to use by adding a slicer visual with the Value.label column on the report:

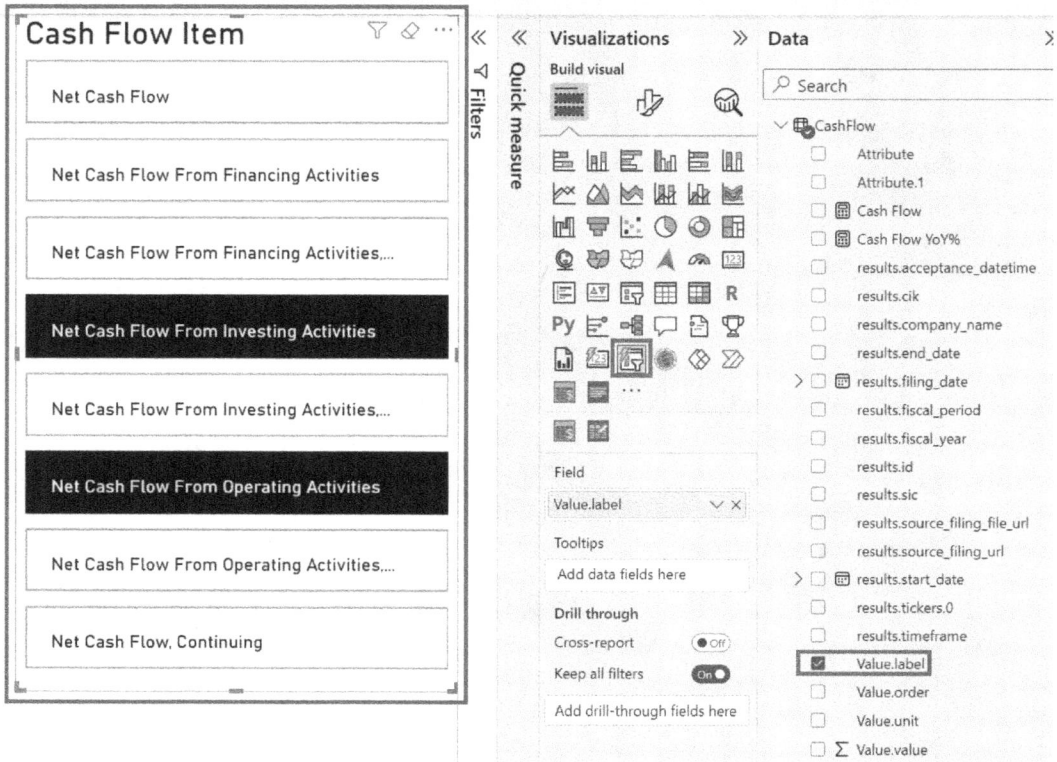

Figure 9.18 – Slicer to select cash flow statement items

For company valuations, a typically used approach is the **free cash flow**, which is calculated by subtracting the **capital expenditure (CAPEX)** from the operating cash flow. As we don't have CAPEX in our source data, we can use the **Net Cash Flow From Operating Cash Flow** plus the **Net Cash Flow From Investing Activities** statement lines as a relatively close compromise.

The actual amount value is in the Value.value column. This comes from the source as a string, so we need to convert this to a decimal number by selecting the column and switching the format to **Decimal Number** in the **Data Type** option in the **Transform** ribbon:

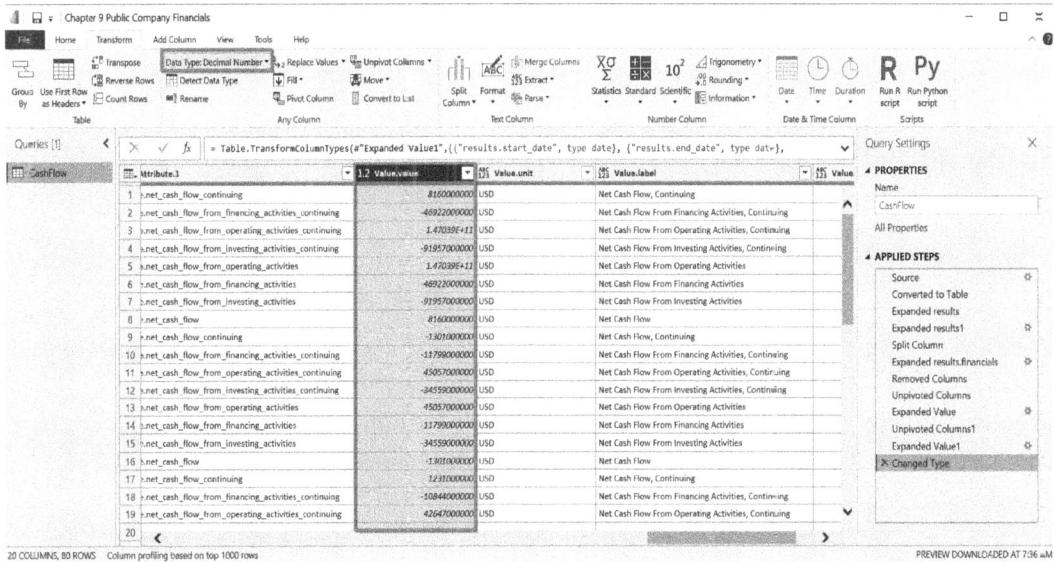

Figure 9.19 – Converting string values to decimal numbers

In our table, we have a variety of time units for our data: **ttm** (which stands for **trailing twelve months**, i.e., the 12 months from the cutoff date of the data), **quarterly**, and **annual**. For our calculations, we need to settle on a single unit. This, in general, depends on the requirements of the analyst. The best approach here is to leave it to the report user and add a slicer for the periodicity of the results.timeframe field.

To allow for period selection, we can add another slicer with the **Year** field from our **Date** table.

Finally, we can just create an explicit measure with the Value.value field:

```
Cash Flow = (sum(CashFlow[Value.value]))
```

We can add that to a card visual on the report. After these steps, our report will look like this, displaying an approximation (as our API data source doesn't provide the exact required details) of the Free Cash Flow of $64.9 billion (the actual one is around $59.5 billion for 2023):

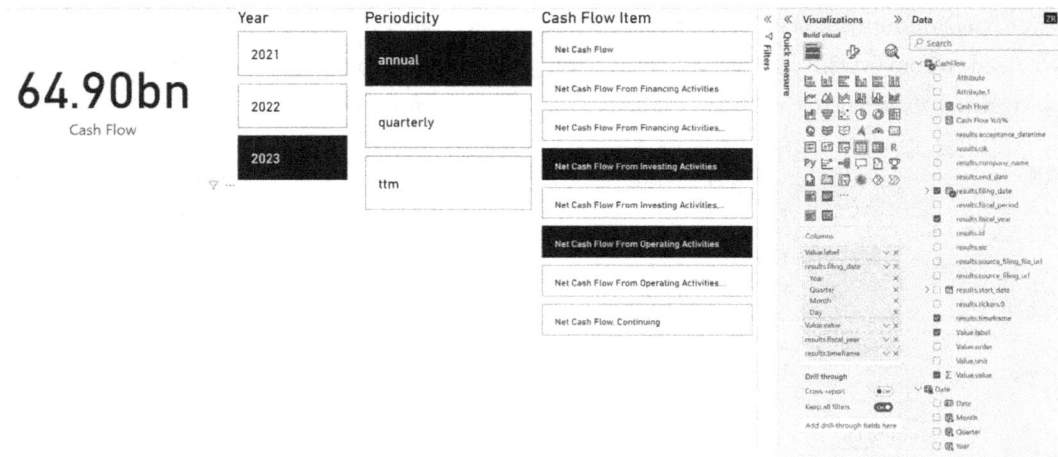

Figure 9.20 – Valuation report

This concludes the necessary transformation steps to obtain the relevant cash flow details from an API source. In the next section, I will cover options on how to handle growth factors and the calculation of the company value.

Calculating the growth factor

To project cash flows in the future, there are a variety of approaches. One option is to look at the growth rate in historic periods. We can calculate annual growth with the following calculation:

```
Cash Flow YoY% =
VAR __PREV_YEAR = CALCULATE([Cash Flow], DATEADD('Date'[Date], -1, YEAR))
RETURN
    DIVIDE([Cash Flow] - __PREV_YEAR, __PREV_YEAR)
```

This returns a growth rate of around 10.5% for the two years of complete data until 2023. The actual growth rate over the last four years was around 12.5%. To have more realistic outcomes, we will use that in our model.

Another option is to use a growth rate factor. But as financial professionals will know, this is not the best approach as it assumes a linear development that does not take into account compound growth. We should take into account the new total changes in the prior period as opposed to just the first base period. The mathematical formula for **compound annual growth rate (CAGR)** is as follows:

```
CAGR = Ending Balance / Beginning Balance ^# Years -1
```

We now have all the required discounted cash flow details to calculate the total company value, which we will look at in the next section.

Calculating the company value

The necessary parameters for the total company value are as follows:

- **FCF**: Projected future free cash flows (in our example, the latest free cash flow with the CAGR applied).
- **n**: The number of future free cash flow periods, for example, four years of forecasted data.
- **r**: A discount rate that brings future cash flows to the **present value (PV)**. Typically, the discount rate is the organization's cost of capital. Usually, the **weighted average cost of capital (WACC)** is the rate that the organization pays on average to all its security holders to finance its assets. In our case, we assume 10%, which is around the average for the total US market in 1/2023.

The calculation for future years is as follows:

```
PV FCF1..n =  FCF Base * Compound Growth Rate / (1 + r)n
```

So, for our requirements, we can calculate these with DAX measures:

```
FCF1 = [Cash Flow]
FCF2 = DIVIDE([FCF1]*(1.125),1.1^2)
FCF3 = DIVIDE([FCF2]*(1.125),1.1^3)
FCF4 = DIVIDE([FCF3]*(1.125), 1.1^4)
```

The value of `1.125` represents the mathematical approach to applying the 12.5% CAGR that we have calculated in the previous section.

In this example, I only use four periods, but these can, of course, be extended/reduced as needed. The total of these is then the first part of the company value. The second part is a terminal value calculation, where the last annual free cash flow is discounted with the discount rate, r, minus a perpetual growth rate, g:

```
Terminal Value = divide([FCF4],1-1.1)
Finally, we can use this terminal value in the full Company calculation:
Company Value = [FCF1]+[FCF2]+[FCF3]+[FCF4]+[Terminal Value]
```

This measure produces a value of $2.23 trillion, which is in the ballpark of the $2–3 trillion market cap at the time of writing of this book.

We can now add all the relevant details to the report. In the sample file, I used this layout:

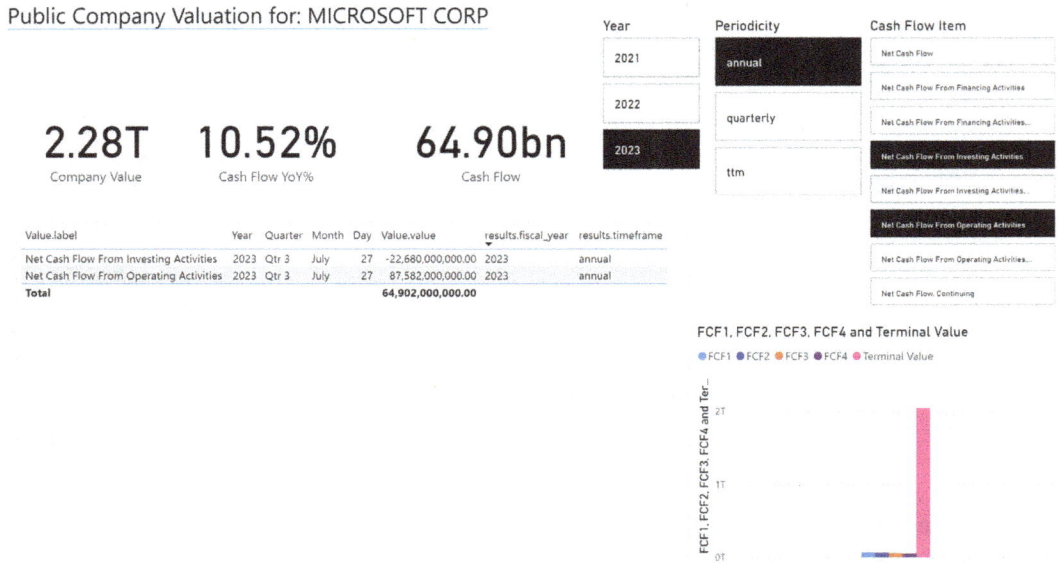

Figure 9.21 – Final report

The title will dynamically change to the company name in the data file if we change the ticker symbol to another company. This is done by using a DAX measure that combines title text and the company name field:

```
Title = CONCATENATE("Public Company Valuation for: ",min(CashFlow[results.
company_name]))
```

We can then use this measure in a reference in a Power BI text box visual at the top:

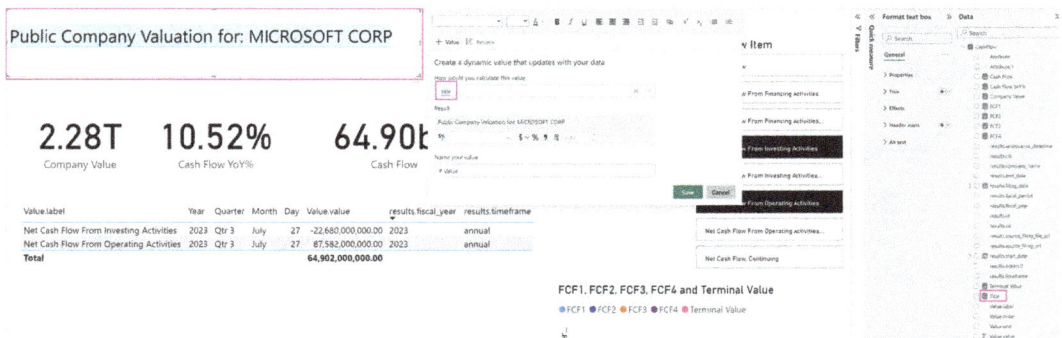

Figure 9.22 – Dynamic title

Here, we now see the complete report that displays the valuation outcome, filter fields, and a table with the quarterly details.

Summary

In this chapter, we saw a comprehensive example of integrating data from a commercial provider of public company fundamentals via a REST API. We then looked at DAX calculations and dynamic report layouts to display public company value estimates using a projected free cash flow approach. Please remember that the methods covered only provide the principal approach using limited sample data that will require further refinement for the particular requirement.

In the next chapter, we will talk about price, volume, and mix variance analysis.

Get This Book's PDF Version and Exclusive Extras

UNLOCK NOW

Scan the QR code (or go to packtpub.com/unlock). Search for this book by name, confirm the edition, and then follow the steps on the page.

Note: Keep your invoice handy. Purchases made directly from Packt don't require one.

10

Price Volume Mix Analysis

In this chapter, we will cover how to utilize **Price Volume Mix (PVM)** analysis, a powerful tool that helps organizations understand how price, sales volume, and product mix changes impact revenue. PVM analysis is particularly important for businesses that sell various products or services at differing prices. Companies can make informed decisions about pricing, marketing, and product development by analyzing the impact of each of these factors on revenue.

Furthermore, we will cover how you can carry out PVM analysis using Power BI and add insightful visualizations.

In this chapter, we will cover the following main topics:

- Preparing the dataset
- Joining the tables
- Adding the PVM logic

Technical requirements

The concepts covered in this chapter can be seen in the `Chapter 10 PVM.pbix` Power BI sample file. All the sample files, including this one, are located in the book's GitHub repository: `https://github.com/PacktPublishing/Power-BI-for-Finance`.

Preparing the dataset

Before we get into the details, we need to look at the data required. PVM analysis requires, at a minimum, the following data details for the current (TP) and a comparison period (CP):

- Product/product category
- Price
- Units sold

In the sample file for this chapter, I have included sample tables in a typical format that exports from a sales and CRM system, as well as from a data warehouse/ planning application. It utilizes the following:

- A sales transaction table with a single value or multiple measure columns (e.g., for price, units, discount, etc.) and all dimension details (e.g., product/customer name, sales outlet, etc.)
- A separate table for price details for multiple scenarios

The separation of prices and sales is particularly relevant in forecasting/budgeting/planning scenarios as users will plan their volumes in detail but will only maintain a price table by product for the entire period and not for every single planned sales transaction.

We now need to join these tables correctly and some modeling to enable revenue and period comparison calculations is necessary.

Joining the tables

To add relationships (a basic Power BI feature covered in *Chapter 1* of this book) between the price and sales tables, we will need a separate dimension table as the direct relationship between two fact tables would be of the many-to-many type (multiple items in one table are linked with multiple in the other, e.g., prices for the same dates in multiple scenarios), which means the direct relationship is not possible.

Link options

One option to do this is adding another **calendar table**. This is possible when we assume that prices and sales transactions are using the same time granularity, for example, a price per month that applies to every monthly sales transaction in our sales fact table. In that case, the relationship is very easy as we can use a single calendar table with a by-month granularity.

In our case (which is generally a common one), we have a price table with only one price for the current year that applies to all transactions in the business year. We can't create a relationship between the sales and price tables using the existing calendar table as we would only get the price for one single date of the year (1st January), which is used in the price table. Theoretically, we could overcome this with DAX calculations, but this is not trivial. A calendar table (or tables) is essential to establish the relationship between the sales and price tables. It enables the use of **time intelligence calculations**, such as computing **prior period** (**PP**) values. We can either create a calendar table in Power Query, for example, with a SQL query, or just use a DAX function to create a table by clicking on **Insert Table** in the **Modeling** ribbon and entering the following:

```
Calendar = Calendar(min(Sales[DimDate]), max(Sales[DimDate]))
```

This will create a calendar table with all dates between the oldest and the newest in the sales fact table.

Having no relationship between the price and the sales table would be OK if we only had prices for a single year, but in our case, we require PP details to calculate the price effects. This means we need a different approach.

One option is to add another calendar table for the price table. As our prices are managed on a yearly basis, we can easily do this by creating a table from the distinct years in our initial calendar table:

```
Year = DISTINCT('Calendar'[Year])
```

To that, we have to add an additional column with a date type so that we can use the time intelligence logic:

```
Year Date = DATE('Year'[Year],01,01)
```

So, the second calendar table will look like this:

Figure 10.1 – Second Calendar table

Now we can create the required relationships between the first Calendar table and sales, the second Year table and the Prices table, and the two calendar tables on the year level. In addition, we need to create new product dimensions so that we have a reference to products that work for both the sales and price tables. This can be done with a single DAX table function by clicking on **Insert Table** in the **Modeling** ribbon and entering the following:

```
Products = DISTINCT(Prices[DimProduct])
```

The new Products table needs to be related to the product columns in the Sales and Prices tables using the Power BI **Model view** pane.

The final result will now look like this:

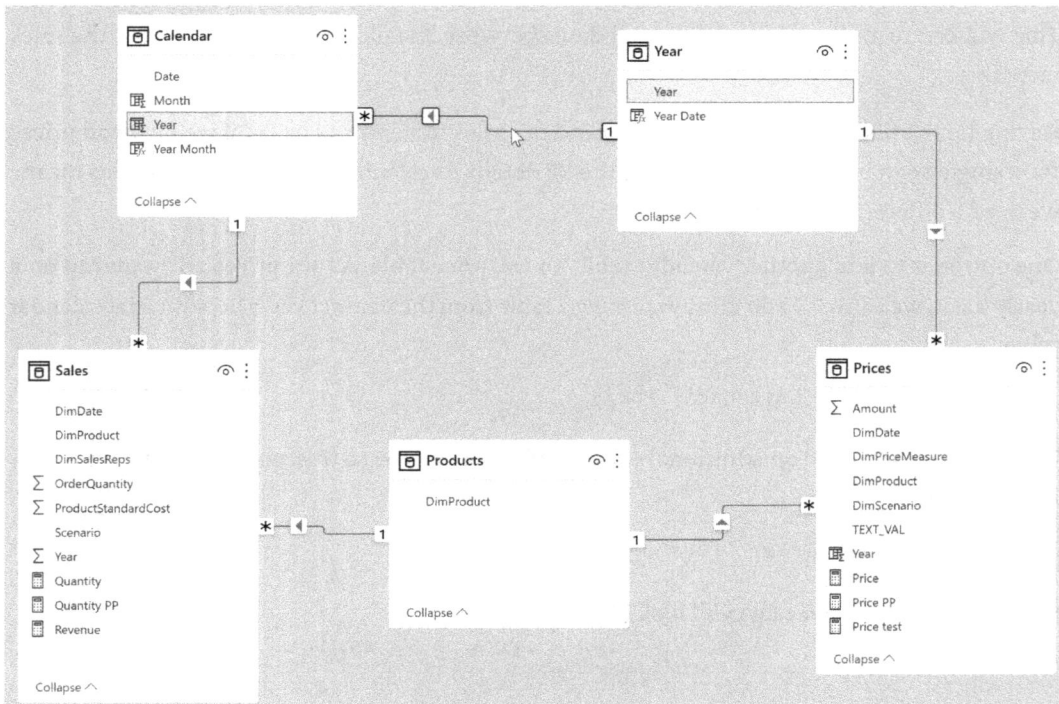

Figure 10.2 – Table relationships

Now that we have all the model components in place, we can calculate the revenue. The necessary measures here are Quantity and Price. Both are already essentially in our tables; we just need to refer to them correctly with the following:

```
Quantity = SUM(Sales[OrderQuantity])
```

We also use the following:

```
Price = AVERAGE(Prices[Amount])
```

But that is not correct as the price is not just the average of all our prices. It needs to be weighted with the quantity sold. If we sell one product for $1000 and one hundred products for $2, the average price is $501 ($1000+$2/2) but that is not correct as it doesn't add up when you multiply the units sold times the average price: 101*501 = $50601. The correct weighted-average price is the total amount sold divided by the units, that is, 1200/101 = $11.8.

So, we first need to first calculate the Revenue. This calculation needs to be a row-level calculation as we only want to calculate revenues on the lowest level. It would make no sense to add up prices and use a total – for example, prices of two periods added up – in revenue calculations for summary hierarchy levels such as a total year. Using a general formula that applies to all levels would result in wrong results as we can't use aggregated prices, as mentioned. So, we need to use a SUMX() formula:

```
Revenue = SUMX(Sales,[Quantity]*Prices[Price])
```

After that we can calculate the weighted average price as:

```
Weighted Avg Price Sold = DIVIDE ( [Revenue], [Quantity] )
```

Now, we can check the calculation outcomes with a Power BI Matrix visual table report and see that the results are correct:

Figure 10.3 – Price Volume Mix report

In addition to the **current period** (**CP**) measures, we also need the PP (in our case, a year) for the coming PVM calculations. With our model properly defined, we can easily do this by using the following formula for the PP quantity:

```
Quantity PP = CALCULATE([Quantity],ALL('Calendar'),ALL('Year'),DATEADD('Ca
lendar'[Date],-1,YEAR))
```

We use the following formula for PP prices:

```
Price PP = CALCULATE(Prices[Price],all('Year'),DATEADD('Year'[Year Date],-
1, YEAR))
```

For visualization purposes at the end, and to control our calculation, it is also useful to calculate the revenue of the previous year. This can be done by calculating price x quantity over the products table:

```
Revenue PP = SUMX(VALUES(Prcducts[DimProduct]),Prices[Price PP]*[Quantity
PP])
```

With the necessary time period parts defined, we can now look at the actual variance calculation.

Adding the PVM logic

Now that we have all the ingredients in place, we can add the PVM logic that calculates the variance with the following calculations.

Price effect

The price effect calculates the monetary impact of changes in price between the two periods. We can calculate this with the price difference between the CP and the PP multiplied by the volume:

```
Price Effect = (Price CP - Price PP) * Quantity
```

In DAX, this is expressed as follows:

```
Price Effect = IF([Price PP]<>blank(),SUMX(Products,(Prices[Price]-[Price
PP])*[Quantity]), blank())
```

This calculation checks that the PP is not blank and calculates the previously mentioned price effect only on the base level (using SUMX()). For summary calculations, for example, quarters, the normal dimension hierarchy logic applies.

Mix effect

Mix effect calculates the impact of changes in products sold, for instance, answering the question: Have I sold more higher-priced products than in the previous period?

The formula for the effect is as follows:

```
MIX Effect   = Quantity Mix Change * (Price PP - AVG Price PP)
```

The quantity mix change is the difference between the share of total product quantity sales in the CP and the PP.

This is a relatively simple calculation in Power BI:

```
Mix Change = [Mix]-[Mix PP]
```

The first part is as follows:

```
Mix = DIVIDE([Quantity],[Total Quantity])
```

The second part is as follows:

```
Mix PP = DIVIDE([Quantity PP],[Total Quantity PP])
```

The mix effect requires the average price across all products of the PP. We need to calculate this by dividing the total revenue by the total quantity. The average across just the price of all products would be wrong as this does not consider the weighting of items; for example, a single item sold of a highly priced product would skew the calculation. We want this average price to be consistent across all products, so we need to add an ALL() function:

```
Average Price PP = CALCULATE([Average Price], ALLProducts),ALL
('Calendar'),DATEADD('Calendar'[Date],-1, YEAR))
```

The final calculation is just the combination of all the preceding parts:

```
Mix Effect = SUMX(Products,[Mix Change]*(Prices[Price PP]-[Average Price
PP]))
```

Volume effect

The volume effect calculates the difference in quantity between the periods multiplied by the average price in the previous period:

```
Volume Effect = SUMX(Products,([Quantity]- [Quantity PP]) * [Average Price
PP])
```

This will give you the correct calculation on the total product level. It gets a little bit more complicated if you want to show the correct results on the single product level. For that, you can add an additional part that calculates the difference between Price PP and Average Price PP times this year's quantity at PP mix minus PP quantity. My thanks go out to Andre Fomin from Obvience, who developed this addition:

```
Volume Effect = SUMX(VALUES(Products),([Quantity]- [Quantity PP]) *
[Average Price PP])
```

We can now add the three effect measures to the table visual in the report. I have also added a simple bar chart for visualizing the total effects:

Price Volume Mix

Year DimProduct	Revenue PP	Quantity	Price Effect	Volume Effect	Mix Effect	Revenue
AWC Logo Cap (223)	41,541.19	493	11,518.45	-213,275.64	6.33	38,394.84
Bike Wash - Dissolver (484)	1,399.62	1763	-758.23	802,360.41	-6.34	2,527.44
Cable Lock (447)	8,370.27	1763	-1,786.32	802,360.41	-6.26	17,863.19
Classic Vest, L (473)	8,072.06	455	-814.00	-235,475.34	6.93	4,070.02
Cone-Shaped Race (178)	1,750,320.00	2553	-306,360.00	96,727.24	1.07	1,531,800.00
Cup-Shaped Race (177-A)	115,043.23	1605	0.00	-251,332.26	12.43	96,068.88
Headlights - Dual-Beam (451)	2,577.49	452	357.59	71,356.16	0.99	3,575.90
Headlights - Weatherproof (452)	128,510.00	452	34,804.00	71,356.16	0.55	195,264.00
Hitch Rack - 4-Bike (483)	62,416.00	455	244,790.00	-235,475.34	6.29	282,555.00
HL Mountain Rear Wheel (421-A)	38,568.29	2913	-10,034.78	830,110.02	-0.77	50,173.91
HL Road Pedal (547)	1,202.88	452	166.88	71,356.16	1.00	1,668.83
HL Road Rear Wheel (424)	54,413.69	452	-15,678.91	71,356.16	0.81	52,263.04
HL Road Tire (540)	3,750.95	452	-780.59	71,356.16	0.99	3,902.93
Total	**40,044,142.71**	**77591**	**1,057,374.00**	**21,038,175.25**	**3.81**	**62,208,820.97**

Revenue PP, Volume Effect, Price Effect, Mix Effect and Revenue

Figure 10.4 – Final PVM report

Summary

In this chapter, we have covered the necessary modeling steps and DAX calculations for variance calculations, such as price volume and mix effects. We see that Power BI is perfectly suited to calculation options that are relatively easy to implement and provides an unparalleled breadth of interactive alternatives to visualize the effects. As already covered in previous chapters, the ease and suitability of the outcome depend on choosing the right data model approach that splits and structures tables connected with the appropriate relationships. Additional options for effect calculations could include foreign exchange, gross margin, and others that follow similar patterns to the ones described.

Moving forward, we will cover options for implementing write-back and planning with Power BI.

Get This Book's PDF Version and Exclusive Extras

UNLOCK NOW

Scan the QR code (or go to packtpub.com/unlock). Search for this book by name, confirm the edition, and then follow the steps on the page.

Note: Keep your invoice handy. Purchases made directly from Packt don't require one.

Part 4

Planning and Forecasting

In this final section of the book, we turn from descriptive reporting to the forward-looking side of finance—building models that not only capture what has happened but also enable users to plan for what could happen in the future. In the final two chapters (13 and 14), we cover how to use advanced analytics, machine learning, and large language models (LLMs) for financial applications in Power BI.

This part of the book includes the following chapters:

- *Chapter 11, Write-Back Options in Power BI*
- *Chapter 12, Case Study – Planning Model*
- *Chapter 13, Advanced Analytics and Machine Learning*
- *Chapter 14, Using Language Models and Copilot in Power BI to Improve Financial Analysis*

11

Write-Back Options in Power BI

Data entry and write-back are key aspects in financial processes like planning, forecasting, and budgeting. Out of the box, Power BI doesn't offer any write-back capabilities apart from a very basic option in Power BI Desktop with the **Enter data** feature. This, though, only allows report creators in Power BI Desktop to create simple tables with no options for end users to change them. Equally, core planning features such as data entry on aggregated levels and collaboration options like commenting are not possible without additional third-party solutions in Power BI.

Write-back allows any users to make changes to write-enabled data sources in any Power BI frontend (Desktop or the service) and have those changes reflected in the reports and dashboards they create in real time. This is the foundation for many typical financial processes, including the following:

- **Collecting planning assumptions**: Enable global subsidiaries to enter/update their plans with immediate insights into the implications for the group as a whole
- **Workflow approvals**: Enable users to approve, reject, and comment on forecasts, budgets, or operational plans that have been submitted
- **Commentary and collaboration**: Capture narrative explanations (commentary) alongside numeric values
- **Operational planning updates**: Allow teams to update operational KPIs (e.g., production volumes, marketing spend, and staffing levels) and instantly see the impact
- **Forecast rolling updates**: Let users continuously update forecasts (rolling forecasts)
- **Master data management**: Allow decentralized updates of master data attributes (e.g., product groupings and customer classifications) directly within reports

- **Initiating new elements or entities**: Create new records, such as new products, customers, projects, or cost centers, inside the reporting environment
- **Task and issue tracking**: Users can log action items, deadlines, and statuses tied to planning or performance metrics
- **Risk and opportunity capture**: Capture/update identified risks or opportunities
- **Driver simulations**: Enable real-time adjustments of planning model drivers (e.g., price, volume, foreign exchange rates, etc.) for reforecasting

In this chapter, we'll cover how to facilitate write-back with the following topics:

- An overview of what write-back options exist in Power BI
- Write-back with Acterys/Dynamics BPP introduction
- Administrating the solution
- Different write-back options with Acterys/Dynamics BPP
- Setting up a test environment

Technical requirements

This chapter only requires a web browser to set up the Acterys trial.

Write-back options

As mentioned in the introduction, the built-in options for write-back in Power BI are very limited, with no options for non-report creators to enter/edit data. The only way to add write-back that caters to financial purposes is commercial third-party offerings. Microsoft offers a (separately licensable) solution to collect data with **Power Apps**. Power Apps is normally a standalone solution that runs in a web browser or mobile app, but there is a visual supplied by Microsoft that enables you to run Power Apps applications in Power BI. This is useful if you need to collect a limited number of inputs, but doesn't cater for entry in tables and other typically required planning features like top-down distributions.

The lack of a write-back solution for finance users inspired me and my team to come up with a solution for it. Having personally worked in the corporate planning space for more than two decades, we developed an add-on solution for Power BI that enables complex enterprise-wide planning scenarios for large user numbers in conjunction with the unparalleled analytics components in Power BI. The result of this is the Acterys ecosystem developed by Managility.

In 2023, Microsoft licensed the Acterys solution to form the basis of a new, optional, extended planning and analytics module, that is, Dynamics **business performance planning (BPP)**, alongside their Dynamics 365 offering.

Both the generic Acterys version and Dynamics BPP are commercial offerings that are not part of Power BI and have to be licensed separately. For further details, please refer to the Acterys website (https://acterys.com) or https://learn.microsoft.com/en-us/shows/dynamics-365-fasttrack-architecture-insights/business-performance-planning for the Dynamics version.

There are other solutions by commercial third-party providers that also offer some planning aspects in Power BI, but given my bias and as it is now the official platform of Microsoft's offering, I will only cover the Acterys option.

Acterys/Dynamics BPP introduction

Acterys is an integrated ecosystem that covers three core requirements, as shown in *Figure 11.1*:

- Automated data integrations from financial ERP systems and others
- A planning engine that manages the write-back process and is administered through the Acterys Modeller web application or Microsoft BPP
- A variety of frontend options to enable users to write back and participate in planning processes, either through Power BI visuals or Excel add-ins

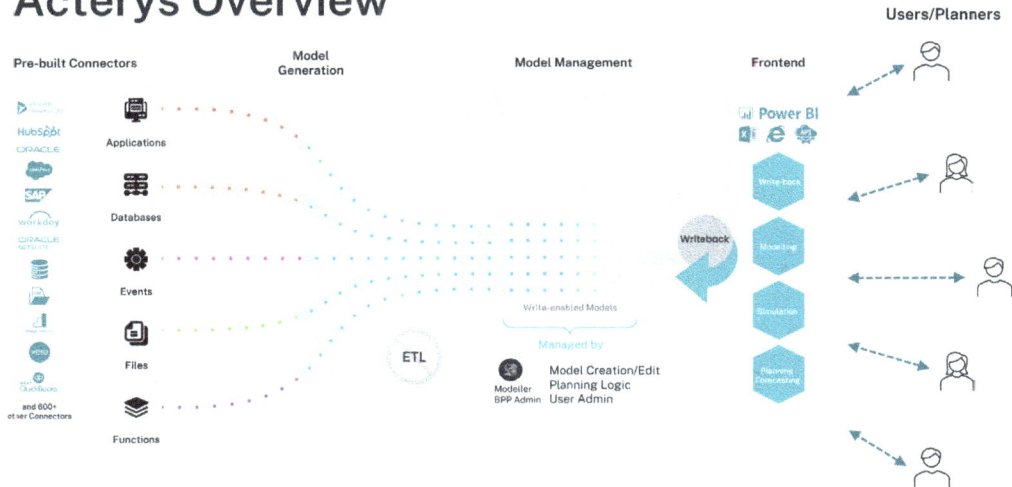

Figure 11.1 – Acterys overview

The core objectives of the solution set are to enable business users without in-depth IT skills to do the following:

- Automatically create Power BI models for the major accounting, CRM, HR, and billing SaaS solutions, including multi-company consolidation and group reporting, as well as best practice, interactive performance management dashboards in Power BI.

- Add and edit models or tables (e.g., account mappings, adding new products for simulation, etc.) from their existing sources, and add write-back and planning capabilities that automatically incorporate best practice modeling principles covered in this book.

- Access and design frontend options for advanced planning use cases that are then directly available in Power BI and Excel/Excel Online. The planning features include a very comprehensive set of entry options from top-down, bottom-up changes, and rolling forecasts, to a variety of specialized financial requirements such as integrated/three-way **profit and loss** (**P&L**), balance sheet, cash flow, sales, HR, and driver-based planning.

Acterys planning engine

At the heart of the suite is the **Acterys planning engine**, an add-on component to **Microsoft SQL Server/Azure SQL**, which is specifically designed to handle large-scale write-back and planning tasks, even when faced with a large number of concurrent users.

The engine offers a diverse range of entry and planning logic options, catering to various needs such as top-down and bottom-up approaches, as well as intricate financial requirements such as **integrated business planning** (**IBP**) scenarios. These scenarios can seamlessly merge different detailed models, such as the interplay between sales and financial data or multiple financial statements, such as *Income*, *Balance Sheet*, and *Cash Flow*.

The engine always takes into consideration the user's rights to read and write transactions that can be defined on any level of the model, including more advanced conditional access logic constraints. Additionally, users are empowered to construct and modify all aspects of their data model, granting them full control over their planning processes.

When users enter data, for example, plan values or edit structures by changing how financial accounts are mapped, they modify data in a standard Microsoft SQL Server write-back table. This is either part of an Acterys model that has been created automatically from a specific source, such as Dynamics 365 (Dynamics xP&A), Xero, and other systems, or from a table that has been added from a generic source, such as any table in Power BI.

Typically, the Acterys planning engine is a cloud-based component that comes bundled with every Acterys/BPP subscription. However, it can also be installed on-premises as an extension, working seamlessly in conjunction with various SQL Server components, such as RDBMS (relational engine), SSAS (Analysis Services), SSIS (Integration Services), and Power Platform offerings (Power BI, Power Automate, and Power Apps).

Acterys models/write-back tables

The planning engine generates and works with Acterys model tables (`https://acterys.com/videos/acterys-training-module-2-the-acterys-data-model/`) that are based on a best practice relational star schema model, which is similar to the optimal approach in Power BI that we introduced in *Chapter 1*. It consists of *dimensions* (dimension tables) that define the structure and *cubes* (relational transaction tables) where data records are stored, as shown in *Figure 11.2*:

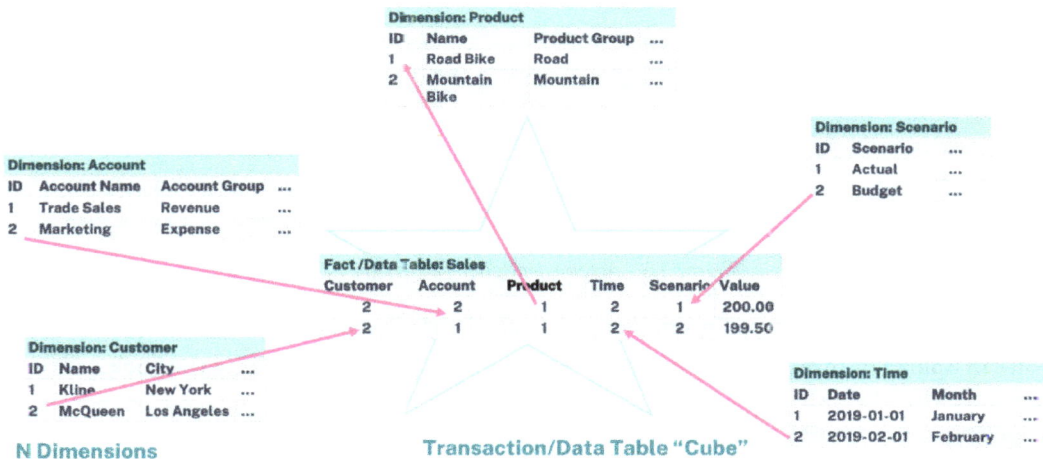

Figure 11.2 – Sample Acterys model

Dimensions

Dimensions in Acterys are relational tables that contain the structure details of your data model, for example, time periods, scenarios, products, customers, organizational entities, and so on, as described in *Chapter 1*. Acterys gives you full flexibility to use as many dimensions as you like for your data model. A dimension consists of one or more columns; for example, a time dimension could contain the date, month name, year, and so on. These columns can then be used in the analysis to create hierarchical structures, such as a drill-down path from *Year* to *Quarter* and date.

In Acterys, every dimension contains at least the ID column, which uniquely defines the element, and the Name column, which is the description of this element. In addition to that, users can add as many additional columns as they like:

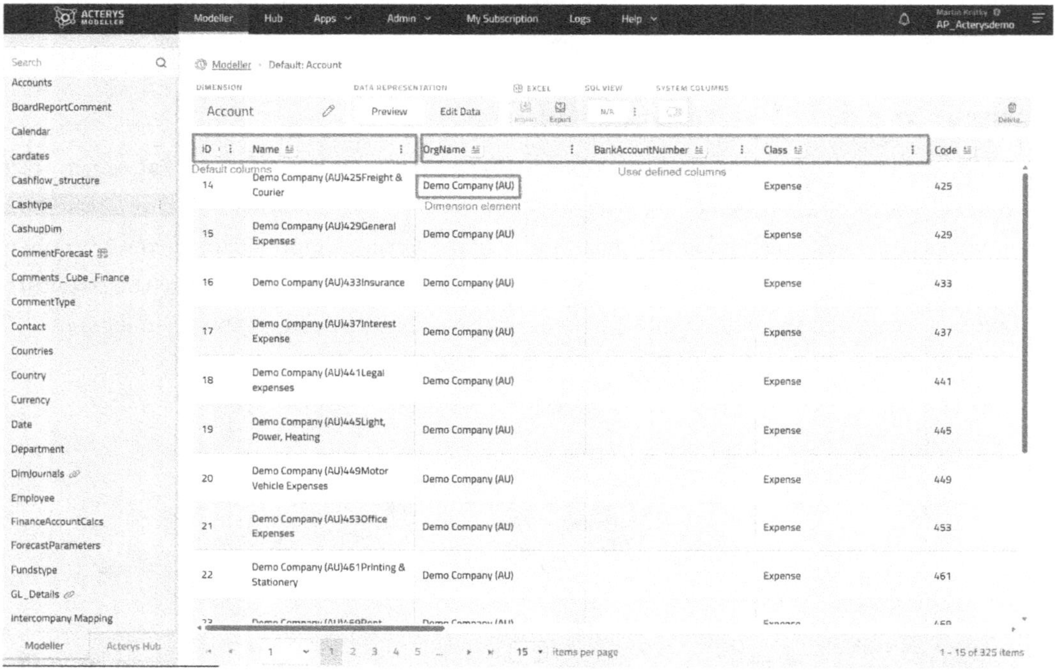

Figure 11.3 – Acterys Modeller dimension view

A dimension can also be used for simple write-back models that only consist of a single table that you can upload from any source, as also covered in the practical examples in the book.

Cubes

Cube is the term for the actual storage container (database table) that contains the data/transaction records of the model. It is defined as a collection of dimension tables, structured in a star schema optimized for analytical purposes and for minimizing query times. You can use the same dimensions in different cubes.

Think carefully about the structure of your cube, as the dimensions used in the cube can't be changed subsequently. If it turns out that you need additional dimensions or need to change the dimensions used, the only way to do this is to create a new cube and import the data from the old cube to the new structure.

In the following screenshot, we can see a cube named **Finance** that uses five dimensions (DimAccount, DimDate, DimDepartmentGroup, DimOrganization, and DimScenario):

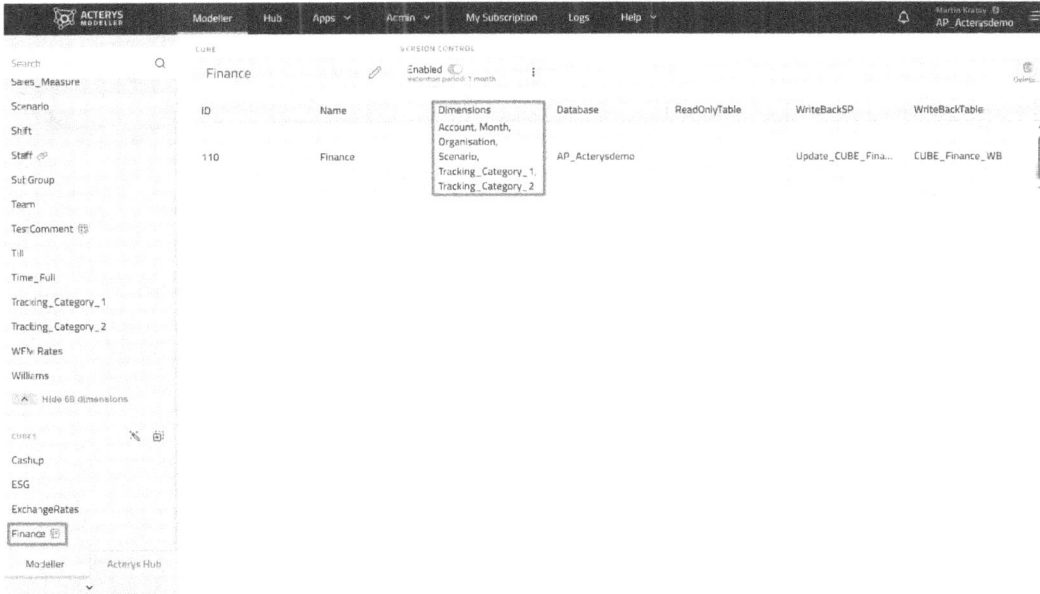

Figure 11.4 – Cube details in Acterys Modeller

The data in the cube is defined by an element of every dimension used and the respective value for that coordinate.

The data in the Acterys model (dimensions/cubes) can be accessed via different frontend options:

- **Power BI**: Using the Acterys visuals: Acterys Matrix, Acterys Comments, Acterys Visual Planning, and Acterys Table Edit, available in Power BI or Microsoft AppSource
- **Excel**: With the Acterys Excel add-ins that can be installed from the **Download** section in the Acterys Modeller (VSTO version) or directly from Excel in the **Add-ins** area (Excel Online version)

In this section, we have covered how Acterys/Dynamics BPP manages write-back tables/multi-dimensional cubes. In the next section, we will look at Acterys Modeller, a web-based application that enables you to manage all aspects of your planning model.

Administering write-back with Acterys Modeller

The administration aspects of the Acterys write-back models are managed in central applications. The first option is Acterys Modeller, a web (or on-premises installed in a company network) browser-based application, as shown in *Figure 11.5*.

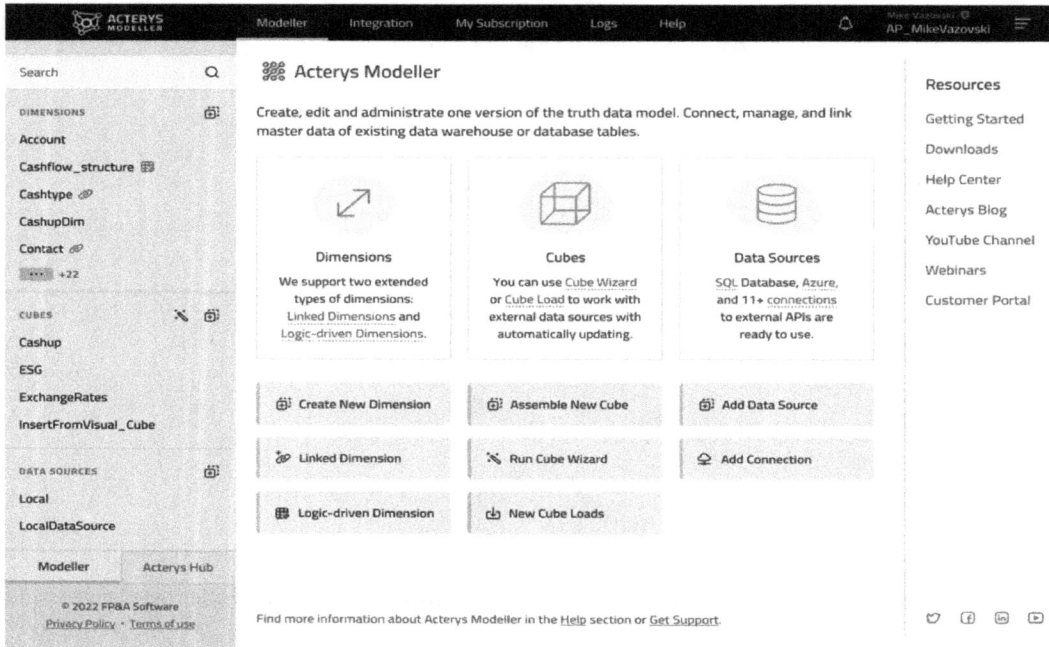

Figure 11.5 – Acterys Modeller home screen

The second setup option is an add-on to Microsoft Dynamics BPP, as presented in *Figure 11.6*.

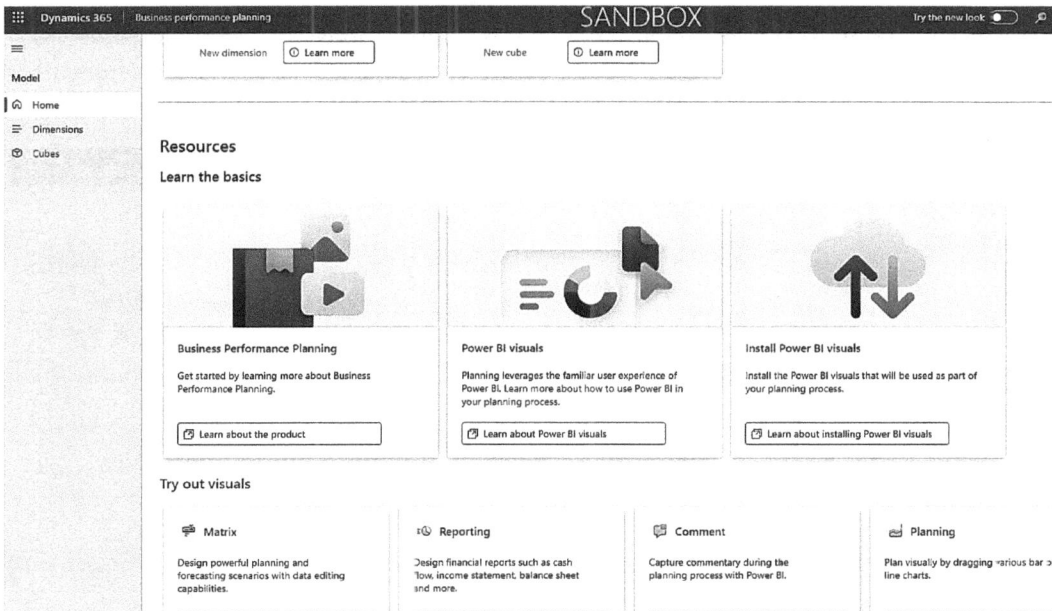

Figure 11.6 – Microsoft BPP administration

In these environments, Power users and administrators can control all aspects of their models/tables, analytical applications/planning logic, and workflows in a single environment. This includes the following:

- Automated model generation (optimal RDBMS star schema plus Power BI/Tabular) for a variety of ERP, SaaS solutions, and Power BI datasets
- Business user-driven creation and editing of star schema data models (dimension and cube tables
- Management of best practice business logic, including time intelligence, FX conversions, as well as planning calculations and workflows, among others
- Effective master data management and linking of existing data warehouse or database tables
- Wizard-driven user rights administration with smart access rules, such as workflow handling (user rights according to workflow status, e.g., "Approved" can't be changed)
- Detailed audit trail of all user activities

Acterys Hub

A recent addition to Acterys Modeller is Acterys Hub. This feature enables you, as a business user, to build and populate data models from a variety of sources. You can load data from other databases, cloud-based files (Excel or CSV) into Acterys dimensions and cubes.

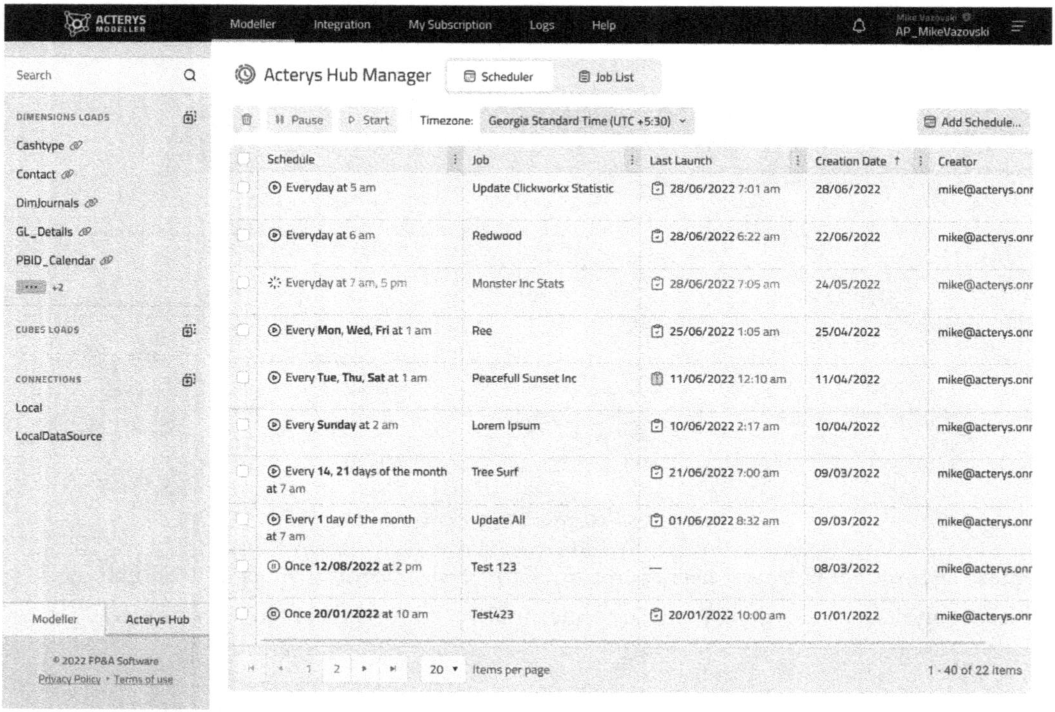

Figure 11.7 – Acterys Hub listing data integration jobs

You can also completely automate the process by setting up scheduled jobs in your required time interval that ensure that the data in your source systems and Acterys models is always up to date without any manual intervention.

Next, let's look at Acterys visuals, which are the actual interface to enable the entry of data into a table from Power BI. They support an extensive array of different write-back use cases.

Acterys visuals

Write-back in Acterys is enabled through nine different Power BI custom visuals. The following table provides an overview of the visuals and their respective planning use case and features:

Visual	Key purpose	Features	Use cases
Acterys Matrix	Multi-dimensional data entry and planning	Data entry at any level, selective expand/collapse, "Enter like" distributions, cell comments, custom calculations, conditional formatting, validation rules, dynamic cell locking, and write-back to SQL	Budgeting, forecasting, driver-based planning, and bottom-up or top-down adjustments in financial models
Acterys Comments	Rich-text or list-based commenting	Rich-text formatting, HTML link embedding, drop-down selection, and integration with the Matrix visual	Adding commentary to forecasts, documenting planning assumptions, and collecting qualitative inputs
Acterys Table Edit	Grid and form-based table editing	Bulk edit, search/filter, image handling, drill through, validations (e.g., by type or choice from list items), Unicode support, formatted text editing, and grouping	Managing master data (products and cost centers), mass updates to table/dimension records, administrative data entry, and risk management classifications
Acterys Variance	Variance and forecasting visualization	KPI cards with absolute/relative/waterfall variance, drag-to-forecast, zooming, drill down, small multiples, and write-back	Analyzing plan vs. actual performance, and adjusting forecasts dynamically based on real-time insights
Acterys Visual Planning	Visual data entry via dragging in charts	Planning via drag/drop in bar, column, line charts, locking, totals/variance display, and drill down	Interactive scenario planning, visual target setting, and reallocation of budgets across categories

Visual	Key purpose	Features	Use cases
Acterys Copy	Scenario and model data copy	Copy data at any granularity across scenarios/models	Rolling forward historical data for new budgets, and setting baseline versions for scenario comparisons
Acterys Reporting	Advanced financial reporting per IBCS	Custom row/column calcs, rich formatting, data-driven styles, variance visualization, and row/cell comments	Financial statement reporting, management dashboards, and variance reporting in board packs
Acterys Gantt	Project management in Power BI	Task hierarchy display, editing, resource assignment, and progress tracking	Planning and managing project timelines, resource allocations, and tracking project deliverables
Acterys Smart XL (not available in Dynamics BPP)	Excel-like planning and reporting in Power BI	Dynamic cell-based reporting, formulas, real-time database integration, and master data management	Migrating Excel-based plans into Power BI, handling complex custom planning forms that require cell-based handling and can't be realized with a standard matrix/pivot format, and editing large datasets collaboratively

Table 11.1 – Acterys visuals: features and use cases

As a general principle, the Acterys/BPP custom visuals can be added to your report from the Microsoft App Store. Following that, you can configure the required write-back tables and a variety of formatting and process options.

The following figure shows three widely used Acterys/BPP visuals (Matrix, Table, and Comment) that are used as part of a planning form, which includes the main pivot table for data entry, a status view, and workflow management option:

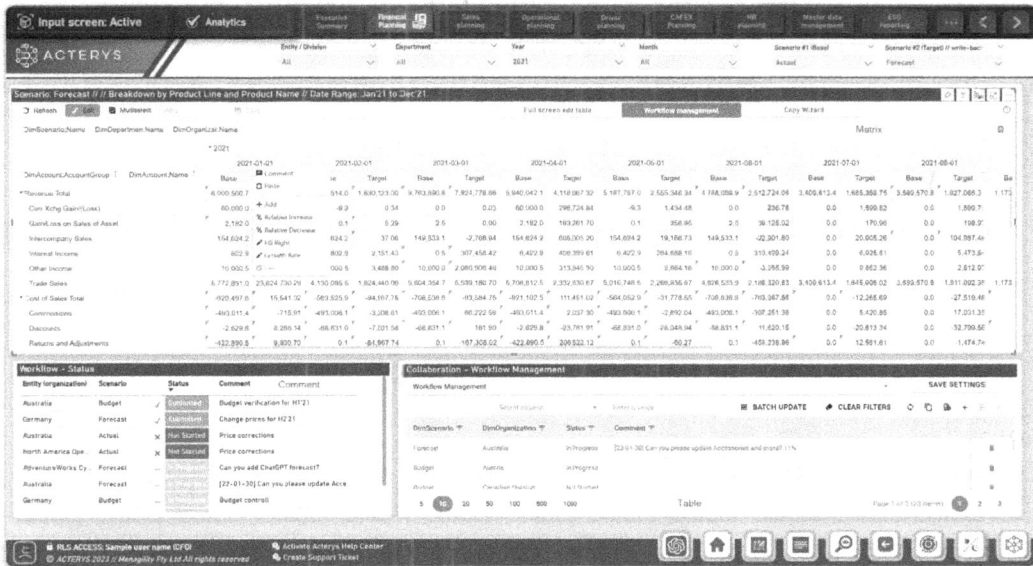

Figure 11.8 – Power BI sample report with Matrix, Comment, and Table visuals

We will cover details on how to configure and use the visuals in an end-to-end case study that includes the most used visuals in *Chapter 12*.

Excel add-ins

In addition to options from Power BI, both Acterys and Dynamics BPP also include Excel add-ins with extensive functionalities for write-back and planning:

- One is based on the traditional **Visual Studio for Office (VSTO)** platform
- The other is a cloud-deployed Office Add-in that runs in the browser and on Mac platforms, in addition to Desktop Excel

The **Acterys Excel** add-in enables users to run planning processes in conjunction with a central data model directly in their familiar, flexible spreadsheet environment. All Acterys planning features, such as top-down, bottom-up data entry, allocations, and so on, are supported in either a pivot table environment or using smart worksheet formulas. Equally, users can edit dimensions and tables with all the ease that Excel provides, such as copy/paste, drag and drop, using formulas, and so on. This is all governed by the normal Acterys user rights and governance processes.

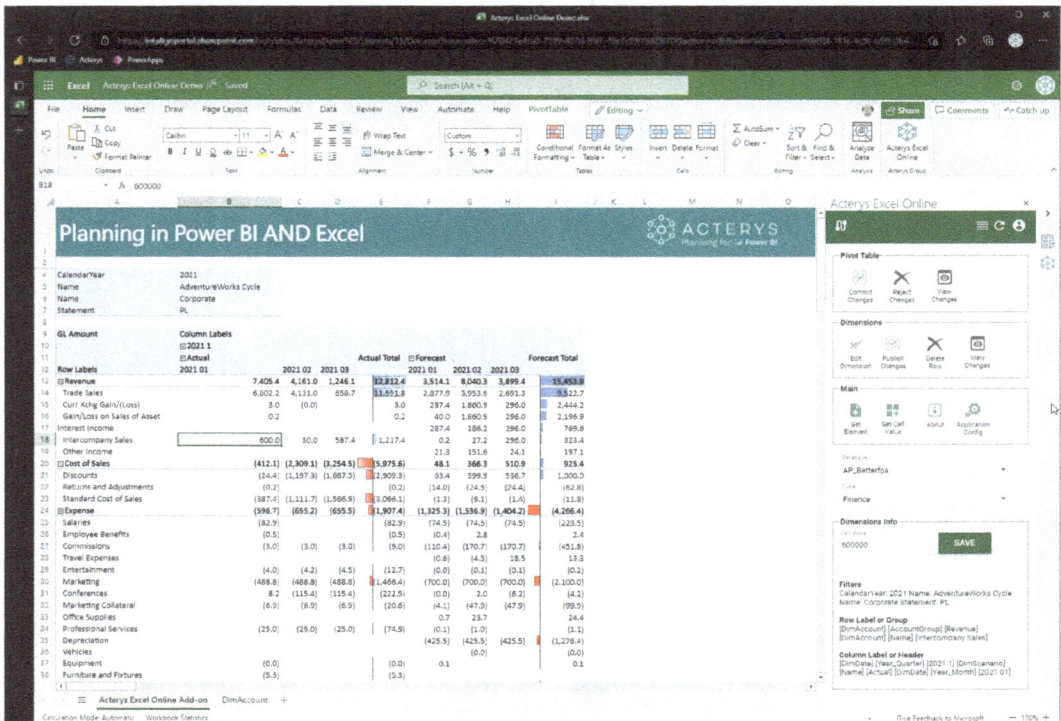

Figure 11.9 – Excel add-in sample report

In the previous sections, we covered the elements of the Acterys/BPP ecosystem. In the final section, I will take you through the necessary options to install the Acterys/BPP setup.

Setting up your sample environment

In this section, I will describe the process from setting up an initial free trial Acterys subscription that is the basis for enabling write-back in Power BI and the subsequent case study in *Chapter 12*.

Provisioning an Acterys trial subscription

Execute the following steps to initiate a trial subscription:

1. Go to https://app.acterys.com/onboarding. Complete the form with your details.

2. When asked for a database name, use a simple term without spaces.

3. Complete the rest of the steps until you get to the message that you will receive an activation email. Check your email client. Sometimes the email ends up in a spam folder. Please check there if you don't receive it within a few minutes. Once you receive the email, click on the activation link.

Your tenant will now be provisioned. This will take a few minutes. Once finished, you will receive an email with your tenant details.

When you log in for the first time, use your initial Acterys admin username and the temporary password sent to you in the email. This has to be changed subsequently to a password of your choosing in the next step.

In Acterys, Microsoft Entra ID/Microsoft password requirements apply: passwords must be at least eight characters, long and include uppercase letters, numbers, and special characters.

Initial configuration

After you have logged in for the first time, you will see the Acterys wizard that takes you through the setup steps:

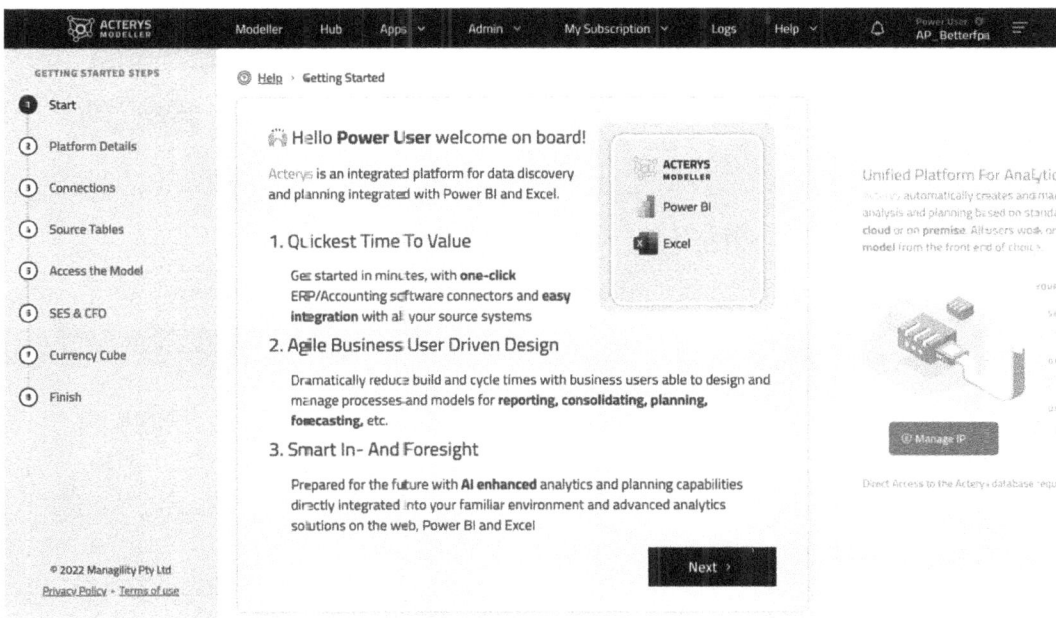

Figure 11.10 – Initial configuration

In the next step of the wizard, key elements of the environment are explained, and you can configure the following:

- Define safe IP addresses to allow access directly to the Acterys database. A step that is only relevant for administrators. Normal access for end users is provided via the Acterys API.
- Link a supported data source to provision end-to-end solutions (data model/Power BI/ Excel reports) available in the Acterys apps.

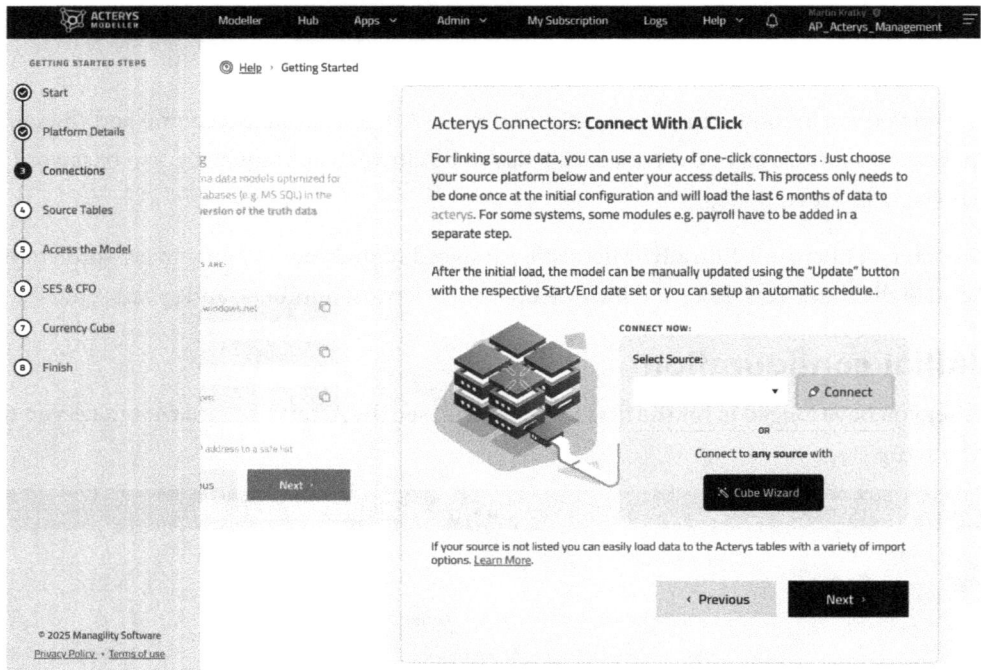

Figure 11.11 – Adding a data source for the Acterys app

- Set application parameters for the financial calendars and currency conversion.

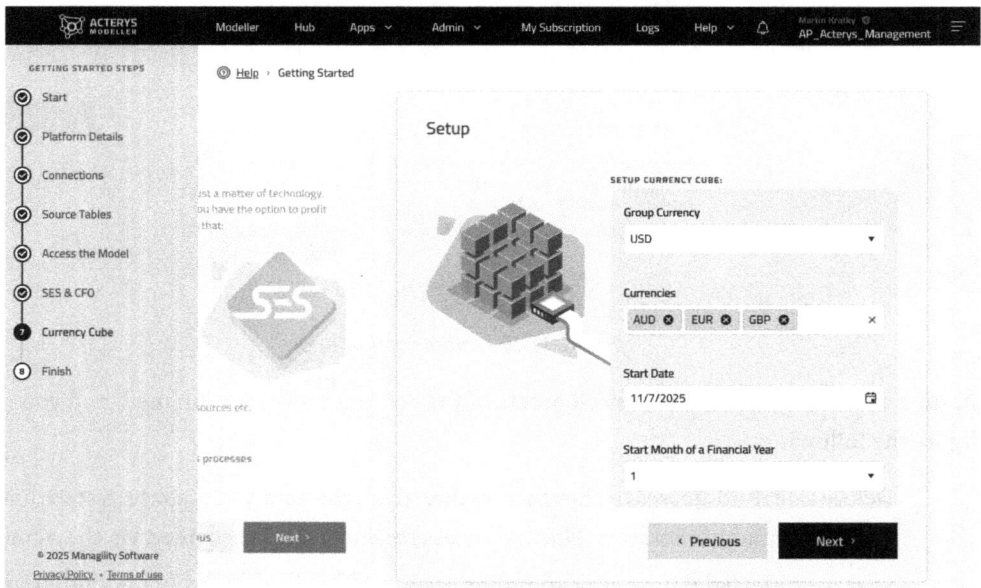

Figure 11.12 – Configuring calendar and currencies

Summary

In this chapter, we introduced the Acterys/Dynamics BPP solutions that add extensive write-back and planning options to Power BI. We also covered how to set up a trial environment and the core concepts of the data model used.

In the following chapter, we will cover how to implement a planning environment, from creating a typical financial budgeting model to finished planning forms in Power BI.

12

Case Study – Planning Model

In this chapter, we will learn how to build a planning form from start to finish. We will initially look at how to build a write-enabled star schema model in Acterys/Dynamics **Business Performance Planning (BPP)**, and following that, we will learn how to design the related planning entry form in Power BI.

In this chapter, we will cover the following main topics:

- Creating the planning model
- Accessing and planning with an Acterys model in Power BI

Technical requirements

To follow the practical examples in this chapter, you'll need the following:

- An active Acterys or Dynamics BPP license account, either as a trial or full account
- The latest version of the Edge or Chrome web browser
- The sample accounting data file, `Accounting Sample Data.xlsx`, in the book's GitHub repository: https://github.com/PacktPublishing/Power-BI-for-Finance

Creating the planning model

In this section, we cover how to create a custom planning model from scratch in Acterys/Dynamics BPP.

In Dynamics BPP, the initial planning model is automatically created for you based on your Dynamics data, so this step is not relevant there. To get started, log in to the Acterys Modeller at `https://app.acterys.com` using your Acterys account and open the Acterys Cube Wizard in the **CUBES** section on the left side pane:

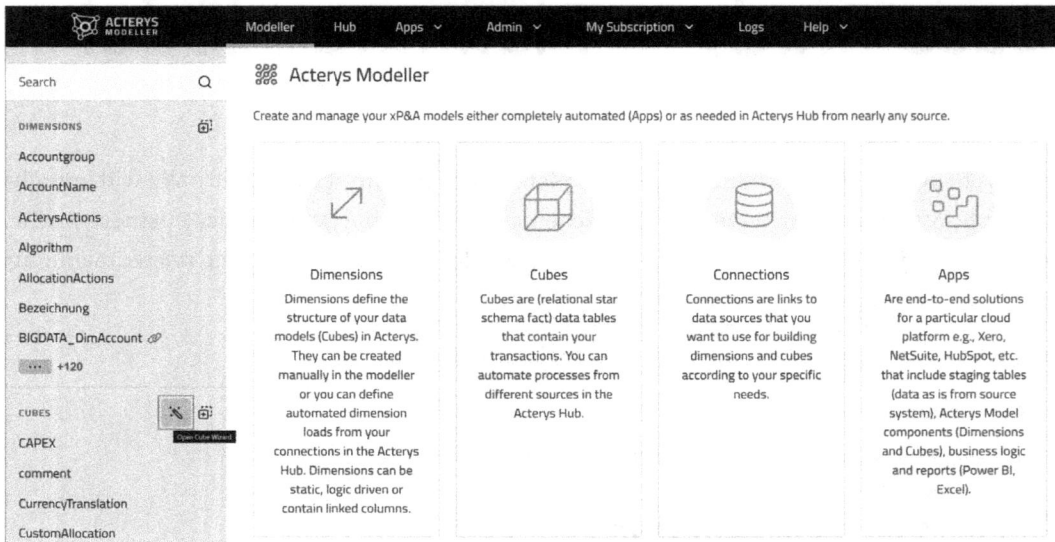

Figure 12.1 – Starting the Cube Wizard

Here, you can now point to the sample accounting data file, `Accounting Sample Data.xlsx`, from the GitHub repository with the **Choose a file** button:

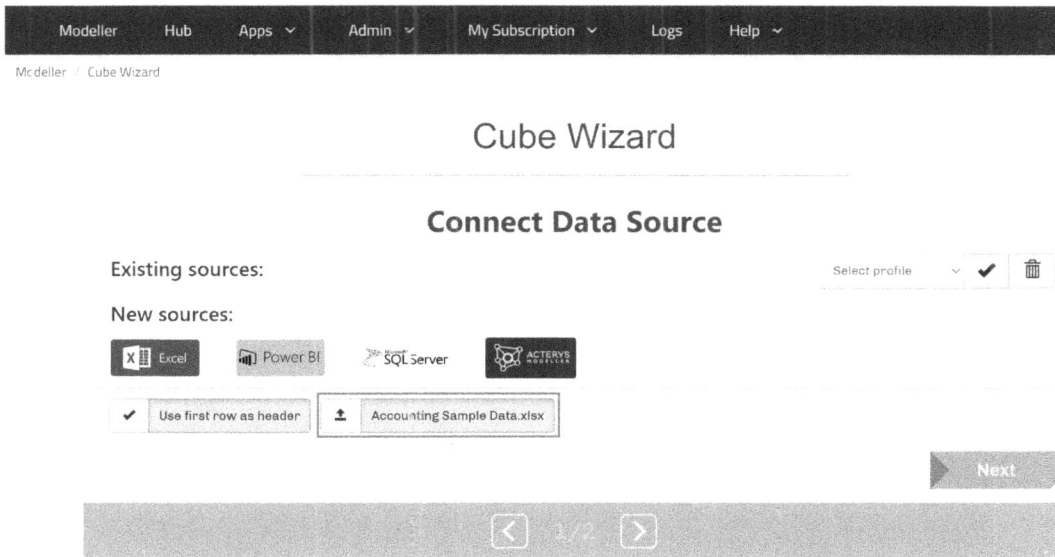

Figure 12.2 – Choosing the data source

After you have clicked on **Next**, you will see a screen to define your dimensions and cubes that shows all columns with sample records of your source file:

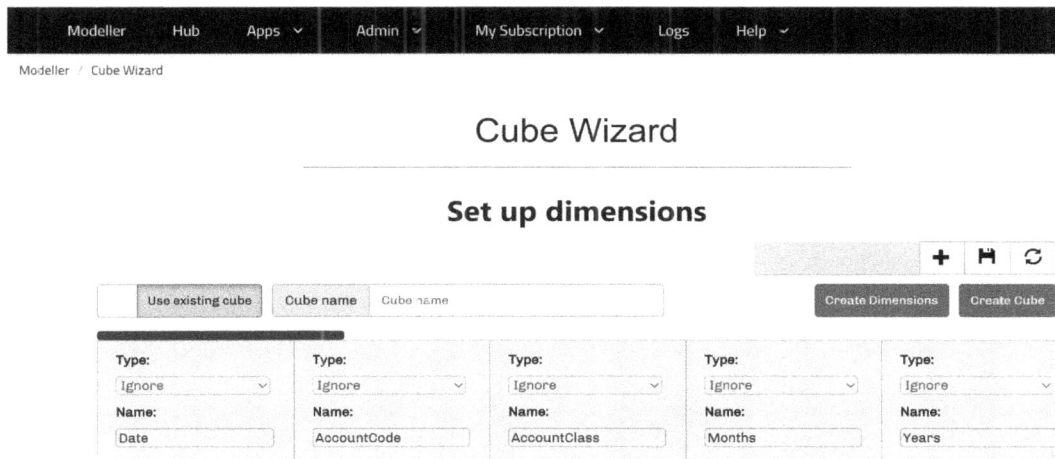

Figure 12.3 – Selecting columns to be used in dimensions

From here, we can now define the necessary dimensions by selecting the columns we want to use and assigning the required dimension type. For example, to set up a time hierarchy, we can click on the top of the first column, **Date**, and select **Time** from the **Type** dialog box. After that, we can specify the granularity (for budgeting purposes, normally **Month**) and start and end dates:

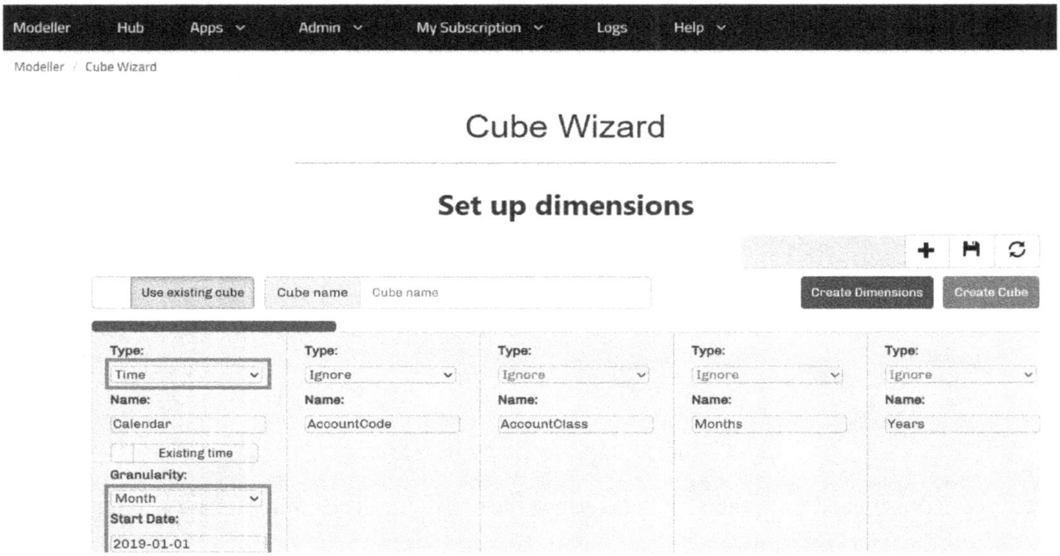

Figure 12.4 – Setting time dimension details

The start and end dates depend on your preferences. Here, we choose just the start and end of the calendar year with typically a few years ahead, so you have options to enter plan data for future periods.

The next dimension to specify is **Accounts**. With that, it is crucial to have a column with unique values that identify the account in place. This can be a challenge when you are working with data from multiple companies that might use, for example, the same account codes. In this case, you must create a new unique key in the source, such as a combination of company code/name plus account code. In our case, we already have the concatenated account key in the Accounts. Account key column. We can scroll there and specify **Type** as **Dimension** and specify the name Account for that dimension:

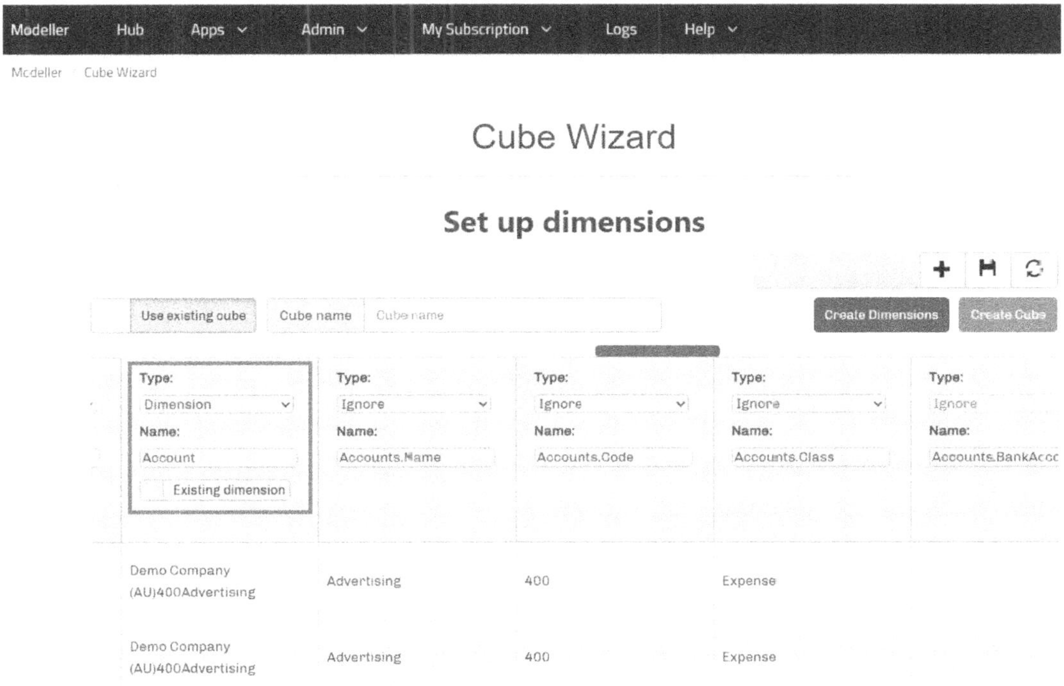

Figure 12.5 – Defining the Account dimension

This step will create the lowest level of the dimension. To add hierarchies to that dimension, we have to specify **Type** as `Attribute` and the related base column/dimension. For example, we can add the `AccountName` on its own without the key information and `AccountClass`:

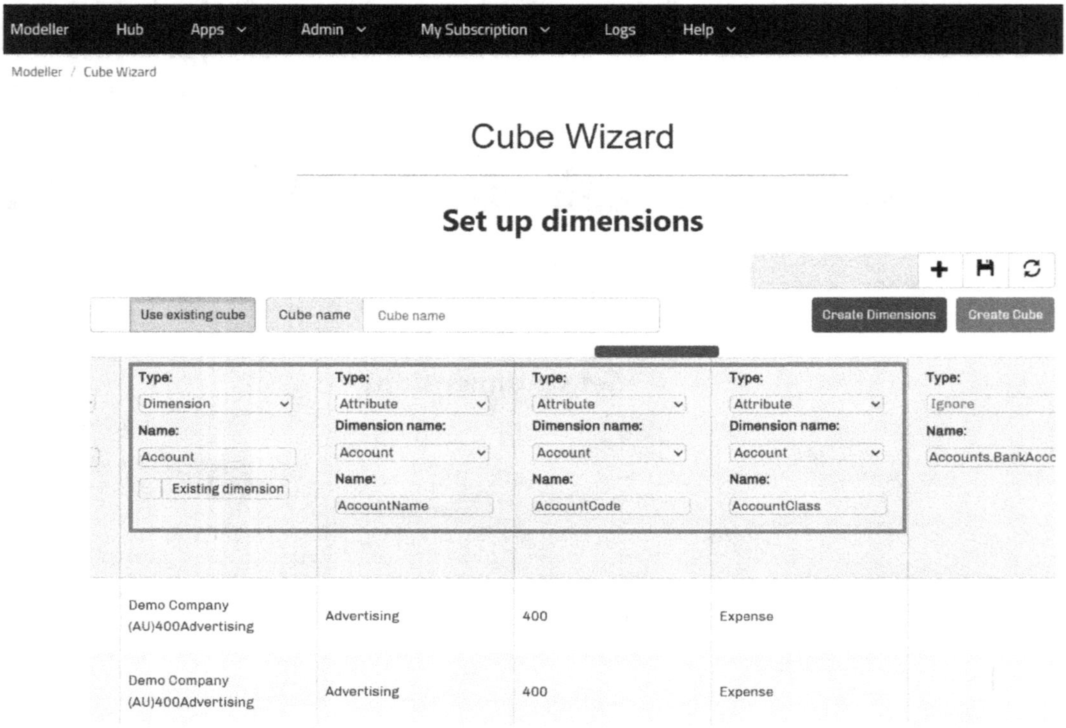

Modeller	Hub	Apps ⌄	Admin ⌄	My Subscription ⌄	Logs	Help ⌄

Modeller / Cube Wizard

Cube Wizard

Set up dimensions

Type:	Type:	Type:	Type:	Type:
Dimension ⌄	Attribute ⌄	Attribute ⌄	Attribute ⌄	Ignore
Name:	**Dimension name:**	**Dimension name:**	**Dimension name:**	**Name:**
Account	Account ⌄	Account ⌄	Account ⌄	Accounts.BankAcco
Existing dimension	**Name:**	**Name:**	**Name:**	
	AccountName	AccountCode	AccountClass	
Demo Company (AU)400Advertising	Advertising	400	Expense	
Demo Company (AU)400Advertising	Advertising	400	Expense	

Figure 12.6 – Hierarchies of the Account dimension

For our model, we add two more dimensions in the same way – Scenario and Organization:

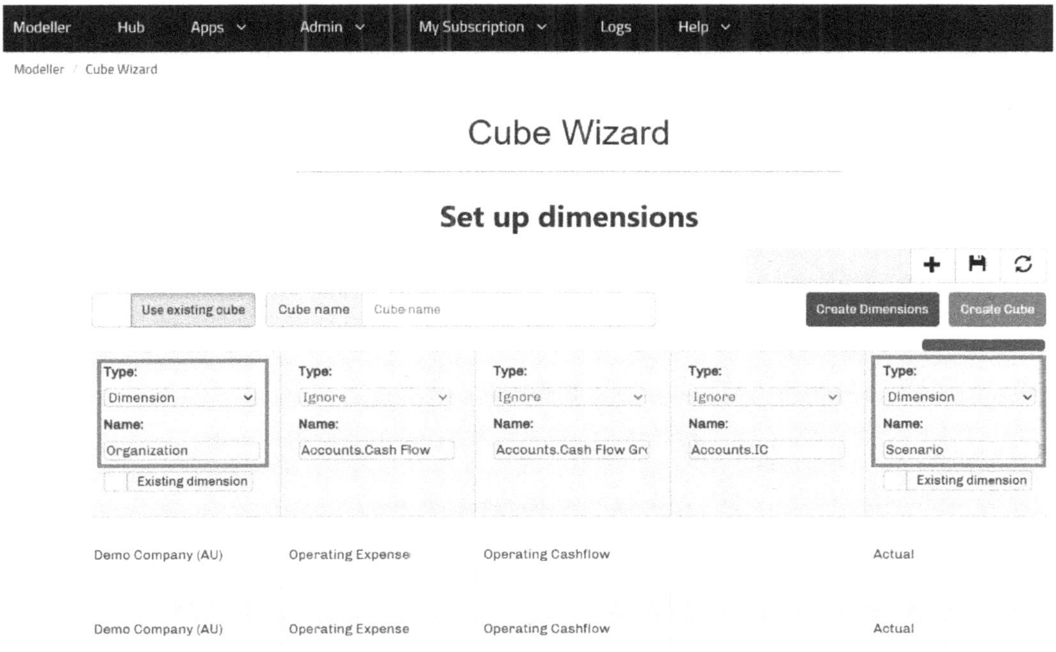

Figure 12.7 – Organization and Scenario dimension definition

The final step is to select the column that contains the actual data. In this case, we will use the transaction balance in the NetAmount_GC column:

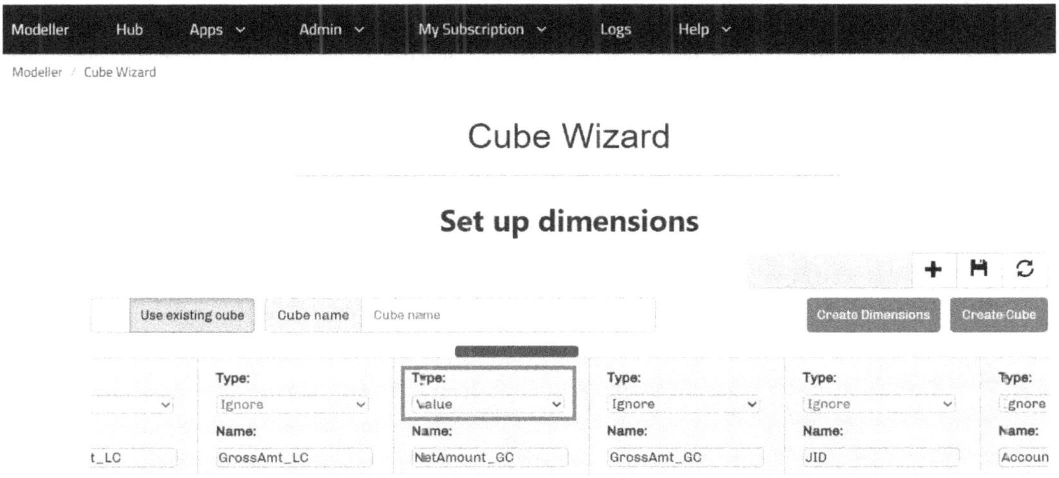

Figure 12.8 – Specification of the Value column

To create the model, we just have to specify its name (for example, Planning) and click on the **Create Cube** button:

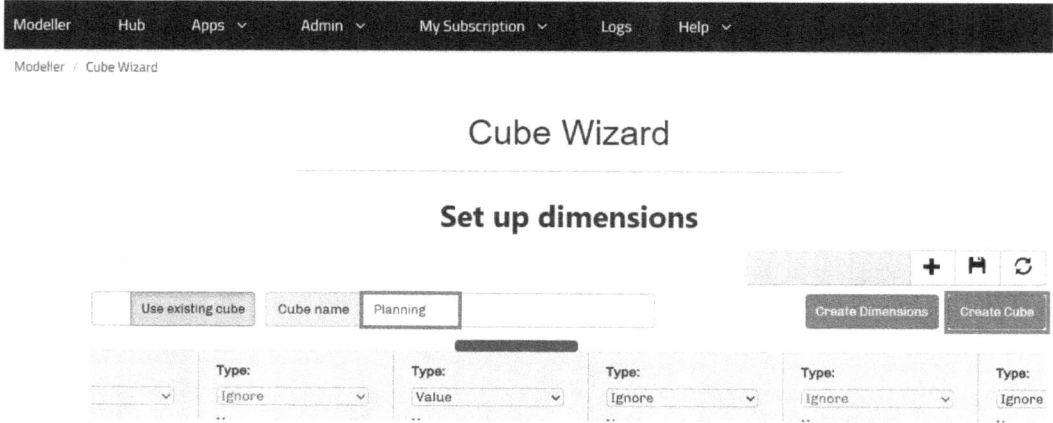

Figure 12.9 – Setting the Cube name

After this, Acterys will automatically create a star schema data model with a transaction table that contains all transactions in the import file and the related dimension tables.

Accessing and planning with an Acterys model in Power BI

Now that we have our model, we just need to connect to it from Power BI and configure the required Acterys custom visuals:

1. Open Power BI Desktop, create a new report, and choose **Get Data**. This will present the following screen:

Get Data

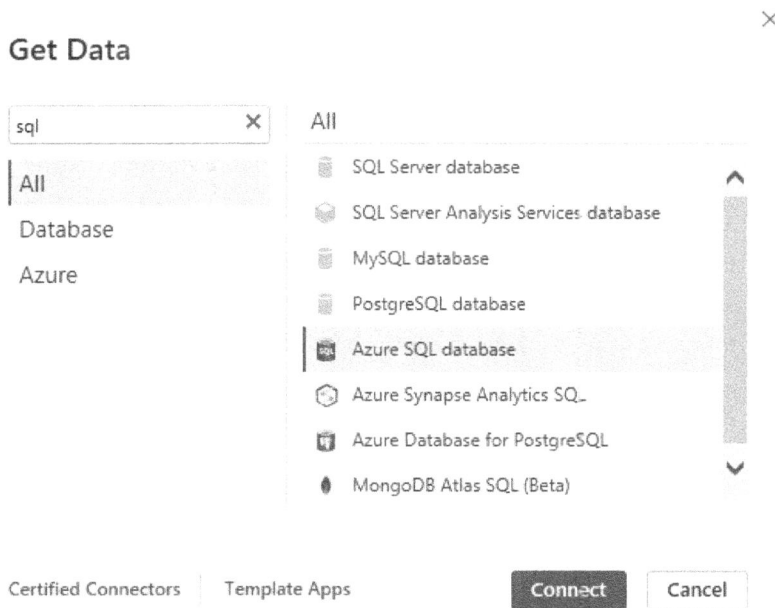

Figure 12.10 – Choosing the Azure SQL data source

2. Add a new Azure/SQL Server data source by specifying your Acterys database details:

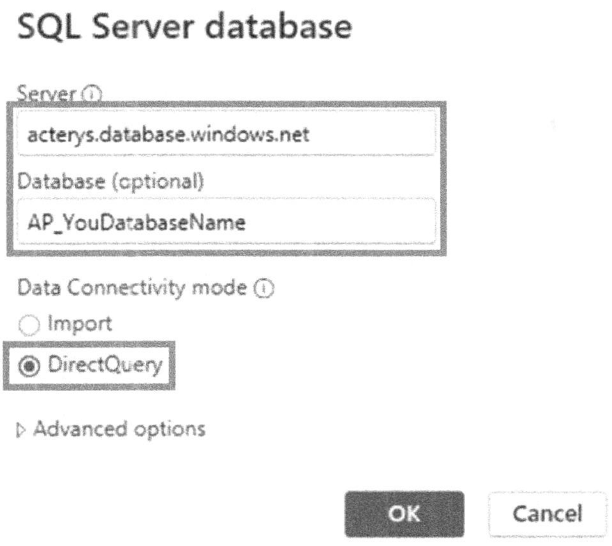

Figure 12.11 – Setting Database details

Fill the respective fields with the following details:

- **Server name**: `acterys.database.windows.net` (this is the default, but that could be different if you are using a dedicated regional data center or your own)
- **Database name**: Your Acterys database name starting with `AP_`
- **Connectivity mode**: Make sure **DirectQuery** is selected

3. Log in with your Acterys user with admin rights and password. Make sure the machine IP where you are logging on from is on the **Safe List** in Acterys (to add your IP, use **Safe IP** in the Acterys Modeller **Admin** menu and click on the **Add New IP** button).

4. Following that, you will see a dialog box with the tables in your Acterys Azure SQL database that contain the transaction/cube tables with the `OLAP.CUBE_` prefix and `_WB` (write-back) suffix, as well as the dimension tables with the `OLAP.` prefix. All tables will use the schema **Online Analytical Processing (OLAP)**.

Here, you can now select the `OLAP.Planning_WB` cube table that we have just created and click on the **Select Related Tables** button at the bottom of the dialog box. This will automatically add all the dimensions for this cube.

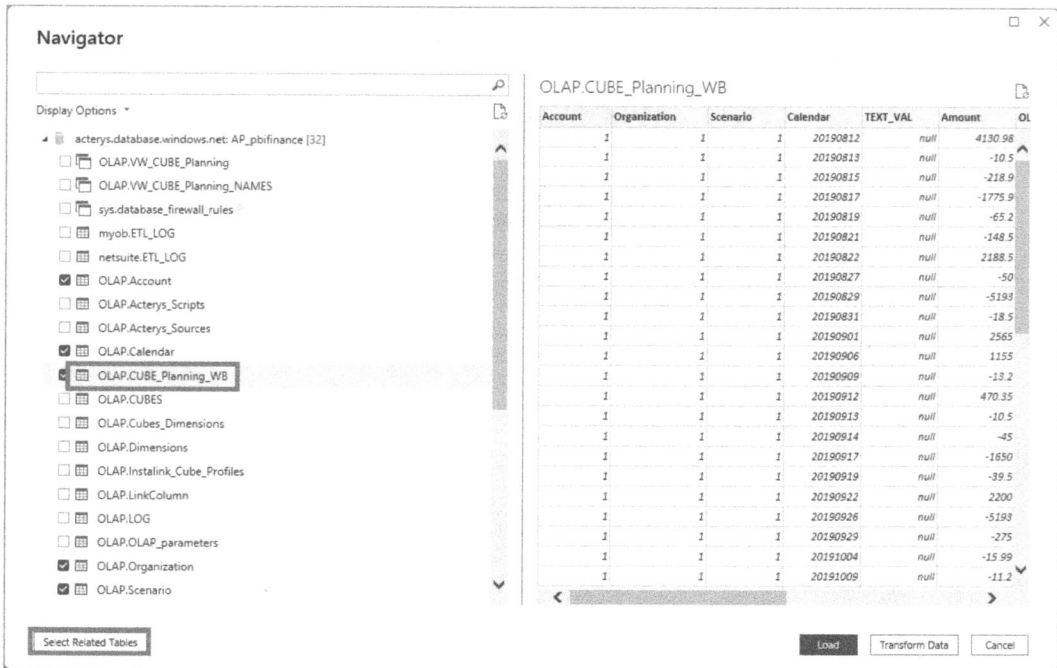

Figure 12.12 – Choosing the cube and related dimensions

Here, we also see the structure of the Acterys write-back table – it contains a column for all dimensions that connect to the dimension table via the ID of the respective element (for example, ID 1 for the Demo Company (AU) organization). It also contains two value columns for amount and comment (TXT_VAL).

This is all we need. We can now load these tables using the **Load** button.

Adding planning visuals in Power BI

In the previous section, we added the Acterys Microsoft SQL Server database to the Power BI semantic model. To use it with the write-back and planning features, we have to add the required Power BI visuals (which are not part of the default Power BI configuration and were described in *Chapter 11*), either in the Acterys or the Dynamics BPP version. All of these can be added by clicking on the three dots in the **Visualizations** pane in Power BI and choosing **Get more visuals**:

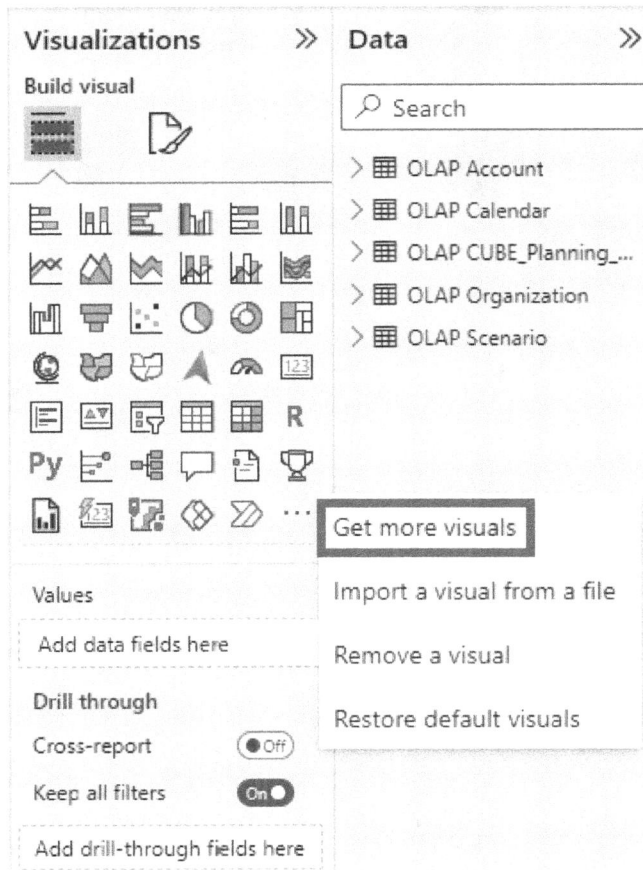

Figure 12.13 – Adding Acterys Visuals

Depending on whether you are using Acterys or Dynamics BPP, we have to select the respective versions:

- **If using Acterys visuals**: In the following dialog box, type Acterys and select the required visual from the list shown. In the following examples, we will be using **Table Edit**, **Matrix**, and **Copy**:

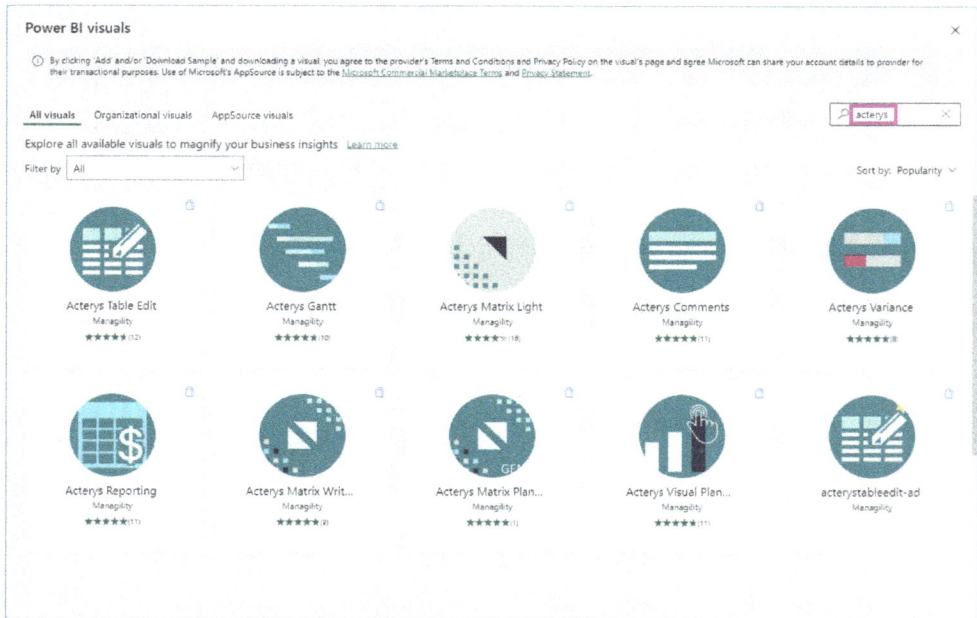

Figure 12.14 – Adding Acterys visuals

- **If using Dynamics BPP**: In the following dialog box, type Dynamics 365 and select the required visual from the list:

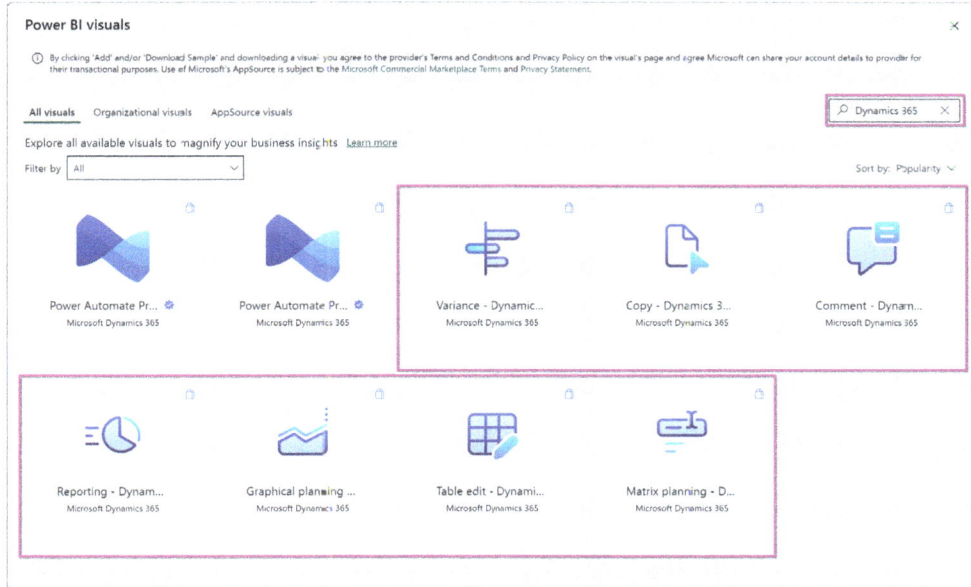

Figure 12.15 – Adding Dynamics BPP visuals

Acterys/Dynamics BPP Table Edit

From the **Power BI visuals** section, we can now add the Table Edit visual by entering the search term Table Edit and choosing **Acterys or Dynamics BPP Table Edit**. This Power BI custom visual allows you to edit any table in your Acterys/Dynamics BPP model. These could either be native dimension tables associated with a cube or any tables that can be linked to Acterys in the supported sources (for example, SQL Server, Power BI – that is, any of the 600+ connectors that Power BI supports – OneDrive, and so on).

To configure the visual with **Active Directory (AD)** authentication, we need to specify **PBI AD Auth** in the visual properties:

Figure 12.16 – Specifying the authentication type (Acterys)

As of the writing of this book, AD authentication is only supported on the Power BI service. This means you will have to publish your desktop file to the service or start the new report directly on the Power BI service.

This is the only configuration necessary in Table Edit. We now have the option to edit any of the dimensions in our planning model in the visual. For example, we can add a new scenario in the scenario dimension, which enables us to plan for variations and simulate different assumptions in all of the other Acterys/BPP visuals.

To add a new scenario, we just select the **Scenario** dimension in the drop-down box of the visual and then add a new record with Plan in the **Name** column:

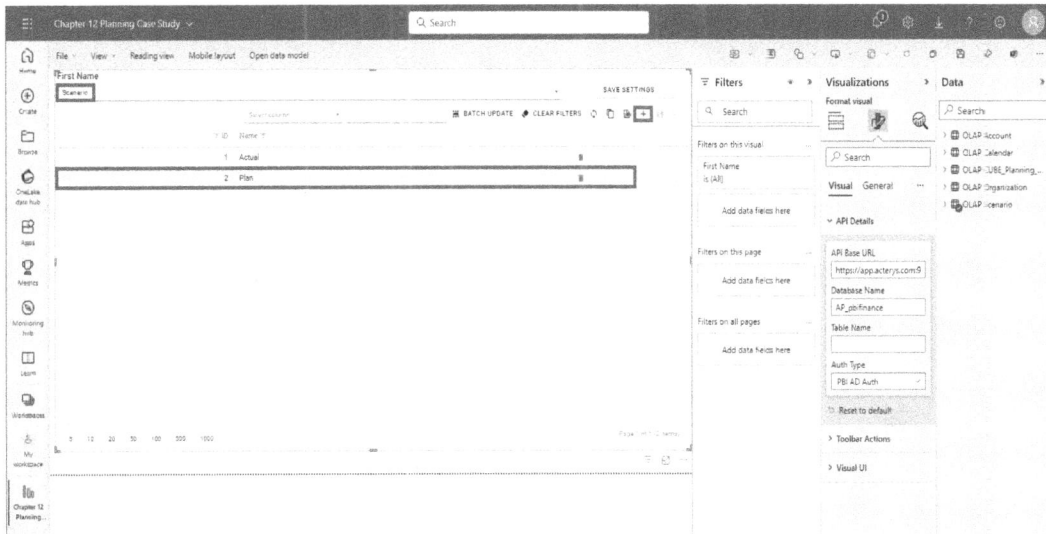

Figure 12.17 – Adding a new record

Acterys/Dynamics BPP Matrix

Acterys/Dynamics BPP Matrix enables editing records and supports the most widely used scenario of row-column (matrix)-based planning forms. To get started, we can again add it from AppSource to our Power BI report. As before, we have to configure AD authentication in the visual properties. In addition, we need to specify other details – at a minimum, the row and column attributes, as well as the values in their intersection, that our new planning form should use. Let's assume a typical case for financial planning with a hierarchy of sales and expenses accounts on the rows and a time hierarchy in the columns, where users can plan by either detail account, account classes, as well as enter monthly and yearly assumptions.

For this purpose, we just need to drag the relevant attributes of our model to the respective row/column section of the visual. In addition, we can set filters in the Power BI **Filters** pane for the Revenue and Expense account classes to limit displayed accounts to income statement/PL items and select a specific scenario (Actual) and company (Demo Company (AU)):

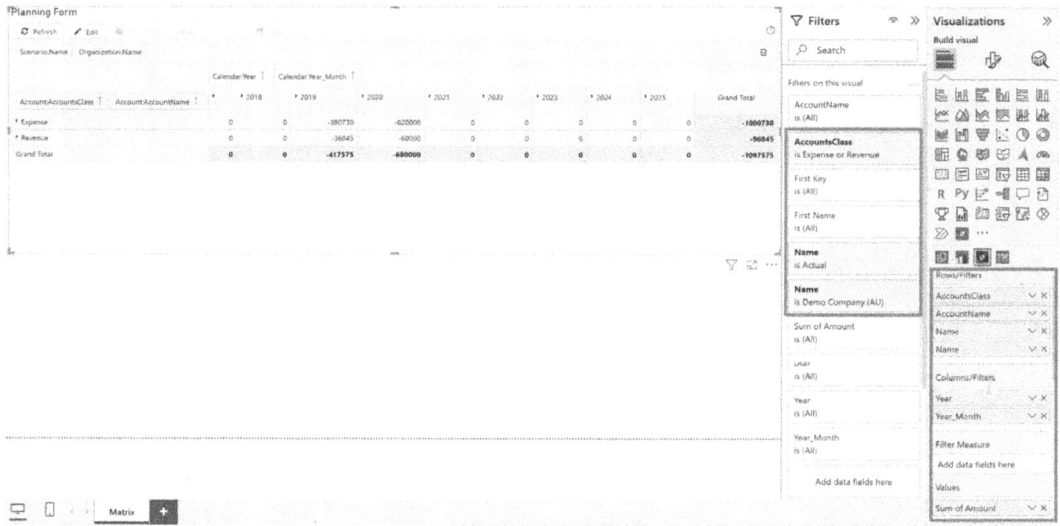

Figure 12.18 – Report configuration

In that layout, we can now see the actual data from the file we imported for the selected filters actual and Demo Company (AU). We could even change that data, as we haven't set a security rule to prevent entries on Actual, which normally should be in place. This is just a simple rule in the Acterys Modeller that prevents that. Let's do that quickly in the **Admin** menu by selecting **Manage Access Rights**, as shown:

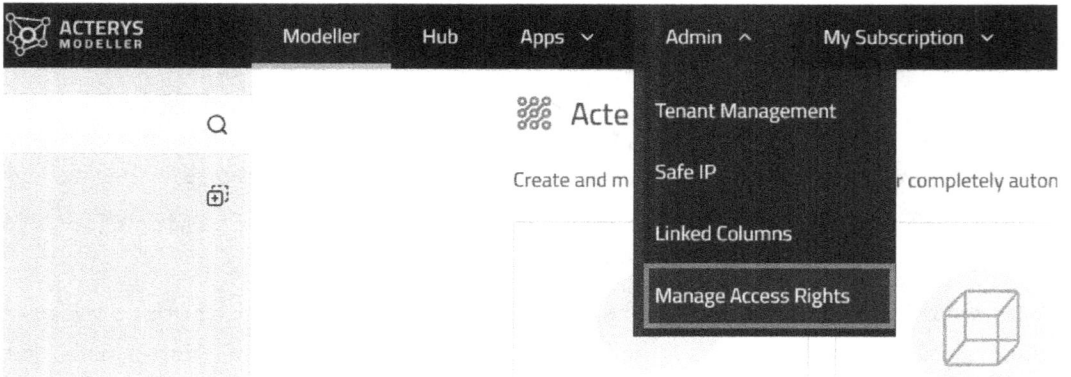

Figure 12.19 – Setting access rights

Here, we now have the option to define a rule for a specific model (cube) or all models that use a dimension. For our requirement, it's useful to have this apply to every model, despite us only having one, as it is unlikely that we want to allow users to change actuals anywhere. So, we can add a new dimension rule by using the **Add Rule** button.

In the drop-down boxes, we select **Dimension** and the restriction that all users can only read the Actual scenario. This prevents anyone from changing actual data in any context.

Now that our model is secured, we can go back to Power BI and try out the planning options. Acterys, in general, allows users to enter and change plans on any level of the model. This means you can change any detail transaction, or in other words, an intersection of a single base level element (no aggregation of other elements) in all dimensions.

For example, we could switch the scenario now to the **Plan** scenario we have added with Table Edit and enter values:

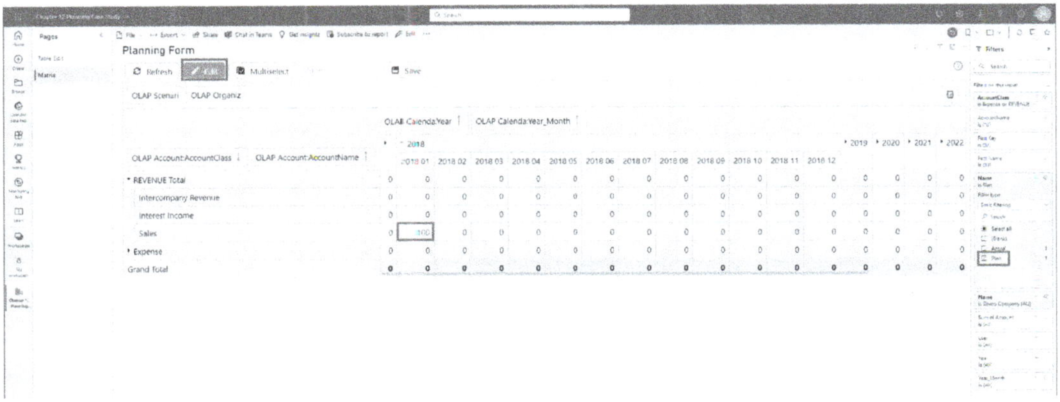

Figure 12.20 – Entering data

The entry of 100 on the **Account|Account Name**: Sales, **Calendar|Year_Month**: 2018 01, **Scenario**: Plan, and **Organization**: Demo Company (AU) base level elements will write one record in the cube database that contains the ID of the elements and the 100 in the **Amount** column.

In this fashion, we can now enter data in any intersection, for example, 50 on `Interest Income`. When we hit **Save** after that and then **Refresh**, we can see the new total for **REVENUE** of 150. What Acterys allows us now is to also change that total. Either just overwrite it with a specific new amount or use one of the special Acterys options that are available with a right click or a prefix:

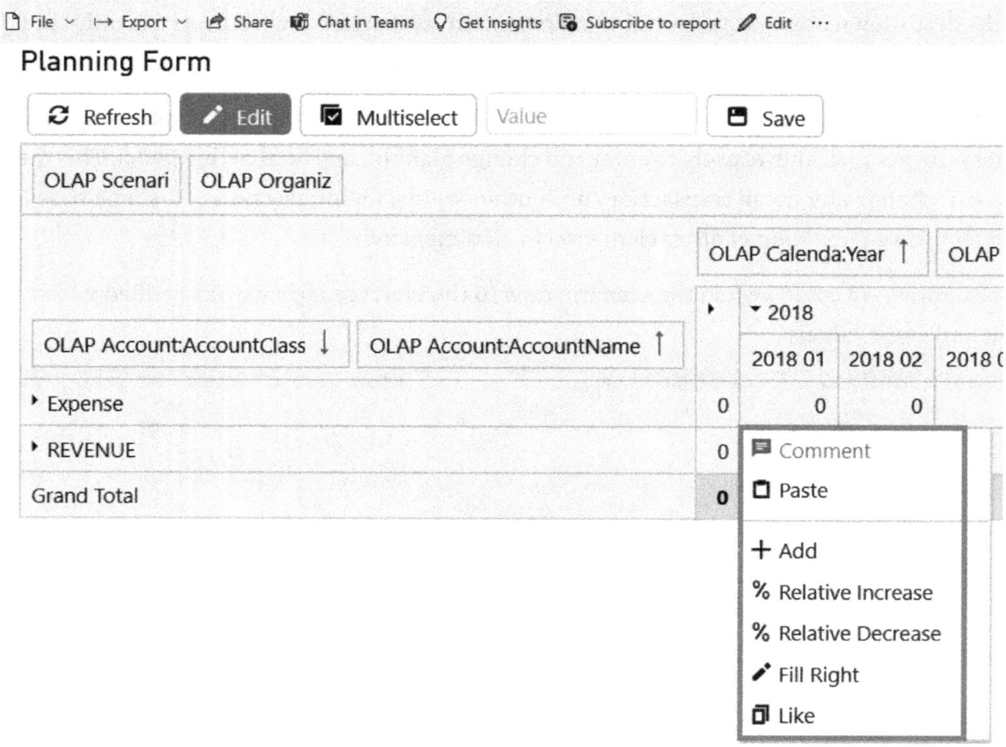

Figure 12.21 – Data entry/planning options

If we choose **% Relative Increase**, we can just enter 10% and see the new total of 165. The same can also be achieved if we enter 10% without using the right-click menu. After we save and refresh, we can see that the amounts for the children (**Sales** of 110 and **Interest Income** of 55) of **REVENUE** were proportionally adjusted to satisfy the change in the total.

Often, it can be convenient to be able to enter a value in the aggregate column total. We can easily do this by collapsing the year and entering an amount for the total year. For example, 1000 entered in the collapsed **2018** and **Intercompany Revenue** will automatically spread the 1,000 over the 12 months:

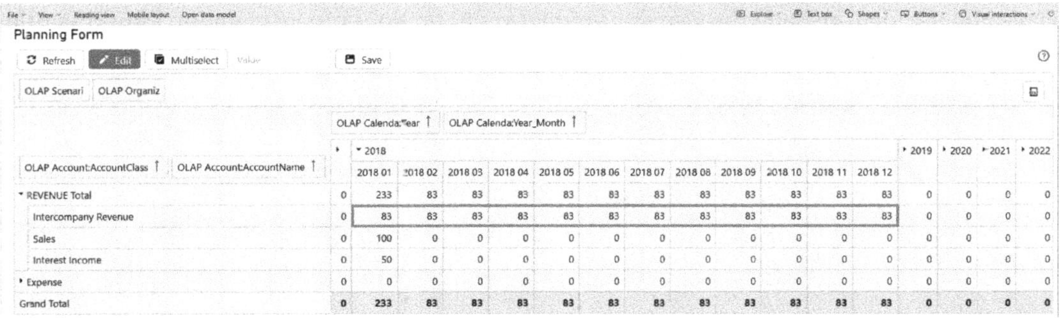

Figure 12.22 – Entry distributed to base level months

Acterys Copy

Starting from scratch is often not the best option. For that reason, Acterys offers another visual to facilitate data transfers – for example, copying the actuals from the previous year to the plan for the new plan year. This visual is called *Acterys/BPP Copy*. The respective versions are also available in the Microsoft AppSource marketplace and can be easily downloaded from the **Downloads** area in the Acterys Modeller:

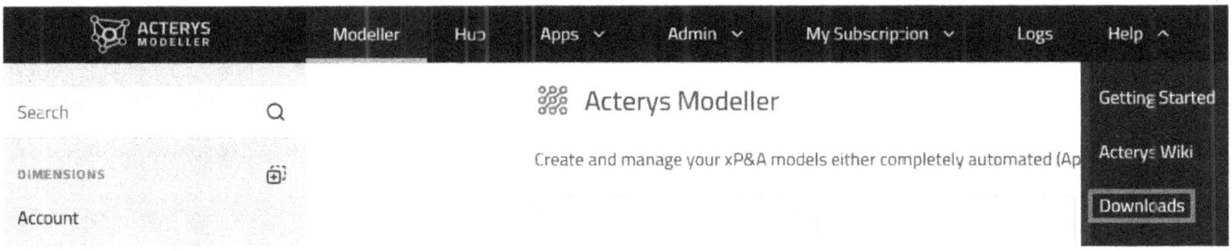

Figure 12.23 – Downloads in Acterys Modeller

Once downloaded, just add the visual to your Power BI report with the planning form (the title for the Copy visual was changed to **Data Management** from the default title):

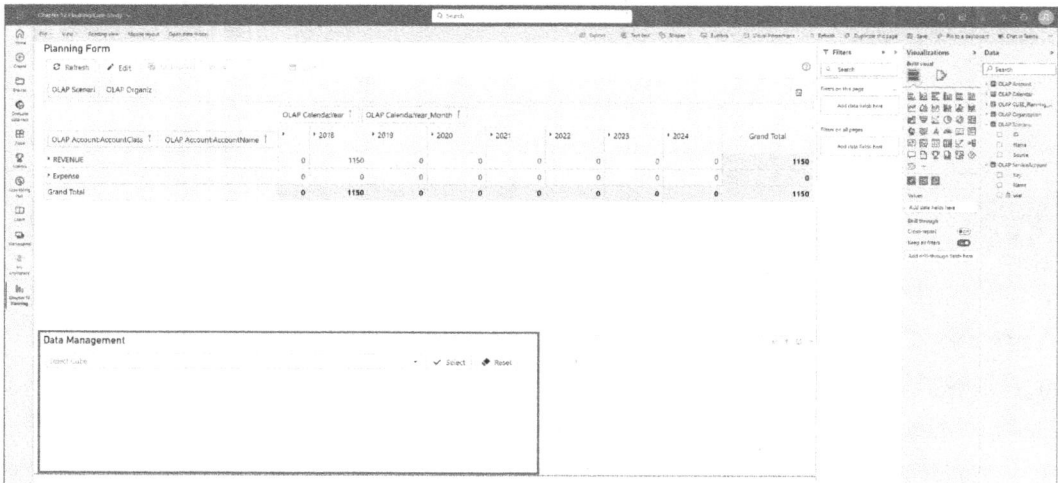

Figure 12.24 – Copy visual added to report

Copying is applied to either all models or a specific one. In our case, we only have the **Planning** cube, so we can select that. Following that, we can specify the dimensions that we want to use for the copy process. In our case, we want to copy the Actuals from the year 2019 to the Plan scenario for the year 2020. To do that, we can click on the plus symbol, add the conditions, and then click on **Copy**:

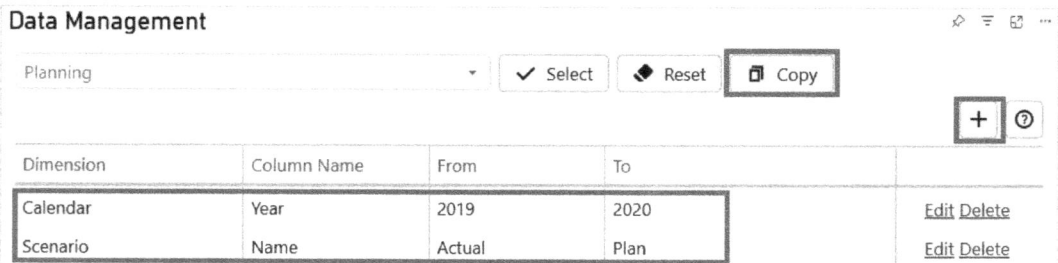

Data Management

Dimension	Column Name	From	To	
Calendar	Year	2019	2020	Edit Delete
Scenario	Name	Actual	Plan	Edit Delete

Figure 12.25 – Adding Copy parameters

Now, when we refresh the Matrix visual at the top, we can see the new populated scenario:

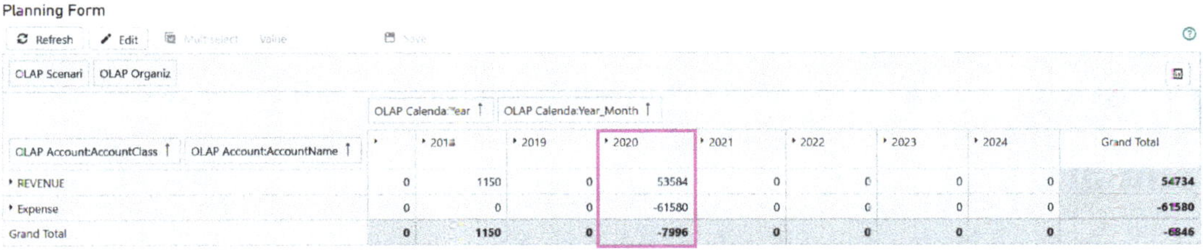

Figure 12.26 – Values were copied to the destination

With that, we now have all the powerful planning functionalities that Acterys offers. For example, we can see what a 10% total revenue increase (entering i10% or using the right-click menu) would do to our bottom line:

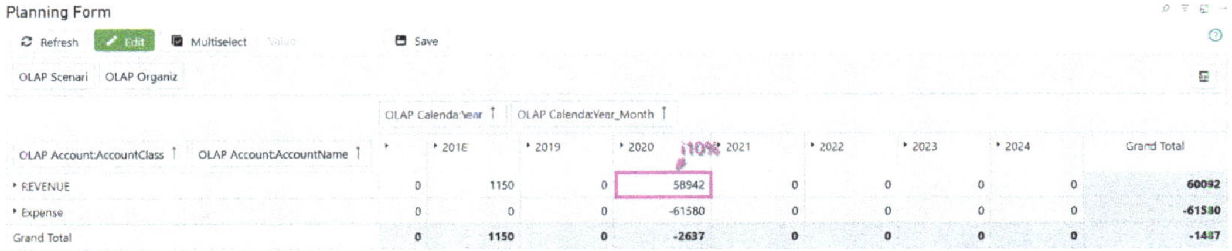

Figure 12.27 – Modifying copied values

We can now also very quickly try some other planning options. For example, the *Visual Planning* visual allows us to plan by dragging on a chart. The only thing we need to do for that is duplicate our report page and change the type of the visual used from the *Matrix* visual to the *Visual Planning* visual. The latter has to be added to the report if not done already, as explained in *Chapter 11*. Once we switch, we can change the used fields/attributes to the hierarchy and filters we want, such as a revenue plan with the option to plan by period, with a drill down to the account detail:

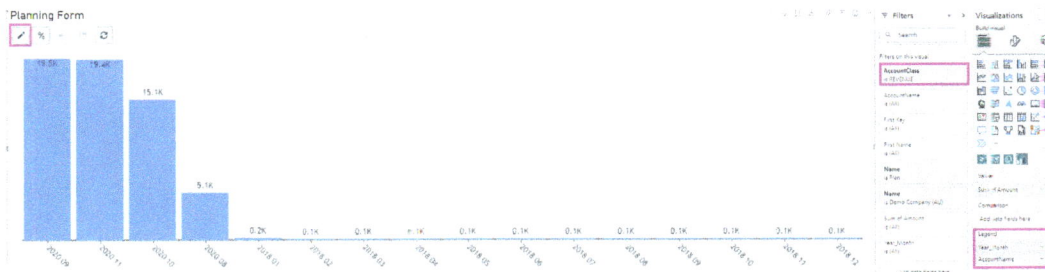

Figure 12.28 – Enabling planning in the Visual Planning visual

With that, the user can now turn on the edit mode with the pencil symbol and drag at the top of the chart or click on the area above or below to plan. This visual also has the option to plan by percentage – that is, change the percentage of a column in regard to total and the option to lock the total so that a change in one column changes all other bars to keep the total fixed.

Summary

In this chapter, we covered an end-to-end sample of how to build a planning system with Power BI and Acterys that combines the unparalleled analytics power in Power BI with the very comprehensive planning options in Acterys/Dynamics **eXtended Planning and Analytics (xP&A)**. We only covered a fraction of the capabilities and some basic scenarios. For more advanced enterprise planning examples, I recommend the Acterys/Dynamics xP&A knowledge base and many training videos and case studies on the Acterys YouTube channel: `https://www.youtube.com/@Acterys`.

In the following chapters, we will do a deep dive into advanced analytics, AI, and machine learning options with relevant examples for finance use cases.

13

Advanced Analytics and Machine Learning

In this chapter, we will cover how advanced analytics techniques that use mathematical methods to identify strategies, uncover patterns, and predict outcomes can also assist with financial requirements.

We will begin with some of the standard features in Power BI and then move on to see how we can extend Power BI's capabilities with even more sophisticated external advanced **machine learning (ML)** services.

In this chapter, we will explore the following topics:

- Advanced analytical methods and their principles
- Implementing AI/ML methods in Power BI
- AutoML machine learning

Advanced analytical methods and their principles

Before we go into a detailed explanation of how to realize applications in Power BI, we should understand the major types of advanced analytical methods (often also referred to as data mining) and the principles involved. This is essential to understand the different options and outcomes that Power BI can deliver.

The most relevant are the following:

- **Anomaly detection**: Anomaly detection is the process of identifying data points that deviate significantly from the expected state of the data. Anomalies can indicate errors, fraud, outliers, or rare events that are of interest or concern.

  Anomaly detection has a variety of use cases for financial aspects, such as variance analysis, error detection, and others. Major methods used include z-score and proximity-based measures.

- **Regression**: Regression is a type of predictive modeling used when the target variable is continuous, meaning it can take on any value within a given range or interval (potentially an infinite number of possible values). It seeks to establish a relationship between input features (independent variables) and a continuous outcome (dependent variable).

  For instance, a typical financial use case could be to predict future sales based on historical data. The algorithms involved include linear regression, polynomial regression, and various ML algorithms such as support vector regression and random forests.

- **Classification**: Classification is used when the target variable is categorical, meaning it falls into one of a limited number of classes or categories. It aims to assign a class label to input data points based on their features.

  For instance, a typical business use case could be fraud detection, where historical transactions classified as regular or fraudulent with relevant attributes (e.g., demographics, transaction amount, etc.) are used to predict high-risk transactions. The algorithms used include logistic regression, decision trees, K-nearest neighbors, support vector machines, and deep neural networks.

  Classification methods typically fall into the **supervised** category, where the analysis is performed with the objective of a particular outcome, such as the identification of whether a transaction is fraudulent.

- **Clustering**: Another method that I would like to cover here is clustering. As opposed to the previous method, this one is typically **non-supervised** (i.e., the analyst applies a method to find "interesting aspects" in the data).

An example is grouping similar data points together based on their features, without any predefined class labels, to uncover hidden patterns or structures within the data. The method is used in customer segmentation for marketing, document categorization, anomaly detection, and image segmentation, among others.

Algorithms include K-means clustering, hierarchical clustering, DBSCAN, and **Gaussian mixture models (GMMs)**.

- **Natural language processing (NLP)**: Finally, there is also an AI-based method called NLP, which focuses on enabling computers to understand, interpret, and generate human language. Its applications include sentiment analysis, chatbots, language translation, and content summarization. These are typically tasks that are less relevant for financial applications.

In the next section, we will review the actual implementation of the aforementioned methods in Power BI.

Implementing AI/ML methods in Power BI

The first built-in option (as opposed to others that require external services, such as Microsoft Azure) that I would like to cover is anomaly detection in Power BI.

Anomaly detection

This feature enables us to identify outliers in the built-in line chart visual. We can use our existing report from *Chapter 4* with our accounting data set and see whether interesting data points are found.

Let's create a new report page, add the line visual with the months from our Calendar table, and either the existing actual (ACT) measure or the net amount in group currency (NetAmount_GC) filtered on the actual scenario from the Transaction table. We also need to filter the Accounts dimension to a single item, as the totals across different measures wouldn't render useful results. In our case, we can, for example, filter on just the Revenue items in the Accounts Class field.

Once you have set the visual fields, we can click on the **Data/Drill** menu and select the **Find anomalies** button in the ribbon. Following that, we will then see a gray area around our line chart, as displayed in *Figure 13.1*. This is the expected range based on the data at hand.

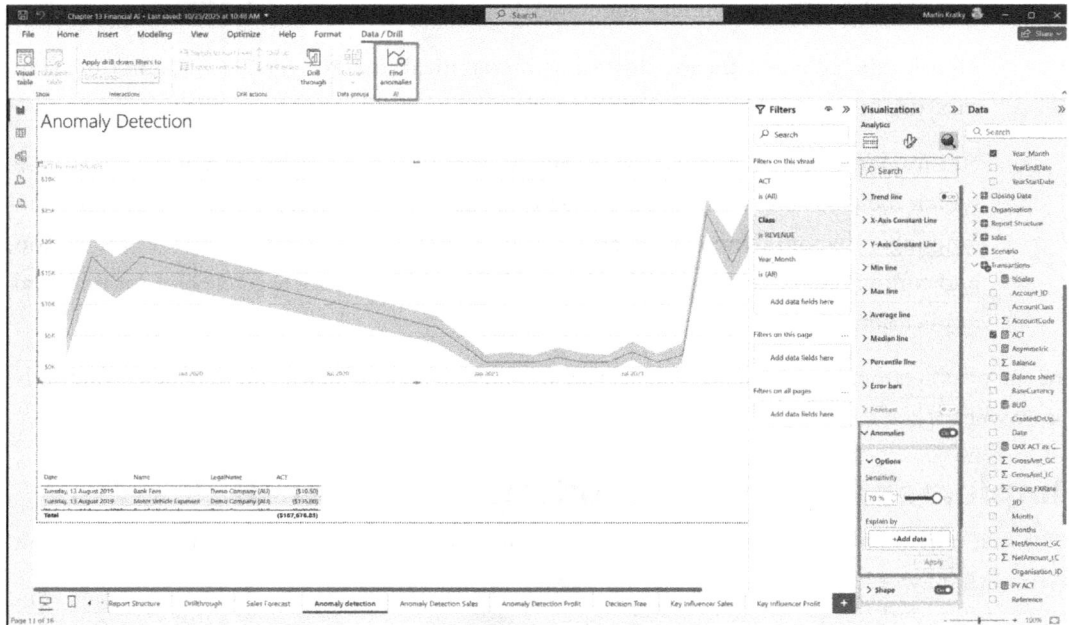

Figure 13.1 – Visualization of anomalies

With the default settings, no anomalies are detected; had any anomalies been detected, they would have been marked. Anomaly detection, like many other ML/AI methods, is dependent on sensitivity settings in the visual.

The default setting for anomalies is a 70% sensitivity. If we increase the sensitivity, the algorithm is more sensitive to changes in our data. In that case, even a less relevant deviation is marked as an anomaly. If you decrease the sensitivity, the algorithm is more selective about what it considers an anomaly.

If we, for example, increase **Sensitivity** to 80%, we see that an anomaly is found:

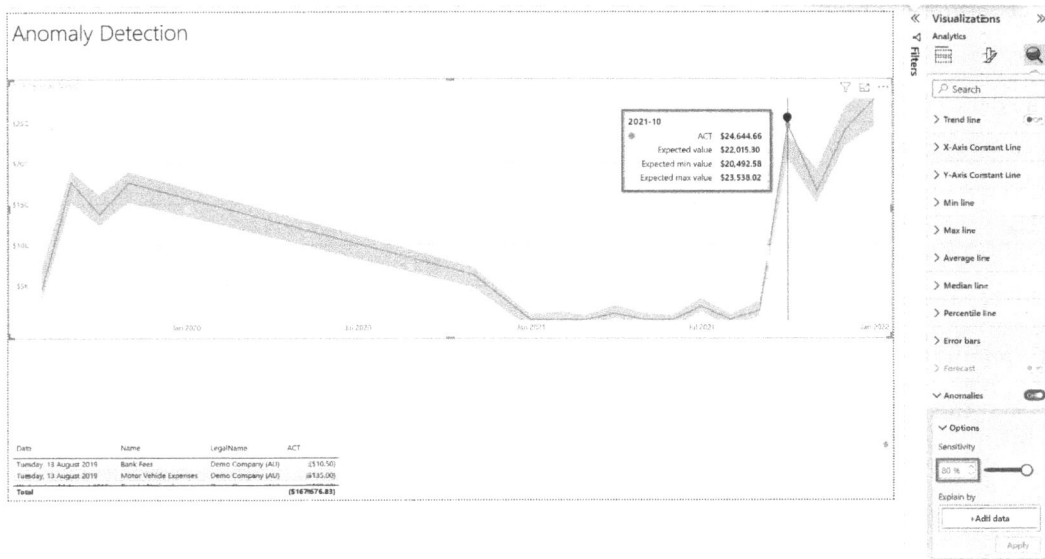

Figure 13.2 – Anomaly details

We can see in *Figure 13.2* that *Month 10* has a value of around $24k, but the expected value is $22k. When we click on this outlier, Power BI can provide additional details. In our case, though, no explanations for this outlier are found.

Based on some practical experience with real datasets, I have to say that the "explanation feature" at the time of writing (July 2025) is of limited use. With my real datasets, I never received any explanations apart from a few non-descript error messages. For that reason, my recommendation is to use other features that support automated analysis – in particular, the CoPilot options covered in *Chapter 14*.

Next, I would like to cover a more extensive end-to-end example of how you can use ML features in Power BI for classification and prediction purposes.

End-to-end classification case study

Let's look at a dataset that contains demographic details of the individual targeted, as well as macroeconomic indicators. In addition, the records in the dataset contain campaign outcomes, such as by what means and how often the person was contacted. The final and most important detail in the set is the success classifier: was the campaign eventually successful or not?

Our problem statement is that, based on this data, we need to develop a prediction algorithm that optimizes who we contact for future campaigns. This objective should also take into account cost restrictions and profit targets.

The dataset that we are using is based on real data from a Portuguese bank published by the University of California/Irvine: https://archive.ics.uci.edu/dataset/222/bank+marketing (Moro, S., Rita, P., and Cortez, P. (2012). Bank Marketing. UCI Machine Learning Repository). Here, we are using a slightly extended file with additional external market columns available at https://github.com/akhil12028/Bank-Marketing-data-set-analysis/blob/master/bank-additional-full.csv.

It contains the following fields:

- **Customer demographic:**

    - age (numeric)
    - job: Type of job (categorical: admin., unknown, unemployed, management, housemaid, entrepreneur, student, blue-collar, self-employed, retired, technician, services)
    - marital: marital status (categorical: married, divorced, single; here, divorced means divorced or widowed)
    - education (categorical: unknown, secondary, primary, tertiary)
    - default: Has credit in default? (binary: yes, no)
    - balance: Average yearly balance, in euros (numeric)
    - housing: Has housing loan? (binary: yes, no)
    - loan: Has personal loan? (binary: yes, no)
    - contact: Contact communication type (categorical: unknown, telephone, cellular)

- **Previous campaign metrics:**

    - day: Last contact day of the month (numeric)
    - month: Last contact month of year (categorical: jan, feb, mar, …, nov, dec)
    - duration: Last contact duration, in seconds (numeric)

- **# other attributes:**

    - campaign: Number of contacts carried out during this campaign and for this client (numeric, includes last contact)

- pdays: Number of days that passed by after the client was last contacted from a previous campaign (numeric, -1 means client was not previously contacted)

- previous: Number of contacts performed before this campaign and for this client (numeric)

- poutcome: Outcome of the previous marketing campaign (categorical: unknown, other, failure, success)

- **Macroeconomic/company metrics:**

  - Emp.var.rate: Employment variation rate – quarterly indicator (numeric)

  - Cons.price.idx: Consumer price index – monthly indicator (numeric)

  - Cons.conf.idx: Consumer confidence index – monthly indicator (numeric)

  - Euribor3m: Euribor 3-month rate – daily indicator (numeric)

  - Nr.employed: number of employees – quarterly indicator (numeric)

- **Output variable (desired target):**

  - y: Has the client subscribed to a term deposit? (binary: yes, no)

The first steps in nearly any ML context are as follows:

1. Get a clear understanding of the data.

2. Clean and restructure data to improve model ML outcomes.

3. Optionally, augment the source with additional relevant details.

The first step is crucial. If there is no clear understanding of the nature of the data, it will be impossible to apply an ML approach effectively.

With Power Query, Power BI provides very helpful tools that profile and visualize data in your dataset columns. This feature is available in either Power BI Desktop or in dataflows in the Power BI service. In the next section, we will cover more advanced methods that are available in dataflows.

Data profiling

For the AutoML machine learning features that I will be covering in the next section, we will require dataflows. As a preparation for that, I will now cover how you can use your data with that component.

The features that we cover require a **Premium per-user (PPU)** trial to go through this exercise. This is currently available free of charge for a limited amount of time.

Let's get started:

1.   Log in to your Power BI service account and create a new **Premium per-user** workspace from the **Workspaces** button on the pane on the right:

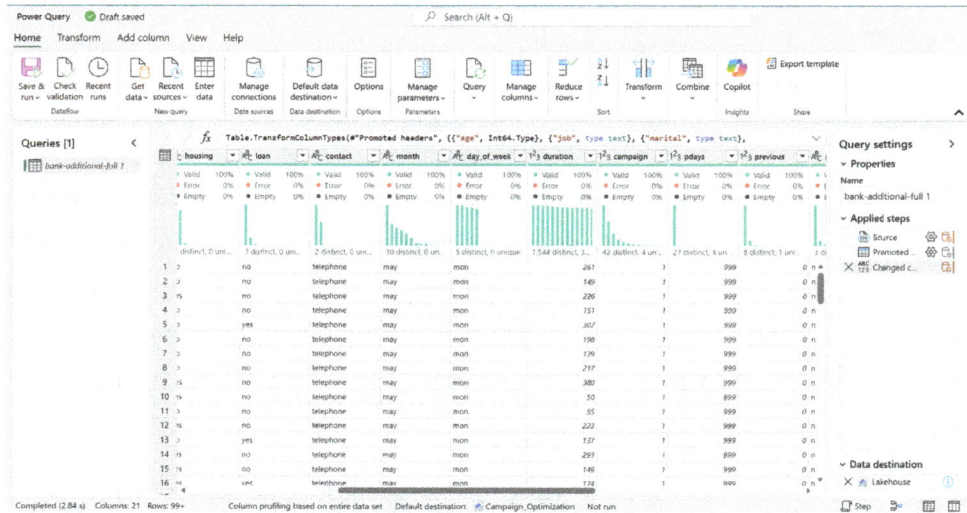

Figure 13.3 – Changing the licensing mode

2.   Next, we can open this workspace and create a new **dataflow** from the vertical pane on the right:

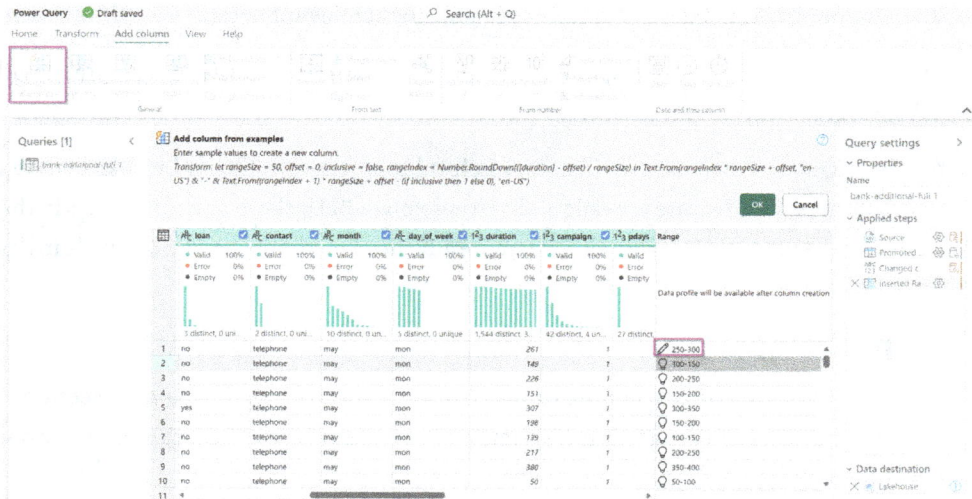

Figure 13.4 – Creating a new dataflow

3. In the next step, we have to add our dataset with the campaign data to the dataflow by using **Add new tables**, choosing the **Text/CSV** type, and uploading the bank-additional-full.csv file.

4. This brings us to the Power Query editor for dataflows, which gives us very good insights into the data profile when column profiles and details are turned on in the **Options** button in the ribbon. I also recommend that, as much as possible, you apply the profile to the entire dataset. Dataflows can typically compute those extremely quickly:

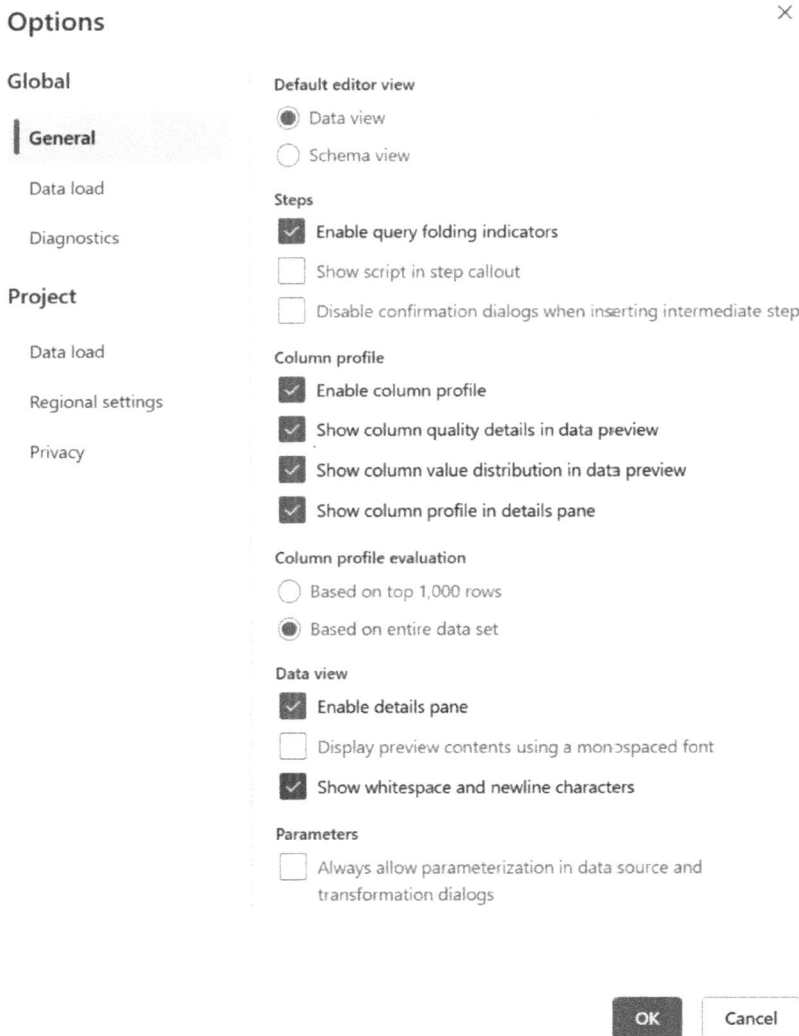

Options   ×

Global

| **General**

Data load

Diagnostics

Project

Data load

Regional settings

Privacy

Default editor view

◉ Data view

○ Schema view

Steps

☑ Enable query folding indicators

☐ Show script in step callout

☐ Disable confirmation dialogs when inserting intermediate steps

Column profile

☑ Enable column profile

☑ Show column quality details in data preview

☑ Show column value distribution in data preview

☑ Show column profile in details pane

Column profile evaluation

○ Based on top 1,000 rows

◉ Based on entire data set

Data view

☑ Enable details pane

☐ Display preview contents using a monospaced font

☑ Show whitespace and newline characters

Parameters

☐ Always allow parameterization in data source and transformation dialogs

OK   Cancel

Figure 13.5 – Column profile options

The profiles shown at the top and for the specific column display comprehensive details such as minimum, maximum, blanks, and errors:

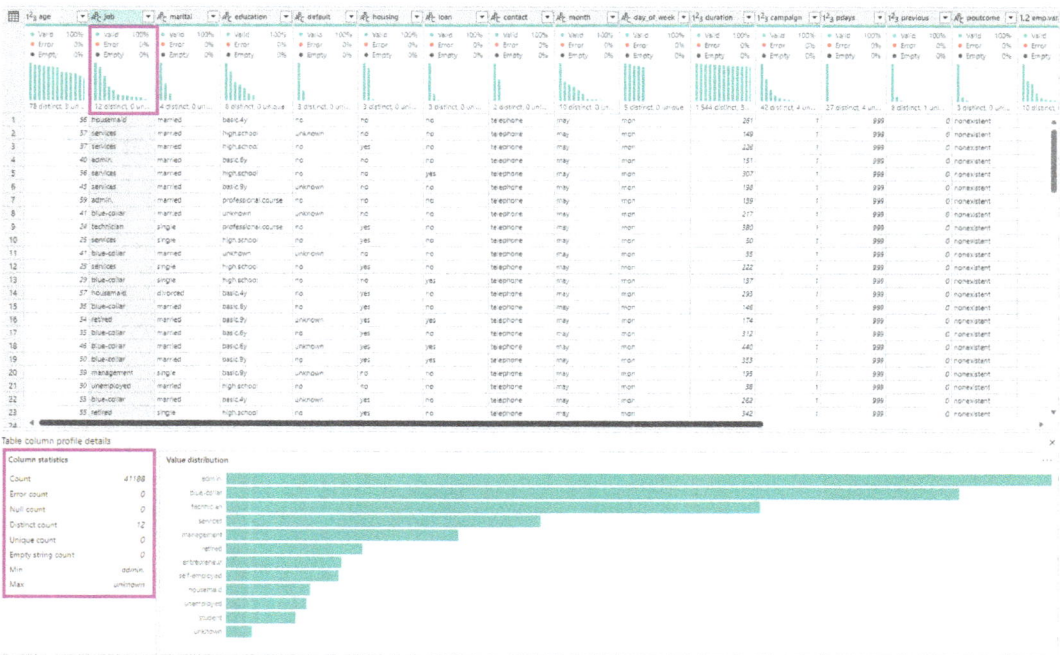

Figure 13.6 – Column profiling

Before proceeding with anything else, you should fix the errors or reduce blank and unknown details as much as possible. It might be necessary to filter out blanks and errors if they can't be fixed in the source.

Cleansing and restructuring

Another important step is to categorize data from continuous to categorical. For example, we have a continuous call duration attribute in our dataset. It is harder to infer relationships from a continuous number of minutes than from a category because the number of possible options is substantially bigger. Power BI gives us great options to do this very easily.

We can select the `duration` column and apply the `column from example` function with either a right click or a click on the **Column from examples** button in the **Add column** ribbon and then enter a category for the value in the first row. In our case, the duration is 261, which we can classify into a `250-300` category by just entering that in the first row of the new column. Following that, we see that Power BI has automatically determined that we want to apply a categorization of the values in the `duration` column in brackets of 50-minute increments and applied that to the rest of the rows:

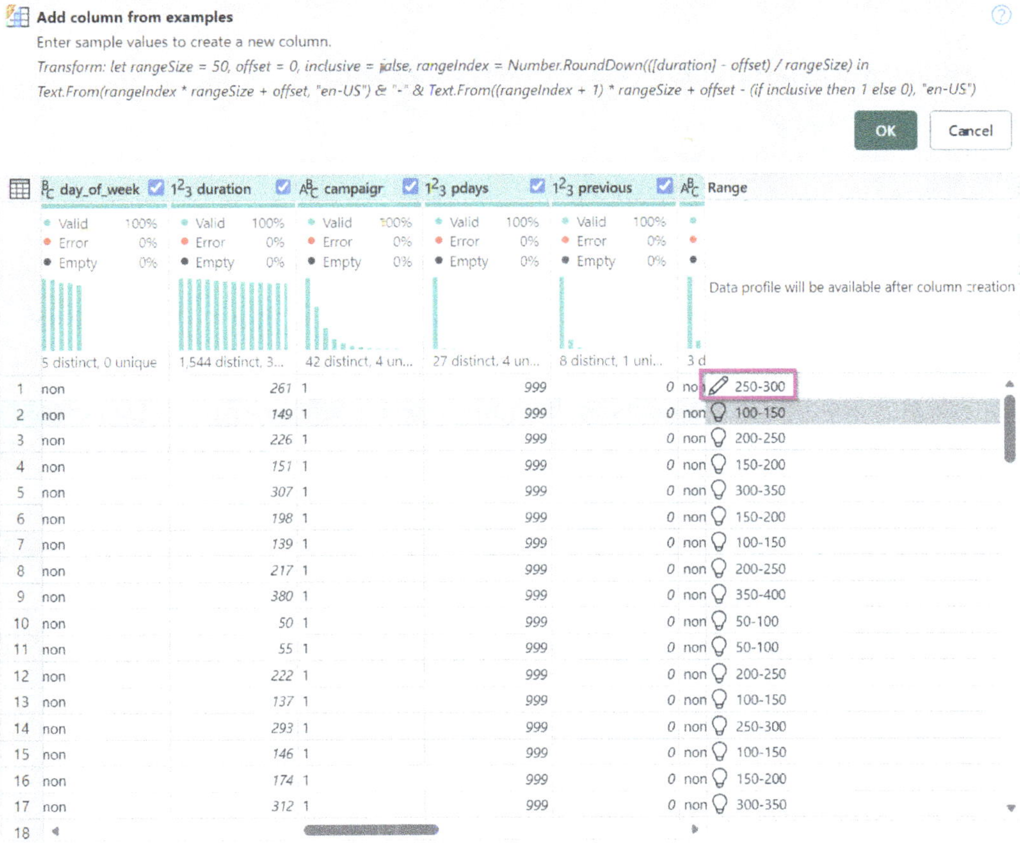

Add column from examples					?
Enter sample values to create a new column.					
Transform: let rangeSize = 50, offset = 0, inclusive = false, rangeIndex = Number.RoundDown(([duration] - offset) / rangeSize) in					
*Text.From(rangeIndex * rangeSize + offset, "en-US") & "-" & Text.From((rangeIndex + 1) * rangeSize + offset - (if inclusive then 1 else 0), "en-US")*					

	day_of_week	duration	campaigr	pdays	previous	Range
	Valid 100%	Valid 100%	Valid 100%	Valid 100%	Valid 100%	
	Error 0%	Error 0%	Error 0%	Error 0%	Error 0%	
	Empty 0%	Empty 0%	Empty 0%	Empty 0%	Empty 0%	Data profile will be available after column creation
	5 distinct, 0 unique	1,544 distinct, 3...	42 distinct, 4 un...	27 distinct, 4 un...	8 distinct, 1 uni...	3 d
1	non	261 1		999	0 no	250-300
2	non	149 1		999	0 non	100-150
3	non	226 1		999	0 non	200-250
4	non	151 1		999	0 non	150-200
5	non	307 1		999	0 non	300-350
6	non	198 1		999	0 non	150-200
7	non	139 1		999	0 non	100-150
8	non	217 1		999	0 non	200-250
9	non	380 1		999	0 non	350-400
10	non	50 1		999	0 non	50-100
11	non	55 1		999	0 non	50-100
12	non	222 1		999	0 non	200-250
13	non	137 1		999	0 non	100-150
14	non	293 1		999	0 non	250-300
15	non	146 1		999	0 non	100-150
16	non	174 1		999	0 non	150-200
17	non	312 1		999	0 non	300-350
18						

OK   Cancel

Figure 13.7 – Adding column from example

With ML models, we also have to be careful about which attributes we can include in the model. For example, the call duration will not be applicable when we run our model against a new set of customers that weren't contacted before, so that detail is not available

Data augmentation

Often, it is useful to add additional details to the data that are not part of the original source. An example of this is the macroeconomic details in the file. In our case, they were already added to the data. Normally, these are likely not part of the original CRM system. With Power BI, you have the simple option to easily add the metrics/columns to a new table in Power Query. We just have to ensure that the data has a date granularity that matches our CRM data and merge the two tables in Power Query.

Advanced data analysis with Power BI visuals

Once we have finished the data cleansing and preparation, it's typically helpful to use Power BI analytics functionalities (in particular, visuals) to get a better understanding of the data beyond the initial column profiling.

The quickest way to do further analysis is with Power BI Desktop.

One very simple but powerful way to get insights into the data is to use the **Power BI Insights** feature, which automatically applies advanced analytics to a Power BI dataset:

1. To get started, we can just publish the Power BI report with a reference to our dataflow to the Power BI service. Once this is done, you can just select the **Get Quick Insights** link from the dialog box:

Figure 13.8 – Link to display Quick Insights

2. Following that, you get to a very comprehensive report with interesting findings that include data structure, anomalies, and others:

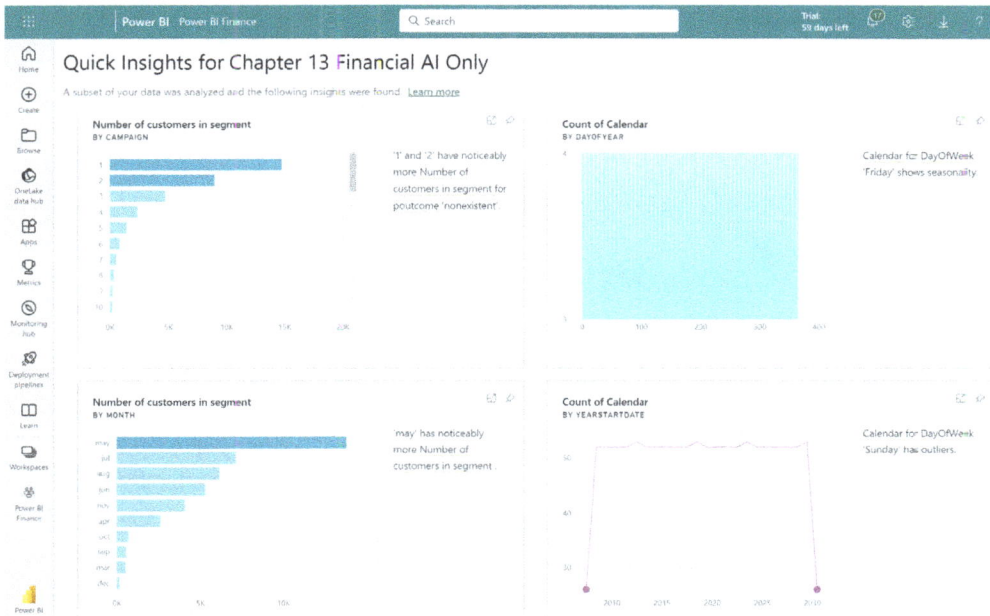

Figure 13.9 – Insights in Power BI

As with many automated, non-supervised (i.e., they just return what the data contains without a specific objective as opposed to supervised methods) advanced analytics approaches, there are irrelevant and trivial results, but also often very helpful findings that are not easily found with manual Power BI visualization techniques.

Also helpful are the **Key Influencer** and **Decomposition Tree** visuals, which we will cover in more detail in the following sections. Scatter charts with regression lines can also provide further insight if you are using continuous as opposed to categorical target variables.

Decomposition tree analysis

In the following screenshot, you can see the settings for the decomposition tree. I am adding the Success supervised variable to the Analyze field and all relevant fields to the Explain by field of the visual. After that, I navigate in the tree by choosing **High value** in the navigation option at the highest value of every level:

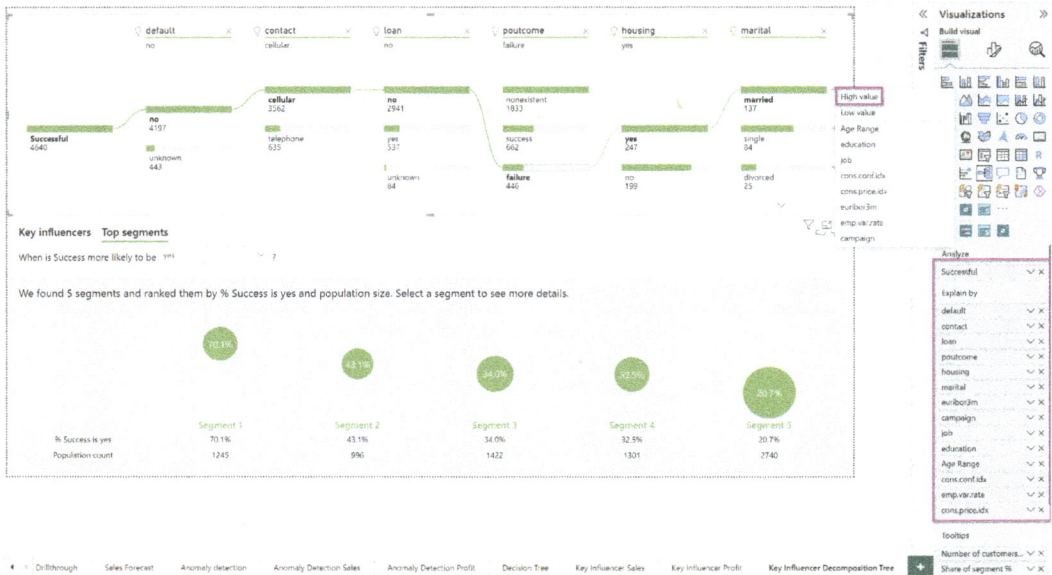

Figure 13.10 – Variables for the Key influencers visual

An interesting calculation to add here is the relevance of the navigation point as a proportion of the total. This can be easily achieved by adding three DAX calculations.

The first calculation summarizes the total number of data points (successful and non-successful). The count can be done on any field that doesn't contain blanks – I have used age here:

```
Number of customers in segment = CALCULATE(count(bank_additional_
full[age]),all(bank_additional_full[Success]))
```

The second calculation just counts the successful outcomes:

```
Successful = CALCULATE(count(bank_additional_full[age]),bank_additional_
full[Success]="yes")
```

And finally, the third one calculates just the share of the two segments:

```
Share of segment % = DIVIDE([Successful],[Number of customers in segment])
```

Now, we can add the three DAX calculations to the visual **Tooltips** field, which gives you an overview when you hover over a node in the tree:

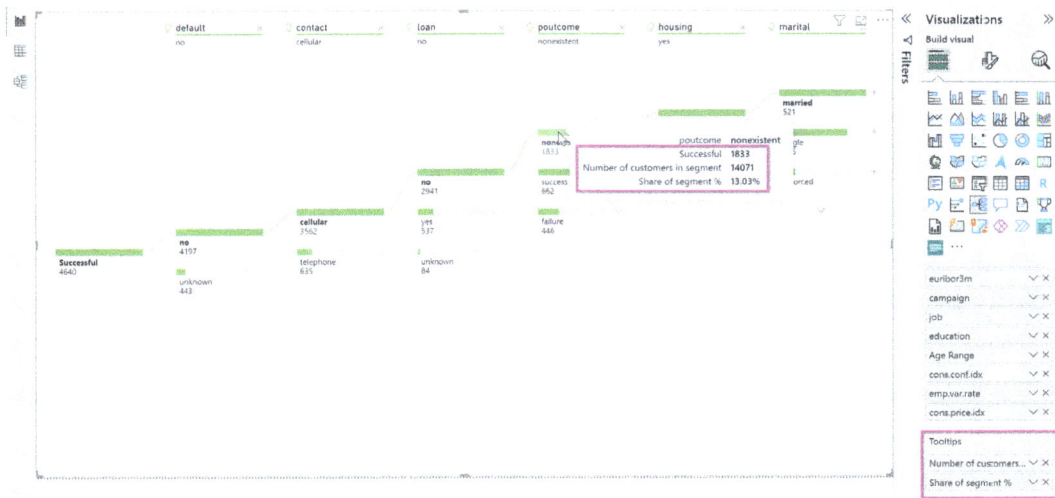

Figure 13.11 – Decomposition tree analysis

Decomposition is an effective option to get a better understanding of the structure of your data. In the next section, we will cover how we can determine drivers for particular outcomes with key influencer analysis.

Key influencer analysis

Even more advanced insights are provided with the **Key Influencer** visual. The configuration is the same as **Decomposition Tree**, so we can just take a copy of that and change the visualization to **Key Influencer**. Following that, we get an overview of key drivers in the dataset that determine the Success outcome. This is provided as single attributes and segments:

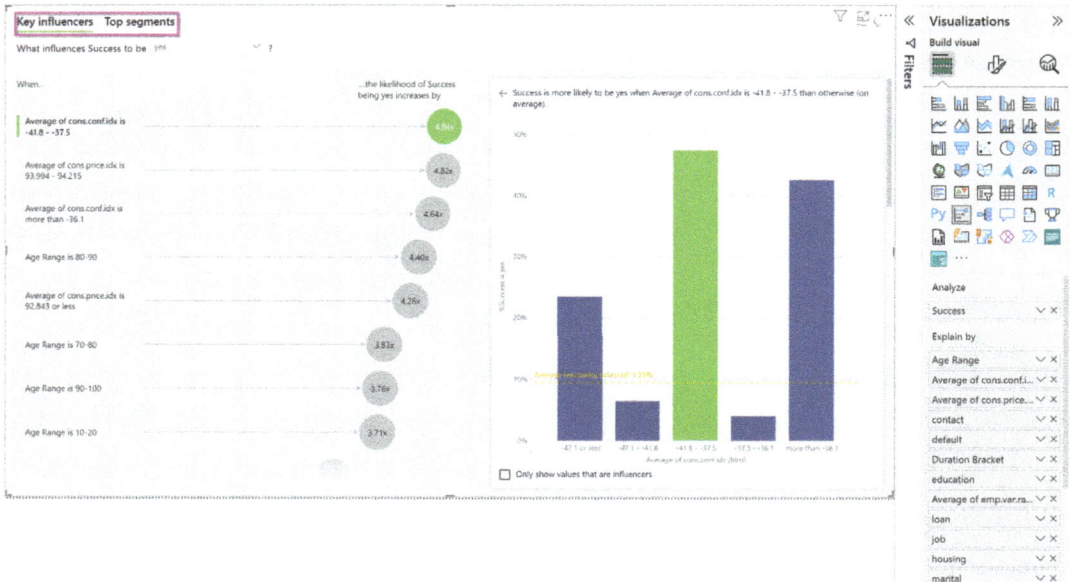

Figure 13.12 – Identified key influencers

We have now covered an end-to-end example of an unsupervised (without a particular objective) ML application in Power BI. In the next section, we'll look at a supervised method.

AutoML machine learning

Now that we have a better overview of the data, we can move to the more advanced ML capabilities in Power BI: AutoML in the Power BI service. AutoML is an approach that automatically applies a combination of ML algorithms and methods optimized for the user's particular dataset and problem case at hand.

> **Important!**
>
> During the publishing process of this book, Microsoft announced that the AutoML technology used in this section will be replaced with a new, scalable AutoML solution in Microsoft Fabric. However, this was not available at the deadline for this book. My assumption (I tried unsuccessfully to confirm with the Microsoft team) is that the process will be very similar to the one that I cover in this section.

As opposed to the previous unsupervised methods, such as key influencer analysis and anomaly detection, this time, we have a particular problem statement that we want to address. Based on the learnings in our dataflow training dataset with our campaign details, we want to optimize outcomes for future campaigns by identifying criteria for customers who are most likely to purchase the service promoted in the campaign. In summary, our objective is to maximize the campaign profitability, taking into account the available budget for marketing spend.

Setting up the Power BI AutoML

As mentioned initially, you will require a Premium capacity or trial. Let's log back in to our Power BI service workspace:

1. Open the dataflow. Here, we can initiate the AutoML features by clicking the *brain* icon:

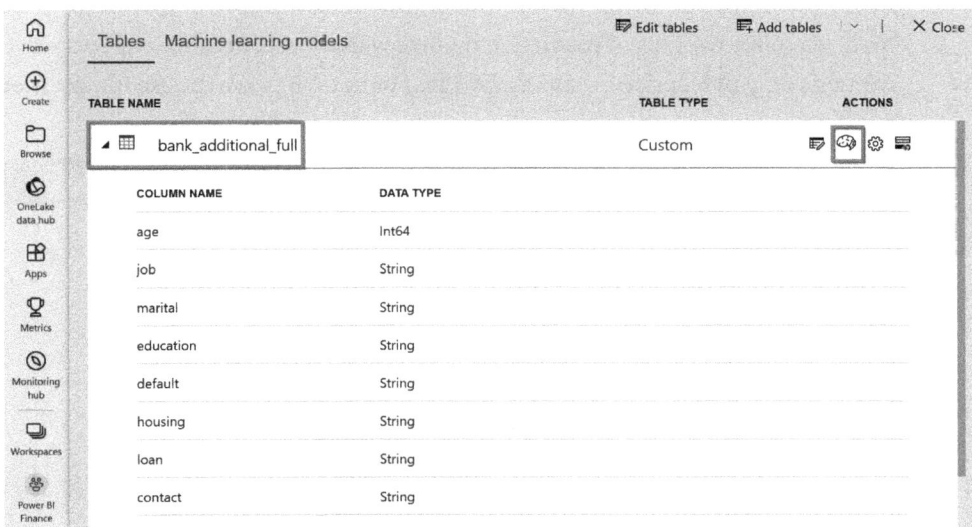

Figure 13.13 – Initiating AutoML

2. Following that, we navigate through a wizard to set up the model. The first step is to specify the (supervised) variable that we want to predict. In our case, this is the Success column that defines whether the campaign was successful or not:

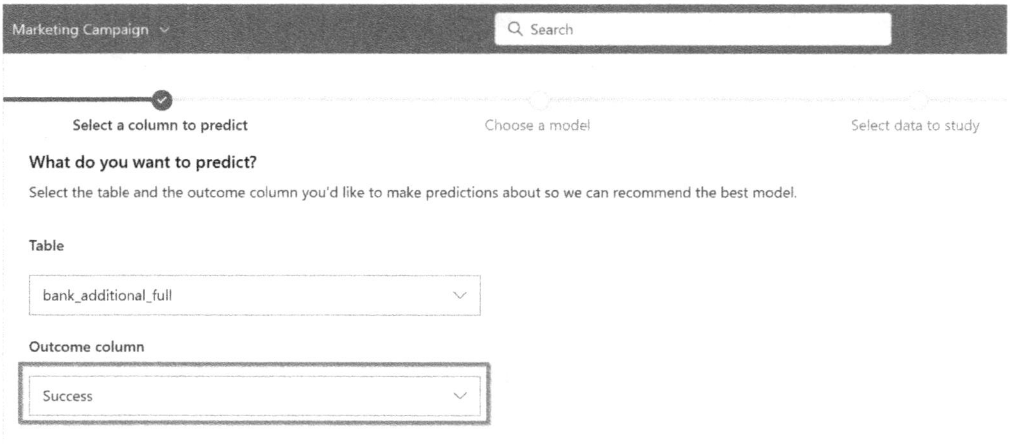

Figure 13.14 – Selecting the Outcome column

3. Next, we select the type of prediction that we want to use. Because our Success column contains only two options – successful (yes) or not (no) – we choose **Binary Prediction** here:

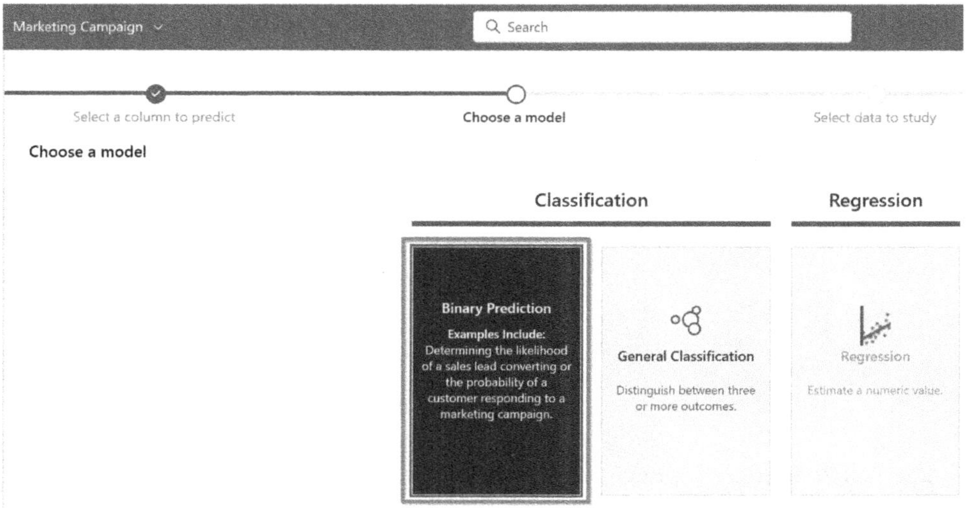

Figure 13.15 – Selecting the Classification type

4. In the following step, we define the success criteria – in our case, yes:

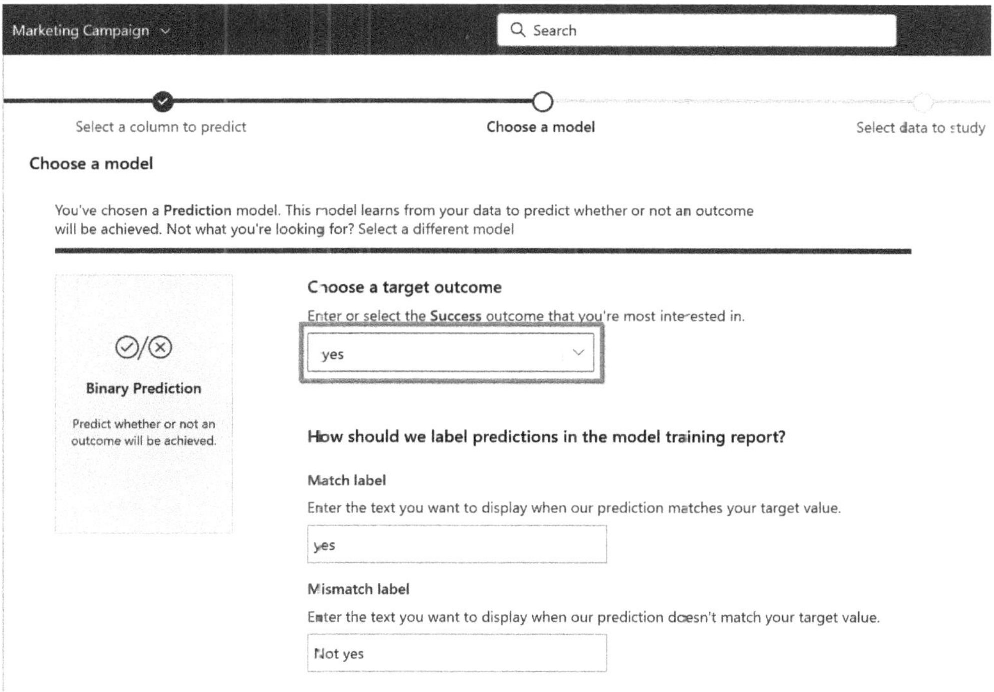

Figure 13.16 – Specifying the target variable

5. Next, we can select the columns that we want to utilize. Power BI automatically makes suggestions and only selects the columns where it detects a correlation. This is based on a subset of data. The correlation with a single column doesn't necessarily mean there are no correlations in combination with other columns, so I recommend using all columns that could be relevant, but also omitting columns that are either definitely not helpful or not known in new datasets, such as the campaign duration:

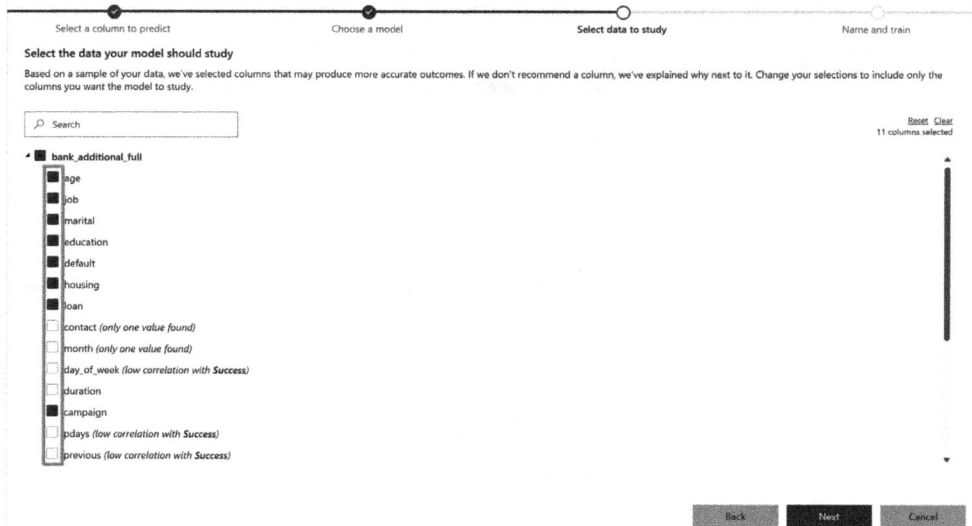

Figure 13.17 – Specifying columns to include

6. In the final step, we set the name of our model and the processing time for the training. My recommendation here is to start with a short duration and see the quality of the model. Following that, you can gradually increase the time and see whether that improves the model:

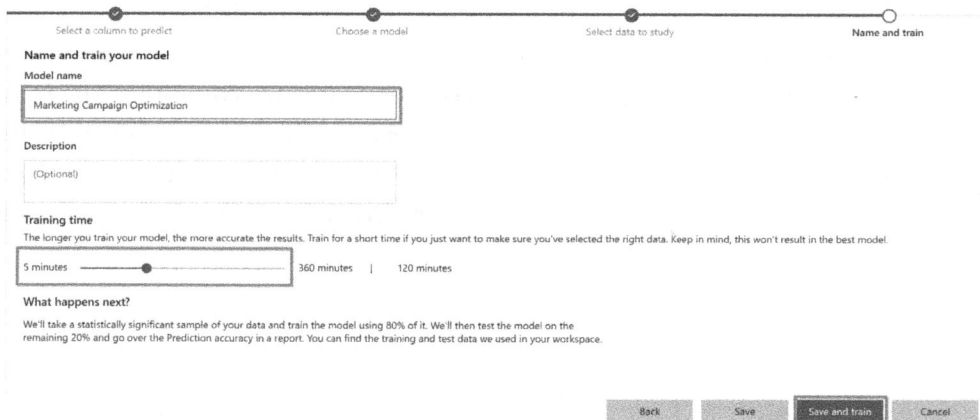

Figure 13.18 – Model settings

7. After clicking the **Save and train** button, the process will run for the selected time, and following that, we can open the new model training report with the name that you have set in your workspace:

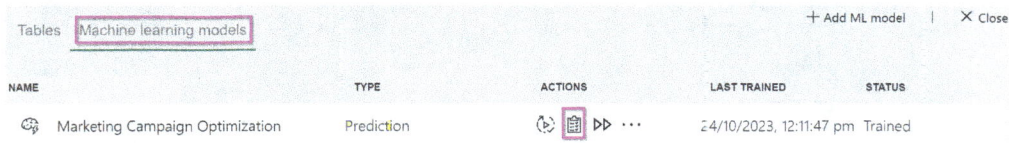

Figure 13.19 – Starting the report

8. After clicking the *report* icon, we get this report, which shows the outcomes of the Power BI ML process:

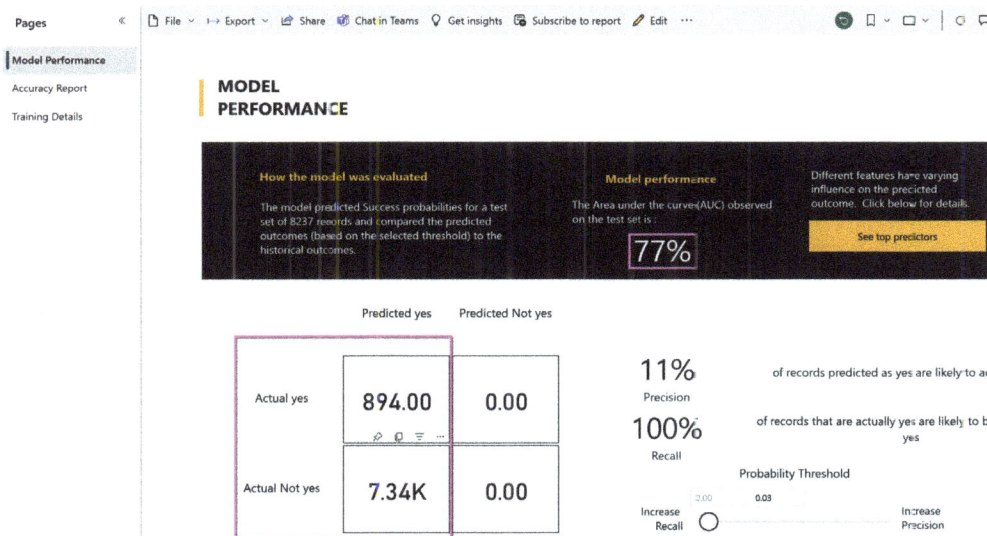

Figure 13.20 – Predictions with a probability threshold of 0.03

The results with the initial settings do not look very good, as more than 90% are incorrectly qualified with the default setting of a **0.03** probability threshold. This essentially means that all records are qualified as the Success criteria, which doesn't make a lot of sense in our case. If we change the probability to higher than 50%, we get a more useful outcome for our case:

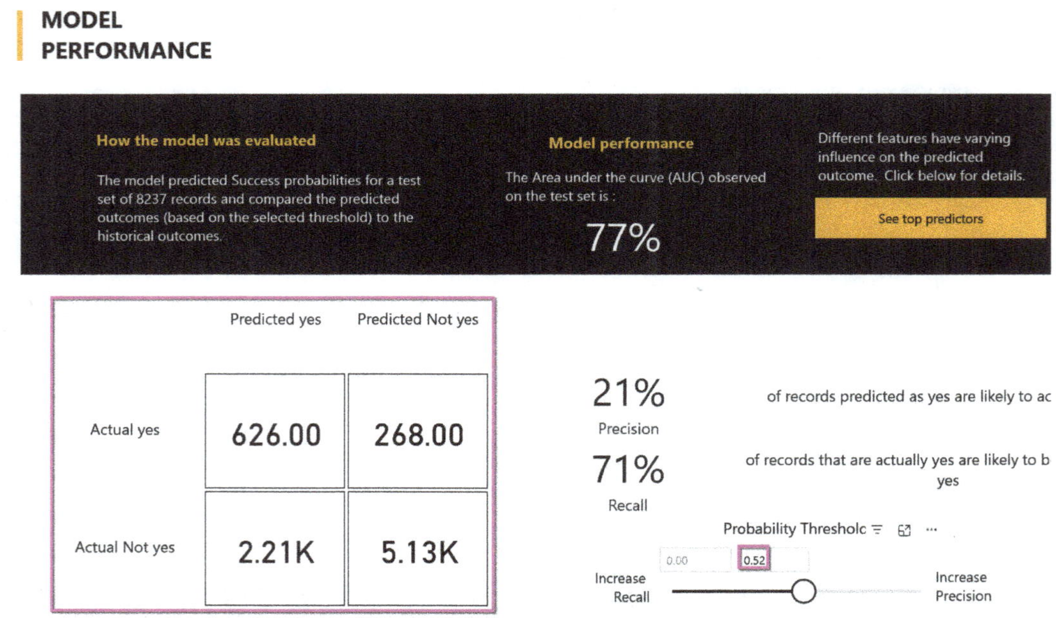

MODEL PERFORMANCE

How the model was evaluated

The model predicted Success probabilities for a test set of 8237 records and compared the predicted outcomes (based on the selected threshold) to the historical outcomes.

Model performance

The Area under the curve (AUC) observed on the test set is :

77%

Different features have varying influence on the predicted outcome. Click below for details.

See top predictors

	Predicted yes	Predicted Not yes
Actual yes	626.00	268.00
Actual Not yes	2.21K	5.13K

21% Precision — of records predicted as yes are likely to ac

71% Recall — of records that are actually yes are likely to b yes

Probability Thresholc

| 0.00 | 0.52 |

Increase Recall —————————◯————— Increase Precision

Figure 13.21 – Predictions with a probability threshold of 0.52

We see that 5,756 (*626 + 5130*) or 71% are correctly classified. This is not an optimal outcome, but typical for initial results. Let's see whether we can improve it. If we increase the processing capacity to 1 hour, it only changes slightly:

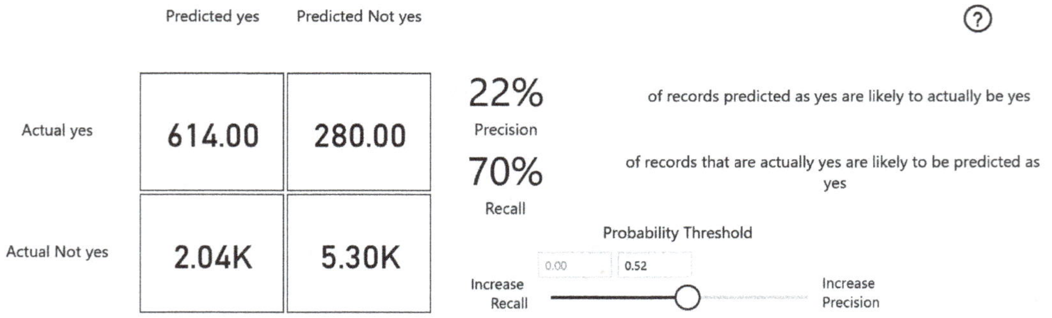

	Predicted yes	Predicted Not yes
Actual yes	614.00	280.00
Actual Not yes	2.04K	5.30K

22% Precision — of records predicted as yes are likely to actually be yes

70% Recall — of records that are actually yes are likely to be predicted as yes

Probability Threshold

| 0.00 | 0.52 |

Increase Recall —————————◯————— Increase Precision

Figure 13.22 – ML-generated predictions with a 1-hour processing capacity

From here, we can now also get to interesting commercial insights. As per our initial objective, we want to optimize campaign outcomes for a given budget. We can immediately do that in this report by scrolling down and entering our conditions, for example, assuming the following:

- A target database of 5,000 contacts
- A cost of acquisition (e.g., telemarketing success fee) of $150
- An expected profit of $1,000 for a successful sale

We see the suggested probability threshold curve and related profits (maximum campaign profit of $191,210) in the report:

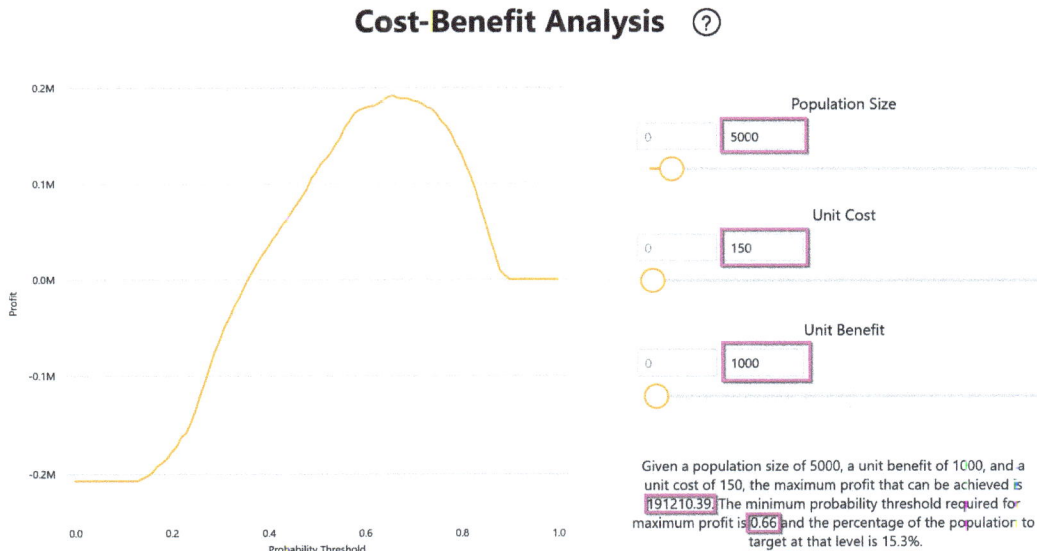

Figure 13.23 – Cost-benefit analysis

To run the actual campaign optimization, you would use the **Apply model** button at the top of the report or in the workspace and point to the dataset with the new data:

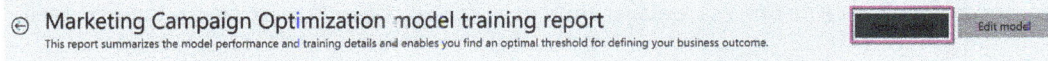

Figure 13.24 – Applying the ML model

This will then apply your model to this data, which will generate a new query with scores in your dataflow. You can now filter this on the TRUE predictions and filter for the desired probability score, and run a campaign on this subset with expected results, as in the cost-benefit analysis:

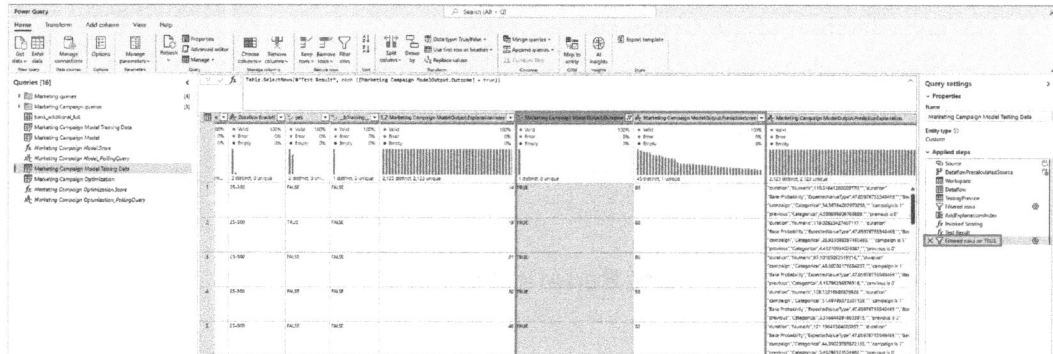

Figure 13.25 – ML-generated scores

Machine Learning in Power BI: Transitioning to Microsoft Fabric AutoML

With the deprecation of AutoML in Power BI Dataflows, Microsoft now recommends using the AutoML capabilities available in Synapse Data Science within Microsoft Fabric. This new approach offers theoretically greater flexibility, scalability, and control over your machine learning workflows, along with all the analysis and visualization benefits that Power BI offers. At the time of finalizing this book, this feature was very immature, and I couldn't get a working result. I still want to provide an outline of how to approach the exercise with the new technology and hope that by the publishing date the issues are addressed.

Business Case

As before, our objective is to optimize future campaign outcomes by identifying customer criteria most likely to purchase the promoted service, while considering budget constraints and profitability targets. The process remains similar, but the tools and environment have evolved.

Setting Up Machine Learning in Microsoft Fabric

Here are the prerequisites for setting up machine learning in Microsoft Fabric:

- Access to Microsoft Fabric (Premium capacity or trial license)
- Data must reside in a Fabric Lakehouse storage item. The **Fabric Lakehouse** enables management of large volumes of structured and unstructured data in an open, scalable format (such as Delta Lake). It is a prerequisite for many advanced analytics, machine learning, and business intelligence workloads in Fabric.

Workflow Overview

We will use Fabric's data engineering tools to ingest, clean, and transform the campaign data. Dataflows (now in version 2) can still be used for ETL, but the machine learning model creation now happens in Fabric's Synapse Data Science environment.

1. The new AutoML implementation in Fabric requires data to be stored in a Lakehouse storage type. To do this, create a new Lakehouse by clicking **New** > **Lakehouse** in your Fabric workspace or select an existing one:

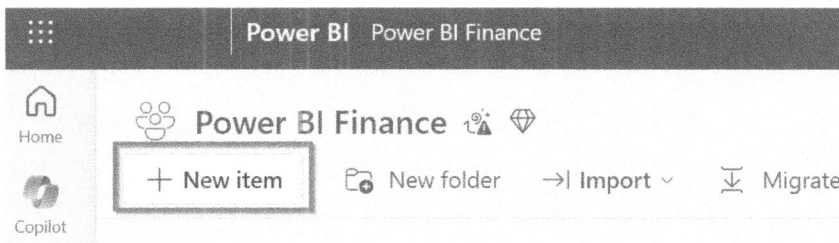

Figure 13.26 – Creating a new Fabric item

2. Select **Lakehouse** in the following dialog box:

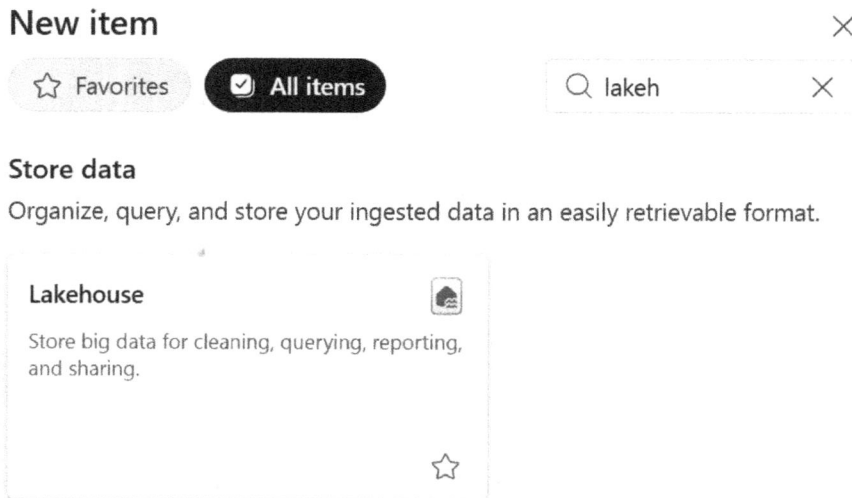

Figure 13.27 – Selecting Lakehouse type

3. Create a new **Dataflow Gen2** from our data file by uploading our transaction file bank-additional-full.csv. For that, first select the file type as shown here:

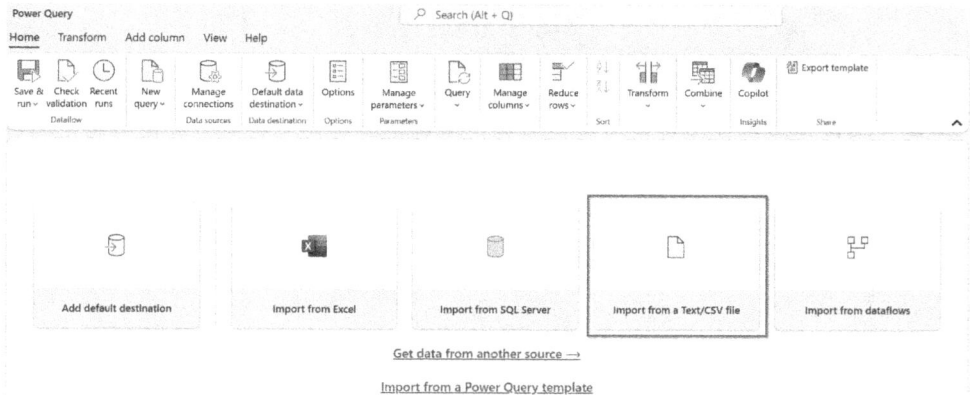

Figure 13.28 – Selecting file type

Then upload the file:

Get data
Connect to data source

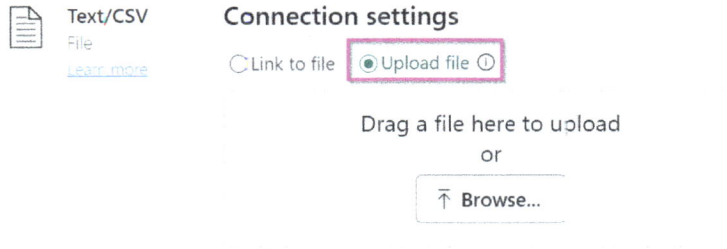

Text/CSV
File
Learn more

Connection settings

○ Link to file   ⦿ Upload file ⓘ

Drag a file here to upload
or

↑ Browse...

Figure 13.29 – Uploading the csv file

4. Now, the Power Query editor opens for the file:

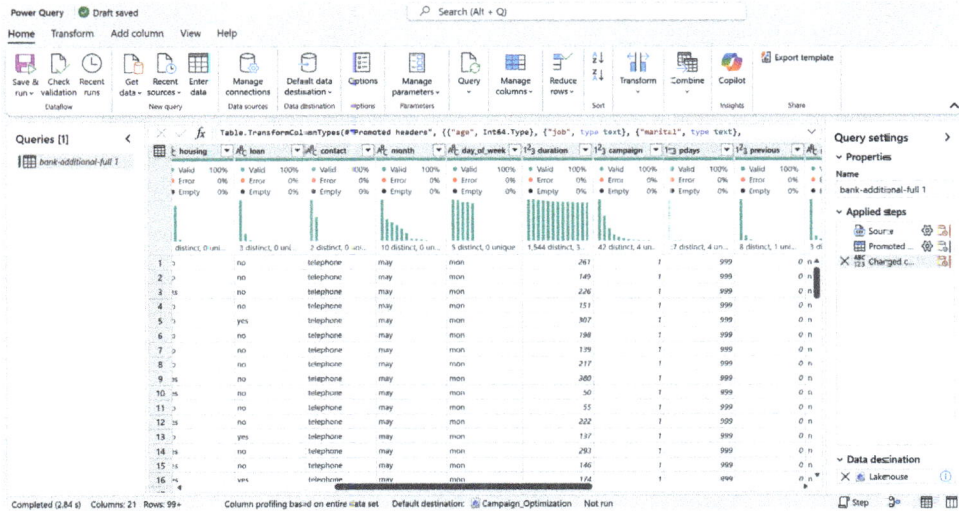

Figure 13.30 – New Dataflow (Gen2)

Here, add the age categorization (By example) by entering an example for the age bracket (55-60) as described in the previous section:

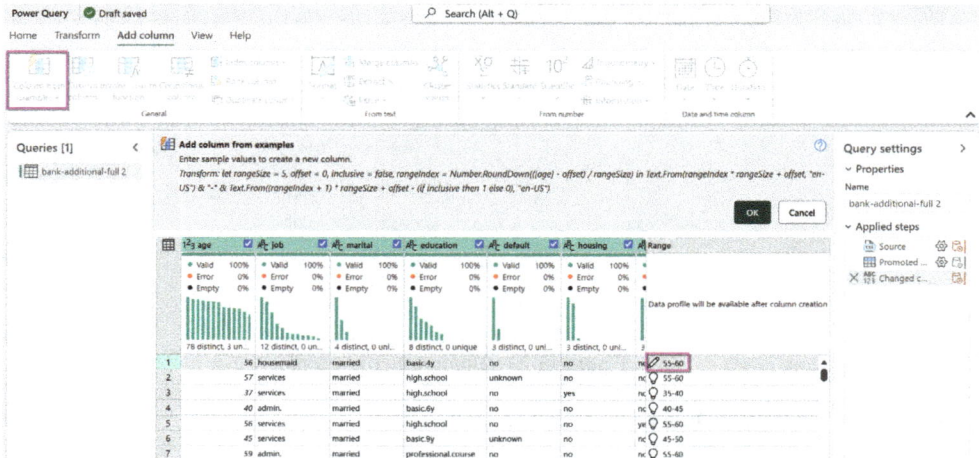

Figure 13.31 – Adding a column from example for age range

5. Then, remove columns that are not relevant, such as "duration", a variable that is not known before the event:

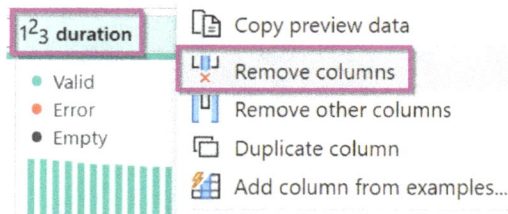

Figure 13.32 – Removing unnecessary columns

6. Click **Save & run** and load the data into the Lakehouse storage:

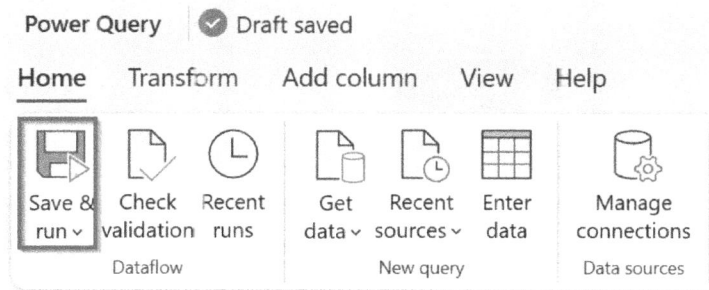

Figure 13.33 – Loading data into Lakehouse

The source data is now ready to be used in the next step, where we implement the machine learning process.

Model Training with AutoML

Follow these steps to apply the ML process:

1. Open your Power BI / Fabric Workspace.
2. From the ribbon on the left, either create a new workspace or select an existing one.
3. In your **Workspace** click on **New Item** at the top:

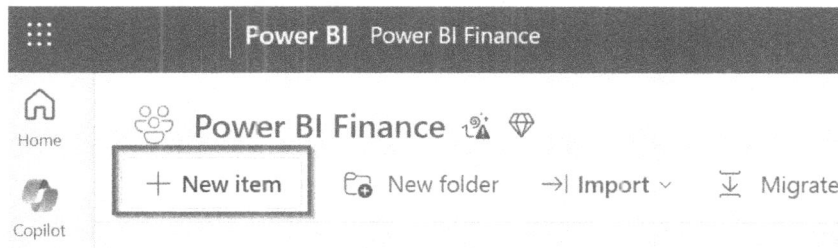

Figure 13.34 – Loading data into Lakehouse

Then, select **Experiment**:

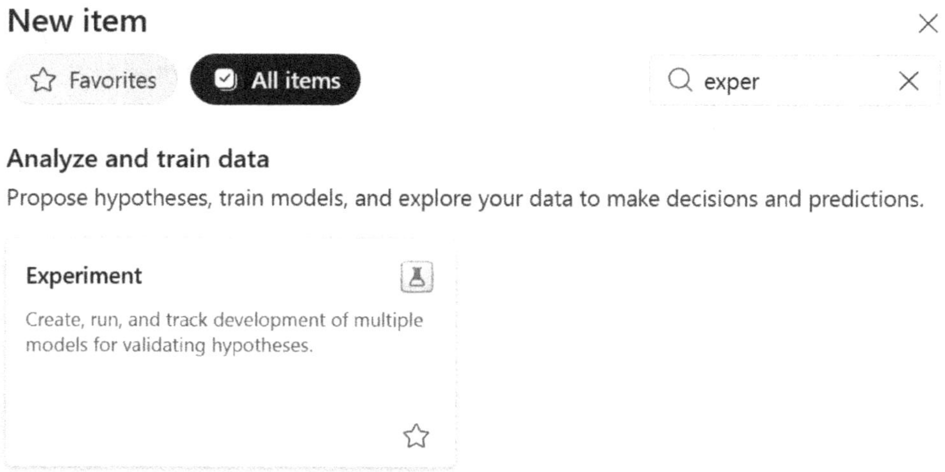
New item
Favorites
All items
exper
Analyze and train data
Propose hypotheses, train models, and explore your data to make decisions and predictions.
Experiment
Create, run, and track development of multiple models for validating hypotheses.

Figure 13.35 – New Experiment item

4. Choose the new Lakehouse to be used with the experiment:

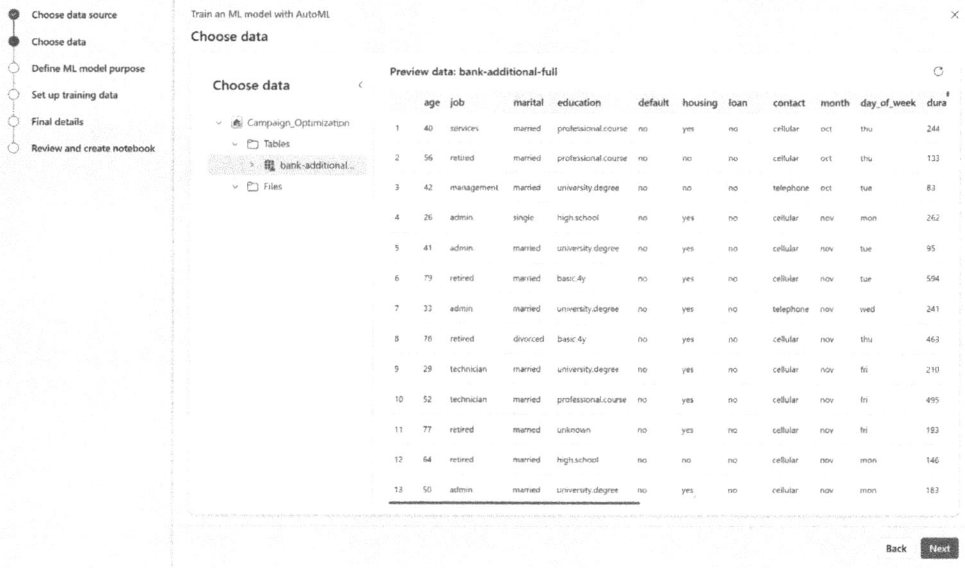
Choose data source
Choose data
Define ML model purpose
Set up training data
Final details
Review and create notebook
Train an ML model with AutoML
Choose data
Choose data
Campaign_Optimization
Tables
bank-additional...
Files
Preview data: bank-additional-full
age job marital education default housing loan contact month day_of_week dura
Back
Next

Figure 13.36 – Selecting Lakehouse table

5. Select our model type as **Binary classification**:

Figure 13.37 – Selecting ML type

After the Review step, the Wizard will generate a Fabric notebook. This interactive workspace lets you write and execute code in languages such as Python, R, or Scala, often leveraging Apache Spark, an open-source, distributed computing system designed for fast processing and analysis of large-scale data analysis including data transformation, machine learning, and real-time analytics across clusters of computers. Notebooks are designed for data exploration, transformation, analysis, and machine learning, allowing users to combine code, visualizations, and narrative text in a single, shareable document. This makes them ideal for advanced analysis, enabling you to document the process, experiment with different models, and visualize results.

In theory, Fabric AutoML should produce similar outcomes as I have covered in the previous section with the now deprecated Dataflows approach, but by the time of publication of this book (November 2025), I was not able to get to a usable outcome. The data preparation steps in the notebook worked, but after that, I only got errors with the Python code generated by Fabric AutoML.

Summary

Power BI's machine learning capabilities have evolved, with Microsoft Fabric now providing the recommended platform for automated ML workflows. The transition offers more advanced tools, scalability, and integration options, ensuring your analytics remain future proof. For users with advanced needs, Azure Machine Learning remains a powerful option, seamlessly integrated with Power BI for custom modeling and real-time scoring.

Recommendation: Begin migrating your machine learning workflows to Microsoft Fabric's Synapse Data Science AutoML. Explore integration with Azure Machine Learning for specialized use cases and continue leveraging Power BI's AI visuals for quick, actionable insights and explanations.

Get This Book's PDF Version and Exclusive Extras

Scan the QR code (or go to packtpub.com/unlock). Search for this book by name, confirm the edition, and then follow the steps on the page.

Note: Keep your invoice handy. Purchases made directly from Packt don't require one.

14

Using LLMs and Copilot in Power BI to Improve Financial Analysis

Since 2020, **large language models (LLMs)** and Microsoft Copilot (2024) – an AI assistant that is an optional component in various Microsoft products, including Power BI – have emerged as powerful tools that add completely new ways to improve efficiency in Power BI model creation and analysis. Some of these improvements are very relevant to financial use cases. These AI-driven solutions can streamline report creation, optimize DAX calculations, automate documentation, and generate valuable business insights.

This chapter explores how LLMs and Copilot can be used in conjunction with Microsoft Power BI to enhance financial analysis and decision-making. By the end of this chapter, you will understand how to harness LLMs and Copilot to optimize Power BI workflows, accelerate report generation, and drive more informed business decisions. The content in this chapter (as of Q2 2025) comes with a word of warning: this is an extremely fast-changing technological environment where content can be quickly outdated. So, I recommend using your LLM of choice to validate the content of this chapter for up-to-date details.

In this chapter, we'll cover the following main topics:

- Understanding LLMs
- Using Copilot for Power BI
- Differences between other LLMs and Copilot
- Practical use cases of LLMs in Power BI

Technical requirements

As with all sample content in this book, all related files from examples covered in this chapter are available in the GitHub repository: `https://github.com/PacktPublishing/Power-BI-for-Finance`. Specifically, we will use the `Chapter 14` sample file.

To follow the examples in this chapter, you will need an active Copilot for Power BI license.

Understanding LLMs

LLMs are based on advanced machine learning algorithms in the deep learning category. They are trained on extensive amounts of textual data to generate human-like responses and understand complex queries, typically in the form of a chatbot. These models, such as OpenAI's GPT-5, Anthropic's Claude, and Google's Gemini, process natural language inputs to perform a variety of tasks, including summarization, content generation, and analytical reasoning.

LLMs rely on deep learning techniques, specifically transformer architectures, to predict and generate text-based outputs based on user queries. They can recognize patterns in data, generate code, automate processes, and provide insights based on pre-existing knowledge. For example, they can automatically generate an in-depth financial analysis based on financial statements that are either already available online or provided as an upload by the user.

Most popular LLMs that can be used with Power BI

While multiple LLMs exist, the most effective ones for use with Power BI include the following:

- **Claude (Anthropic):** Very strong with coding and particularly relevant in our context with its ability to generate interactive analysis applications. It is also helpful for summarization and business report writing.
- **Microsoft Copilot (integrated with OpenAI's ChatGPT):** Ideal for requirements that involve the entire model (structure and data) in the Power BI model and the generation of visuals and reports directly in Power BI.

- **Gemini (Google)**: Strong at pattern recognition and contextualizing business data.
- **ChatGPT (OpenAI)**: Excellent for DAX generation, report documentation, and natural language queries.
- **Llama (Meta)**: An open-source alternative useful for customizable business intelligence solutions.
- **DeepSeek**: A powerful AI model designed for structured data analysis and reasoning, making it particularly useful for creating efficient Power BI data models and generating DAX calculations.

Each of these LLMs has unique strengths that make it suitable for different Power BI applications. For example, ChatGPT excels at generating complex DAX formulas and automating report documentation, making it ideal for users looking to streamline repetitive tasks. Gemini, on the other hand, is highly effective at identifying patterns within large datasets, helping analysts uncover trends and anomalies. Claude is particularly useful for writing code and full analytical applications, summarizing reports, and generating detailed business narratives, which can enhance presentations and decision-making. Meanwhile, Llama's open-source nature makes it a strong choice for organizations requiring custom AI-driven solutions tailored to specific Power BI workflows.

Apart from Copilot, the covered LLMs have no direct integration with Power BI; you have to input your queries (e.g., DAX queries to be reviewed) in the respective chatbot. The only one with a direct integration in Power BI is Microsoft Copilot, which we will cover in the following section.

Using Copilot for Power BI

Microsoft Copilot is an AI-powered assistant that leverages OpenAI's LLM capabilities integrated into Power BI to help users generate reports, create DAX formulas, and gain insights from data using natural language. By leveraging Copilot, users can quickly configure Power BI visuals, summarize findings, and even automate repetitive tasks.

To follow these examples, you will need an active Copilot for Power BI license. Copilot is included in Microsoft Fabric editions starting with at least F64, which costs approximately $8,400 per month as of the time of publishing this book (Q2 2025), but it can be used on an hourly basis for a cost of around $10 per hour. The latter would be my suggestion for this demo. Just create a capacity in your Azure environment and make sure you only have it active (start and pause when you use it – otherwise, it will get very expensive!).

Let's discuss a few examples of Copilot usage for financial analysis.

Data exploration/analysis assistants

Users can ask Copilot open-ended questions, such as *What are relevant questions to analyze in the context of this model?*, and receive typical, useful angles to improve analysis. For example, in our Chapter 4 Power BI sample report, we can open the Copilot assistant and start with the following prompt: `what are interesting questions to ask in the context of this model`, and receive the following helpful breakdown:

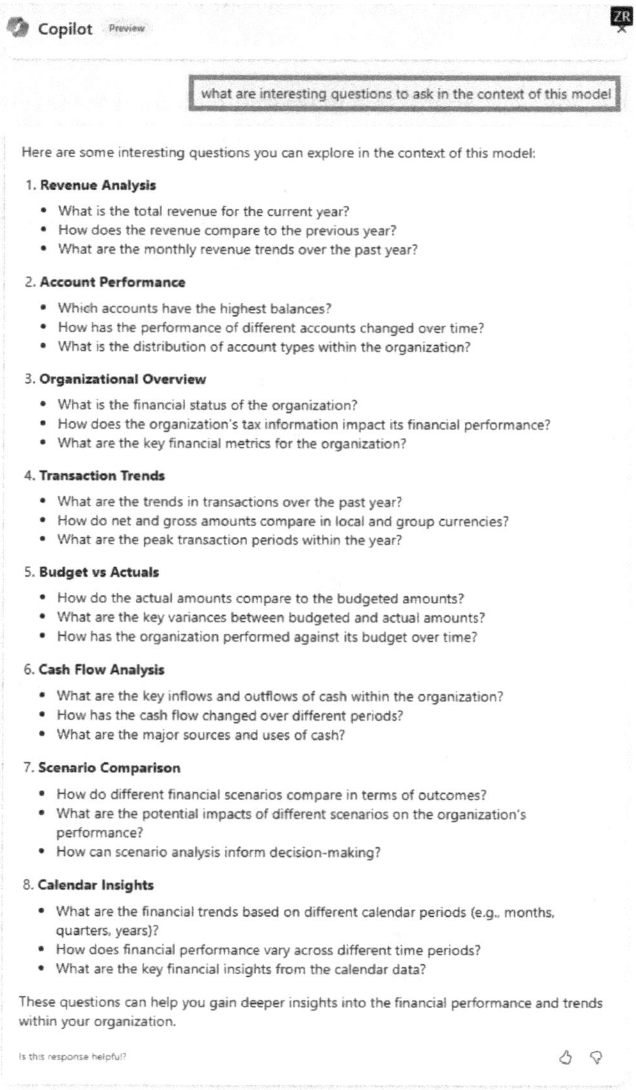

Figure 14.1 – Support with helpful questions for analysis

Creating completely new reports/visuals

In the Chapter 14 Power BI sample file, I have included a demo sales model with fictiti sales across different geographies and sales reps, which is used for some of the following examples on how Copilot can be used for completely new models:

Filename	Type	Likely Role
DimDate.csv	CSV	Date dimension (calendar attributes)
DimProduct.csv	CSV	Product dimension (product details)
DimSalesMeasures.csv	CSV	Measures dimension (KPIs, metrics)
DimSalesReps.csv	CSV	Sales reps dimension (employee info)
DimScenario.csv	CSV	Scenario dimension (forecast vs actual)
Sales_Chapter_14.csv	CSV	Transactions for Sales fact table

Table 14.1 – Sales model tables

These were imported into the Power BI with the **Get Data** option that we discussed in previous chapters. We can now test how Copilot can assist with generating reports and provide helpful insights.

Initially, we can see what reports can be created automatically by entering this prompt in Copilot: create a useful sales dashboard. This creates a very good result with the key requirements in a sales context (which were automatically detected), such as sales over time, by product, by sales rep, and by geographic distribution:

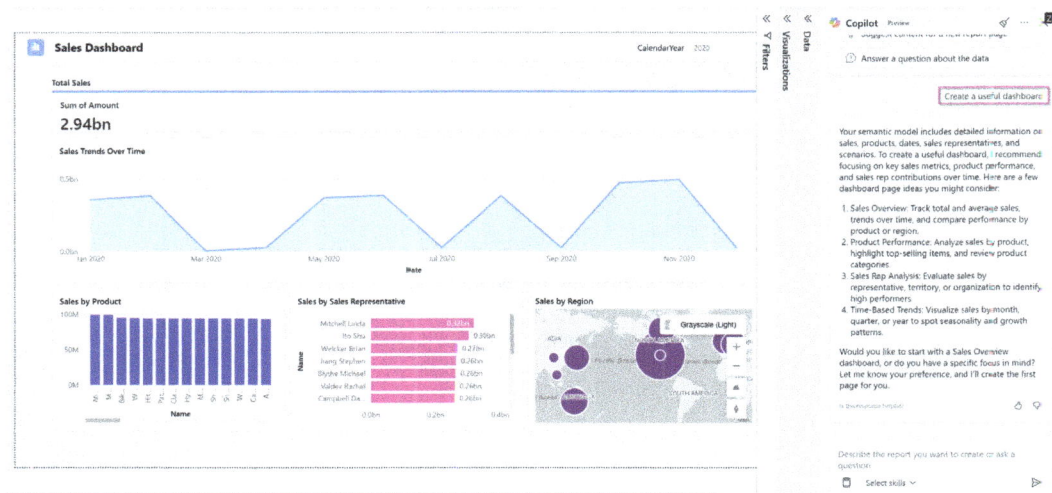

Figure 14.2 – Dashboard generated by Copilot

The initial results are useful, but it would be better if the user had the option to filter them. We can test whether the output can be improved by prompting add filter for year, and we see that the existing results can also be easily adapted:

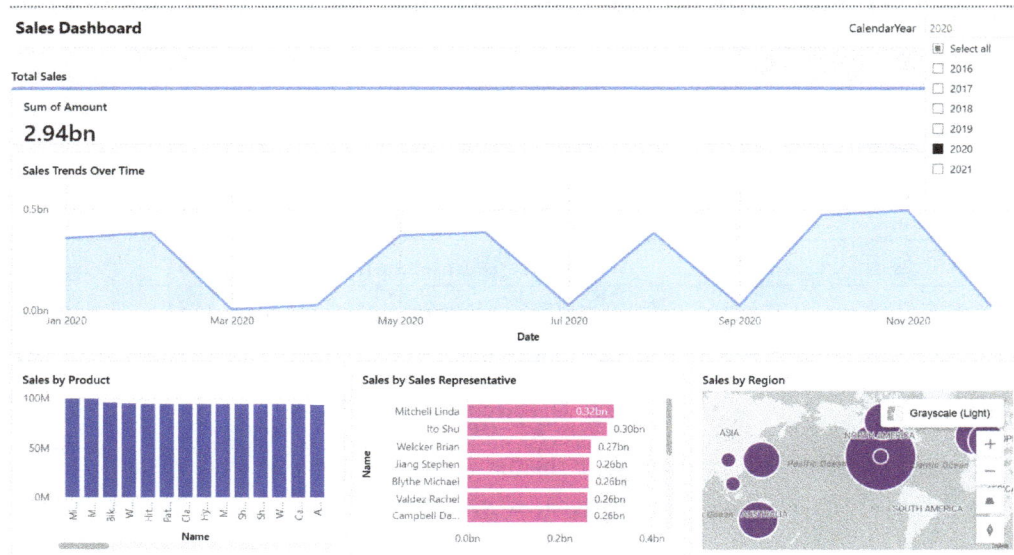

Figure 14.3 – Added filter

Now that we have a useful initial dashboard, we can try to see whether Copilot can find insights by asking: What are the interesting insights?. This now gives us a list of relevant findings with the interesting additional benefit that we can highlight the visuals related to the finding by clicking on the number next to the insight:

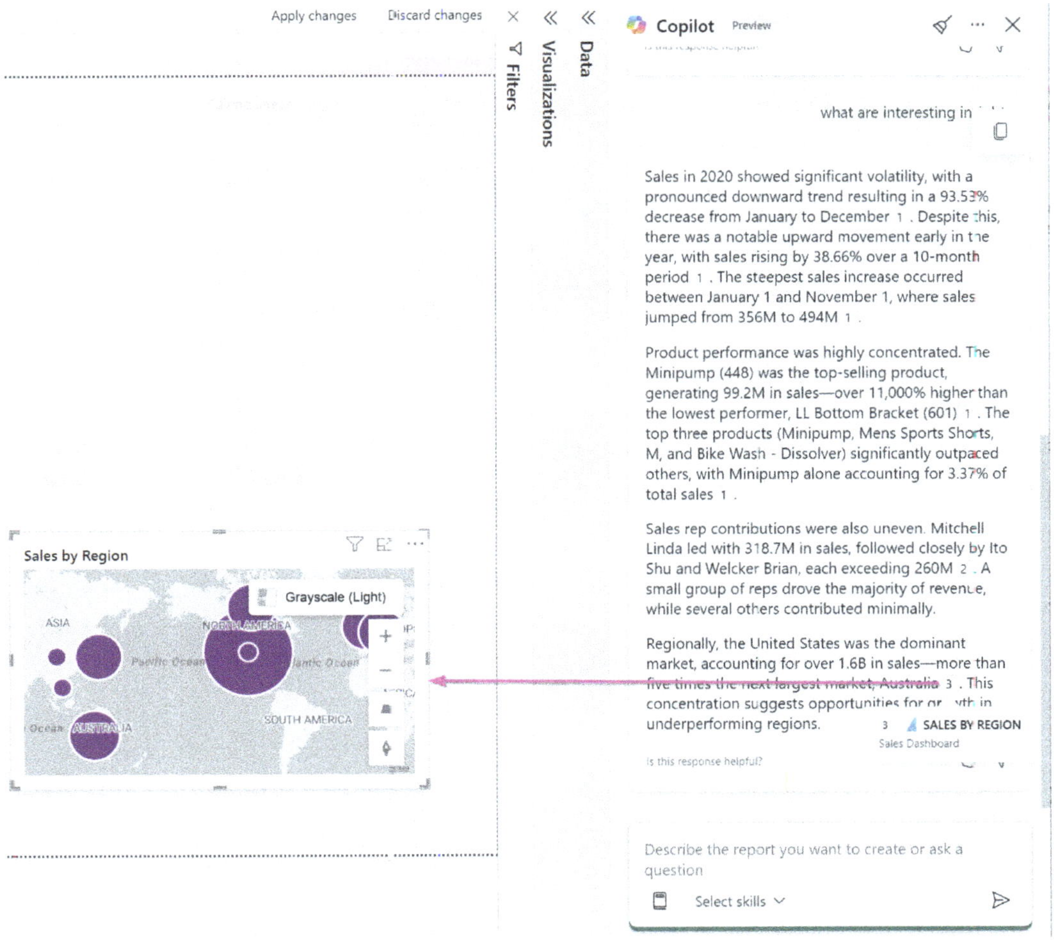

Figure 14.4 – Interesting insights and highlighting

Creating financial metrics with DAX

Power BI Copilot can also assist users with generating useful calculations, such as financial metrics, using DAX. To calculate the gross margin (revenue minus direct costs), for example, a user can request, Create a DAX measure for Gross Profit Margin, and Copilot generates a helpful response that is also correct in the context of the model (identifying that standard costs are in the product dimension, DimProduct):

To create a DAX calculation for gross margin, you need to have the necessary fields in your semantic model. Typically, gross margin is calculated as follows:

```
[ \text{Gross Margin} = \frac{\text{Total Sales} - \text{Cost of Goods
Sold (COGS)}}{\text{Total Sales}} ]
```

From the schema provided, it appears that you have a `Total Sales` measure but not a `Cost of Goods Sold (COGS)` measure. If you have a field that represents the cost of goods sold, you can use it in the calculation. Assuming you have a `COGS` field in the `Sales` table, the DAX formula for `Gross Margin` would be as follows:

```
Gross Margin =
DIVIDE(
    SUM(Sales[Amount]) - SUM(Sales[COGS]),
    SUM(Sales[Amount])
)
```

If you do not have a `COGS` field, you will need to identify the appropriate field that represents the cost of goods sold in your model. If you have a `StandardCost` field in the `DimProduct` table, you can use it to calculate `Gross Margin` as follows:

```
Gross Margin =
DIVIDE(
    SUM(Sales[Amount]) - SUMX(Sales, RELATED(DimProduct[StandardCost])),
    SUM(Sales[Amount])
)
```

At the time of writing this book, my tests around generating useful DAX measures without a specific prompt didn't produce useful enough results to include in this book. Copilot was also not able to create the measures directly; the results produced must be copied manually. So, I suggest you try your own variations of this prompt: `Generate useful DAX measures in the context of this model`.

Analyzing financial statements

Copilot can calculate financial metrics (current ratio and quick ratio) and profitability ratios (ROE and ROA) automatically and generate visual breakdowns over different periods.

We can test these capabilities with our financial statements (balance sheet, income statement, and cash flow statement) model from *Chapter 4* and enter What are interesting financial insights in this model? in the Copilot prompt. This gives us a few different options of areas to analyze, such as **Revenue Trends, Budget vs Actual Performance**, and so on:

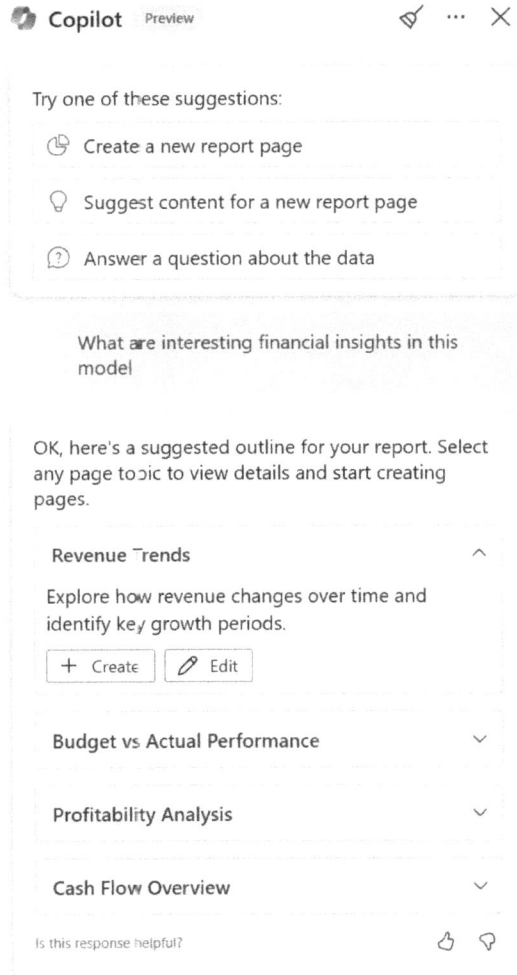

Figure 14.5 – Copilot options

For example, we can now click on the **Create** button in the **Revenue Trends** option and get very detailed insights:

Explore how revenue changes over time and identify key growth periods.

Revenue shows significant fluctuations over the observed periods. In late 2019, revenue was strong, with values such as $4,600 in August, $17,686 in September, $13,700 in October, and $17,500.96 in November. There is a notable gap in revenue data for much of 2020, with only November showing $6,305.17.

In 2021, revenue starts lower, with $747.26 in January and $753.06 in February, but then increases to $1,494.78 in April and $2,366.08 in July. A substantial spike occurs in October 2021, where revenue jumps to $24,644.66, followed by $16,576.18 in November and $24,069.57 in December. The upward trend continues into January 2022 with $27,797.72.

Key periods of revenue growth are observed in:

- September to November 2019
- April to July 2021 (steady increase)
- October 2021 to January 2022 (sharp growth, peaking at $27,797.72)

These periods represent the most significant increases in revenue over time, with the most dramatic growth occurring in late 2021 and early 2022 [1].

Is this response helpful?

Figure 14.6 – Revenue trends analysis

The other options also generate in-depth results that would take a qualified analyst substantial time, even considering the not very realistic character of the demo data.

Variance analysis and forecasting

Variance analysis to compare actual financial performance to budgets or previous periods is the second option that Copilot suggests with our data model. This equally returns very useful insights that definitely outperform the basic methods in Power BI visuals that we reviewed in *Chapter 13*:

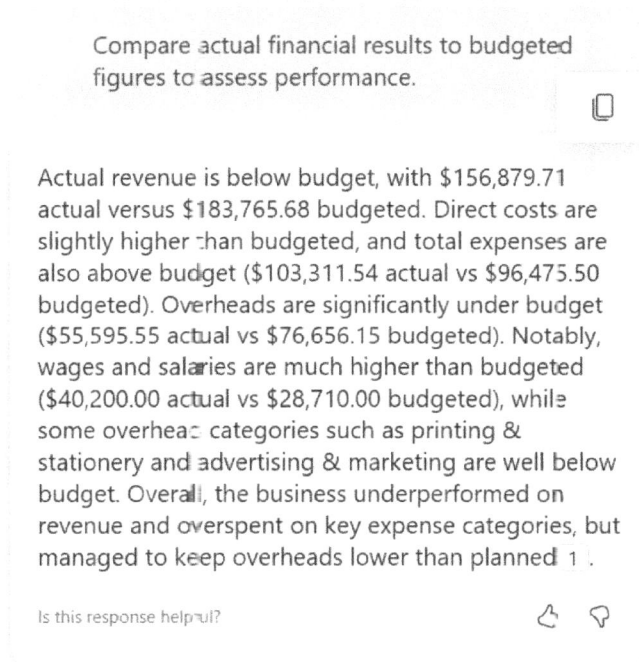

Compare actual financial results to budgeted figures to assess performance.

Actual revenue is below budget, with $156,879.71 actual versus $183,765.68 budgeted. Direct costs are slightly higher than budgeted, and total expenses are also above budget ($103,311.54 actual vs $96,475.50 budgeted). Overheads are significantly under budget ($55,595.55 actual vs $76,656.15 budgeted). Notably, wages and salaries are much higher than budgeted ($40,200.00 actual vs $28,710.00 budgeted), while some overhead categories such as printing & stationery and advertising & marketing are well below budget. Overall, the business underperformed on revenue and overspent on key expense categories, but managed to keep overheads lower than planned 1 .

Is this response helpful?

Figure 14 7 – Copilot variance analysis results

Cash flow analysis

The third option that we are given is **Cash Flow Overview**. When we choose **Create** here, we again get textual explanations, and in this case, we also get a chart that we can add to our report. At the bottom, we also have the option to see how Copilot arrived at this and what measures were used:

Based on the available data, cash flow patterns show significant volatility, with strong inflows early in the year followed by substantial outflows in later months. This suggests challenges in maintaining consistent liquidity and operational efficiency throughout the year.

Sum of NetAmount_GC by Month and Cash Flow Group

Cash Flow Gr... ● (Blank) ● Operating Cashflow

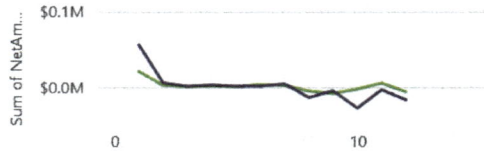

+ Add to page   ⟨⟩

∧ How Copilot arrived at this

You asked: "Review cash flow patterns to understand liquidity and operational efficiency."

Data used

▯ Cash Flow Group
Σ Month
Σ NetAmount_GC

Filters applied ⓘ

None

To improve results, prep your data for AI.

Is this response helpful?   👍 👎

Figure 14.8 – Copilot cash flow analysis

In addition, we can also always process our own specific questions, such as `Generate a DAX measure for Free Cash Flow`:

- Free Cash Flow DAX measure:

```
Free Cash Flow = [Operating Cash Flow] - [Capital Expenditures]
```

Another area where Copilot can assist that is very relevant for finance professionals is risk management. For example, it can help identify financial risks in large datasets or anomalies, such as the following:

- Sudden spikes in operational expenses
- Unusual revenue fluctuations compared to historical trends
- Accounts receivable aging trends that indicate potential bad debts

For Power BI users, Copilot offers the easiest available option to leverage the power of LLMs, but there are good arguments to review other LLMs, which we will cover in the next section.

Differences between other LLMs and Copilot

To utilize LLMs, Power BI users can either use one of the generic models (GPT-x, Gemini, DeepSeek, etc.) or the built-in Microsoft Copilot feature. The latter, though, is only available with high (and costly, starting in the $10 range per hour) Premium/Fabric tiers.

The following table outlines the key differences:

Feature	Copilot	LLMs
Integration	<ul><li>Deeply integrated with Microsoft's ecosystem, not just Power BI (Office, Windows, Edge). Combines ChatGPT capabilities with Microsoft's specific tools (Power BI Q&A feature set) and services.</li><li>Contextual awareness of user data within Microsoft's environment. Can create Power BI reports, pages, and visuals.</li><li>Available both as a standalone assistant and integrated into Microsoft products.</li><li>Works predominantly with data in the model but can consider external details in prompts.</li></ul>	<ul><li>Via chatbot, external APIs, or self-hosted models. Can only access data provided (copy/paste/model structure upload), which typically only includes non-sensitive (companies typically disallow any upload of sensitive data to externally hosted LLMs), structural, model data.</li><li>Cannot directly manipulate Power BI or other applications.</li><li>Standalone solution.</li><li>Works with any data presented in prompts and accessible to the LLM.</li></ul>

Feature	Copilot	LLMs
DAX support	Direct formula suggestions.	Requires external queries for formula generation.
Cost model	Power BI/Fabric Premium licensing.	Free or usage-based pricing or self-hosted options.
Customization	Limited to Power BI features.	Fully customizable for different use cases.
Data security	Hosted in a Microsoft environment.	Depends on hosting model (cloud vs. self-hosted).
Contextual financial intelligence	As described in the previous section, Copilot automatically provides contextual financial insights (trend, variance, and cashflow analysis).	Specific analysis requirements are typically specified by the user, but these can be generic.

Table 14.2 – Comparison of Copilot and external APIs

In the previous section, we covered LLM concepts and the differences between generic LLMs and Power BI Copilot. In the next section, we will cover more extensive practical use cases.

Practical use cases of LLMs in Power BI

You can use an LLM with direct prompts. For example, you can copy and paste a DAX measure in the prompt and add—Can this DAX measure be improved?—or a more generic question on how to realize a general requirement with DAX. Another option is to use a **Business Intelligence Model (BIM)** file. Let's see how we can combine these two methods for comprehensive financial analysis.

Analyzing Power BI model structures using PBIP and BIM files

This contains details about the semantic model in human-readable form used in a Power BI file (pbix/pbip). This includes tables, columns, DAX measures, queries, and so on, but it does not contain any data details. Using a BIM file is an approach I would recommend when using Power BI with general LLMs for use cases that need to take the entire model into account, such as the following:

- **Automating model optimization**: LLMs can analyze BIM files to detect inefficient relationships, unnecessary columns, and performance bottlenecks

- **Enhancing documentation**: By extracting metadata from a BIM file, an LLM can generate comprehensive documentation, including table descriptions and measure explanations

- **Refactoring DAX measures**: LLMs can suggest optimizations for existing DAX measures based on the structure stored in a BIM file

- **Validating model design**: AI-driven analysis of BIM files can highlight missing relationships, redundant tables, or suboptimal indexing

How to generate a BIM file

As of June 2023, BIM files are part of **Power BI Project** files, known by the .pbip extension, which were introduced as a preview feature in Power BI Desktop. This new format allows for better integration with version control systems such as Git, facilitating collaborative development and **continuous integration/continuous deployment** (CI/CD) processes. In August 2024, with the release of Power BI Desktop version 2.132.908.0, .pbip files transitioned from preview to general availability, enabling all users to utilize this feature without enabling any preview settings. As of Q1 2025, saving as a PBIP file still needs to be enabled in **Preview features** under **Options**. Also, make sure that **Store semantic model using TMDL format** is not enabled, as shown in *Figure 14.9*:

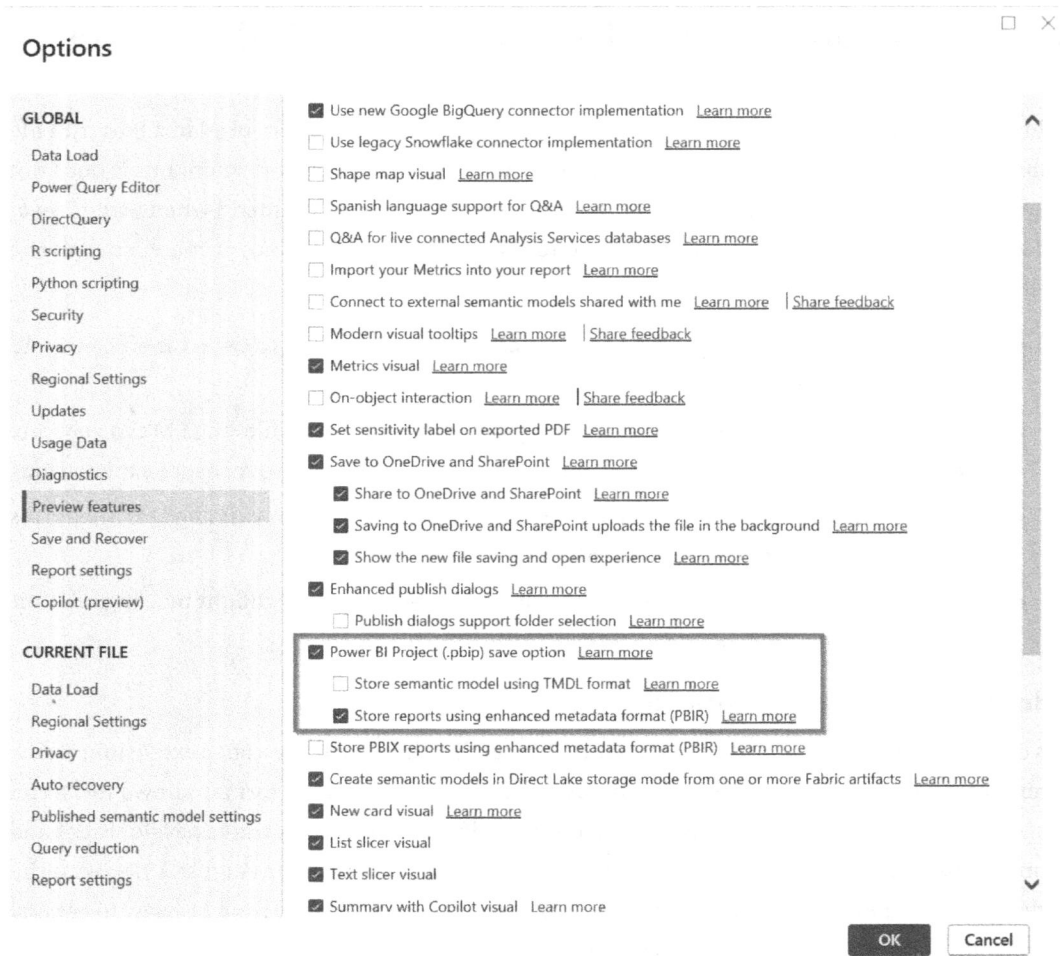

Figure 14.9 – Enabling a BIM file

To use the BIM file, you first have to save your Power BI file in PBIP format using the **Save As** dialog in the **File** menu:

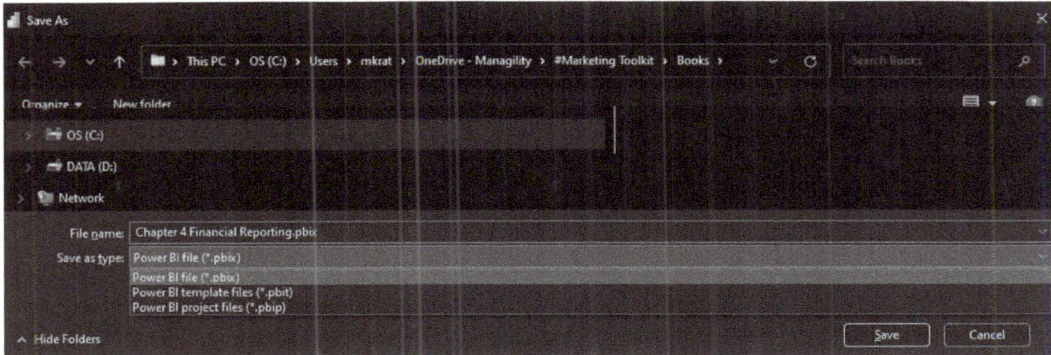

Figure 14.10 – Saving a Power BI file as PBIP

This PBIP file format generates two folders: yourfilename.Report and yourfilename.SemanticModel. The latter contains, among others, the BIM file with the name model.bim:

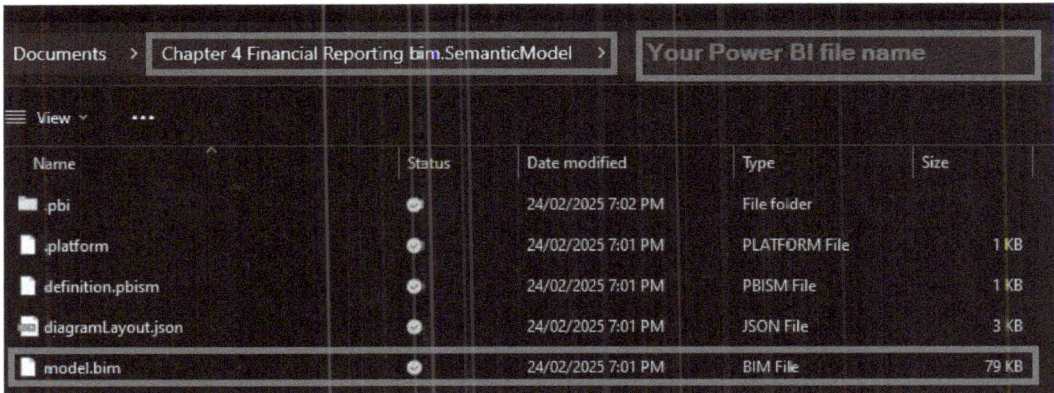

Figure 14.11 – Using the .bim file with LLMs for structural analysis

The .bim file can now be uploaded into a prompt of the LLM of choice (ChatGPT, Gemini, Llama, DeepSeek, etc.) with text instructions on what analysis the users require.

Use cases and prompts for analysis

Examples of use cases and prompts for the LLM could include the following:

Purpose	LLM prompt text
Documenting Power BI models. Proper documentation is crucial for collaboration and maintainability. LLMs can automate the following: • Generating explanations of data relationships • Creating data dictionaries for different tables and columns • Providing descriptions of calculated columns and measures For example, an LLM can generate a full report detailing all tables, relationships, and measures within a Power BI model for easy reference.	`Create documentation for this Power BI .bim file`
Analyzing and improving the model	• Can you recommend relationships between tables using primary and foreign keys? • Suggest calculated columns and financial measures based on common KPIs, such as Total Sales, Profit Margin, and Customer Retention Rate • Identify potential performance bottlenecks in the model • Identify unnecessary relationships and fields • What can I do to improve data refresh efficiency?
Analyzing DAX measures	Can you propose an improvement for DAX measure xyz?

Purpose	LLM prompt text
Generating specific or generic insights	`Track financial performance across multiple regions and product categories`
Improving analysis options and questions relevant to the context	<ul><li>`What are relevant questions that could improve insights?`</li><li>`Recommend ways to segment and analyze data for deeper insight`</li></ul>
Generate relevant metrics	`What metrics can I add that would add value in the context of this model?`

Table 14.3 – LLM sample prompts

In the previous sections, we covered the enormous opportunities of using LLMs in Power BI in a financial context. It is important to be aware that LLMs are not 100% reliable and can return inaccurate results. In the following section, I will juxtapose rewards with risks and associated mitigation strategies.

Risks and rewards of using LLMs and Copilot for financial analysis in Power BI

As we have seen, LLMs can generate impressively coherent and contextually relevant content, but it is important to note that they also come with significant risks that users and organizations must understand. Among the most concerning challenges is the phenomenon of hallucinations: instances where these models confidently generate information that is factually incorrect or fabricated. Unlike human errors that often come with visible uncertainty, LLM hallucinations can be presented very confidently as accurate information, making them particularly dangerous.

The risks of hallucinations are particularly relevant in a financial context, where the accuracy of information is paramount.

So, the importance of human verification of LLM outputs is absolutely crucial. In the following overview, we cover the rewards and risks:

- **Rewards:**
    - **Increased efficiency**: LLMs and Copilot automate repetitive tasks, such as generating DAX measures, structuring financial reports, and summarizing financial trends, significantly reducing the time analysts spend on manual work.

- **Enhanced accuracy**: AI-driven insights help reduce errors in financial calculations, ensuring consistency and adherence to financial standards.

- **Improved data accessibility**: Business users with minimal technical expertise can leverage Copilot and LLMs to interact with financial data using natural language.

- **Advanced predictive capabilities**: AI-driven forecasting models offer the opportunity to incorporate vast external information sources and forecasting logic alongside internal data.

- **Risks:**

  - **Data privacy concerns**: Using AI tools such as LLMs in relation to sensitive financial data requires strict security policies to prevent privacy infringement, unauthorized data exposure, and potential regulatory violations. One option to address data exposure risks is using local LLMs without an internet connection. I recommend reviewing tools such as LM Studio and GPT4, which make this very easy to set up, even for business users without an in-depth IT background.

  - **Dependence on AI accuracy**: While LLMs and Copilot provide valuable insights, they may generate incorrect or misleading information if not properly validated.

  - **Cost implications**: AI-powered tools require significant investment, with costs varying based on usage, licensing, and required infrastructure.

  - **Model transparency issues**: AI-generated recommendations may lack full transparency, making it difficult for financial analysts to understand how conclusions were derived.

  - **Regulatory compliance challenges**: Organizations must ensure that AI-driven financial analysis aligns with legal and compliance requirements.

- **LLM costs:**

  - **GPT-4 (OpenAI API)**: Some free tiers. Pricing depends on usage tiers, typically charged per 1,000 tokens.

  - **DeepSeek and Gemini**: Available under different licensing models, with Enterprise plans for larger organizations.

  - **Self-hosted LLMs (Llama, Claude, etc.)**: May require investment in computing infrastructure, though open-source options reduce software licensing fees.

Summary

The integration of LLMs with Power BI has the potential to revolutionize business intelligence workflows. From automating data model creation to generating powerful DAX formulas and improving report accessibility, LLMs and Copilot have the potential to provide immense value to Power BI users, but they have to be very carefully validated, particularly in a financial context, where accuracy is the priority over everything else.

Still, by leveraging these AI-powered tools, finance professionals can enhance analysis insights and decision-making and substantially increase process efficiencies.

Concluding your journey with Power BI for Finance

Congratulations on completing *Power BI for Finance*! If you've read the chapters, built the examples, and applied the concepts to your own scenarios, you've accomplished something significant. Throughout this journey, you built a comprehensive skill set on financial analytics in Power BI:

- You began by understanding the building blocks of Power BI and how to structure data models for financial requirements. You learned that data modeling isn't just a technical nicety but the foundation of everything else.

- You then implemented financial logic through DAX calculations, created interactive financial statements, and built sophisticated reporting structures that go far beyond traditional tools. You tackled real-world complexities like multi-currency handling, management reporting, and advanced planning scenarios.

- Most importantly, you learned to think differently about financial data. Instead of static spreadsheets that become outdated quickly, you can now create dynamic, interactive reports that update automatically and provide insights with unprecedented speed and detail.

The dynamic Power BI/Fabric ecosystem

Power BI and Microsoft Fabric are constantly evolving. New features, integrations, and capabilities are released regularly, and the broader ecosystem—including third-party visuals, integration tools, and complementary solutions such as Dynamics BPP and Acterys for planning—continues to expand.

Your learning doesn't stop here. The principles and patterns you've mastered will remain relevant, but staying current is essential. Follow the Power BI blog, join community forums, and experiment with new features as they become available.

Where to go from here

The skills you've developed open many doors. You might focus on becoming the Power BI expert in your organization, helping colleagues transition from spreadsheets to modern analytics. Or you could specialize in areas like planning, forecasting, or advanced analytics.

Whatever direction you choose, you now have the foundation to keep building. Every financial mode you design, and every insight you uncover will strengthen your expertise. Don't be afraid to experiment, try new approaches, and push the boundaries of what's possible.

Stay connected and share your feedback

Your experience with this book matters, and I would appreciate hearing from you. What worked well? What challenges did you face? Your feedback helps make future editions better for the entire finance community. I invite you to connect with me on LinkedIn and share your thoughts, questions, or success stories. Whether you've implemented a solution that transformed your reporting process, encountered a unique challenge you'd like to discuss, I'm here to listen and help where I can.

Get This Book's PDF Version and Exclusive Extras

UNLOCK NOW

Scan the QR code (or go to packtpub.com/unlock). Search for this book by name, confirm the edition, and then follow the steps on the page.

Note: Keep your invoice handy. Purchases made directly from Packt don't require one.

15

Unlock Your Exclusive Benefits

Your copy of this book includes the following exclusive benefits:

- ☁ Next-gen Packt Reader
- 📄 DRM-free PDF/ePub downloads

Follow the guide below to unlock them. The process takes only a few minutes and needs to be completed once.

Unlock this Book's Free Benefits in 3 Easy Steps

Step 1

Keep your purchase invoice ready for *Step 3*. If you have a physical copy, scan it using your phone and save it as a PDF, JPG, or PNG.

For more help on finding your invoice, visit https://www.packtpub.com/unlock-benefits/help.

> **Note:** If you bought this book directly from Packt, no invoice is required. After *Step 2*, you can access your exclusive content right away.

Step 2

Scan the QR code or go to `packtpub.com/unlock`.

On the page that opens (similar to *Figure 15.1* on desktop), search for this book by name and select the correct edition.

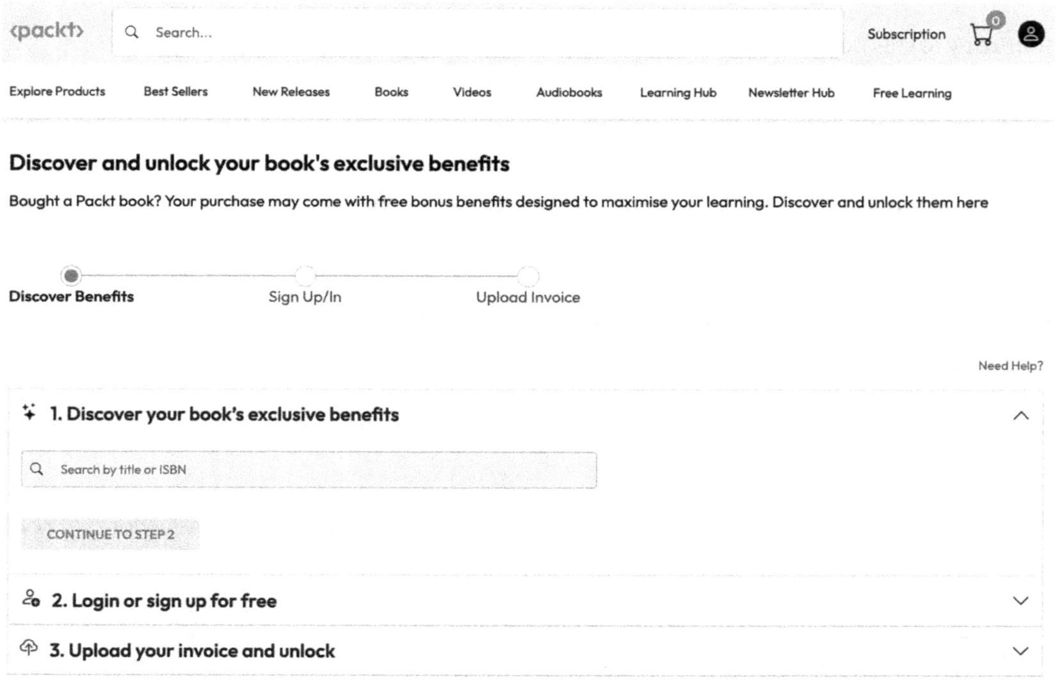

‹packt›   Q Search...   Subscription 🛒 👤

Explore Products   Best Sellers   New Releases   Books   Videos   Audiobooks   Learning Hub   Newsletter Hub   Free Learning

Discover and unlock your book's exclusive benefits

Bought a Packt book? Your purchase may come with free bonus benefits designed to maximise your learning. Discover and unlock them here

●————————————○————————————○
Discover Benefits   Sign Up/In   Upload Invoice

Need Help?

✦ **1. Discover your book's exclusive benefits**   ∧

 Q Search by title or ISBN

 CONTINUE TO STEP 2

👤 **2. Login or sign up for free**   ∨

☁ **3. Upload your invoice and unlock**   ∨

Figure 15.1: Packt unlock landing page on desktop

Step 3

After selecting your book, sign in to your Packt account or create one for free. Then upload your invoice (PDF, PNG, or JPG, up to 10 MB). Follow the on-screen instructions to finish the process.

Need help?

If you get stuck and need help, visit `https://www.packtpub.com/unlock-benefits/help` for a detailed FAQ on how to find your invoices and more. This QR code will take you to the help page.

Note: If you are still facing issues, reach out to `customercare@packt.com`.

‹packt›

packtpub.com

Subscribe to our online digital library for full access to over 7,000 books and videos, as well as industry leading tools to help you plan your personal development and advance your career. For more information, please visit our website.

Why subscribe?

- Spend less time learning and more time coding with practical eBooks and Videos from over 4,000 industry professionals
- Improve your learning with Skill Plans built especially for you
- Get a free eBook or video every month
- Fully searchable for easy access to vital information
- Copy and paste, print, and bookmark content

At www.packtpub.com, you can also read a collection of free technical articles, sign up for a range of free newsletters, and receive exclusive discounts and offers on Packt books and eBooks.

Other Books You May Enjoy

If you enjoyed this book, you may be interested in these other books by Packt:

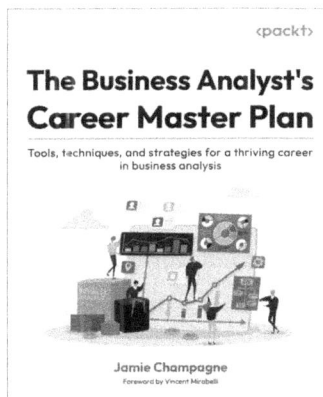

The Business Analyst's Career Master Plan

Jamie Champagne

ISBN: 9781836206859

- Master foundational business analysis skills and apply them to real-world scenarios
- Explore techniques for effective requirements elicitation and modeling
- Improve stakeholder communication, ethical decision-making, and leadership capabilities
- Plan career progression by setting realistic goals and creating a roadmap
- Explore business analysis specializations and find your path
- Understand how emerging technologies are impacting analysis work
- Use assessment tools and guided techniques to evaluate your skills and drive long-term career success

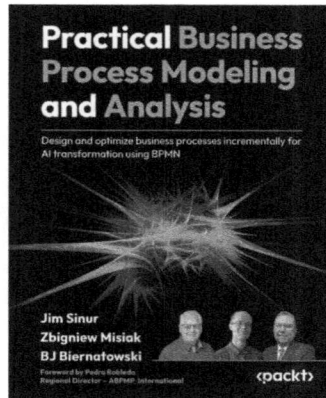

Practical Business Process Modeling and Analysis

Jim Sinur, Zbigniew Misiak, BJ Biernatowski

ISBN: 9781805126744

- Explore the role of business process in digital transformation
- Build scalable process architectures for long-term efficiency and adaptability
- Find out how to avoid common pitfalls in digital transformation and automation programs
- Apply real-world strategies and frameworks to optimize operations effectively
- Discover methods and tools to enhance business process analysis and decision-making
- See how the BPMN can be extended for scenarios like process simulation and risk management
- Measure and maximize business value from process transformation efforts

Packt is searching for authors like you

If you're interested in becoming an author for Packt, please visit authors.packt.com and apply today. We have worked with thousands of developers and tech professionals, just like you, to help them share their insight with the global tech community. You can make a general application, apply for a specific hot topic that we are recruiting an author for, or submit your own idea.

Share your thoughts

Now you've finished *Power BI for Finance*, we'd love to hear your thoughts! Scan the QR code below to go straight to the Amazon review page for this book and share your feedback or leave a review on the site that you purchased it from.

https://packt.link/r/1837635013

Your review is important to us and the tech community and will help us make sure we're delivering excellent quality content.

Index

www.ingramcontent.com/pod-product-compliance
Lightning Source LLC
Chambersburg PA
CBHW081051220326
41598CB00038B/7058